D1095858

Meditating the Gospels

MEDITATING

THE GOSPELS

Emeric Lawrence, O. S. B.

The Liturgical Press
St. John's Abbey
Collegeville, Minnesota

Nihil obstat: John Eidenschink, O.S.B., *Censor deputatus. Imprimi potest:* † Baldwin Dworschak, O.S.B., Abbot of St. John's Abbey. *Imprimatur:* † Peter W. Bartholome, D.D., Bishop of St. Cloud, August 15, 1956.

To the Community
of St. John's
Abbey

PREFACE

The apostles' request to Christ: "Lord, teach us to pray!" is itself one of the most human of prayers. I doubt that anyone is ever completely satisfied with his or her prayer life or convinced that it could not be improved. For years I have been reading about the Bible as the source and sustenance of mental prayer. But I have not been able to find completely satisfactory selections of the Bible so prayed.

The following meditations (if they may be called such) are therefore the result of a search. Surely they are very personal, as private prayer must be. But if they give others the idea to create their own, they will serve a good purpose.

After having experimented for some time with this kind of writing, I was pleased to find a certain justification for it in Louis Bouyer's *The Meaning of the Monastic Life*. He says: "If it is to be *truly* God whom we seek, we have to seek Him as a person. Martin Buber, in fact, the Jewish philosopher whose meat and drink has been the mysticism of the Hassidim, in which a last living thread of the tradition of the prophets lingers to the present day, has expressed this very adequately: 'a person is only sought as a person, in dialogue. It is only in the "I to Thou" relationship that the person remains personal for us. Someone of whom we get into the habit of speaking as "he" is no longer a person for us'" (p. 8).

These, then, are attempts to know the Christ of the gospels by means of dialogue. It is admittedly quite a one-sided dialogue, but I think I know Him better as a Person than when I began some years ago to talk to Him.

In relation to participation in the Liturgy, I concede that this is strictly private prayer. But since one of the purposes of private prayer is to help prepare us for more intelligent participation in the Liturgy, I would hope that this might be the kind of prayer that could fulfill Father Roguet's expectation: "The word of God (he is talking about the epistles and gospels at Mass) is not only meant to instruct, or rather, if it instructs, it is not merely to enlighten the intellect; it is in order to reveal the greatness of God and to call forth praise" (*Holy Mass*, p. 26). Thinking out and writing each of these meditations has helped me to appreciate God's greatness and made me want to praise Him. I hope that others will likewise benefit and that they will use the meditations as a springboard for their own intimate and personal reaction to the personality and word of our Lord as His inspired Gospels reveal Him.

Each meditation is headed by a summary of the day's gospel and ends with a sentence that has been called "Prayer for the day." I consider these direct quotes from the sacred text all-important and strongly recommend that they be memorized and then recalled again and again during the day and thus used to promote the living conversation with our Lord of which these meditations are only a start. All too few of us Catholics are able to recall and use *exact* quotes from the Scriptures, and our spirituality has suffered considerably from this failure. It is by every word that comes forth from the mouth of God that man lives.

I wish to express my sincere gratitude to so many confreres and friends without whose help the book could hardly have been made ready. I want especially to thank Abbot Baldwin Dworschak, O.S.B., Fathers Godfrey Diekmann, Gregory Roettger, William Heidt, Henry Anderl, Eric Buermann, Jeremy Murphy, Hugh Witzman, Alberic Culhane, Alcuin Siebenand, Mr. and Mrs. Emerson Hynes, Mr. and Mrs. Al Veranth, and Mr. John Dwyer.

EMERIC A. LAWRENCE, O.S.B.

St. John's Abbey
Collegeville, Minnesota

INTRODUCTION

For a long time I have felt (and I am sure many have shared the feeling) the need for a book of meditations on the gospels of the Mass. Those whose appreciation of the Mass impels them to attempt daily participation in the Holy Sacrifice, surely have progressed to the point where they need daily mental prayer as part of their spiritual program. Fifteen minutes (or more) given to mental prayer in the morning before Mass, or on the previous evening, will be an excellent preparation for one's access to the altar. If the mental prayer centers on the gospel of the day's Mass, the preparation would seem ideal.

Perhaps it is repeating the obvious to point out the difference between mental prayer and vocal prayer, but it is better to be obvious than to be obtuse.

Vocal prayer is prayer in which we make use of words to express our thoughts and sentiments to God. Even though we pronounce the words silently in our mind, it still is vocal prayer. A characteristic of vocal prayer is that we do the talking, while God listens.

In mental prayer we largely dispense with words, aside from asking the assistance of the Holy Spirit as we begin and thanking God for His graces and lights when we finish. But in mental prayer, it is the mind and heart rather than the vocal organs which do most of the work; and in mental prayer God has more opportunity to speak to us.

We begin a mental prayer by choosing some topic as a springboard for our thoughts. It may be some truth, some incident in the life of Jesus or of His Blessed Mother, some parable or other words

of our Lord. In a spirit of quiet prayerfulness we examine the topic
we have chosen, we turn it over in our minds, asking ourselves,
"What message does this have for me? How can I apply it to my
own life? What is God trying to say to me here?" As I ruminate,
my mind and heart are fixed on God with attention and with love.
Given the opportunity, God will speak to me. He will direct my
thoughts. Before I am finished, I shall see a path of action opening
up before me (it may be a very hidden action) which I had not even
thought about before. This is mental prayer; or, to give it its more
common name, this is meditation.

There must of course be some element of meditation in every
vocal prayer or it is not prayer at all. And there often is some use
of interior speech in mental prayer. The principal difference is one
of quantity and of emphasis. Vocal prayer is not to be belittled and
all of us must use it; but mental prayer is a higher kind of prayer
and a great accelerator to spiritual growth.

For those who are intent upon such growth and who wish to
practice daily meditation, but find themselves perplexed in the daily
choice of a topic, Father Emeric's book *Meditating the Gospels* will
come as a welcome aid. *Meditating the Gospels* is a meditation book
with a difference. Instead of proposing some general truths for consideration, truths for each reader to ponder and apply for himself,
Father Emeric actually makes the meditation for us, insofar as it
can be done.

Addressing himself to our Lord Jesus in a personal You-and-I
relationship, Father Emeric thinks out loud, and lets us share the
fruit of his thinking. There is still work to do for ourselves, particular applications to individual problems of which only we ourselves
can know. However, with reverent familiarity Father Emeric
initiates with the Master a conversation in which each of us can
participate, a conversation which each of us may expand and pro-
long according to our needs.

It is the Christ-minded layman especially who will welcome
this work of Father Emeric's. It is a book which will be a natural
companion to one's daily missal. Daily meditation is a highly desirable practice for anyone, even for those — *especially* for those —

for whom daily Mass is impossible. But the combination of meditation plus Mass, particularly meditation keyed to the Mass, will make for a power-charged, Christ-centered lay apostolate.

Father Emeric's book will be acclaimed by all — priests, religious, and laity — who see that apostolate as today's most urgent need.

FATHER LEO TRESE

CONTENTS

COMMON GOSPELS OF THE SAINTS

VOTIVE MASSES

PROPER GOSPELS OF THE SAINTS

Meditating the Gospels

FIRST SUNDAY OF ADVENT

Summary:

Christ describes the Last Judgment. There will be signs above the world, on the earth, and fear in the hearts of men as the Savior returns in glory.

LIFTING UP MY SOUL

Lord Jesus, why do You talk to us on this first Sunday of Advent about Your second coming in Judgment at the end of the world? Are we not supposed to be preparing for Your coming at Christmas? Is there a closer relationship between these two comings than we think?

Your description of Last Judgment is surely vivid enough. The signs in the sun and moon and stars will produce fear in men's hearts. You say that they will faint for fear and for expectation of the things that are coming on the world. And then You will come, Lord Jesus! Son of God and Son of man, You will come on a cloud with great power and majesty. You, the Child of Bethlehem whose birth I so desire now, You will come as Lord and Judge. And on this first Sunday of the year, You want us to see that second coming in majesty as the glorious culmination of Your and our whole life. Your coming at Christmas calls for and points to Your coming in glory.

I don't know if I shall be on the earth on that last day. But what I do know is that there is going to be a meeting face to face between You and me some day quite soon and that I want no irrational and slavish fear spoiling my love for You when that meeting comes. There is only one thing that makes me hope that our coming together will be happy, and that is my desire and my love for You.

This is Advent, Lord Jesus, the time of hope, expectation, desire. You and Your Church begin this new year by making us pray: "To Thee, O Lord, have I lifted up my soul: in Thee, O my God, I put my trust" (introit).

You have loved me, You have called me, You have filled my bottomless heart with longing and desire for You. This is Your doing, this deep yearning for You, and I can't help myself. I wouldn't want it otherwise. I know enough about life to realize that if I try to satisfy that desire by anything or anyone else than You, I shall be disappointed and frustrated. Human love is good; it is a sharing in the love that You and Your Father have for one another. But unless I make human love a part of my love for You—which means making it take second place to love for You—it can destroy both me and all love. And, of course, I know how senseless it is for me to set my heart on anything like riches, food, drink or any other man-made attraction. Experience has shown so often that these material things, far from filling the deep spiritual emptiness of our hungry hearts, only make the hunger the more keen.

COME, LORD JESUS

To You, Lord Jesus, I lift up my soul. Show me Your ways. Teach me Your paths in this year. Show me Your mercy and teach me Your salvation. I must seek You during this year, I must desire You. St. Benedict tells us that to seek You is the principal vocation and work of a monk. I believe that it is also the mark of every Christian. My wanting You is already the sign and pledge of the fulfillment and completion that You will grant. "All they that wait on Thee, shall not be confounded, O Lord" (gradual).

MARANATHA! Come, Lord Jesus! Come now during this holy season of Advent and purify my being of the works of darkness that have taken root in me: the pride, the bitterness, the impatience, and all the forms of self-indulgence that I am subject to. Come now, and come at Christmas. Come and destroy the fear of living and the fear of dying that haunt my life, so that on that great day of our mutual meeting I may lift up my head and know that my salvation is indeed at hand. Come, Lord Jesus!

Prayer for the day:
YOUR REDEMPTION IS AT HAND.

SECOND SUNDAY OF ADVENT

Summary:

Christ cites His miracles of healing to prove to the disciples of St. John the Baptist that He is the expected Messias. He then gives a beautiful tribute to John, claiming him as His Precursor.

MORE THAN A PROPHET

Lord Jesus, You see the two disciples of John coming, and You know their question before they ask it: "Art thou he who is to come, or shall we look for another?" You know the answer that will convince them: "Go and report to John what you have heard and seen: the blind see, the lame walk, the lepers are cleansed, the deaf hear, the dead rise, the poor have the gospel preached to them."

They who know the ancient prophecies so well cannot fail to see that You claim to fulfill the sign concerning the Messias given by Isaias: "God himself will come and save you. Then shall the eyes of the blind be opened: and the ears of the deaf shall be unstopped. Then shall the lame man leap as a hart, and the tongue of the dumb shall be free."

Your answer, revealing so well Your heart of mercy, satisfies them, and they go back to John. I can see John's smile as they report. This is what he wants. Personally he has no doubts about You. But he is beginning to fear that these good followers of his are perhaps more attached to him than they should be; for he knows that his mission is to bring souls to You, not to keep them for himself. Now they will know the truth and will follow You. That's the kind of man John is. I can well understand why You should esteem him so highly.

Lord, Your tribute to John also tells us a lot about the qualities You prize in Your followers. Your love for John leaps out of the sacred text: "What did you go out to the desert to see? A reed shaken by the wind? A man clothed in soft garments? But what did you go out to see? A prophet? Yes, I tell you, and more than a prophet. This is he of whom it is written, 'Behold, I send my messenger before thy face, who shall make ready thy way before thee.'" John is no indecisive cowardly character who can never make up his own mind. Nor is he a weak-kneed dandy, interested only in soft living and the self-indulgence that usually goes with that kind of living. He is Your man, Your precursor, and You love him very, very much.

PREPARING THE WAY

Lord Jesus, I tend too much to think of John as being sent exclusively to the Jews. That is not Your intention or that of Your Church. Am I wrong in judging that You send John to *us*, to disturb our complacency as Catholics, to chide us for softness to ourselves, to make us feel our insufficiency without You, and to sharpen our longing desire for You?

We Catholics are supposed to be Your precursors today to our world. We are supposed to prepare the way for You. By our proud joy in possessing You, we are intended to awaken longing for You in the hearts of our contemporaries. You want so to use us.

Lord Jesus, to be Your precursor! To be another John! To do his work! But when I compare myself with John and the standards You lay down in this gospel, I am afraid. But You can make me what You want me to be. John was strong in love for You because You were first strong in him by Your grace. Dear Lord, use that method on me too. Come, Lord Jesus! Come and possess me as You did John so that You can also use me in the same way You used him. Come and stir up our *hearts* to prepare thy ways!

Prayer for the day:
BEHOLD, I SEND MY MESSENGER BEFORE THY FACE.

THIRD SUNDAY OF ADVENT

Summary:

John the Baptist denies he is the Messias or Elias, but claims to be the Precursor. He is not worthy, he says, to be compared to Jesus.

JOHN'S WORK TODAY

Lord Jesus, John the Baptist was one of the greatest and holiest of Saints. But because he knows himself so well, he is the humblest. The messengers of the Pharisees ask him, "Who are you?" With his reputation for holiness, he might have claimed to be a great prophet, or even Your position, that of Messias. But his vocation is to prepare Your coming to us this year by preaching a baptism of penance. He does it by his personal example of self-denial. But above all, he does it by being himself.

He is the living example of humility to me this year. If I am to be ready for Your birth this year and above all for Your second coming at death or the end of time, I must be humble. That is, I must know myself as I am. This knowledge will reveal me to myself in all my naked need. I need You. You are my completion. Any other desire I've ever had is sickly and wan alongside this essential desire of my life. The psalmist's words are mine: "As the deer longs for the streams of water, so does my soul long for Thee, O God. My soul thirsts for God, for the living God: when shall I come and see the face of God?"

But this is my better self speaking, Lord. It is a busy world we live in; there are so many distractions, so much to do, so much to read and look at. Too often in the past these words of St. John are verified in me: "There has stood one in your midst that you know not." All my life You have been near and with and in me, and I have not known. Oh, I've known about You. I've known certain Christian slogans. But I've not known You sufficiently as a person, as my beloved Lord and Savior, as the fulfillment of my heart's desires.

7

REJOICE ALWAYS

And I haven't known You because, besides being so busy with so many things, I have felt sufficient unto myself. And I needn't tell You what happens to those who are sufficient unto themselves: they find out the truth the hard way. Overconfidence easily develops into that fear and despair that drive out joy. And joy is my heritage as a member of Your body. What shall I do? You tell us in this Mass: "Rejoice in the Lord always: again I say, rejoice. Let your modesty be known to all men: for the Lord is nigh. Be nothing solicitous: but in everything let your petitions be made known to God."

Well then, here is my petition: Stir up, O Lord, Your power and come to save us! Enlighten the darkness of our minds by the grace of Your visitation. Come and help us to live justly and piously in this life, looking for the blessed hope and looking, too, for Your coming at the end. Come, Lord Jesus! You must come, You will come. But in these few days that remain before Your birth, purify all my hopes. But since I know that You will come and fill me only in proportion to the immensity and intensity of my desire for You, then increase the humility whereby I may know my utter need for You! Come, Lord Jesus!

Prayer for the day:
MAKE STRAIGHT THE WAY OF THE LORD.

EMBER WEDNESDAY IN ADVENT

Summary:
God sends Gabriel to Mary to get her consent to be Mother of His Son. Learning that she will remain a virgin and still be the Mother, she consents.

BLESSED ART THOU

Lord Jesus, Mary looks up from her prayer (or is it her housework?) and sees the angel. Not many people see angels because they are pure spirits and it isn't every day that they take a human form. But this is a very special day. Gabriel greets her: "Hail, full of grace, the Lord is with thee. Blessed art thou among women." Such a wonderful greeting can have its origin only in the heart of God, and it is more than a greeting: it is the statement of a condition of sinlessness and purity that our world has never seen since (or before).

But the greeting troubles Mary, and Gabriel sees her questioning mind. "Do not be afraid, Mary, for thou hast found grace with God. And behold, thou shalt conceive in thy womb and shalt bring forth a son; and thou shalt call his name Jesus. He shall be great, and shall be called the Son of the Most High; and the Lord God will give Him the throne of David, His Father, and He shall be king over the house of Jacob forever; and of His kingdom there shall be no end." This is a very brief, but very exact biography of You, Lord Jesus.

But Mary is still a little troubled. There is that vow of virginity that You have inspired her to make and which You want her to keep. "How shall this happen, since I do not know man?" And the angel answers and says to her, "The Holy Spirit shall come upon thee and the power of the Most High shall overshadow thee; and therefore the Holy One to be born shall be called the Son of God."

The angel talks in the future, but we know he is stating what inevitably will take place. The Holy Spirit, He who is creative Love in Your Trinity of Persons, will work in her His unutterable act of Love; the power of the Father will overshadow her, and You, Son of God, Second Person of the Godhead, God of God, Light of Light, born before all ages, You will come into her womb, to take from her the body that You will later offer to the nails and to the soldier's lance and to us as food for our life.

You, the Father, and the Holy Spirit—You who are God, you wait for the consent of this girl. And it is proper that she should give that consent, for that is the way You have made Your creature, man. It is in our freedom that we most resemble You; and You have always wanted us to exercise it. For freedom and love are twins, the one cannot exist without the other.

HANDMAID OF THE LORD

Mary chooses, she gives her consent; but she does it out of love and out of desire for the one thing she has wanted and does want and will want all the rest of her life: the will of God. "Behold the handmaid of the Lord; be it done to me according to thy word." "Lift up your gates, O ye princes: and be ye lifted up, O eternal gates, and the King of glory shall enter in" (gradual), so pleads salvation-hungry mankind. Mary hears, she consents, she opens up the gate of her womb, and there You are, Lord Jesus! You who are God are now man, You are Mary's Son, You are one of us, You are our life, our hope, our love.

"Behold the handmaid of the Lord . . ." What a full and magnificent expression it is! It is love-motivated consent to divine motherhood, yes. But it is more than that. It is love-motivated, total and complete, gift of the creature to the Creator. It is abandon, trust, obedience to compensate for and overcome the disobedience and self-love of the first Adam and the first Eve. Little wonder that a Son of a Mother like Mary will later on say to the world: "I seek not my own will but the will of him who sent me" (John 5:30).

Lord Jesus, this is a beginning . . . for You, for Mary, for all of us. You asked Mary's consent to be Your Mother. That same respect that You have for her freedom You show to each of us. Lord Jesus, here we are. Come into us all, take possession of our whole being, grow and develop in us, help us to think as You think, to love as You love, to judge as You judge; so that using us as You will, You may continue saving the world in and through us.

Prayer for the day:

BEHOLD THE HANDMAID OF THE LORD, BE IT DONE TO ME ACCORDING TO THY WORD!

EMBER FRIDAY IN ADVENT

Summary:

Mary goes to visit her cousin Elizabeth and is
greeted as the Mother of God.

BLESSED ART THOU

Lord Jesus, the very last words that Archangel Gabriel speaks
to Your Mother before You come into her womb tell her about her
cousin Elizabeth's miraculous conception. Elizabeth is old, she has
been barren all her life, and now she is with child, for, as the angel
says, "Nothing shall be impossible with God."

Mary gives her consent, she becomes the Mother of the Son of
God, and immediately she rises up to visit Elizabeth, carrying You
in her womb.

Lord, this is significant of Your future life: Your first work,
even before You are born, is an errand of mercy. Your Mother enters Zachary's house and greets her cousin. It is an historic moment,
this coming together of two mothers and two sons, the sons not even
born yet. In his mother's womb John recognizes You and leaps for
joy. He is the representative of humanity rejoicing in salvation after
all those thousands of years of death and exclusion from heaven.

He rejoices most of all because You the Bridegroom come to him
who will some day call himself the friend of the Bridegroom. You
come to him so that later on he can go before You, preparing the
way for You. John's love for You has a very early history.

Elizabeth feels John's gladness, and filled with the Holy Spirit,
she cries out with a loud voice, saying, "Blessed art thou among
women and blessed is the fruit of thy womb! And how have I deserved that the mother of my Lord should come to me? For behold,
the moment that the sound of thy greeting came to my ears, the
babe in my womb leapt for joy. And blessed is she who has believed,
because the things promised her by the Lord shall be accomplished."

Lord Jesus, it is well that the evangelist tells us that Elizabeth is
filled with the Holy Spirit, for her greeting and her feelings about
You and Mary have an everlasting destiny: "Blessed art thou among

11

women and blessed is the fruit of thy womb . . . Blessed is she who has believed!" These sentiments are ours now.

MAGNIFYING THE LORD

How typical is Mary's answer! He who is mighty has done great things for her, and holy is His name. Her reaction is simple, child-like, natural: "My soul magnifies the Lord, and my spirit rejoices in God my Savior."

To magnify the Lord and to rejoice in God. Lord, these are things that Mary does with perfection; they are things that each one of us can do, and all because she consents to be Your Mother . . . and then comes to us bearing You in her womb. We do not have her extraordinary privileges. But You do come to us in grace and in Communion, so that we can say in all truth: "My soul magnifies the Lord . . . He who is mighty has done great things to me."

In a few days it will be Your birthday, Lord Jesus. Mary is about to bring You to us in another blessed visitation. Thou art near, O Lord, and all Thy ways are truth (introit). Like John we can leap for joy. Like Elizabeth we can cry out to Your Mother, "Blessed art thou among women and blessed is the fruit of thy womb!" And like Mary herself, we can magnify the Lord and give full sway to our spirit as it rejoices in God our Savior. Show us, O Lord, Thy mercy, and grant us Thy salvation (offertory).

Prayer for the day:
MY SOUL MAGNIFIES THE LORD.

EMBER SATURDAY IN ADVENT

Gospel same as for tomorrow, the Fourth Sunday of Advent.

FOURTH SUNDAY OF ADVENT

Summary:

At a definite moment in history God sends John to preach the baptism of penance for the remission of sins. John thus fulfills the prophecy of Isaias: Prepare ye the way of the Lord: make straight his paths.

DESIRED OF NATIONS

Lord Jesus, the scene described in this gospel took place originally when You were thirty years old. John's first preaching prepared the way for Your public life. But Your Church uses John — his words and example — to prepare us for Your birth this Christmas.

The moment is at hand when the prophecy of Aggeus is to be fulfilled: "Behold the Desired of all nations shall come: and the house of the Lord shall be filled with glory." You are the Desired of all nations. And our parish church, or chapel, is the house that You by Your birth will fill with glory. Could I not say that I too am called to be the "house of the Lord" that You will fill with Your glory?

But first I must attend to those words of John: Prepare ye the way of the Lord, make straight His paths. Lord Jesus, I must be convinced that the baptism of penance is as necessary for me as it was to those who longed and hoped for Your first coming. I cannot expect You to come and live and grow in me if my heart is divided between You and sinful self-love. Everything about You implies purity and holiness; and You want to share that holiness with me. "The house of the Lord shall be filled with glory."

I can say that I long for Your coming, that I want You to be born in me at Christmas, and that I desire lasting union with You forever. But how much do I mean what I say? One of Your good friends, Abbot Marmion, tells us that a man is worth what he desires. Would this mean that my desiring You would make me worth You? How wonderful that would be! How wonderful it is! You, God, lift me up to oneness with You!

13

Yet most of the time I seem to want to be worth, not You, but a luxurious meal, a stimulating drink, a movie, a new car or even a sinful thought, word, or act. If I experience the need of creatures so that I am sinfully attached to them, then I cannot say that I seek and desire You solely. And in that case You cannot give Yourself wholly to me. You cannot lift me up to a share in Your worth.

MY HEART SPEAKS

Lord Jesus, this desiring You solely does not mean that I cannot have any human loves or friendships or that I cannot love and appreciate created things. No, human affection and the good things of life reflect Your goodness and beauty. They tell me that if they, being only shadows, are good and beautiful, how much more beautiful and good are You, the Reality of Realities. But always I must love and desire You more, much more. And from time to time, I must give up these things, practicing fast and abstinence, so that my desire for You may be increased.

And so, Lord Jesus, come and tarry not: forgive the sins of Thy people! "My heart speaks to Thee, my face seeks Thee; Thy face, O Lord, I seek" (Ps. 26). You tell us in this Mass that You are near to all who call upon You in truth. I call upon You. Lord, have mercy. As the parched earth calls for refreshing, life-giving rain, I call for You. "Drop down dew, ye heavens, from above and let the earth be opened and bud forth a Savior" (introit). Come to me, be born in me, grow in me so that this dry piece of earth which I am may bring You forth as a Savior to others. "O God, Thou art my God: earnestly I seek Thee. My soul thirsts for Thee, my flesh longs for Thee like a dry and parched land without water" (Ps. 62). *Maranatha! Come, Lord Jesus!*

Prayer for the day:
PREPARE YE THE WAY OF THE LORD.

VIGIL OF CHRISTMAS

Summary:

Joseph is told in a dream not to be afraid to
take Mary as his wife, for that which is begotten in her is of the Holy Spirit.

A JUST MAN

Lord Jesus, You have not prepared Joseph for Your birth in
exactly the same way that You prepared Your Mother Mary. Joseph
is to be Your foster Father: You do not take Your origin from him,
and therefore an immaculate conception in Joseph is uncalled for.
But to be the husband, protector and provider for Your blessed
Mother, You want the best that the human race can offer. Joseph
is Your man.

There is in him the same element of calmness regarding the
course of events and of confidence in the workings of Providence
that we find in Mary. But He is a man, a husband. Therefore his
great love for his precious wife-to-be must make the discovery of
her pregnancy all the harder to take. According to the custom, he
could repudiate her and throw her out unto the mercy of the Pharisees with whom she will find small mercy. But what will such
harshness accomplish? Nothing at all. Besides, his very love for
Mary forbids it. So he decides simply but with a heavy heart to tell
her to leave quietly, and she will hear no more from him.

When he comes to this decision, it is time for You to act. You
cannot afford to lose a foster father like Joseph, nor can Mary lose
so perfect a husband. You therefore send him an angel while he
sleeps who says to him: "Do not be afraid, Joseph, son of David, to
take to thee Mary thy wife, for that which is begotten in her is of
the Holy Spirit. And she shall bring forth a son and thou shalt call
His name Jesus; for He shall save His people from their sins."

St. Matthew tells us Joseph rises from his sleep and takes unto
him Mary his wife. In taking her, he also takes You. You will be
his foster Son; and I don't know who is more pleased at the bargain
— You or he.

15

ALL FLESH SHALL SEE

So now the stage is set, Lord Jesus, for Your birth into the world. "Lift up your gates, O ye princes: and be ye lifted up, O eternal gates, and the King of glory shall enter in" (offertory verse). "Tomorrow shall the wickedness of the earth be abolished: and the Savior of the world shall reign over us" (alleluia verse).

The longing of the ages, humanity's thirst for God, the yearning of the human race for salvation is now concentrated in the hearts of these good and just people whom You have gathered around You — Mary, Joseph, Elizabeth, John. They will not be disappointed. "The glory of the Lord shall be revealed; and all flesh shall see the salvation of our God" (communion verse).

Lord Jesus, help us to make their longing desire our own. Come, show us Thy ways, teach us Thy paths. Grant us, we beseech Thee, Almighty God, that, as we anticipate the adorable birthday of Thy Son, so we may joyfully receive His everlasting gifts (secret prayer).

Prayer for the day:
THOU SHALT CALL HIS NAME JESUS.

CHRISTMAS

Summary:

The Son of God, born before all ages, becomes Man as He is born in a stable of Mary, His Virgin Mother. Angels announce His birth to shepherds who hasten to adore Him.

GOOD NEWS

Lord Jesus, the great temptation to be avoided as I record my reactions to Your birth is that of being over-dramatic. Here, if ever, it is necessary to be simple and open — as were Mary, Joseph, and the shepherds.

There is a poor cave in a hillside that has been used as a barn.

A man and his wife are waiting there. They are waiting for You. For nine months the woman has been carrying You in her womb. How she has longed to see and hold You! Suddenly You are there. With infinite love and gratitude, she takes You into her arms and wraps You up and lays You in a nest of straw in the manger. Then she and Joseph look at You, they admire You, they love and adore You.

Outside the cave, on the hills there are some shepherds and some sheep. The shepherds watch the sheep as they watch the stars; and as they watch they think of You, their promised Messias. Maranatha! Come, Lord Jesus! So do they pray. They do not expect to see anything out of the ordinary out there on the hills. Nothing ever happens out there. That's what they think, Lord Jesus. But they are wrong. Angels do not appear on hillsides ordinarily. But this is not an ordinary night. First one angel appears and speaks to them: "Do not be afraid, for behold, I bring you good news of great joy . . . for today has been born to you a Savior who is Christ the Lord." Then a multitude of angels appear; they sing, "Glory to God in the highest, and on earth peace among men of good will."

The shepherds do not waste any time. They hurry to Your cave. They enter and look at You with all their love and admiration. So that now You are surrounded with the love of angels, of men, and of animals. Lord Jesus, royal Child, let me add my love to theirs!

THY GREAT GLORY

Why do You do it, Lord Jesus? You who are the Lord God, why do You come as an infant? Babies are lovable, of course, and You want to be loved. There is nothing You and Your Father want more, is there? But I think You want more than this yearly, passing stirring-up of our emotions. There is always an over-supply of that. You want to be loved in fact and in truth so that we will freely give ourselves and our lives to You and Your transforming power all through the year.

I think You came as a child because You want us to *be* children. This is what Christianity means. To be a Christian means to be a child, to be *like You, to be one with You.* Later on when You grow up You are going to tell us: "Unless you turn and become like little children, you will not enter the kingdom of heaven." How could You ever make such a demand on us unless You are first a child Yourself?

In Your becoming a child, You show us what we must always be: full of trust, of love for Your and our Father, of abandonment into His hands. This is the feast of Your birth. It is also the feast of the Father's love. Your childlikeness, Your response to the Father's love, is Your life, not just in the cave, but all the way through to the end. So it must be mine. And so it is mine by the grace of this feast, the wherewithal to be a child, which You will give to me in proportion to my love and my desire.

And now if I am a child, if I have the grace of childlikeness, then I have a right to a child's joyful enthusiasm. So here goes: "Glory to God in the highest. We praise Thee, we bless Thee, we adore Thee, we glorify Thee. We give thanks to Thee for Thy great glory."

> *Prayer for the day:*
> TODAY A SAVIOR HAS BEEN BORN TO YOU WHO IS CHRIST THE LORD!

December 26, ST. STEPHEN

> *Summary:*
> The gospel relates the treatment that Jerusalem gives to the men of God whom Jesus sends. He foretells the punishment that will come upon the city.

THOU WOULDST NOT

Lord Jesus, when You talk about the prophets and wise men You have sent to the Jews, You speak as God for whom there is no past, no future, but only the living present. You think of Jeremias, Isaias, and all the other prophets who preceded You on earth. You think of Your own apostles and their successors.

You say: "Some of them you will put to death and crucify, and some you will scourge in the synagogues and persecute from city to city."

If they will treat Your prophets so shamefully, why do You send them? Why do You come Yourself — for You know they will treat You as badly? I can think of only one answer, the one given by Your disciple John: "God so loved the world that He gave His only-begotten Son" (John 3:16). And You are willing to be given: You love the world too.

There is something mysterious, dear Lord, about this love of Yours for men. You lavish it upon them with the full knowledge that they will fail to love You in return, some of them at any rate. What tender mercy is there in Your words in this gospel: "Jerusalem, Jerusalem (It could just as well have been "New York, or Paris, or Rome, or Berlin, or Moscow" or my own village or city) thou who killest the prophets, and stonest those who are sent to thee! How often would I have gathered thy children together, as a hen gathers her young under her wings, but thou wouldst not! Behold, your house is left to you desolate."

Lord, I think that those words "Thou wouldst not" are about the saddest You have ever spoken. Refusal to love is always tragic, but never so much as when You are the one whose love is turned down.

RECEIVE MY SPIRIT

You know this will be mankind's way with You when You are born. But You have come anyhow. And so it will always be. Many will reject and ignore and hate You. But some will return Your love, and by the intensity of their devotion to You, they will more than make up for the refusal of the rest.

This surely is the case with this young man, Stephen. He loved You so much that his love draws from You the idea and the courage to pray for those who are stoning him.

Lord Jesus, I must always be grateful to You for inspiring Your Church to put Stephen's feast right after your Birthday. For no one tells me more plainly than he what to be and do about that birth. There is nothing that Stephen did that I cannot do. Like him I can by my love make up for the refusal of so many. Like him I can look up steadfastly to heaven, see "the glory of God and You, Jesus, standing on the right hand of God." Like him I can say, "Lord Jesus, receive my spirit," confident that such a prayer at the heart of my life will help me, like Stephen, to fall asleep in the Lord, that is, in You.

Prayer for the day:

HOW OFTEN WOULD I HAVE GATHERED THY CHILDREN TOGETHER AS A HEN GATHERS HER YOUNG UNDER HER WINGS, BUT THOU WOULDST NOT!

December 27, ST. JOHN THE EVANGELIST

Summary:

Jesus tells John that He wishes him to remain until He comes.

DO THOU FOLLOW ME

Lord Jesus, it is proper that we should celebrate the feast day of Your beloved disciple, John, so soon after Your own birth. But I could have wished that the section of the gospel that Your Church uses could have been a little less mysterious. The time of the gospel is after Your resurrection. You are speaking to Peter: "Follow Me." It isn't the first time that Peter hears Your invitation. You have invited him first at the beginning of Your public life. He obeys and You choose him to be the head of Your Church. He wants to follow You. But Peter is still human and still curious.

Your relation to John has always been something special. It is accepted among the apostles that Peter is their leader. Likewise is it common knowledge and completely taken for granted that John is Your beloved disciple. He is the one who leans on Your breast at the Last Supper and asks You the fateful question, "Lord, who is it that will betray Thee?"

So now You are beckoning to Peter, and Peter will obey; but there is John. He cannot keep his curiosity under control any more: "Lord, and what of this man?" Your answer is hardly illuminating either to Peter or to us: "If I wish him to remain until I come, what is it to thee? Do thou follow me."

The disciples have their own interpretation of Your words: they think You are promising that John will not die. John himself corrects that impression. He says that You do not promise he is not to die, but rather that You wish him to remain until You come . . . and what is it to them? And that is not so plain either. Until you come . . . what do You mean, Lord Jesus? Until You come at the end of time? Is John still alive somewhere in this world? Hardly that. But maybe I'd better not worry about it any more and simply listen to Your words to Peter, accepting them as addressed now to me: "If I wish John to remain, what is that to thee? Do *thou* follow me."

REMAIN TILL I COME

As a matter of fact, Your command is possible of fulfillment . . . with Your help. John does remain. He remains among us as a living member of Your Mystical Body, exceedingly concerned with making us share his knowledge of You and his love for You. He remains in our midst in a very special way in his gospel. There we can see his love for You, Lord Jesus, and his tender desire to share You with us. He is the bridge between Your mind and Your heart and our minds and hearts today.

Lord Jesus, give us all the impulse to use John as he wants to be used. Reading his gospel will be like entering into his mind. But being guided by John there is only one place where we can end up — in Your own heart. Then it will be easy to accept Your invitation, "Do thou follow me."

Prayer for the day:
DO THOU FOLLOW ME.

December 28,
FEAST OF THE HOLY INNOCENTS

Summary:

Warned by an angel, Joseph takes Mary and Jesus and flees into Egypt: Herod has the boys under two years killed.

WEEPING AND LAMENTATION

Now, Lord Jesus, Your angel appears again to Joseph, this time to warn him of danger to You and Your Mother. Herod wants to seek You — not as the shepherds and the Magi and all decent people do: because they need You and want You and love You — but rather to destroy You. This is something to contemplate: a man called Herod — a small-minded politician, envious, self-centered — seeking to remove from his path the Power and Love of God in person: You, God's Son, Savior of the world. Poor Herod, how little he knows about life and about God's irresistible will to give Himself to men!

When he finds that he has been shown up by the Magi, who do not come back to the palace to tell him Your whereabouts, Herod adopts a heartless plan for catching You. It is the dragnet. You aren't more than a few days old; but just to make sure he doesn't miss anyone, he commands that all male children under two years of age shall be killed. You are gone, safe in Your Egyptian refuge. Herod's soldiers work his destructive will on the babies. And these become the first human beings to give their lives for You, the first martyrs and the first virgins.

Then is fulfilled what was spoken through Jeremias the prophet, saying, "A voice was heard in Rama, weeping and loud lamentation. Rachel weeping for her children, and she would not be comforted, because they are no more."

Lord Jesus, this feast and its meaning is dear to Christian consciousness. The idea of confessing You by dying is thus early and firmly established in Your Church. "Out of the mouth of infants and of sucklings, O God, Thou hast perfected praise, because of

Thy enemies. O Lord, our Lord, how admirable is Thy name in the whole earth" (introit)!

DESTROY SIN IN US

Lord Jesus, the thought strikes me that this feast represents much more than the martyrdom of a number of babies, precious as that is to You. The whole incident is a kind of preview and foreshadowing of what will happen to You at the end of Your life. Here there are a lot of innocent children who give their lives for You; then You, *the* innocent one among all the sons of men, You will give Your life for them and for all mankind. Here there are broken-hearted mothers who give their sons to death because of You; then there will be another broken-hearted Mother, Your own, who will understand their grief and will make up for the love they understandably lack here. And both You and they can say: "Our soul has been delivered as a sparrow out of the snare of the fowlers; the snare is broken, and we are delivered" (offertory verse).

"O God, whose praise the martyred Innocents did this day proclaim, not by speaking, but by dying, do to death in us all the malice of sinfulness, that our lives may also proclaim the faith, which our tongues profess" (collect).

Lord Jesus, the praise begun by the Holy Innocents can be continued in our lives. The obstacle is the malice of sinfulness within us. Kill, destroy it, so that our profession of Christianity may be a true confession, a readiness for any kind of martyrdom or suffering, according to Your will. In the martyrdom of the children of Bethlehem and the martyrdom of the broken hearts of their mothers You are already active with Your grace and consolation.

So will You be active in our lives, too. Make us to see our closeness — to the Holy Innocents and their mothers, to Mary, Your Mother (and theirs and ours, also), and to You, the center of life then and now.

Prayer for the day:
HEROD WILL SEEK THE CHILD TO DESTROY HIM.

SUNDAY WITHIN THE OCTAVE OF CHRISTMAS

Summary:

Old Simeon blesses Jesus and prophesies that a sword shall pierce the soul of Mary.

LIGHT OF REVELATION

Lord Jesus, Simeon has been waiting long years for this moment; and now as he holds You in his arms, the Holy Spirit inspires him to cry out those glorious words: "Now thou dost dismiss thy servant, O Lord, according to thy word in peace, because my eyes have seen thy salvation, which thou hast prepared before the face of all peoples: a light of revelation to the Gentiles, and a glory for thy people Israel." All the longing love of centuries of Jewish holiness are in his voice and heart. And now we can join our love to his.

Naturally, Your mother and Joseph are astounded at their (and Your) reception by Simeon; but they have been so wrapped in the supernatural these past few months, that they just marvel, without being surprised. Simeon blesses them both and then turns to Your Mother Mary: "Behold, this child is destined for the fall and rise of many in Israel, and for a sign that shall be contradicted. And thy own soul a sword shall pierce, that the thoughts of many hearts may be revealed."

It is not necessary to point out how exactly this prophecy will be fulfilled. You will hang on the sign of contradiction, the cross, and beneath it, looking up at You, will stand Your mother, her heart pierced again and again with swords of sorrow because You whom she loves is so hated and mistreated.

The scene is completed with the incident of Anna. She too has been longing for this hour. She never leaves the temple, worshiping with fastings and prayers night and day. She sees You in Simeon's arms and enlightened from on high, she begins to give praise to the Lord. Then immediately she rushes out to tell of her discovery to all who are awaiting the redemption of Jerusalem. So now age bears witness to You, Lord Jesus. Simeon holds You and Anna rushes out to tell the world about You. There is no doubt in their minds — You have been well worth waiting for, and how their enthusiasm contrasts with our indifference and complacency!

THE CHILD GROWS

Your Mother and St. Joseph fulfill the prescriptions of the Law of Moses for the birth of a little Jewish boy — although You are certainly above such laws — and then they return to Nazareth where You are to live the life of the family and grow up and become strong as a carpenter and worker. The Evangelist says that You are full of wisdom and the grace of God is upon You. It would seem to be a considerable understatement of the true facts. For You are Wisdom, You are the Word in which all Wisdom and Knowledge are expressed; and you have in You the fullness of divine life. But I must not seem to quibble with St. Luke, for his is a wonderful way of saying that as a boy already You are on Your way to becoming "the beautiful one above all the sons of men," and by Your bruises all will be healed.

Lord Jesus, You whom Simeon holds in his arms, You whom Anna proclaims, You now become food for our souls. You are ours much more than You are theirs. "By the operation of this mystery, O Lord, may our sins be purged, and our just desires fulfilled" (post-communion). This is a good prayer for us. Cleanse us more and more from our sins, for it is sin and sin alone that prevents or diminishes just and holy desires to possess You and have You grow in us even as You grow in Nazareth.

Lord Jesus, hasten in our lives the accomplishment of Simeon and Anna, so that soon we may recognize clearly that You are our salvation, that You are the light of revelation to us, that You are the glory of Thy people now.

Prayer for the day:
THY OWN SOUL A SWORD SHALL PIERCE.

December 29,
ST. THOMAS OF CANTERBURY

Summary:

Jesus claims to be a good shepherd because He knows His sheep and His sheep know Him, but most of all because He lays down His life for the sheep.

GOOD SHEPHERD

Lord Jesus, this gospel of the Good Shepherd is used on the Second Sunday after Easter, and at that time it sums up perfectly the whole of Your life and work. You claim to be a Good Shepherd and by laying down Your life for us, Your sheep, You prove that You deserve the title.

The Saint of today is also a good shepherd, a pastor of his flock, who as Your representative fulfills all the requirements of a shepherd. The king wishes to subjugate Thomas and his flock to the throne. Thomas resists and is rewarded with imprisonment and finally in his own cathedral of Canterbury he lays down his life for his flock. But his death wins the grace of conversion for the king: he changes heart and restores full rights to the church. Thomas is a good shepherd, not only because he lays down his life, but most of all because he is strong in principle in resisting the invasion of the rights of Your flock.

Lord Jesus, few of us are bishops. That is one fact; another fact is that so few of us ever think of what a bishop really is and how closely a bishop is called to be a stand-in for You. If we sometimes find them wanting — according to our uncharitable way of judging others — perhaps it is mainly because the ideal You set for them is so very exalted. As You could say, "I am the Good Shepherd . . . I know mine, and mine know me . . . and I lay down my life for my flock," so must every bishop *try* to say and think the same way.

CHILD AND SHEPHERD

But here it is only a few days since Your birthday, Lord Jesus.

At first it seems a little strange to think about the gospel of the Good Shepherd while You are still so fresh in our minds as a child. But it is good for us to see the close relationship between You the Child and You the fully grown and responsible pastor of Your flock.

For no better image than the Good Shepherd could bring home to us the *purpose* You have in mind in becoming Man (namely, to lay down Your life for us); and above all, no other symbol could bring home to us the *love* that inspires both Your incarnation and Your redemption. And nothing, finally, could tell us more eloquently the deep attachment to Your Father's will that is going to inspire all Your life from this crib in Bethlehem to the final laying down of Your life.

All in all, it is a blessed inspiration that causes Your Church to put St. Thomas' feastday so soon after Your own birth and to choose this gospel. And we can therefore quite readily consent to the exhortation of the introit: "Let us all rejoice in the Lord, celebrating a festival day in honor of blessed martyr Thomas: at whose martyrdom the angels rejoice, and give praise to the Son of God."

We cannot all be bishops; but all the qualities that You show us in this parable can become part of our life and make us better followers of Yours. In accordance with our vocation, we can want to help You to save others; we can grow more and more in the love that this parable proclaims so gloriously; we can grow more and more in complete dedication to the Father's will which is the foundation of all apostolic action.

You have laid down Your life for us. You say: "Other sheep I have that are not of this fold, them also I must bring, and they shall hear my voice, and there shall be one fold and one shepherd." As long as You can say that, there is work for all of us to do.

Prayer for the day:
I LAY DOWN MY LIFE FOR MY SHEEP.

December 30,
MASS WITHIN OCTAVE OF CHRISTMAS

Gospel of Mass of Our Lady on Saturday, Between Christmas and Purification, page 283.

December 31, ST. SYLVESTER, POPE.

Gospel No. 2, page 242.

January 1, FEAST OF THE CIRCUMCISION.

Summary:

Eight days after His birth, Mary's Child is circumcised and given the name Jesus.

FIRST BLOOD

Lord Jesus, for a week now Mary and Joseph have had You with them. I don't suppose any couple ever enjoyed a week more than that one. "A child is born to us, and a Son is given to us." For the first time in the history of the world, You, who are God, dwell physically among men.

But Mary and Joseph are Jews, subject to the laws of their God-given religion. You know about that, too. One of the laws that You as a Jew must obey is that of circumcision. Circumcision is a sign of that alliance that Your heavenly Father made with Your earthly ancestor, Abraham. It marks You as one of the Chosen People.

It is Joseph, I suppose, who performs the operation. Your blood

28

flows for the first time. It will not be the last. You know that already. You who founded the law, who are above the law, You submit to the law in order that, as St. Paul put it, You might "redeem them who were under the law: that we might receive the adoption of sons" (Galatians 4:5).

I doubt that Mary and Joseph are very sympathetic to this operation. But it isn't what they think that matters. This is to be Your life: to submit to law, to be obedient to the will of others even if it means shedding Your blood.

Does Mary, seeing Your blood for the first time, know that this is the beginning of Your passion? The angel has told her that she is to give You the name Jesus because You will save Your people from their sins. I don't suppose she knows how the salvation will come about; it doesn't matter at present. What does matter is that Mary is with You in Your obedience to the will of the Father now at Your circumcision as she will be with You all Your life. The blood You shed now and at the end of Your life had its source in her holy body. Little wonder that Your Church sees this feast as Your Mother's feast, too. "Behold Mary hath brought forth unto us a Savior, whom John, beholding, cried out: Behold the Lamb of God, behold Him who takes away the sins of the world" (vespers antiphon).

RESTRAINT

You, the Lamb of God, will be slain in sacrifice, Your blood will be poured out. You will humble Yourself, becoming obedient unto death, even the death of the cross. This is what Your circumcision tells me. You do not need the purification that the rite of circumcision symbolizes. I need it. I need the restraint, the cutting out of self-will, the uprooting of pride that it indicates.

This then is the way I see Your circumcision in relation to my self: blood poured out is a striking sign of Your love for me and of the purification I must go through this year in order to make myself more worthy of that love. May the vision of Your blood shed for the first time in obedience to the will of the Father, together with the unbloody sacrifice of Your mother Mary, convince me of Your love and draw from my reluctant heart the desire and the will to do violence to myself, to die to sin, in order to live unto You, my God!

Prayer for the day:

HIS NAME SHALL BE CALLED JESUS.

FEAST OF THE HOLY NAME

Summary:

At His circumcision the Child is named Jesus.

NAME FOR A CHILD

Lord, Your name is no accident. It has been planned for all eternity, and Mary has known it ever since that first visit from the angel nine months ago. Joseph has known it too. I recall how the angel appears to him when he discovers that Your Mother is pregnant to tell him that "that which is begotten in her is of the Holy Spirit. And she shall bring forth a son, and thou shalt call his name Jesus; for he shall save his people from their sins" (Matthew 1:20-21).

During those nine months it isn't as with other parents who wonder if this Child will be a boy or a girl. They know. Mary is carrying a man-child and His name is Jesus. She is carrying You. But although Your name has been ordained from eternity, it is to be their privilege to confer it officially. As the ceremony of circumcision concludes, Joseph, in his capacity as head of the family stands before You there in Mary's lap: "Your name shall be Jesus."

Joseph, the creature, gives a name to You, the Creator, and You accept it. You accept all that it will entail by way of blood to be shed and a heart to be broken. Jesus is Your name. So You are named because You will save Your people from their sins. "O Lord, our Lord, how wonderful is Thy name in all the earth!"

Lord Jesus, I marvel at the effect of Your name. St. Paul says that in Your name every knee shall bow in heaven, on earth, and under the earth. And let that knee bow, he says! But we always come back to the meaning of the name. Jesus . . . Savior. And we come back to how the name is used. It is how I use that name that makes the difference as to whether or not You will be a Savior now.

SANCTIFYING NAME

If I talk to You, call You by Your name, Your name saves me now. It is like a sacrament. It makes You real to me. It produces a union of friendship and love between You and me. It sanctifies me, saves me. "Call his name Jesus," the angel says to *me* as he said to Joseph, "Because if you do He will save you from your sins. Call Him Jesus again and again."

Lord Jesus, how wonderful is Your name in all the earth! Now that I think of this, I don't wonder at the daring with which St. Bernard (was it he?) wrote of You:

> Jesu, the very thought of Thee
> With sweetness fills my breast,
> But sweeter far Thy face to see
> And in Thy presence rest.
>
> Jesu, our only joy be Thou,
> As Thou our prize wilt be,
> Jesu, be Thou our glory now,
> And through eternity. Amen.   (vespers hymn).

Lord Jesus, it is how I use Your name that makes the difference. Jesus! Savior! How wonderful is Thy name in all the earth!

> *Prayer for the day:*
> **HIS NAME SHALL BE CALLED JESUS.**

January 6,
EPIPHANY OF OUR LORD JESUS CHRIST

Summary:
Magi, led by a star, come to adore Jesus, offering Him gifts of gold, frankincense, and myrrh.

GIFTS FOR THE KING

Lord Jesus, this is a very mysterious event. Rich Magi from Persia, guided by a star, are irresistibly drawn to the side of a Child in a stable in Bethlehem. They are drawn to You. You have to admit that this is not an everyday incident, and further, that they do go to a lot of trouble for You. But they do not seem to mind it at all. Seeing You, Your Mother, and Joseph is a joy that doesn't often come to human inhabitants of this world.

They do not seem at all surprised at the surroundings of the "newly born King of the Jews," namely You. The star has been guiding them. It now stops and indicates the cave where You are housed. They get off their camels, enter the cave, and prostrate before You in worship.

Then one of them breaks silence for the first time. I hear him say: "We brought You some gifts." They give You gold, incense, and myrrh. You are too young to receive the gifts into Your arms. Joseph accepts them and lays them at Your feet. But You are not too young to receive the obedience, the love, the complete self-dedication with which the Magi offer the gifts. You are a Child, You love to receive presents. You are God, You love to receive love.

But the giving has not been all one-sided. There has been an exchange. They give and You give. You reward their generosity by opening their eyes to what and who You are. You reveal Yourself to them as their King, their God, their Savior.

I don't suppose they want to leave, and I don't blame them. But they have work to do back home. They who come to the Light, guided by a light, must bear the responsibility of the gift they have received. Enlightened by the loveliness of Your divinity, they must return to carry You to their people. They have come seeking, and they have found. So they don't really leave You at all.

MAKE CAREFUL INQUIRY

Lord Jesus, it isn't only Your divinity and Your kingship that You manifest in this feast. It is the way of life that You would have me live. You could just as well have enlightened the Magi back in their own country. But You wanted them to bestir themselves and come to You. So You want me to be human, too. You want me to seek You actively with my human faculties of mind and body. You want me to come to You bearing my heart, my devotion, my life, my labor. You insist on my seeking. For that is the condition of Your giving.

Where is the newly born King of the Jews? Where are You, Lord Jesus? You are in this feast and in every feast. You are in this Mass and every Mass. You are in the epistles and above all in the gospels. Herod said something I can be grateful for (I don't imagine he ever thought of himself as a spiritual director): "Go and make careful inquiry concerning the Child." That I shall always try to do, for the end is so mysteriously rich. It is the same end for me as it was for the Magi: You are the end. "Mercifully grant that we, who know Thee now by faith, may be led even further to gaze on the beauty of Thy Majesty."

> Prayer for the day:
> FALLING DOWN THEY WORSHIPPED HIM.

FEAST OF THE HOLY FAMILY

> Summary:
> Mary and Joseph lose Jesus. After three days they find Him in the temple teaching the teachers. He returns to Nazareth and is subject to them.

SUBJECT TO THEM

Lord Jesus, I hesitate to try to get into Mary's heart and mind during those three days of separation. With all her faith and obedience to the will of Your Father, she is still human, still a mother. The pain of losing You is so heavy that for the first and only time in her life she complains: "Son, why hast thou done so to us? Behold thy father and I have been seeking thee sorrowing."

You must admit that Your answer doesn't help her much. "How is it that you sought me? Did you not know that I must be about my Father's business?" They do not understand Your words. Not then, at any rate. But Your Mother keeps these words carefully in her heart. You are now twelve years old. Years will pass. Understanding will dawn gradually until the day when she will stand beneath Your cross looking up at You, saying to herself: "This is what You meant that day in the temple. This is what Your Father's business is." And, of course, the full vision of that business of Your Father will come to her when You appear to her the morning of Your glorious resurrection. Then she will understand everything.

But this is the Feast of the Holy Family, and Your Church wants us to think more about the thirty years of Your life together with Mary and Joseph in Nazareth than about the three days of Your separation from them when You were twelve.

St. Luke says that You went down with them and came to Nazareth, and that *You were subject to them*. You who created not only them but the wood You formed into chairs and doors in Joseph's shop, and the food You ate and the water You carried — You are subject to them in obedience. You work together and You live and pray together. You grow up and they grow old; and all three of You grow towards that climax of Your Father's business, the cross.

SHOW YOURSELVES THANKFUL

You who are God are subject to Your creatures in order to show us how we must live in our families, our parishes, our schools and religious houses. To be subject to another means to be selfless instead of selfish, to put one's life at the service of the common good. Through St. Paul in today's epistle, You give details of family living that You have practiced Yourself at Nazareth. You tell us to "bear with one another and forgive one another, if anyone has a grievance against any other . . . But above all things have charity, which is the bond of perfection . . . Show yourselves thankful. Let the word of Christ dwell in you abundantly (that is what I want to do in these meditations, dear Lord — to make Your word, to make *You* dwell in me abundantly) . . . Whatever you do in word or in work, do all in the name of the Lord Jesus Christ."

You give the example of family living. More than that, in this feast You give the grace to carry the example into effect in our life.

Which means that You are not only subject to Joseph and Mary, but also to me! Any time I want, I can have You subject to me; I can bring You into the family life in which my vocation places me. All I have to do is to seek You as Mary and Joseph did . . . and to keep Your words, the words of these gospels, carefully in my heart.

Prayer for the day:
>JESUS ADVANCED IN WISDOM AND AGE
>AND GRACE.

January 13, BAPTISM OF JESUS

Summary:
>John the Baptist relates how he saw the Spirit descending on Jesus at the moment of His baptism.

BEHOLD THE LAMB

Lord Jesus, John the Baptist is talking to his disciples when he sees You coming towards him. You are on the threshold of Your public life, just fresh from Your baptism by John. John's disciples must wonder at the extraordinary way in which he describes You: "Behold the lamb of God, who takes away the sins of the world! This is He of whom I said, After me there comes One who has been set above me, because He was before me."

It is a wonderful and very exact description, not only of Your Person, but of Your work. John is a great man to these disciples (You Yourself say there is none greater); but he tells them that You are set above him because You were before him, which is just a human way of saying that You are God, You are He Who Is. Yet, God though You are, You are now also man: You are man so completely and fully that You are going to be the new head of the race, offering Yourself in sacrifice as the true Lamb of God, so that the sin of the world will be taken away. He can call You Lamb of God because already in Your heart is that same core of sacrifice — that dedication to Your Father's will — that will carry You aloft to the cross and to death.

John then describes the events of Your baptism: "I beheld the Spirit descending as a dove from heaven, and it abode upon Him. And I did not know Him. But He who sent me to baptize with water said to me: He upon whom thou wilt see the Spirit descending, and abiding upon Him, He it is who baptizes with the Holy Spirit. And I have seen and have borne witness that this is the Son of God." John is indeed a witness of You to us.

PERFECTION OF SONSHIP

We are still celebrating Your Epiphany, the Manifestation of Your divinity. I am much impressed at the Father's eagerness to show forth who and what You are, Lord. Both with the Magi and here at Your baptism He does not spare miracles; and I am convinced that these miracles and the divinity that they prove as Your essence are for us as much as for John and his disciples. Your Father's desire to show You forth is understandable, for He is a Father and You are the perfection of sonship. But He is also our Father, and He knows that You are our greatest need. Loving us, He wants to give You to us.

Lord Jesus, help me to be worthy of the Father's gift and above all of His great love. And to be properly appreciative. "We bring Thee offerings, O Lord, for the epiphany of Thy Son that is born, humbly beseeching Thee that as He is the author of our gifts, so also He, Jesus Christ our Lord, may mercifully receive them" (secret). In short, may we be received by Him, but first let Him perfect the gift of our hearts.

Prayer for the day:
THIS IS THE SON OF GOD.

SECOND SUNDAY AFTER EPIPHANY

Summary:

At the request of His Mother, Jesus changes water into wine at a wedding feast. This first of His miracles won the belief of His disciples.

NO WINE

Lord Jesus, I never thought much before about that sentence of Mary's: "They have no wine." Am I hearing right? Does Mary actually say that to You who are the Son of God? Not to have wine seems so inconsequential and unimportant alongside of all the sickness and sin and evil in the world, and maybe it is. But Mary thinks that the reputation of a young married couple is not inconsequential; nor is the bewilderment of those disciples of Yours who still haven't made up their minds about You. Neither is the right attitude that men of all times should have about drink, sex, and marriage unimportant.

Your Mother is a wise woman, Lord Jesus. She knows what she is doing when she says to You: "They have no wine." And she isn't turned back by Your apparent rebuff. "Do whatever He tells you," she says to the waiters. Mary, Your Mother, is a woman; and women, it is said, have a way of getting what they want.

You look at the young couple and observe their chagrin. You look around at the guests — Your disciples among them — and see their long faces. You look at Your Mother. Then for the first time in Your public life You issue a command. Again, it seems so unworthy a command for You, but there it is: "Fill the jars with water." They obey, but if Mary hadn't told them to do so, they would probably have refused.

Then You say: "Draw out now, and take to the chief steward." Again they obey. But what is this? As they pour out the jars they see that the "water" is now red. The steward tastes it. It is wine. Where did it come from? He calls the bridegroom. "What's the idea? You've kept the good wine till now!"

The bridegroom says that he didn't buy the wine. It's a surprise to him, too. Then the waiters let the story out. "Mary told us to do what Jesus said. Jesus told us to fill the jars with water and we did. That's all that's to it."

MANIFESTING YOUR GLORY

So they all have enough wine. The young couple come to You and Mary to express their thanks. You smile at them and bless them and their marriage. They will never forget that day; they will never forget You and Mary, Your thoughtful Mother.

Lord, this is still the Epiphany idea. You are still manifesting Yourself to men, still showing forth Your divinity . . . and Your love. The disciples believe in You. Maybe some of them — remembering the wine — figure You are a good Man to be around. I don't blame them: they are still young in the faith. I wonder if they see, not only Your divine power, but also Your love and mercy. You manifest Your glory. Yes, but You also manifest Your heart. And there is nothing like manifesting Your heart to win the hearts of others.

You still manifest Your glory and Your love. I have never tasted water changed into wine. But I have tasted bread changed into Your Body and wine changed into Your Blood. Of course, they still taste like bread and wine. But I know better because I believe in You and in Your power to make these changes. But most of all, I believe in Your love: for the young couple . . . and for me!

What a wonderful chain reaction Mary started that day when she said: "They have no wine." It was an important sentence after all. Now and hereafter when I think of it, I'll feel like shouting with joy to God and singing a song to His name and inviting all to "come and hear, and I will tell you, all ye that fear God, what great things the Lord has done for my soul" (offertory verse).

Prayer for the day:
DO WHATEVER HE TELLS YOU.

THIRD SUNDAY AFTER EPIPHANY

Summary:

Jesus cleanses a leper. A centurion tells Him his servant is sick. Jesus offers to come and heal the servant and praises the centurion's faith.

ONLY SAY THE WORD

Lord Jesus, the first thing that strikes me about today's gospel is Your eagerness to help. The leper says: "Lord, if thou wilt, thou canst make me clean." You touch him and say, "I will; be thou made clean." Immediately the man's leprosy is cleansed. These words of today's offertory verse express what he must have felt: "The right hand of the Lord hath wrought strength . . . I shall not die, but live, and shall declare the works of the Lord."

You really like the centurion. He is a pagan, a man of means, power, and position. He is also a man of heart. You are as pleased with that quality as with his faith. His servant is paralyzed and in much pain. He presents these facts to You. You say: "I will come and cure him." There's that eagerness again.

The centurion knows You mean it. He also knows that one so ready and capable of curing paralysis is more than man. And he knows himself for what he is: "Lord, I am not worthy that thou shouldst come under my roof; but only say the word, and my servant shall be healed."

Only say a word, that's all that will be necessary. Because You are God and You are merciful. That is faith, the kind of faith that immortalizes the centurion and makes him — pagan Roman soldier that he is — the model of all future Christians in high places or low. You love him for his heart and for his faith. "Amen I say to you, I have not found so great a faith in Israel." Then You send him away with these words: "Go thy way; as thou hast believed, so be it done to thee." And the servant was healed in that hour.

BE MADE CLEAN

Lord Jesus, this centurion is one of the men I am most anxious

to meet when and if I get to heaven. Think of all the good his attitude and words have accomplished these many years since he first
spoke. They have probably made a lot of saints. Or rather, You
make the saints, but with the help of those wonderful words of the
centurion, "Lord, I am not worthy . . ."

I think that You are as eager to help me as You were to help
the leper and the centurion's servant. "I will, be thou made clean,"
You say to me when I ask You in confession to take away the
leprosy of sin. "I will come and cure you. I will strengthen you, I
will feed you with My own body and blood," You say to me daily.
And I answer, "Lord, I am not worthy that thou shouldst enter
under my roof." Which would be wonderful if I only knew what I
was saying. But You know how often I go through the words and
motions of the Mass without really sacrificing my self-will, without
being afire with charity, without adverting at all to my careless and
neglectful heart.

Lord Jesus, help me to mean this: I am not worthy that Thou
shouldst enter under my roof. *But only say the word,* and my soul
shall be healed!

Prayer for the day:
    I WILL COME AND CURE HIM.

FOURTH SUNDAY AFTER EPIPHANY

Summary:

A storm rises while Jesus sleeps in the boat.
His disciples, frightened, awaken Him, and He
calms the storm.

YOU OF LITTLE FAITH

Lord Jesus, it must have been a very violent wind. Old sailors
like Your apostles do not easily scare. Still, there is nothing like a
tossed boat to make people realize how truly dependent they are on

their God. As they approach the center of the lake, and the storm, their uneasiness changes to terror.

They look around, they look at one another. But mostly they all look at You. You are asleep. You must have been very tired to be able to sleep through all that racket. What can they do? Fear for self conflicts with their knowing that You are exhausted. Finally fear wins. One of them touches You. You open Your eyes to the terror in theirs. They all cry out: "Lord, save us! We are perishing!"

For a moment You seem displeased. But it is not at having missed Your sleep. "Why are you fearful, O you of little faith?" You of little faith — that gives the cue. You are hurt because of their lack of faith in You. You are telling them that they should have been reassured simply by Your presence among them — awake or asleep.

But then You realize again what is in man: his weakness, his need to learn gradually, above all, his need to learn by seeing and doing. They will never forget what You now do and say. St. Mark gives Your exact words: "Peace, be still." And immediately there comes a great calm over the sea. It is a reflection of the calm that settles in their minds and hearts.

They marvel, saying, "What manner of man is this, that even the wind and the sea obey him?" It is a good question, Lord Jesus. And it takes us back to the idea of the Epiphany. With us as with the apostles, You are seeking to drive home the lesson that You are God. You first reveal Yourself as God to the Magi; then to the disciples and guests at Cana when You change water into wine. You cleanse a leper and heal a centurion's servant. In all these miracles, You show Yourself to be the Lord of creation. Nature and all of nature's laws bow to Your will. And today's acknowledgment of Your Godhead is surely one of the most spectacular of all. "Peace, be still!"

WHAT MANNER OF MAN

The impact of the fact of Your divinity is inescapable . . . and so good for me to know. It is so good because it means that You are with us today — in Your Church, in the midst of our families, our parishes, our schools. The climate of fear that we breathe today seems to grow more and more dense. Your words come to *us:* "Why are you fearful, O you of little faith?"

That, too, is a good question. Why am I afraid? Because of my little faith? But why the little faith? Because I do not know You? That could be it. *I do not know You as You are today.* I have known of a Christ who lived 2,000 years ago. But I have not sufficiently known You in this new presence of Yours in our midst, in Your Church, in my brethren.

Lord Jesus, if You could calm the storm, You can help me to grow in true knowledge of You in the year ahead. You can show Yourself to me in these meditations. That will help me grow in faith, the faith will help me grow in trust, and trust will lead to love. Further than that I do not want to go.

Prayer for the day:
LORD, SAVE US! WE ARE PERISHING!

NOTE: If the Church calendar requires the celebration of the Fifth and Sixth Sundays after Epiphany at this time, the gospel meditations for these Sundays may be found just before the Twenty-fourth Sunday after Pentecost, page 231f.

SEPTUAGESIMA

Summary:
Jesus compares His Church to a vineyard to which He constantly invites workers. All receive the same wage whether they work little or long.

I AM GENEROUS

Lord Jesus, You hire workers and agree with them on a just wage. You hire new workers throughout the day. In the evening You pay them off. Those who work all day object to being paid the same wage as those who come to work just before quitting time. You say, "Friend, I do thee no injustice; didst thou not agree with me for a denarius? Take what is thine and go; I choose to give to this last even as to thee. Have I not a right to do what I choose? Or art thou envious because I am generous?"

Of course, You are talking about Your Church and our life in Your Church today. Why do the workers object to Your giving the same wage to all? Could it be that they lose sight of You whose work it is they are doing? You hire them. You work through them. You will pay them. And the pay will far exceed the value and amount of the work done, whether it be all day, all of life, or just a short time. "I am generous," You say.

Work in Your vineyard, Your Church, is religion. The grumbling workers think religion is mainly for themselves. You are trying to tell them and us that it is for God. Or maybe it is more exact to say that religion is Your and our work together. It is working for You. It is spreading Your kingdom. You once took Your human body from Mary, so that You spoke with the tongue and mouth You received from her and did all those other blessed acts with the body she gave You; so now You want to use me — my body, my heart, my whole being — to build up Your Church.

By being a good worker in Your vineyard, I can do Your will; and doing Your will in turn brings You more and more into my life to perfect me. Redemption thus becomes personal to me.

But I must not think too much about becoming perfect. I must rather think about You, about the task of developing Your vineyard and helping You to bring in more members; I must let thoughts of personal perfection be absorbed in love for You. If I have You and Your cause, Your kingdom, as my one great concern in life, then I shall be saved any such foolish pitfalls as being jealous of those whom You call late in life to membership in Your Church and then to eternal life. True love for You will make me happy that You have acquired more workers to develop Your vineyard and to add to and build up more love for You.

All this sounds very good in theory, Lord Jesus. But "the groans of death surrounded me, the sorrows of hell encompassed me." This is my life as a Christian in the world. The heat of day, the temptations, the resistance to Your way of thinking from within me and from without — all point up the vastness of the work to be done.

What can I do, Lord Jesus? In my affliction I shall call upon You, and You will hear my voice from your holy temple. Indeed, Lord, You are generous. "I will love Thee, O Lord, my strength: the Lord is my firmament, and my refuge and my deliverer" (introit).

Prayer for the day:

GO YOU ALSO INTO THE VINEYARD, AND I WILL GIVE YOU WHAT IS JUST.

SEXAGESIMA

Summary:

Jesus teaches that only seed sown in good ground can grow and bear fruit. The seed He sows is His word, Himself.

SOWING SEED

Lord Jesus, it is a very great crowd that gathers around You this day. Why do they come to You? They are hungry for truth, and they think You have it. They will not be disappointed.

But what kind of teaching is this parable method? "A sower went out to sow his seed. The seed falls on the wayside, on rock, among thorns, on good ground." I can excuse Your hearers if they are a little puzzled. But You do not leave them perplexed long. You say: "The seed is the word of God." Men are the soil. There are various kinds of soil as there are various kinds of men. But there is only one kind of seed: You, Your word, Your truth — You are the seed.

Lord Jesus, it is obvious that You want to give Yourself to men. You have come for that — to give and to be life and truth. You first sowed Yourself in Mary, Your Mother. She was good soil. She brought forth fruit a hundredfold. And so did St. Paul, who tells the story of his being sown by You and his own sowing of You in today's epistle. Ever since You have wanted to sow Yourself in men.

I am far from being good soil as Mary and Paul were. I am so changeable. At various times in my life I am like a highway filled with the rush of traffic, too busy even to think of You. Again I am like rock. I might accept You for the moment, and You might sprout out a little in me. But You cannot penetrate rock; so You wither and die. The thorny soil of materialism and worldliness — I have been that, too, perhaps more than any other kind; and You have small chance of growing in such ground.

LET HIM HEAR

But, Lord Jesus, soil can be changed and renewed. You do that, too. By Your inspirations and Your grace You constantly work in us to fertilize us and then to water the seed You plant. But You do require some cooperation. The coming together of seed and soil is like marriage. Both soil and seed must surrender themselves one to the other. Then and only then will there be a hundredfold of new grain, new life.

Lord Jesus, Your cry comes to me across the years: "He who has ears to hear, let him hear!" There is a note of divine intensity and urgency in your tone. You know better than I how much I need You.

Renew me, Your soil, in this approaching Lent. Do it by awakening me to my condition of spiritual erosion and to the dangers of being over-busy, spiritually flighty, blowing now hot, now cold, of being worldly and worried and given over-much to pleasure.

I beseech You in this matter as St. Paul did when he was troubled with his weakness. You answered him: "My grace is sufficient for thee, for strength is made perfect in weakness." Lord Jesus, You who planted Yourself in Mary, in the Apostles, and in all the saints down through time, You now wish to plant Yourself in me. The result of Your union with them was their own holiness and the spread of Your Church. Maybe it will happen again if I can only say in my heart, using Paul's words, "Gladly I will glory in my infirmities, that the strength of Christ may dwell in me" (epistle).

Prayer for the day:
THE SEED IS THE WORD OF GOD.

QUINQUAGESIMA

Summary:

Jesus predicts His death and resurrection to His apostles who do not understand. He heals a blind man who cries to Him for help.

GOING TO JERUSALEM

Lord Jesus, You could hardly have chosen plainer words to describe Your coming passion and death: "Behold, we are going up to Jerusalem, and all things that have been written by the prophets concerning the Son of Man will be accomplished. For he will be delivered to the Gentiles, and will be mocked and scourged and spit upon; and after they have scourged him, they will put him to death; and on the third day he will rise again."

The apostles look at one another, as they so often do when You speak mysteriously. You, their Hope, You are to be put to death? You are to rise again? They ask: "What is He talking about?"

Lord, they will soon find out what You are talking about. You know. You turn it over in Your mind as You walk along. You are walking to Good Friday. But You are also walking towards Easter. You are walking to us, to Your new presence in Your Church. Truly, "You are the God that alone dost wonders."

Near Jericho a blind man, hearing the passing steps of Your group, cries: "Jesus, Son of David, have mercy on me!" He is all excited, for he has heard of You and Your merciful works. How many times he has said to himself: If only He would come my way! Now You are there. As blind men do, he walks around in circles, hands outstretched. "Have mercy on me!"

His cry reaches Your ears. "Bring him here," You say. Then You ask him, "What wouldst thou have me do for thee?" You know his answer before he speaks. "Lord, that I may see!" You give in to the longing in his voice. "Receive thy sight, thy faith hath saved thee."

And at once he receives his sight, and follows You glorifying

46

God. And all the people upon seeing it give praise to God. Lord Jesus, let their praise — and the blind man's — be continued in my mouth! Because exactly what happened then is going to take place again now during this Lent. Now it is to us that You say, "Behold, *we* are going up to Jerusalem . . . The Son of Man will be put to death; and on the third day He will rise again."

RECEIVE THY SIGHT

That is what this Lent is all about, Lord Jesus. At least, that's the way You want it. "Behold, *we* go . . ." You seem to want company. You seem to want us to share, if not Your actual dying, at least Your sacrificial will to die. Unless I can see this fact — I am blind. More blind than the apostles, than the blind man of the gospel, blind without even knowing that I am blind. But his prayer is mine: "Jesus, Son of David, have mercy on me!"

I shall repeat that prayer over and over again. It is sure to bring forth Your consoling question: "What wouldst thou have me do for thee?" You know my answer: "Lord, that I may see!" And I know Your reply: "Receive thy sight." That will be Easter.

Lord Jesus, I want to follow You forever, glorifying God. "Sing joyfully to God, all the earth: serve ye the Lord with gladness. Come in before His presence with exceeding great joy: know ye that the Lord He is God. He made us, and not we ourselves: but we are His people, and the sheep of His pasture" (tract). Lord Jesus, "In Thee have I hoped, let me never be confounded: deliver me in Thy justice, and set me free" (introit).

Prayer for the day:
LORD, THAT I MAY SEE!

ASH WEDNESDAY

Summary:

Jesus gives directions for fasting: it should be done—not to win praise from man—but from God.

WHEN YOU FAST

Lord Jesus, how well You know human nature! And how fitting is this advice about the manner of fasting at the beginning of Lent! We are going to fast and abstain, and we will not go through the first day of Lent without being tempted to think that we are close to being great saints. I am talking from my own experience.

But You tell me: When you fast, don't tell everybody about it either by word or by your long, sad face. Don't *pretend* to be an ascetic. But You do want me to fast, don't You? I should not excuse myself from mortification on the grounds that it might make me proud. What You want is sincerity. You want me to mortify myself, but You want me to see my mortification not as an end but as a means to an end.

You tell us the deep meaning of fasting in today's epistle. You say: "Be converted to me with all your heart, in fasting, in weeping, and in mourning. And rend your hearts and not your garments, and turn to the Lord your God."

HAVE MERCY ON ME

This is what my Lenten life must be: being converted to You, turning to You, my God. But to turn to You, I must first turn away from self. Only then will I experience the truth that you are "gracious and merciful, patient and rich in mercy" (epistle). Fasting then is the symbol of my turning away from self and self-centeredness. It is also the guarantee of final success. For the end of my Lenten fasting will be to so live in You that Your mind and Your will become mine.

Lord, Thou hast mercy upon all, overlooking the sins of men for the sake of repentance, and sparing them: because Thou art the

48

Lord our God. Have mercy on me, O God, have mercy on me; for
my soul trusteth in Thee (introit).

Lord Jesus, help me to keep my fasting sincere so that by it I
may learn that Thou art the Lord my God. Not food or drink or
my own will, but Thou. "O Lord, I have cried to Thee, and Thou
hast healed me" (offertory verse).

> *Prayer for the day:*
> DO NOT LAY UP TREASURES ON EARTH.

THURSDAY AFTER ASH WEDNESDAY

Summary:

Admiring the humility of the pagan centurion,
Jesus consents to heal the man's sick servant.

NOT WORTHY

Lord Jesus, this centurion is a very exceptional man, a fact that
You seem to recognize immediately. It is not customary at this
time in human history for a man of his position to show such compassion for a servant, nor for a pagan to be so humbly respectful
of Your holiness and dignity. Even before he asks You to cure his
servant, You say: "I will come and cure him." The faith of the
centurion, his kindness to his servant, and above all his faith and
humility win Your admiration.

He says: "Lord, I am not worthy that thou shouldst come under
my roof; but only say the word, and my servant will be healed."

You say: "Go thy way; as thou hast believed, so be it done
to thee."

Lord, one day of Lent is gone. There are many left, and the
prospect is not pleasant. I seem to feel as though there are two men
in me. The one, my better self, is like the centurion. The other is
another self, an I that is sick. My better self knows this sickness
and comes to You, the only One who can cure me. This gospel

convinces me that You are as eager to heal me of spiritual sickness as You were to heal the centurion's servant. Lord, I am not worthy that You should bother about me. But "Hear, O God, my prayer and despise not my supplication: be attentive to me and hear me" (introit). Only say a word and I shall be healed.

Lord Jesus, this is a perfect gospel for the second day of Lent. Your Church recognizes that we are spiritually sick, that we have grown lax, that sloth has eaten away zeal and brought imitation of You to a standstill. She shows us the remedy in the living example of this pagan soldier. Your response, Your readiness to heal us is the one thing we need at this moment. You tell us: "I will come and heal you; but you must do something: you must trust in My love and in My power, in My interest. Cast your care on Me, and I will sustain you."

SUCH GREAT FAITH

Then there is something else, perhaps more necessary for us than Your compassion for the sick servant. You say: "Many will come from the east and from the west, and will feast with Abraham and Isaac and Jacob in the kingdom of heaven, but the children of the kingdom will be put forth into the darkness outside; there will be the weeping, and the gnashing of teeth." In other words, You are warning us now to take advantage of Lent, of this time of great grace. You want us to come to You with the loving desire and the tremendous trust of the centurion. Above all, You want us to be compassionate for our fellow men. If we do not, You warn us, we will run the risk of being put forth into the darkness outside where there will be eternal weeping and gnashing of teeth.

Lord Jesus, I am sick, my faith is not strong, I could lose You forever. But "To Thee I lift up my soul: in Thee, O my God, I put my trust; let me not be ashamed: neither let my enemies laugh at me: for none of them that wait on Thee shall be confounded" (offertory verse).

Prayer for the day:

ONLY SAY THE WORD AND MY SERVANT WILL BE HEALED.

FRIDAY AFTER ASH WEDNESDAY

Summary:

Jesus tells us to love and do good to enemies as well as to friends and not to make a display of alms-giving.

DO GOOD

Lord Jesus, during this Lent You want more than anything else that I become charitable. Last Sunday Your Church gave us the ideal in St. Paul's beautiful hymn of charity. And now today You Yourself speak of it. You command us — it is more than a mere request — to love even our enemies. "Do good to those who hate you, and pray for those who persecute and calumniate you." Then You give the reason for love of enemies. "That you may be children of your Father in heaven."

At first it is not easy to see the connection between being a child of God and love of enemies, Lord Jesus. But You are the Father's Son; and no one has ever loved anyone, friend or enemy, as You have. What You are saying is that my love for enemies can make me Your brother, a son of the Father, like unto both Him and You. Love, forgiveness, mercy — such is the proper activity of You who are God. I can hear Your voice from the cross, "Father, forgive them, they know not what they do."

You have to admit that what You command here is hard. But, You come right back at me, of course it is hard. Anybody can be good to those who are good to him. But You want more than the ordinary. Your Father is always forgiving us who are sinners, us, therefore, who are His enemies. You say: "You therefore are to be perfect, even as your heavenly Father is perfect." There is only one way I can think of whereby I can fulfill commands like these: You must love in and through me, I must be perfect in and through You.

WHEN THOU GIVEST

But I think Your Church wants us to concentrate today on the second part of today's gospel. On Ash Wednesday You held up for us the ideal for *fasting;* yesterday the centurion showed us the need for *prayer* and how to pray well; today You teach the true spirit behind *almsgiving.*

We must give alms, You tell us, but not so that everyone finds out about our generosity. To publicize our good deeds is to receive the praise of men as a reward, and that serves only to puff us up. Let your almsgiving be in secret, You tell us, "and thy Father, who sees in secret will reward thee."

Lord, You are simply telling me to keep self out of the picture . . . all the way. Almsgiving diminishes attachment to possessions; doing it secretly diminishes self-love and puts the credit for a good action where it belongs — in the inspiration and the love that arises from Your heart and communicates itself to me.

Lord Jesus, I think I see the connection now between loving my enemies and giving alms secretly. In both cases we do something outwardly that manifests the gift that is dearest to us — our hearts, our wills. And it is this that makes us children of our Father, sharing His nature, being like unto Him. For He gave what is dearest to Him, namely You, Lord Jesus. "I will extoll Thee, O Lord, for Thou hast upheld me: and hast not made my enemies to rejoice over me" (introit).

Prayer for the day:
> YOU ARE TO BE PERFECT, EVEN AS YOUR HEAVENLY FATHER IS PERFECT.

SATURDAY AFTER ASH WEDNESDAY

Summary:
> Jesus walks on the waves and calms the storm and heals as many sick as touch His garment.

THE WIND FELL

Lord Jesus, You are watching Your apostles out there on the sea; perhaps You hear them better than You see them, for it is very early in the morning and still quite dark. "They are having a hard time," You say to Yourself. "I'll go and help them." So You start out walking on the waves towards them. Walking on waves is no problem for You who are nature's Creator and Master.

You pretend to pass them by. But they, seeing You walking on the sea, think You are a ghost and cry out. They are troubled, and well they might be, for they are not used to seeing men walk on waves. You settle them down: "Take courage; it is I, do not be afraid." And as soon as You get into the boat with them, the wind dies down. Calm comes upon the sea . . . and fear leaves their hearts, giving place to astonishment.

"Who is He?" they say to one another. You have multiplied loaves and fed thousands; You have walked on the water; You have calmed the storm. They cannot answer their question, they can only wonder. Nor do You answer it now by word. They will see many more marvels before You are through with them, so much so that finally the conclusion will force itself from their minds and they will answer the question themselves: "He is God!"

The people at Genesareth do not know who You are either. But they do know what kind of a heart You have. They know You as the Healer. Wherever You go You always find Yourself in the midst of a sea of sickness and pain. You sort of belong there, Lord. Wherever You go, they lay the sick in the market places, and entreat You to let them touch but the tassel of Your cloak; and as many as touch You are saved. You are mercy incarnate. You are God.

DO NOT BE AFRAID

As God and as mercy incarnate, You live now. You are present to us. As You come to the aid of the apostles tossed about on the churning waves, and as You come to the sick at Genesareth, so do You come to our aid now. You are almost fatally drawn to people in trouble. You are concerned about our bodies as well as our souls. You heal our illness, You comfort us in our fear, You attract our love.

We are just now launched on the sea of Lent. There is much resistance from our weakness within and from the world and the devil without. But here You are, coming up to our boat, saying: "Take courage; it is I, do not be afraid." I'll take You at Your word,

Lord Jesus. With You in our ship, we are safe. We will surely
reach the port of Easter and Resurrection and final union with You
when the voyage is over. It is Your closeness that makes me desire
that end. "One thing I ask of You, this I seek after: that I may
dwell in the house of the Lord. That I may see the delight of the
Lord, and be protected by His holy temple" (gradual).

Prayer for the day:
TAKE COURAGE; IT IS I, DO NOT BE AFRAID.

FIRST SUNDAY OF LENT

Summary:

After fasting forty days and nights, Jesus resists Satan's temptations.

IT IS WRITTEN

Lord Jesus, You now know hunger. You know what it means to
starve. You also know what it means to be tempted to think or do
wrongly. You know what it means to be one of us.

For forty days You have dreaded Satan's approaching visit. Not
that You are afraid of him. It is rather that he is evil in person:
he is the enemy, Your enemy and the enemy of those You love.
Now he faces You who are goodness incarnate. He uses his old
methods on You — appeal to the weakness of the flesh, appeal to
pride, appeal to power. Turn stones into bread, jump from the roof
of the temple, possess all worldly riches and power.

But the values Satan proposes to You are straw compared to
those You have in Your heart. You love Your Father with a boundless love. The devil would have You trade that love for bread, for
the acclaim of men, for the possessions and kingdoms of the world.
Your thundering response still echoes over the years: "Begone,

Satan! for it is written, '*The Lord thy God shalt thou worship and Him only shalt thou serve.*'"

Satan obeys. He leaves and angels come to serve You.

Lord Jesus, Your words are addressed to the devil, to be sure. But You also mean them for our world, for me: The Lord *Thy* God shalt *thou* worship. Those words do Satan no good. They are poison to him, they plunge him deeper and deeper into his hatred and misery.

But to me Your statement brings light and life . . . and a way of life that brings joy to me. Worship is the expression of loving dependence. "Worship the Lord, your God," You tell me. "Tell Him by word and sign that without Him you are helpless and hopeless."

UNDER HIS WINGS

But how can I worship, Lord Jesus? Am I right in thinking that fasting, self-denial, overcoming my pride and my desire for power can be worship? One thing I am sure of: I can worship Your Father with You at Your Mass. There with my gifts of bread and wine, I can express my conviction that the Father's will alone matters. There I give myself wholly to Him, to be used as He wills. I say: "Thou art my protector and my refuge: my God, in You will I trust" (tract).

But in worship I give myself to a Person so that a real relationship of love is set up between Him and me. Your Father is my Father too. In receiving me He says: "Because you have hoped in Me, I will deliver you; I will protect you, because you have known My name. You will call upon Me, and I will hear you: I am with you in tribulation. *I will deliver you, and I will glorify you; I will fill you with length of days, and I will show you My salvation*" (tract).

Lord Jesus, now I think I can see Lent a little more in its true context. Fasting, mortification, overcoming temptations and all that goes with Lent re-enacts Your victory over Satan and prolongs it into our time.

Lent is therefore the acceptable time, the day of salvation, because it is the time of my growing away from self-love and Satan into Your spirit of loving, absolute trust in Your Father. "Under His wings I shall trust: His truth shall compass me with a shield."

Prayer for the day:
THE LORD THY GOD SHALT THOU WORSHIP!

MONDAY, FIRST WEEK IN LENT

Summary:
Jesus describes the Last Judgment in terms of works of mercy done to the unfortunate . . . or left undone.

YOU DID IT FOR ME

Lord Jesus, during this Lent I am supposed to be renewing my Baptism, that is to say, I am supposed to be renewing my being, my inner self, as Your follower. There will come a day when You will call me to account in this matter: You will judge me. It is this judgment that You describe in today's gospel.

You will separate the good from the bad, the sheep from the goats. To the good You will say, "Come, blessed of my Father, take possession of the kingdom prepared for you from the foundation of the world; for I was hungry and you gave me to eat; I was thirsty and you gave me to drink; I was a stranger and you took me in . . . sick and you visited me." Then the just will answer You saying: "Lord, when did we do all this?" And You will reply: "Amen, I say to you, as long as you did it for one of these, the least of my brethren, you did it for me."

Then the same process will take place again with the damned on Your left hand. They have not performed these work of mercy. They say: "Lord, when did we see thee hungry, or thirsty, or a stranger, or naked, or sick, or in prison and did not minister to thee?" Your answer will be plain and sharp and irrevocable: "Amen, I say to you, as long as you did not do it for one of these least ones, you did not do it for me." And these will go into ever-lasting punishment, but the just into everlasting life.

"As long as you did it for one of these, the least of my brethren, you did it for *me*." Then, Lord Jesus, the sick man or the sick woman is not John or Anne or Walter or Florence: he, she, is You. The poor, the aged, the imprisoned, the stranger, the hungry, the thirsting—each is You. A bum accosts me on the street, asking for a dime. You, Lord? An old woman lies dying in rags. You? A criminal is strapped to the electric chair. Is it You?

EVERLASTING LIFE

Lord Jesus, do you really mean what You are saying in this gospel? Is it possible for a human being to do what You ask here? Don't You see that obeying You in this matter will turn my life upside down? I know your answer: "As long as you did it for one of these, the least of my brethren, you did it to me." You say to me: "Turn your life upside down. It won't be so difficult if first you change your thinking, that is, if you turn away from yourself and your worldly values and let Me do your thinking and judging for you."

All right, then, Lord Jesus; if You can do this during Lent and the rest of my life, then go ahead: think and judge in me. If this is the renewal of my being that You require, then I can only pray: "Convert us, O God our salvation, and that the Lenten fast may be of profit to us, *instruct our minds* with heavenly discipline" (collect). "As the eyes of servants are on the hands of their masters: so are our eyes unto the Lord our God, until He have mercy on us: have mercy on us, O Lord, have mercy on us. To Thee have I lifted up my eyes: who dwellest in heaven" (introit).

Prayer for the day:
COME, BLESSED OF MY FATHER.

TUESDAY, FIRST WEEK IN LENT

Summary:

Jesus casts out the buyers and sellers from the temple and rebukes the Pharisees for being jealous of His popularity.

HOUSE OF PRAYER

Lord Jesus, the people see You entering Jerusalem, and all the city is thrown into commotion, saying, "Who is this?" But the common people know You. "This is Jesus the prophet from Nazareth of Galilee," they say. And they crowd around You as always, sure in their hearts that You will say or do something that will be good for them.

They are not disappointed. They follow You to Your Father's house, the holy temple. But what do You see here? Is this the public square or a holy place? You take in the hustle and rush of business being carried on, the shouting, scheming, cheating, bargaining. You see men and women intent, not on the glory of Your Father and reverence for His House, but only on themselves and their personal gain. Your divine temper blazes up and drives them out, Your burning words scorching their fleeing backs: "My house shall be called a house of prayer; but you have made it a den of thieves."

I can well imagine that You do not endear Yourself to certain interests that day. They will not forget the brash action of a country upstart who has dared to disrupt a profitable venture. Their day — with its revenge — will come. But what matter? There are others whose love and longing compensate for the hatred of Your enemies — people who cannot see and who walk only with painful difficulty. They flock to You there in the temple in the midst of the overturned tables, and Your face melts into pity. You cannot help Yourself: a look, a touch of Your hand, a word of compassion, and all are healthy and new again.

But Your miracles cause another noise. However, this is a noise that neither You nor Your Father mind. Children join their voices to those of the newly cured and shout: "Hosanna to the Son of

David!" They are praising Your Father and You, and this is what Your Temple is for — the praise of God!

PERFECTED PRAISE

But the Pharisees don't think so. Indignantly they want You to repudiate the children's praise. "Dost thou hear what these are saying?" they ask. You answer, "Yes, of course, I hear, and I like it. Have you never read, 'Out of the mouth of infants and sucklings thou hast perfected praise'?" With that rebuke You leave them in their anger and jealousy, smile once more at Your friends, the children and the ex-invalids, and go out of the city to Bethany where You will remain . . . for a while.

Lord Jesus, it is so easy for us to look down on the Jews and especially these profaners of Your Father's house, these merchants. But actually, in a pinch, would I be among the children who shout hosannas or among those who buy and sell? I suspect that You are just as concerned about Your temple, Your Church, now as You were then about the structure in Jerusalem. You want Your Church to be a house of prayer then, now and always. You want it cleared of all self-seeking so that all its members have at heart but one thing: the perfecting of praise for Your Father.

You have plenty of purifying of Your temple to do this Lent, Lord Jesus. We all admit our need. "Look down upon Thy household, O Lord, and grant that our souls, chastened by the mortification of the flesh, may glow in Thy sight with the desire for Thee" (collect). "Lord, I have put my trust in Thee, I said: Thou art my God, my times are in Thy hands" (offertory verse).

Prayer for the day:
MY HOUSE SHALL BE CALLED A HOUSE OF PRAYER.

WEDNESDAY, FIRST WEEK IN LENT

Summary:

Jesus says that those who do the will of His Father in heaven are His brother and sister and mother.

EVEN AS JONAS

Lord Jesus, the Pharisees ask You to show them a sign; they want You to prove to them that You are the Messias. You should work a miracle just to satisfy their curiosity (and if You did, they would explain it away as they have so often already tried to do).

You answer them: "An evil and adulterous generation demands a sign, and no sign shall be given it but the sign of Jonas the prophet. For even as Jonas was in the belly of the fish three days and three nights, so will the Son of Man be three days and three nights in the heart of the earth." You are speaking of Your death and resurrection. This will be the sign they will get, like it or not. It will be the greatest miracle the world has ever seen. If anything should prove Your genuineness, this should be it. But they will not believe.

Lord Jesus, there is more in this gospel for us than for the Pharisees. For You go on to talk about the need for repentance in all men. This is what You expect of us during Lent this year. You want us all to do penance like the people of Ninive of old who "repented at the preaching of Jonas." But You are greater than Jonas: You, Your preaching and Your example. It is by doing penance that we drive out the devil; there is no substitute for penance. But the devil never lets us alone. If he tempted You, we must expect it too.

But most of all that scene at the end of today's gospel tells us what You expect of us. You say: "Who is my mother and who are my brethren?" and You go on to answer Your own question: "Whoever does the will of my Father in heaven, he is my brother and sister and mother."

WHO IS MY MOTHER

Where have I heard that before? My doing the will of Your Father will make me Your brother, Your sister, Your mother. To do the will of Your Father is nothing else than to *be* what You and Your Mother Mary *are*. To do the will of Your Father is what You and she have been doing ever since the moment You became man in her womb: that is Your inner sacrifice of self that You are going to manifest outwardly when You fulfill Your promise to the Pharisees to give them a sign: when You die and are buried.

You invite us to join ourselves to Your sacrificial sign. You ask us to sacrifice ourselves with and for You, to die, to go into the tomb with You. If we can bring ourselves to give ourselves to You and Your Father's will, then we will be a sign to our world of Your continued saving presence in the world.

Lord Jesus, I see the necessity of doing Your Father's will. My profession of Christianity is hypocrisy (like that of the Pharisees) if I do not sincerely will that union of wills. But can I do it? No, not without Your special help. Therefore I pray again and again: "To Thee, O Lord, do I lift up my soul: in Thee, O my God, I put my trust" (introit). "Understand my cry: hearken to the voice of my prayer, O my King and my God: for to Thee will I pray, O Lord" (communion verse).

> Prayer for the day:
> WHOEVER DOES THE WILL OF MY FATHER IN HEAVEN, HE IS MY BROTHER AND SISTER AND MOTHER.

THURSDAY, FIRST WEEK IN LENT

Summary:
Jesus praises the faith and perseverance of a Canaanite woman who insists that He heal her daughter.

SON OF DAVID

The apostles are disturbed about her. Too much noise. "Send her away," they ask of You, "for she is crying after us." Crying women are always embarrassing to men. But she has a sick daughter who "is sorely beset by a devil," and she, knowing You, is not going to let this saving opportunity pass.

"Have pity on me, O Lord, Son of David!" It is a mother's plea. It is her daughter who is ill, but she says, "Have pity on *me*." A mother who is a true mother feels her children's ills as though they were her own. (I suspect that that is the way Mother Church feels about us, her children, tempted and sometimes victims of Satan that we are. She comes to You during this period of Lent and pleads with You to help and heal us. You must not let her down.)

But back to the lady. She cries out again and again, but You continue to ignore her. She insists in spite of the pained looks of the apostles and Your own apparent lack of interest. Finally she breaks You down. "I was not sent," You say, "except to the lost sheep of the house of Israel."

She doesn't quite understand what You are getting at; and it doesn't matter to her. She may not belong to the house of Israel, but she has a daughter who is in distress. So she falls at Your feet, adoring You, saying: "Lord, help me!" You begin to weaken. (Isn't that what worship usually does to You and the Father? It wipes out the resistance of God!)

GREAT FAITH

"It is not fair to take the children's bread and to cast it to the dogs." You know You can't get away with a statement like that, Lord Jesus. And the woman knows it too. She senses victory. Does she mind being compared to a dog? Not at all. All she cares about is that daughter of hers. Thus her answer is quick and to the point: "Yes, Lord; for even the dogs eat of the crumbs that fall from their masters' table."

Have You had enough, Lord Jesus? You are helpless before that kind of repartee, that kind of mother-love, and above all, that kind of faith and humility. The pagan Canaanite woman wins the praises of the Son of God . . . and an answer to her prayer: "O woman, great is thy faith! Let it be done to thee as thou wilt." And her daughter is healed from that moment.

Lord Jesus, have pity on us! We are troubled by our own weakness within and by the devil from without. You can heal us and make us strong again. And You will heal us. "The bread that I will give is my flesh for the life of the world," You answer us (communion verse). Your flesh is the bread of the children of Your kingdom, the bread of the strong, the bread that restores health, that even now gives a foretaste of heaven. Lord Jesus, grant us a portion of the faith of this pagan woman so that we may cry out from the depths of our being: "O taste and see that the Lord is sweet" (offertory verse)!

Prayer for the day:
HAVE PITY ON ME, O LORD, SON OF DAVID!

FRIDAY, FIRST WEEK IN LENT

Summary:
Jesus heals a man who had been sick thirty-eight years.

TAKE UP THY PALLET

Lord, what a desperate sight the pond "called in Hebrew Bethsaida" must be with its porticoes filled with all sorts of "sick, blind, lame and those with shrivelled limbs, waiting for the moving of the water" by the angel of the Lord. And what a scramble to get into the pool at the exact miraculous moment. What discouragement for the mass of unfortunate ones to have to return to the porticoes after an unsuccessful attempt.

Here You are in their midst. You stop before one of the oldest and worst-appearing of the derelicts. Thirty-eight years of infirmity is his record, and St. John says that You know that he has been in that state a long time. You ask: "Dost thou want to get well?"

He thinks You are offering to help him to get into the water. "Sir, I have no one to put me into the pool when the water is stirred." You have no intention of putting him into the pool. *You* should wait for an angel to impart miraculous power to the water? You simply say: "Rise, take up thy pallet and walk." At once the man is cured. Off he goes, walking upright for the first time in all those years, obediently carrying the old sack of a bed with him.

Oh, but it is the Sabbath. And people don't go carrying beds around on that day. So say the Pharisees. But this is something special. A man thirty-eight years a cripple ought to be able to obey the One who has healed him. He makes his point: "He who made me well said to me, 'Take up thy pallet and walk.'" "Who is he?" they ask, knowing in their hearts that it can only be You . . . and jealously angry already at Your greater interest in a sick person than in their narrow, literal, heartless interpretation of the Law.

The man doesn't know who You are, cannot give Your name, and You have slipped away. You meet him a few minutes later in the temple (Is he there to thank God?). You look at him and say, "Behold, thou art cured. Sin no more, lest something worse befall thee." And he goes and tells the Pharisees that it is You who have healed him.

SIN NO MORE

Lord Jesus, there is no need for me to point out that You have performed this same miracle for me hundreds of times. You have made me whole — cured me of my infirmities and sins in holy confession. And each time You have said to me, "Behold, thou art cured. Sin no more." But before that You say to me exactly what you say to the cripple: "Dost thou want to get well?" It is a crucial question. Do I really *want* to get well, to be healed of my sinful habits and tendencies? Over and over again I go through the process of sorrow, confession, firm purpose of amendment, forgiveness . . . and then sin again.

Why is this, Lord Jesus? Am I not honest? Is my sorrow a fake, my love a sham? I know at least part of the answer: I know that I do not sufficiently realize the horror of sin in the light of Your dazzling holiness. Nor do I actually grasp the vast extent of Your love and goodness. My knowing You is still limited and imperfect and distant. Do You suppose You could, during the rest of Lent, enter into my mind and heart and remedy these defects?

I know You cannot force my will; but You can "Help us, O God of mercy, and show to our minds the light of Thy grace" (prayer over the people). For my part I can and shall really try to "bless the Lord and never forget all that He hath done for me: and my youth shall be renewed like the eagle's" (offertory verse).

You say to me: "Do you want to get well?" Lord Jesus, here is my answer: "To Thee, O Lord, do I lift up my soul: In Thee, O my God, I put my trust" (introit).

> *Prayer for the day:*
> BEHOLD, THOU ART CURED. SIN NO MORE.

SATURDAY, FIRST WEEK IN LENT

Summary:
Jesus is transfigured on the mountain before Peter, James and John.

UP A HIGH MOUNTAIN

Lord Jesus, You tell Peter, James and John to come with You. As they walk behind You up the mountain, they must be looking at one another and shrugging their shoulders quizzically. You say nothing; but in a moment You will appear to them as they have never seen You before; and this appearance will tell them more than any number of words what and who You really are.

Years later, Peter will remember this scene when he writes: "For we were not following fictitious tales when we made known to you the power and coming of our Lord Jesus Christ, but we had been eye witnesses of His grandeur. For He received from God the Father honor and glory, when from out the majestic glory a voice came down to him, speaking thus: 'This is My beloved Son in whom I am well pleased.' And this voice we ourselves heard borne from heaven when we were with him on the holy mount" (2 Peter 1: 16-18).

So, Lord Jesus, You are transfigured: You who are God-man momentarily appear as God, and it is as grand and blessed a sight for us today as it was for the apostles then. It is good for us to be here. "How lovely is Thy dwelling place, O Lord of hosts, my soul yearns and pines for the courts of the Lord" (Psalm 83:1).

But somehow, even though this scene on the mountain is made present for us in every Holy Mass in which You also feed me with the transfiguring power of Your body and blood, a sense of being out of place plagues me. What right have I to be on the mountain with You and the apostles?

Like them I hear the voice of Your Father: "This is My beloved Son, in whom I am well pleased; hear Him." You are God, Lord Jesus, God's own Son. What have I to do so close to You? I, who am so earthly, so worldly and self-centered? There is only one logical place for me: on my face with Peter, James, and John. But what is that hand on my shoulder, and whose is that voice: "Arise, and do not be afraid"?

NO ONE BUT JESUS

Lord Jesus, thank You for those words. More than my fear, even more than an expression of unworthiness, You want my desire; desire for You that is strong and courageous and all-embracing can wipe out sin. "O Lord my God, in Thee do I put my trust" (communion verse). "By Thy sacred mysteries, Almighty God, may our vices be cured and Thy everlasting remedies granted unto us" (secret).

It seems, Lord Jesus, that I come back more and more and again and again to *total* dependence on You for everything. But after all, who is it who says: "I am the vine, you the branches"? You are and You must be everything for and in me. "Let my cry come in before Thee, O Lord" (offertory verse).

Possess and transform me by Your strong grace, sanctify and intensify the self-denial that is my small share in my coming transfiguration. "Look down upon Thy household, O Lord, and grant that our souls chastened by the mortification of the flesh, may glow in Thy sight with the desire for Thee" (collect, Tuesday of this week).

> Prayer for the day:
> ARISE, AND DO NOT BE AFRAID.

SECOND SUNDAY OF LENT

Summary:
Peter, James and John see Jesus transfigured on the mountain and hear His Father say: "This is My beloved Son, in whom I am well pleased."

GOOD TO BE HERE

Lord Jesus, it is best for me to try to understand Your transfiguration by trying to grasp what it meant to the three apostles. For nearly three years now they have been with You. They have heard You speak and their minds delighted in Your divine truth. You have spoken to each of them man to man, heart to heart; and they have received Your friendship with gladness and joy.

They have also seen Your mercy towards the poor and sick. They have been constantly proud of You, for You have been so true, so good. But in all these experiences with You, You have appeared to them only as man.

Now for the first time they see with their eyes that You are more than man. Your face shines as the sun, and Your garments become white as snow. They love it, especially Peter. He wants to settle down with You right there: "Lord, it is good for us to be here."

But their experience of Your divinity and glorification is just beginning. You have spoken to them before of Your Father. Now for the first time they hear the Father's voice: "This is My beloved Son, in whom I am well pleased; hear him."

It is the Great God speaking, the God of Abraham, of Moses, the God of the Ten Commandments! God whose face no man can see with human eyes and remain alive. And He calls You "Beloved Son." Struck with awe, they fall on their faces.

You do not leave them long in their fear. They have seen and heard enough. Peter feels Your hand on his shoulder, and Your familiar voice comes: "Arise, and do not be afraid." Obeying You, they raise their heads, stand and look around. The vision — and the heavenly voice — is gone. But You remain. You, and they, have work to do.

But now things will no longer be quite the same between You and them. Ever after, when looking at You and listening to You, they will remember how You looked with Your face shining like the sun. They will hear Your Father's voice, and they will remember how very good it was to have been there.

THINGS TO COME

Lord Jesus, today You do not take Peter, James, and John to the mountain. You take us. Because You died and rose again and instituted Your Church in which You yearly renew Your earthly life, we can now live that life with You. Today You are transfigured before *us*. Your transfiguration is a living experience for us. We see You, we are with You. Your Father says to us: "This is My beloved Son, in whom I am well pleased; hear Him. Contemplate Him, love Him."

I think I am going to enjoy obeying this command of Your Father, Lord Jesus. I want to look at You, I want to hear You all my life and all of eternity. But Your Church puts this gospel at the beginning of Lent. It is a preview of things to come. It pictures Easter to us. It is a foretaste of heaven. But no man — least of all I — has a right to Easter and heaven without first dying to sin and to self. For You between the Mount of the Transfiguration and the broken tomb of Your resurrection there lies the mountain of Calvary arising out of the valley of the shadow of death. Can I expect anything less?

What is Lent with its insignificant bit of fasting and abstaining! What is life, with its work, even its pain! Easter and Transfiguration into You will be the reward. "Give glory to the Lord, for He is good: for His mercy endureth forever" (tract). "To Thee, O Lord, have I lifted up my soul: in Thee, O my God, I put my trust" (introit). Lord Jesus, it is indeed good to be here!

Prayer for the day:
THIS IS MY BELOVED SON . . . HEAR HIM.

MONDAY, SECOND WEEK IN LENT

Summary:
Jesus, in conflict with His enemies, announces His relationship with His Father and His approaching death.

I AM HE

Lord Jesus, now You are face to face with Your enemies. You tell them what they are thinking, what they intend to do, and what the result will be. "I go, and you will seek me, and in your sin you will die. Where I go you cannot come." Their answer is not very complimentary. "Will He kill Himself, since He says, 'Where I go you cannot come'?"

No, You will not kill Yourself, Lord Jesus. Others will very well take care of that. "You are from below, I am from above. You are of this world, I am not of this world . . ." Strange words, You speak to them, Lord, and they hardly understand You.

"Who art thou?" they ask harshly. You do not answer the question directly, but exclaim: "Why do I speak to you at all! I have many things to speak and judge concerning you; but he who sent me is true, and the things that I heard from him, these I speak to the world." But they do not understand that You are speaking about Your Father.

You go on to explain the relationship You have with Your Father: "When you have lifted up the Son of Man, then you will know that I am he (the Messias) and that of myself I do nothing: but even as the Father has taught me, I speak these things. And he who sent me is with me; he has not left me alone, because *I do always the things that are pleasing to him.*"

"I do always the things that are pleasing to Him." Lord Jesus, You come back to that again and again — this doing what Your Father wills. You know, of course, where that sort of thinking is going to lead You — to Your being lifted up by these enemies of Yours. That is what they want — what they seek; and it seems to be what Your Father wants, too. The result will be the world's salvation. But not their salvation: they do not seek You in the right way.

THINGS PLEASING

Lord, at my Baptism I was plunged into You, into Your passion and death and resurrection. That means that I am plunged into Your attitude to the Father. Therefore, I should be thinking and saying, "*I* do always the things that are pleasing to Him." But it isn't quite the case, not yet. I am still more interested in the things that are pleasing to myself.

It is this situation that You must remedy in the days that remain of this Lent. If I cannot yet say that I do always the things that please the Father, then help me to say: *I want to* do those things. "Be thou my helper and my deliverer: O Lord, make no delay" (gradual). You can make my wanting bear fruit.

Lord, help me to be sincere in this willing what Your Father wills. For this sincerity is the one condition for fruitful sharing in this Mass. It is the one condition for active and intelligent and loving participation in the forthcoming redeeming Act that You are going to make present in Your Church. "Redeem me, O Lord, and have mercy on me . . . I have put my trust in You, and shall not be weakened" (introit).

> *Prayer for the day:*
> I DO ALWAYS THE THINGS THAT ARE PLEAS-
> ING TO HIM.

TUESDAY, SECOND WEEK IN LENT

Summary:

Jesus criticizes the hypocrisy of the Scribes and Pharisees: whoever exalts himself shall be humbled, and whoever humbles himself shall be exalted.

OBSERVE AND DO

Lord Jesus, You concede that the Scribes and Pharisees, as official teachers of the people, have an honorable position. "All things that they command you, observe and do. But do not act according to their works; for they talk and do nothing." They have long since lost sight both of the dignity and worth of the people whom they are to serve, and they have forgotten that they are to lead people to Your Father who has a great love for souls.

Religion for them is more a means of imposing their will on men for selfish purposes than of trying by effective leadership to draw men to offer their lives freely and lovingly to God. This makes them about as different from You as it is possible for men to be.

Don't be like them, You tell us. Don't be insincere, don't seek self-advancement, don't look for the first places at the feast-tables. "Do not you be called 'Rabbi' (master); for one is your Master, and all you are brothers. And call no one on earth your father; for one is your Father, who is in heaven. Neither be called masters; for one only is your Master, the Christ. He who is greatest among you shall be your servant. And whoever exalts himself shall be humbled, and whoever humbles himself shall be exalted."

Lord Jesus, what You are really doing here is describing Yourself, the ideal teacher, the exact opposite of the self-seeking Scribes and Pharisees. You are the perfect guide and teacher; for not only do You teach us pure doctrine from Your Father — telling us that He really is our Father — but You live that doctrine.

So also do You teach and live the doctrine that we are all brothers and that we must love our Father above all things and our brother as ourselves. Finally, You the Master, the greatest among

us, You become our servant. I can already see You at the Last
Supper, washing the feet of the apostles and telling them: If I the
Lord and Master have washed your feet, you also ought to wash
one another's feet.

THY FACE, O LORD

Lord Jesus, "You are my light and my salvation: whom shall I
fear" (introit)? Only One is our Master — You. And You are working at Your task now. If You teach nothing else, You bring home
to me the contrast between what You want and what I am, either as
teacher or follower. Again I am forced to find a way out of my con-
tradictions; and even that You provide me. "My heart hath said to
Thee: I have sought Thy face. Thy face, O Lord, will I seek: turn
not away Thy face from me" (introit).

To seek Thy face, Lord Jesus. This is the essential vocation and
prayer of the Christian as he stands looking on the ideal that You
present. It is the prayer of man as he stands at the Redemption that
You make present at every Mass. Those that seek shall surely find.
That too, I have on Your word. "Cast thy care upon the Lord, and
He shall sustain thee. When I cried to the Lord, He heard my
voice from them that drew near to me" (gradual).

> *Prayer for the day:*
> HE WHO IS GREATEST AMONG YOU SHALL
> BE YOUR SERVANT.

WEDNESDAY, SECOND WEEK IN LENT

> *Summary:*
> Jesus announces His crucifixion and resurrec-
> tion to the apostles; the Mother of James and
> John asks Him to give her sons places of pref-
> erence in the kingdom.

OF MY CUP

Lord Jesus, You again announce Your coming passion, death

and resurrection. You will be betrayed to the chief priests, delivered to the Gentiles to be mocked and scourged and crucified. But on the third day You will rise again. You hardly finish this momentous announcement when the mother of James and John (being a mother she is probably less to be blamed than they) comes up to You to ask that her sons might sit the one at Your right hand, the other at Your left hand in Your kingdom.

How much to the point is Your response: "You do not know what you are asking for. Can you drink the cup of which I am about to drink?" They say to You, "We can." And knowing that some day they will really understand You and the nature of Your kingdom, and thinking outright of their martyrdom, You assure them: "Of my cup you shall indeed drink: but as for sitting at my right hand and at my left, that is not mine to give you, but it belongs to those for whom it has been prepared by my Father."

The mother asks You for an earthly favor: You promise the cross.

Then, noticing the anger of the other apostles at the ambition of the two brothers, You put them straight. What right have they to be critical of James and John? Have they never been selfishly ambitious? You tell them: "You know that the rulers of the Gentiles lord it over them, and their great men exercise authority over them. Not so is it among you. On the contrary, whoever wishes to be first among you shall be your slave; even as the Son of Man has not come to be served but to serve, and to give his life as a ransom for many."

They probably — at that moment — understand little of what You say, Lord Jesus. We do not understand too well even now after we have repeatedly beheld Your victory.

BUT TO SERVE

Lord, the Church is our Mother; she pleads with You today in our behalf. But she knows better than the mother of James and John what she is asking for; she knows the true nature of the kingdom in which she wants us to be seated. But no matter; Your question to us is the same as to them: "Can you drink the cup of which I shall drink? Are you willing and ready to accept anything My Father chooses to send you by way of suffering, pain, disgrace, death? Do you desire to give yourselves to the Father and to trust in Him, holding back nothing of your own will? And, in your relations to your fellow-men, are you their minister, their servant? Do you really try to imitate me, I who am 'not come to be served, but to serve, and to give my life as a ransom for many'?"

Like the mother of James and John, our mother the Church pleads for us. You save us by uniting us by Your holy sacrament of Baptism to Your death and resurrection. Can I drink of the cup that You will drink? Lord, I won't say with James and John, "I can," but rather, "I want to and I'll try." As a matter of fact, in and through You, but only in and through You, I can do all things. "Unto Thee have I cried, O Lord my God, be not Thou silent to me" (gradual). In this very Mass I shall drink of Your cup. Here I shall give myself to Your death and resurrection. "To Thee, O Lord, do I lift up my soul; in Thee, O my God, I put my trust" (offertory).

> Prayer for the day:
>
> **CAN YOU DRINK THE CUP OF WHICH I AM ABOUT TO DRINK?**

THURSDAY, SECOND WEEK IN LENT

Summary:

Jesus draws a contrast beween the beggar Lazarus who suffers in this life and is rewarded in the next and a certain rich man who goes to hell because of his worldly attachments.

I AM TORMENTED

Lord Jesus, the rich man in Your parable today with the best clothes, food, and furnishings is completely unmindful of the sore-covered Lazarus begging outside his gates, "longing to be filled with the crumbs that fall from the rich man's table." Death comes to both and now the tables are turned. The rich man looks up from his place in hell to see Lazarus in the glorious company of Abraham in heaven. He cries out to Abraham: "Father Abraham, have pity on me, and send Lazarus to dip the tip of his finger in water and cool my tongue, for I am tormented in this flame."

Then Abraham explains the reasons for his condemnation and for Lazarus' success: the rich man has had his reward in this life, and he has ignored the beggar; whereas the beggar has suffered with patience. Besides, Lazarus cannot come to the rich man in hell because there is a gulf between those in heaven and those in hell that cannot be bridged.

The rich man next asks Abraham to send Lazarus to warn his five brothers against undue attachment to riches. Abraham says: let them listen to Moses and the prophets: "If they do not hearken to Moses and the prophets, they will not believe even if someone rises from the dead."

Lord, what are You trying to teach? The rich man doesn't seem like a bad sort. He doesn't scorn the poor beggar; and once he is in hell, he even seems to develop a kind of social consciousness: he wants Lazarus to help save his five brothers on earth.

FROM THE DEAD

Why is he in hell? Would it be mainly because he simply *ignores* Lazarus? Because his food and drink and comfort are more precious to him than the *person* of one of the poor? It would seem that You want to bring home to us that preferring things to persons is to expose oneself to the loss of all things, all persons, and to find utter loneliness, hell.

Lord, You are just the opposite of the rich man. You love us as persons. You never look through us, never ignore us in our rags and misery and moral sores. You want us with You forever in Your Kingdom. That is why again and again in Lent and in the gospels You feel the need to warn us of our attachments. You tell us that we can go to hell if we make riches, food, clothing, and any kind of self-indulgence our god and close our hearts to the plight of the poor and sick.

Your prophet Jeremias puts it well in today's epistle: "Cursed be the man that trusteth in man and maketh flesh his arm, and whose heart departeth from the Lord . . . Blessed is the man that trusteth in the Lord." What and whom do I trust — things or my God? I must answer that question. Now, this Lent. On the honest answer I give to it will depend my lot for all eternity.

Lord Jesus, give efficacy to our fasts and prayers, for by them we can be delivered from undue, dangerous attachments. Give us Your negative and Your positive treatment: "Forgive us our sins, O Lord . . . Help us, O God, our Saviour: and for the honor of Thy name, O Lord, deliver us" (gradual).

> *Prayer for the day:*
> THEY HAVE MOSES AND THE PROPHETS. LET THEM HEARKEN TO THEM.

FRIDAY, SECOND WEEK IN LENT

> *Summary:*
> Jesus foretells His death and resurrection, the rejection of His people and the election of the gentiles.

THIS IS THE HEIR

Lord Jesus, four weeks from today will be Good Friday, the day of Your death on the cross. In today's gospel You tell a parable which describes how Your people will reject You and put You to death.

The householder who plants a vineyard is Your Father. He sends His servants to collect the rent. The vine dressers maltreat and kill them. They do the same with a second and larger group. Finally the owner sends his son. They kill him too.

Then You ask: "What will the owner of the vineyard do to those vine dressers?" The people answer: "He will utterly destroy those evil men, and will let out the vineyard to other vine dressers, who will render to him the fruits in their seasons."

In all this You are speaking of the manner in which the chosen people have received the prophets . . . and You. They will put You to death: You are the Son whom God the Supreme Owner sends. But death will not be Your end, You tell them. "Did you never read: 'The stone which the builders rejected has become the cornerstone; by the Lord this has been done and it is wonderful in our eyes'? Therefore I say to you, that the kingdom of God will be taken away from you and will be given to a people yielding its fruits."

Lord Jesus, it must be with infinite regret that You tell them this parable, knowing that it will be literally enacted. Rejection by one's own is never easy to take. But self-pity has never been Your favorite pastime. More distressing to You is the fact that by treating You thus they will destroy themselves. So this is a warning to them. You tell them in advance how evil their thinking and acting will be. And they know You are talking about them. But they have hardened their hearts. Your prophecy will be fulfilled.

SPEAKING ABOUT THEM

Well, the first Good Friday profits them little. Will the one to come be different for us? It depends on our relation and attitude to You. Surely there is no hatred in us as there is in them. But there can very well be a lot of indifference to and rejection of Your way of life. We must not think that mere membership in the Catholic Church will save us. We have to die with You. And that is what every Mass and every Lent is all about.

I must die daily to self by this Lenten life. This dying is a progressive advance towards the climax of Good Friday. There is a mentality in me that rebels against this dying. Therefore, Lord Jesus, "Grant that cleansed by this holy fast, we may be brought by Thee with pure hearts to the holy season to come" (collect).

With our fasting and Your leading us on, we prepare for our Good Friday this year. But death is far from the end either for You or for us. You die and You rise. "As for me, I will appear before Thy sight in justice: I shall be satisfied when Thy glory shall appear" (introit). "Look down, O Lord, to help me" (offertory verse).

Prayer for the day:

THE STONE WHICH THE BUILDERS REJECTED HAS BECOME THE CORNERSTONE.

SATURDAY, SECOND WEEK IN LENT

Summary:

Jesus in His parable of the Prodigal Son reveals the deep mercy of the Father towards sinners.

PRODIGAL SON

Lord Jesus, in this parable You characterize each of us with an exactness that is as true today as it was in Your own time. Man is self-centered, pleasure-directed, careless, foolish; he is bent towards fast living and sinning . . . and alternately towards conversion when the money runs out.

I think there is sincerity in the prodigal son's conversion even though it seems motivated more by memory of the good life in his father's house than by a deep love. He does turn away from his sinful life, and from eating with swine, to find his way back to his father. He says: "Father, I have sinned against heaven and before thee. I am no longer worthy to be called thy son; make me as one of thy hired men."

Lord Jesus, if no one has ever known the heart of man as You have, surely no one has better known the heart of God either.

Seeing the son coming from afar, the father (he has been waiting and watching each day) runs to meet him. And, as Peguy points out, it is the father who weeps. His boy's confession is hardly heard: the important thing is to show the lad how welcome back he is. The loved one has returned. Robe, ring, fatted calf are prepared.

"Let us eat and make merry; because this my son was dead, and has come to life again; he was lost, and is found."

Lord Jesus, You are thinking first of all of the human race. Mankind is the prodigal son who goes off to a life of sin and then comes to his senses and returns to the Father. But humanity is individualized in each of us, in me. I don't have to go off on a spree of riotous living to be a prodigal son.

NO LONGER WORTHY

Selfish doing of my own will in a single fall from grace effects the resemblance. And the result of sin — great or small, few or many — is always the same: the food of swine causing me to recognize my betrayal. Confession, conversion, fall. So it goes again and again. And the Father always there, waiting, waiting. I am no longer worthy to be called thy son; make me as one of thy hired men.

Lord Jesus, is there no limit to His patience and to His mercy? Not that I want a limit. If there is anything I need, it is His mercy. But more than all else I need conversion: real, all-embracing, deeply-penetrating conversion of the sort that springs more from love of the Father than from any kind of self-interest or fear. The kind that forces this admission from my heart of hearts: Father, I have sinned against *Thee.*

But the way back to the Father's house is narrow, steep, hard. You are leading me along, helping me each time You absolve me from my sins in confession, each time You join me to Your Sacrifice of the Mass and feed me with Your body and blood. By this help and by the Lenten life You are gradually turning the center of my life away from myself to You and the Father. Lord Jesus, grant that Easter will bring about the final reunion.

Prayer for the day:
I AM NO LONGER WORTHY TO BE CALLED THY SON.

THIRD SUNDAY IN LENT

Summary:

Jesus confounds critics who accuse Him of casting out devils in the name and power of Beelzebub.

BLESSED ARE THEY

Lord, I am going to pass over most of this gospel to concentrate on the last scene. You drive a devil out of a man who had been dumb and he now speaks sanely. Some of the people marvel. Others object absurdly that You and Satan are in partnership together. You are superb in laying that accusation: "If Satan is divided against himself, how shall his kingdom stand? If I cast out devils by the finger of God, then the kingdom of God has come upon you . . . He who is not with me is against me."

All this is build-up for that wonderful display of enthusiasm on the part of that nameless woman of the crowd and an equally wonderful lesson in Christian living for all of us.

The woman has been watching You. She has seen the miracle and heard You rebuke Your enemies. You have been growing on her. Now she can no longer hold back her conviction about You. She shouts aloud the thought that has been forming in her woman's mind: "Blessed is the womb that bore thee, and the breasts that nursed thee!"

You have to admit, Lord Jesus, that few tributes to You and Your Mother in Your day or since have ever equalled this one in intensity of love, feeling, and beauty of imagery. Why then do You rebuke her . . . or seem to? What do You mean by those mysterious words, "Rather, blessed are they who hear the word of God and keep it"?

Are You saying that to hear Your word and keep it is a greater thing than being Your mother in the flesh? It would seem so; and if such is the case, what a vision of life You give to all of us! Of course, Mary comes off better than anyone else in meeting this standard of Yours, because no one has ever approached her perfection in doing Your will, in hearing the word of God and keeping it.

But You seem to say that it was her doing God's will rather than her physical motherhood that made her great.

WHO HEAR THE WORD

Lord Jesus, I am overjoyed at the new meaning Your teaching gives to my own life. I can hear Your word, and with Your help I can keep it. I can do Your will. I can say with Mary, "Be it done to me according to thy word," and if I try to follow through on that with all sincerity and honesty, holding back nothing of my own will, Your words can be true of me: "Rather, blessed is he who bears the word of God and keeps it."

How this teaching can transform daily living and suffering, Lord Jesus! A man might be a hopeless victim of cancer, doomed to early death. A woman might be old and arthritic and plagued with the feeling that she has out-lived her usefulness. A youngster, crippled with polio, might say, "What kind of future do I have in this condition?"

Straight and clear Your words come to these and all of us: "Blessed are they who hear the word of God and keep it!" And if we take that word of Yours and keep it and try with all our might in our weak human way to make it the single, underlying principle of our lives, then we become new beings, each of us bearing a remarkable resemblance to You and to Your Mother, Mary.

It is breath-taking. But You say it, and it must be true.

Lord, now is the time for me to make the decisive step. Now, this Lent. My baptism has made me one with You who said, "My meat is to do the will of Him who sent me." I have heard Your word. Help me, make me, keep it. "My eyes are ever towards the Lord: for He shall pluck my feet out of the snare: look Thou upon me, and have mercy on me, for I am alone and poor" (introit).

Prayer for the day:
BLESSED IS THE WOMB THAT BORE THEE.

MONDAY, THIRD WEEK IN LENT

Summary:

Jesus is rejected by the people of His home town, but He escapes their attempt to kill Him.

NO PROPHET ACCEPTABLE

Lord, there is no hurt more painful than that caused by those You love. These are Your own people. You have grown up with them, You have made furniture for them in Joseph's shop. You were friends with them. Then You went away and became famous. They have heard about You and Your growing reputation and have wondered when You would come home. Now You are there. You have just finished reading a portion of the prophecy of Isaias. The prophecy describes the Messias to come. You claim to be the fulfillment of the prophecy, You claim to be the Promised of the Nations, You, the boy of Nazareth!

At first they receive the announcement with joy. This will bring honor to their town. Then doubt rises and begins to spread. Can any good come out of their town? Do they want any good to come out? "Is not this Joseph's son?" You are watching them, You see their enthusiasm, poisoned perhaps by jealousy and pride, turn to skepticism and then to open enmity.

You now speak to them: "You will surely quote me this proverb, 'Physician, cure thyself! Whatever things we have heared of as done in Capharnaum, do here also in thy own country!' Amen I say to you, no prophet is acceptable in his own country."

Your subsequent references to the pagan widow to whom Elias was sent and to the pagan Naaman whom Eliseus cured indicate to them Your opinion that just being members of the Chosen Race will not save them. Doubt and jealousy have now grown violently into wrath. They rise up, grasp You angrily, push You through the village to the top of the hill on which their town is built. They want to destroy You! But Your hour is not yet. You stop and look around at them. They fall back in fear. Sadly You pass through their midst down the hill, out of the town. Will Nazareth ever see You again?

THROUGH THEIR MIDST

Lord Jesus, they reject You. Your old friends will have nothing to do with You. Do You see in the distance that other hill, Calvary? But there it will be strangers who will reject and crucify You. Here it is Your own. "My people, what have I done to thee? Or in what have I grieved thee? Answer me" (Reproaches of Good Friday).

Poor, unhappy Nazareth, to have so refused her Savior! And yet, what have Nazareth's citizens done that we have not done thousands of times? When we sin, we thrust You out of the city of our life, we rush You to the top of the hill of our pride, ready to cast You off. What can we say? There isn't much that we can say or do except, "I confess to Almighty God . . . that I have sinned exceedingly in thought, word, and deed. Through my fault, through my fault, through my most grievous fault . . . Kyrie, eleison, Christe, eleison. Lord have mercy, Christ, have mercy, Lord, have mercy!" Sorrow, confession, regret — these are our part. "Make, O Lord, the gift of our service, which we offer unto Thee, into a saving sacrament" (secret). "Hear, O God, my prayer, and despise not my supplication: be attentive to me and hear me" (offertory verse).

> Prayer for the day:
> BUT HE, PASSING THROUGH THEIR MIDST, WENT HIS WAY.

TUESDAY, THIRD WEEK IN LENT

Summary:
Jesus teaches the necessity of fraternal correction, the power of binding and loosing in His Church, and our need to forgive those who offend us.

BOUND ALSO IN HEAVEN

Lord Jesus, You seem to believe that correcting the faults of our brethren is much more important than we think. We are very good at talking about others' faults behind their back: few of us have the courage to do it to their face. You insist that it has to be done. You say: if the erring brother does not listen to the first correction, one should take two or three other brothers and try again. If that attempt is not successful, there should be an appeal "to the Church." If he refuses to heed the Church, let him be to us "as the heathen and the publican."

Then You tell the apostles: "Whatever you bind on earth shall be bound also in heaven; and whatever you loose on earth shall be loosed also in heaven. I say to you further, that if two of you shall agree on earth about anything at all for which they ask, it shall be done for them by my Father in heaven. For where two or three are gathered together for my sake, there am I in the midst of them." Finally, You tell Peter that Your followers are to forgive injuries again and again, without counting the number, "seventy times seventy times."

Lord Jesus, in all this — in commanding that faults be corrected, in granting the power to bind and loose, in requiring forgiveness — You show Your vital concern for the most intimate details of our family community life. You know men — how capable and proficient they are in letting faults of character spoil both their own personalities and the common life of the family.

You also know how capable they are in coming to their senses and how they therefore need forgiveness again and again. You know that there can be no true community life if You are not in its midst; and You cannot exist where there is hatred and a spirit of revenge. You are love.

BINDING AND LOOSING

"Where two or three are gathered together for my sake, there am I in the midst of them," You say. And You are there for one purpose only — to bring abiding love.

Lord, You have lived Your temporal life in Palestine in order to make a community. I recall Your prayer at the Last Supper: "Father . . . grant that they may be one as Thou in me and I in Thee: grant that they may be one in us." Your death and resurrection establishes Your Church, Your living community. It is this living community of Yours, it is Your Mystical Body, Your Church that You are concerned with today. And Your main concern? Unity, love, forgiveness among us, the members. Your living in Your Church now, this Lent, Your daily offering of Your holy Sacrifice of the Mass aims at consolidating what You begin in Your historical life.

Lord, I am constantly appealing to the power of binding and loosing that You have given to Your Church, and I am being forgiven again and again. My prayer has been: "From my secret sins, cleanse me, O Lord: and from those of others spare Thy servant" (gradual). Please, Lord Jesus, along with Your forgiveness of my evil-doing, give me the grace to forgive. For that is the grace that will make me like unto You who prays, hanging on the cross, "Father, forgive them, they know not what they do."

> *Prayer for the day:*
>
> WHERE TWO OR THREE ARE GATHERED TO-
> GETHER FOR MY SAKE, THERE AM I IN THE
> MIDST OF THEM.

WEDNESDAY, THIRD WEEK IN LENT

Summary:

Jesus condemns the pharisaical following of the letter of the Law to the neglect of the spirit of love it contains.

THINGS THAT DEFILE

Lord Jesus, You sum up today's gospel thus: "The things that proceed out of the mouth come from the heart, and it is they that defile a man. For out of the heart come evil thoughts, murders, adulteries, immoralities, thefts, false witness, blasphemies. These are the things that defile a man: but to eat with unwashed hands does not defile a man."

The occasion for this clear doctrine is another brush You have with the insincerity of the Pharisees and Scribes. They *seem* to love

God's law. They talk that way and go through the motions of devotion to it. But, as You say, "This people honors me with their lips, but their heart is far from me."

You know, I think You are so "touchy" about this point because You really love the Law. You see the Law as the tangible manifestation for men of Your Father's holy will and therefore as a wonderful challenge to holiness. Not only a challenge, but an invitation and a help. It is the Father's direction and guidance towards the goal that He has set for us: happiness forever.

But that is hardly the way the Scribes and Pharisees conceive it. Instead of seeing Your Father as the source and end of the Law, they look at the mere word and command, completely unrelated either to man or to God. They make their slavish observance of the letter of the Law into a prideful gratification of their own ego instead of a personal outpouring of love. And so they would have everyone else act.

Their trouble is utter lack of love, of love springing freely from adoring hearts. Their sterile interpretation of the precepts has replaced the spirit of divine, fatherly solicitude for men with which the Law was first given by Your Father.

WAYS OF LIFE

You can take that kind of man-made religion just so long. Today You sharply revolt against it. You make it plain that neglecting to wash one's hands before eating — to say nothing of all the rest of their narrow interpretations — is utterly insignificant as an offense against God compared to the horrid violations of His love that are brewed in man's heart, whether they are expressed or not.

Lord Jesus, it is good for You to recall this to us. We modern Christians are very inclined to be critical of the Pharisees. But we forget that the spirit of Phariseeism — the tendency to see the letter of the Law instead of You and Your Father's loving will in the Law — is subtle enough to possess any of us.

Lent is a time for us to purify our motivation, our ideals, our hearts. It is a time for us to return to fundamentals; the basic fundamental of all is *sincerity* in our relations with You. This is essential for us not just that we may avoid the condemnation that You level against the Pharisees. But rather that we may have You and Your Law in the midst of our hearts and thus be led by it to the heart of our God. "Thou hast made known to me the ways of life" (communion verse). Your laws, the Ten Commandments, the commandments of the Church, and especially Your "new" law of love of one another are ways of life. They express Your will. Lord Jesus, in this Mass, in the rest of Lent, fill me with zeal to obey the Law with love so that in the end You may fill me with the joy of Your countenance.

Prayer for the day:
THIS PEOPLE HONORS ME WITH THEIR LIPS, BUT THEIR HEART IS FAR FROM ME.

THURSDAY, THIRD WEEK IN LENT

Summary:
Jesus cures Peter's mother-in-law of her fever and then all manner of other victims of disease and diabolical possession.

A GREAT FEVER

Lord Jesus, it is easy — and pleasant — to picture this scene in Peter's house. You arrive there and someone tells You that Peter's mother-in-law is in bed with a "great fever." In that condition how can she prepare meals for You and for the disciples? Would You help her? they ask. Yes, You would. You stand over her, rebuke the fever, and it leaves her. At once she gets up and sets about preparing the dinner with which she will reward You.

Word spreads that You are in town. By sundown all the neighborhood families flock to You with their sick. You go from one to another, lay Your hands on them and they are well. Disease flees at Your word; so do the devils that possess some of the unfortunates.

All through the night You labor at Your healing. Little wonder that the crowds seek You out in Your hiding place at dawn and plead with You not to depart from them. But You belong, not to just one little town in Palestine, but to the country, to the world. You tell them: "To the other towns also I must proclaim the kingdom of God, for this is why I have been sent."

Off You go then, but You leave behind a village full of love and gratitude. So it is with You, Lord Jesus, with Your great heart so full of pity, compassion, sympathy! How perfectly do these words of today's introit fit into Your mouth: "I am the salvation of the people . . .: from whatever tribulation they shall cry to me, I will hear them: and I will be their Lord forever."

Lord, You do exactly the same things for us that You do for those Palestinians. You still say: "I *am* the salvation of the people." And how we need Your healing hand! There are still the same diseases of our souls. "Our fever," says St. Ambrose, "is avarice; our fever is caprice; our fever is luxury; our fever is ambition; our fever is inclination to anger" (Homily at Matins).

ALL HOPE IN THEE

Lord Jesus Christ, have mercy on us! You are our salvation, our health, when in Your sacrament of Penance You take away the guilt of our sins and fill us with the health which is Your own divine life. Above all, You are our health when You feed us with Your body and blood in this and every Mass. "The eyes of all hope in Thee, O Lord; and Thou givest them meat in due season. Thou openest Thy hand, and fillest every living creature with blessing" (gradual).

Lord, what is this "health" which You say You are? From Your point of view, it is Your own divine life shared with us. You literally dwell in us. For us it implies conversion, the deep-seated, radical will to turn away from self in order to live for You. That is why You tell us: "Attend, O my people, to my law: incline your ears to the words of my mouth" (introit).

"If I shall walk in the midst of tribulation, Thou wilt quicken me, O Lord: and Thou wilt stretch forth Thy hand against the wrath of my enemies, and Thy right hand shall save me" (offertory verse). Your will to save is obvious as always, so also Your desire for

our cooperation, our attending to Your law. Lord Jesus, help us all
to come together with You in this Your desire.

Prayer for the day:
THOU ART THE SON OF GOD.

FRIDAY, THIRD WEEK IN LENT

Summary:

Jesus speaks to the sinful Samaritan woman
and reveals Himself to her as the Messias.

LIVING WATER

Lord Jesus, the first thing I notice in this experience of Yours
with the Samaritan woman is that it is You who make the first
approach and request. "Give me drink," You ask her. It is something of a shock to her: hearing a demand like that from a man, and
a Jew at that! Between Jews and Samaritans there is little communication and little love lost. But this is Your way of doing things. It
is still Your way. People think they are seeking God, but if they
seek Him, it is because You first seek them.

The woman is interested. It is probably the first time any man
has made a decent request of her and treated her as a person, with
any kind of respect. She hears Your words: "If thou didst know the
gift of God, and who it is who says to thee, 'Give me to drink,'
thou, perhaps, wouldst have asked of him and he would have given
thee living water."

She has a hard time making out what You are talking about.
She is thinking of ordinary water: You are speaking about water
as the symbol of the Life of God, divine grace. With no experience
of this Life, she can hardly know that the living water is in fact
divine Life, divine Love and friendship which You are eager to
share with her. "Whence hast thou living water?" she asks. She is

falling into Your hands, Lord Jesus. Just a few more words from You, and her eyes will be opened up to a great new world. You tell her: "He who drinks of the water that I will give him shall never thirst: but the water that I will give him shall become in him a fountain of water, springing up into life everlasting."

Surely, these are strange words for a woman to hear who is as careless of morality as she is. But You have her now. She asks: "Sir, give me this water that I may not thirst, or come here to draw." She still thinks You are talking about the clear, cool flow of a human-dug well. *But she has made a demand of You.* She has prayed. She has sought You. And how You answer her seeking! You reveal to her—to this sinful woman with five ex-husbands—the fact that You are the Messias!

TO SEE A MAN

There has been a wonderful exchange here: You ask her for water, and she asks You; and You are both happy with the results. She rushes off to tell all the men and women in town about You: "Come and see a man who has told me all that I have ever done. Can he be the Christ?" You see her coming back to You, at the head of a line of villagers, fulfilling woman's finest vocation—that of leading men to You. Thus does she answer Your request to her: "Give me to drink."

Lord Jesus, do I hear You say to me, "Give me to drink"? Does just the fact that I am thinking about this incident (and all the others) mean that You seek me even as You have sought the Samaritan?

Here we are at holy Mass, the fountainhead of the living water You describe to her. Here we hear You say to each and all of us: "I who speak with thee am the Messias." Here You become our food, our drink . . . and our truth . . . but only in proportion to our desire for You, our willingness to accept You into the whole of our lives.

Lord, make us want You, fill us with deep desire for You, make us sincere when we pray: "In You has my heart confided, and I have been helped: and my flesh has flourished again, and with my will I will give praise to You. Unto Thee will I cry, O Lord: O my God, be not Thou silent nor depart from me" (gradual).

Prayer for the day:

MY FOOD IS TO DO THE WILL OF HIM WHO SENT ME, TO ACCOMPLISH HIS WORK.

SATURDAY, THIRD WEEK IN LENT

Summary:

Jesus rescues an adulteress from being stoned to death and forgives her.

CAUGHT IN ADULTERY

Lord Jesus, the woman has been caught in the act, and according to Your Father's own Law, she deserves to be stoned to death. There is sin and sin; but adultery is a crime that violates both divine law and a human contract. It is the worst possible insult to married love.

So there she is before You, the focus of a multitude of scornful despising eyes, knowing in her heart her guilt, and terrified at the consequences of her act. The pious voice of one of the Pharisees states the situation: "Master, this woman has just now been caught in adultery. And in the Law, Moses commanded us to stone such persons. What, therefore, dost thou say?"

It's a tricky question. If You say, "Oh, it's nothing, let her go," You will be accused of belittling the Law. If You say, "Go ahead and stone her," Your reputation for mercy and compassion will suffer in the eyes of the common people.

You look at them and You look at her. You look into them and into her. In them You see corruption piled high, and in many cases aggravated by ugly pride. You see corruption in her, too, but also grief, regret, sorrow. You stoop over and begin to write in the sand with Your finger. They wait for Your answer, but You keep writing, apparently uninterested in their trap. Your silence becomes a voice that reaches into the depths of their souls. Finally You put in words the judgment that they already know: "Let him who is without sin among you be the first to cast a stone at her." And they slink away one by one, the oldest first.

If it were to go no further, it would be a beautiful story, Lord Jesus. But You are not finished with the woman. Now You are alone with her. She has been a great sinner and was caught in the act. You are infinite holiness, yet You do not seem at all uncomfortable in her presence. "Woman," You ask, "Where are they? Has no one condemned thee?" She raises her head, looks around, looks at You. "No one, Lord." Your next words burn into her soul, never to be forgotten: "Neither will I condemn thee. Go thy way, and from now on sin no more." I'm sure she will obey You.

GO THY WAY

Lord Jesus, why? Aren't the Pharisees right? Doesn't she deserve death? Yes, she does. The Law is right. But You are telling us that it is not man—especially not sinful, holier-than-thou, hypocritical judges of human guilt—who have a right to determine guilt and punishment. It is You, God. Sin can be big, but Your forgiveness can be greater . . . if You see humble sorrow and regret and longing love in the heart of the sinner. And evidently You see plenty of that in her.

Lord Jesus, comparisions are odious, so I won't put myself in the place either of the Pharisees or the adulteress. But I know where I belong: at Your feet. All sin is a kind of adultery: it is a violation of love binding creature to Creator. It deserves death and hell thereafter. But up to now it seems that Your love for us will not be destroyed even by our weakness. Again and again, in Your holy sacrament of Penance, You forgive. Again and again You invite us back into loving union with You and You cement the union at the wedding feast of Holy Mass. Again and again during this holy Lenten season and all the Lenten seasons of our life, You say to us: "Go thy way, and from now on sin no more." Lord, I shall try to obey. My success will be in proportion to the clean and new heart

You create in me. "Direct my steps according to Thy word: and let no iniquity have dominion over me, O Lord" (offertory verse).

Prayer for the day:
> GO THY WAY, AND FROM NOW ON SIN NO MORE.

FOURTH SUNDAY IN LENT

Summary:
> Jesus feeds a great multitude by multiplying five barley loaves and two fish; and afterwards the disciples gather up twelve baskets of leavings.

THE PEOPLE RECLINE

Lord Jesus, a great crowd follows You, because they see the signs You work upon those who are sick. You are sitting there on the slope of the mountain. The people mill around, they look at You, they wait.

They do not know exactly what they are waiting for, but they know that being with You is wonderfully satisfying and all that matters.

You look at them, too. You see that they are hungry, perhaps without even knowing it. You know men—that they have bodies as well as souls. So You say to Philip: "Whence shall we buy bread that these may eat?"

That starts the drama. A young boy stands before You. He has been fishing and has had just fair luck. He has seen the crowd and concluded that he might be able to sell his catch. But fish need something to go with them, so he has also picked up some bread.

You ask if he is willing to give You the bread and the fish. Without hesitation he holds them out, and You accept. You give thanks to the Father (and surely to the boy, too) and begin to distribute the bread and fish to the people.

I can't picture the multiplication, Lord Jesus. I don't suppose it is necessary that I should. The people eat. They eat as much as they want—till they are filled. And as they eat, their eyes open to what is taking place. They have seen or heard that there were only five loaves and two fish at the start. Now it dawns on them that the food they eat is miraculous—like the manna their ancestors ate in the desert. They see it coming from Your holy hands.

But what are they thinking of? Are they filled with the realization of Your great goodness and mercy? Are they grateful to You for Your kind thoughtfulness and understanding of their needs?

No. Judging them by myself, I am afraid their ideas and then their talk are colored by the vision of how useful You could be to them. You could be a King to end all kings, a ruler who rules, yes, but also one who feeds all his subjects—and with the minimum amount of effort for them as well as for Yourself.

You see into those minds, and You say to Yourself: "They are thinking of laying hands on me and making me their king. I shall be their king all right, yet not in the way they want. But the time is not quite here. Then You slip away up the mountain, alone by Yourself.

BREAD OF LIFE

Lord Jesus, by multiplying loaves and fishes, You are preparing Your disciples, the Jews, and us to believe that You can change bread into Your body and wine into Your blood. And when the people find You again the next day, You will say: "I am the bread of life . . . the bread that I will give is my flesh for the life of the world" (John 6). It is that Bread that I eat, Lord Jesus. I greatly prefer it to the miraculously multiplied bread You gave to the Jews.

But I cannot forget the boy who had the bread and the fish. It was his bread and fish that You multiplied! He has provided material for Your miracle. The rest of his life he will think about this and boast a little. "I gave Him the bread and the fish," he will say to his grandchildren. And he will be glad.

Lord Jesus, I haven't any bread and fish to give You; but if I give You this daily Lenten life of mine, will You change it into Your passion? If I give You my heart, will You give me Yours in return? If I give You all that I am and want to be and will be, will You accept me and give thanks and multiply and distribute me? There is only one thing I want in return: the will and the desire always to praise You, for You are good and to sing to Your name for You are sweet (offertory verse).

Prayer for the day:

THIS IS INDEED THE PROPHET.

MONDAY, FOURTH WEEK IN LENT

Summary:

Jesus cleanses the temple of the merchants and predicts His resurrection.

HOUSE OF MY FATHER

Lord, You go to Jerusalem to celebrate the great feast of the Passover. The first place You visit, naturally, is Your Father's House, the temple, the place where His glory dwells. But what is this You find there—a regular market-place where cattle are bought and sold! It is an insulting violation of the sacredness of the place and the reverence that is due to God. And when there is any question of Your Father's honor and of the respect that is due Him and His holy places, You cease to be "tolerant" or "meek" or "easy-going." Money-making has no place whatsoever in God's dwelling-place.

This is a truth You will drive home to them (and to all men of all time) in as dramatic a manner as possible. They will long remember the sting of Your whip in their bodies and the anger that blazes in Your eyes. Out with them! Out with their cattle! Out with their doves and money! "Take these things away, and do not make the house of my Father a house of business!"

You are a different and strange Jesus to the disciples now. And then one of them remembers the prophecy: "The zeal for thy house has eaten me up." It is well put. The incident reveals in clear light the whole extent of man's relation to his God. Is God to be God, the supreme Lord and Ruler who has rights that He cannot give away or play down? or is He merely a convenience of man who can be shoved aside at the slightest provocation? I remember Your words to Satan at the beginning of Your public life: "Begone, Satan, the Lord thy God shalt thou worship and him only shall thou adore!"

It is to re-establish God in His rightful place in men's lives that You have come to earth and will suffer and die and rise again.

But here are the Pharisees with some questions for You. Who are You, they want to know. What right have You to show such possessive authority? "What sign dost thou show us, seeing that thou dost these things?" Your answer is something of a puzzle to them (and to us): "Destroy this temple, and in three days I will raise it up." St. John explains that You are speaking of the temple of Your body.

IN THREE DAYS

They are going to obey You, Lord Jesus. They are going to destroy the temple of Your body when they hang You on the cross with nails through Your hands and feet. But by that very destruction, they are going to give You the opportunity to fulfill the second part of Your prophecy: "In three days I will raise it up." And then the disciples will remember the prediction of this day and will believe "the Scriptures and the word" that You speak here today. Then, too, You will show them the sign that the temple is not only Your Father's house, but also Yours; and that the only fitting activity for that house is to hear Your word and to respond to it with loving worship and adoration and thanks.

Lord Jesus, this preview of Your Passion and death is not easy for You to take. Already You experience the hatred that they will vent upon You on that terrible day. The words of today's introit fit Your mouth: "Save me, O God, by Thy name, and in Thy strength deliver me: O God, hear my prayer; give ear to the words of my mouth. For strangers have risen up against me: and the mighty have sought after my soul."

Lord Jesus, we are Your temple now; but unhappily we have

introduced into Your temple unworthy ways of thinking and acting
that are as hateful to You as the buying and selling of the Jerusalem
merchants of Your day. You must enter into this temple and drive
out all corruption. Purify us, cleanse us, sanctify us. "From my
secret sins, cleanse me, O Lord: and from those of others, spare
Thy servant" (communion verse).

> **Prayer for the day:**
> **DO NOT MAKE THE HOUSE OF MY FATHER A
> HOUSE OF BUSINESS.**

TUESDAY, FOURTH WEEK IN LENT

Summary:
> Jesus faces His enemies and asks why they want
> to put Him to death.

SEEKING HIS DEATH

Lord Jesus, it is painful to observe the cold hatred Your enemies
have for You. They act more like jealous children than intelligent
and learned doctors of the Law. One can feel their anger, their
envy, jealousy and hatred gradually combining into a mass of murderous intent. You sense it with deep sadness. "Why do you seek to
put me to death?" You ask.

Their answer is as wild as the errant minds that concoct it:
"Thou hast a devil." You, the wonder-worker, the compassionate
healer of minds and bodies, the light of the world, the supreme
teacher of Your Father's truth—they accuse You of being possessed
by a devil! That must be pleasant for You to take!

You justify Yourself for having healed a man on the Sabbath (for
that seems to be what is eating them these days): "If a man receives
circumcision on a Sabbath, that the Law of Moses may not be broken, are you indignant with me because I made a whole man well
on a Sabbath?"

It is no use trying to make them see truth, Lord Jesus. Their hearts are hard, and they have closed their eyes and minds. Hatred is going to grow in them until it forces Your blood from Your body. They will get You, it is inevitable, but not yet. They want to seize You now, but no one dares lay hands on You, because Your hour is not yet come.

There is something very mysterious here, Lord Jesus. The hatred of Your enemies is apparently the necessary means for sending You to Your redeeming death. Yet You act and talk in Your own defense and as though You are hurt by their attitude. Is it because You love them and do not want to see them injured by their own hatred?

NO HANDS ON HIM

The introit of today's Mass fits well Your frame of mind, Your great inner unhappiness and sorrow: "O God, hear my prayer, and hide not Thyself from my pleading, listen to me and answer me. In my anguish I am bewildered and troubled at the voice of the foe, the cry of the sinner. For they bring evils upon me and with fury they attack me."

I cannot solve this mystery, Lord. But with Your help I can and I shall see to it that no thought or action of mine will join me to the ranks of the Pharisees and cause You to say to me: Why do you seek to put me to death? But that is mostly negative action. Best of all, in this and all future Masses I can and will enter into Your inner passion and make it my own. With You I can say: "Behold I come; in the book it is written of me: To do thy will, O my God, is my delight, and thy law is in my very heart" (Psalm 39).

For You the Passion and death are the prelude to resurrection. So it must be for us. On that day we will rejoice in Your salvation: and in the name of our God we shall be exalted (communion verse).

Prayer for the day:

MY TEACHING IS NOT MY OWN, BUT HIS WHO SENT ME.

WEDNESDAY, FOURTH WEEK IN LENT

Summary:

Jesus restores sight to a man born blind and again incurs the displeasure of the Pharisees.

BORN BLIND

Lord Jesus, You say: "As long as I am in the world, I am the light of the world." This is good news, for light is good, Your kind of light especially. It is so good that it is a kind of foretaste of heaven. It is this principle of Yours that prompts You to open the eyes of the man who has been born blind. It hurts You to see eyes that cannot behold the beauty that You have created, the beauty that tries in its own imperfect way to reflect You who are infinite beauty. You are the light of the world, You are the light of eyes.

There is much drama in the chain of events that Your miracle unleashes. The Pharisees, of course, realistically continue to play their role as villains. They are blind, too. A man, blind from birth, can now see. That stupendous fact is apparently very insignificant to them compared to Your "crime" in spreading a mixture of Your spittle with soil on the poor fellow's sightless eyes. He can see now; but You have done Your mixing on the Sabbath, of course, and that is bad . . . in their view.

Then there is the ex-blind man himself. He is very upright and honest and down to earth. After all those years of darkness, he thinks that seeing is pretty wonderful and the world very beautiful. And, in spite of the displeasure of the Pharisees at Your action, he thinks that You are pretty wonderful, too. He doesn't at all go along with their attempts to discredit You. He teases them: "Whether he is a sinner, I do not know. One thing I do know, that whereas I was blind, now I see . . . Would you also become his disciples?" They can't take that, and soon he finds himself thrown out of the synagogue.

LIGHT AND LIFE

You must enjoy keeping in the background and observing Your

99

new friend cross swords with Your enemies, exposing them as the quibblers they are. You think, he will be a very valuable disciple now that he sees . . . and loves. You find him and say: "Dost thou believe in the Son of God?" "Who is he, Lord, that I may believe in him?" You answer: "Thou hast both seen him, and it is he who speaks with thee." Then comes his confession of faith: "I believe, Lord." And falling down he worships You.

Lord Jesus, You say today, "As long as I am in the world, I am the light of the world." As You have given light to the blind man, You now give light and life — You give Your very Self — to us in Baptism. You touch him, You touch us. It is You who act in every sacrament. Baptism fulfills Your prophecy in us: "You shall be cleansed from all your filthiness, and I will cleanse you from all your idols. And I will give you a new heart, and put a new spirit within you: and I will take away the stony heart out of your flesh, and will give you a heart of flesh. And I will put my spirit in the midst of you . . . and you shall be my people: and I will be your God" (epistle).

You have actually done all this to and for us. What You do for us in Baptism is much more wonderful than what You have done for the man born blind. For because of the faith that You give us in Baptism, we now can see with Your eyes and love with Your heart.

Lord Jesus, we have allowed this faith and love to become darkened. Come to us in this Mass and restore our sight so that we can be ready on Holy Saturday night to greet You with our most joyous cry: "Light of Christ . . . Thanks be to God." Blessed be God who hath not turned away my prayer, nor His mercy from me (offertory verse).

Prayer for the day:

AS LONG AS I AM IN THE WORLD I AM THE LIGHT OF THE WORLD.

THURSDAY, FOURTH WEEK IN LENT

Summary:

Jesus, touched by the grief of a widowed mother, restores life to her son.

DO NOT WEEP

Lord Jesus, all Your holy activity reveals Your hatred of any kind of negation, neglect, or abuse of any of the powers You put in man. Eyes are made to see: You constantly give sight to the blind. Legs are made to carry a person: You make cripples walk. The human body is made for life: thrice at least You restore life to dead men.

Today You confront death in the young man of Naim. You do not like death at all, nor do You like the pain it brings to those who are left behind, especially if they are mothers. This woman is a widow, alone in the world now, for the corpse there on the stretcher is her only son. Just a glance at her grief is enough to make up Your mind. "Do not weep," You tell her.

You touch the stretcher. The bearers stand still. The tense crowd then hears words that the world has seldom if ever heard before: "Young man, I say to thee, Arise!" (Who but a wild man . . . or God Himself, would dare such a command!). There is movement on the stretcher; eyes open, a smile forms, the boy sits up, gets up, stands before You, begins to speak.

You look at him: this is the way he should be, alive, well, happy. You take his arm and lead him to his mother's embrace, and there is no point here in being too specific about her outpourings of love, delight, joy, gratitude. How many mothers have ever had dead sons returned to them alive and healthy? The people sense their unworthiness to be in the presence of One who can so command death. Fear seizes upon them, and they begin to glorify God, saying: "A great prophet has risen among us," and "God has visited His people."

VISITED HIS PEOPLE

Lord Jesus, if dead bodies and crippled limbs hurt You, how much more must You rebell against dead souls! "Arise!" is a cry

101

and a command that death forces from You; and it doesn't matter whether the death is physical or spiritual, nor how many times You face it.

A child is baptized by a priest. It is You who baptize, You who say: Young man, I say to thee, arise! And where there was separation from God, absence of His divine Life, there is now Life, Your Life.

A confession is heard by a priest. It is You who hear it, You who say: I say to thee, arise! And where there was spiritual death, sin, there is now Life, grace.

Holy Mass is celebrated. It is You who invite us to be present at Your death and resurrection there made present, You who invite us to die and rise with You, You who feed us with Your sacred body and blood in Holy Communion.

Lent makes its yearly visitation to Your Mystical Body, Your Church, filled as it is with some members who have become spiritually ill, careless about their love for You, or others who have fallen away completely into spiritual death. You speak again: Men, women, children, I say to you all, Arise! Live! Grow! And in the glorious renewal of our baptism on the night before Your resurrection, You will bring us to life again and restore us refreshed and renewed to our holy Mother, our Church. You continue to visit Your people.

O Lord, I will be mindful of Thy justice alone: Thou hast taught me, O God, from my youth: and unto old age and gray hairs, O God, forsake me not (communion verse). Let the heart of them rejoice that seek the Lord; seek Ye the Lord . . . seek His face evermore. Give glory to the Lord, and call upon His name (introit).

Prayer for the day:
YOUNG MAN, I SAY TO THEE, ARISE!

FRIDAY, FOURTH WEEK IN LENT

Summary:

Jesus restores life to Lazarus who had been four days dead.

HOW HE LOVED

Lord Jesus, in this incident I see You at Your most human and Your most divine. Martha and Mary send You a message: "Lord, behold, he whom thou lovest is sick." Knowing You as they do, they are sure their brief word will be sufficent. They are not disappointed.

"Let us also go, that we may die with him," Thomas suggests to his companions when You make it plain that You are going back into Your enemies' territory. (Lord, Thomas could hardly have characterized better the manner in which we should participate in Holy Week).

Now You are there at Lazarus' home. Martha says to You: "Lord, if thou hadst been here my brother would not have died. But even now I know that whatever thou shalt ask of God, God will give it to thee." And You answer: "Thy brother shall rise . . . I am the resurrection and the life; he who believes in me, even if he die, shall live; and whoever lives and believes in me, shall never die."

Martha wants Mary to hear ideas like that and rushes off to find her. "The Master is here and calls for thee," she tells Mary. Mary loses no time. In a moment she is at Your feet. "Master, if thou hadst been here, my brother would not have died." "Where have you laid him?" You ask. "Lord, come and see." And You weep, Lord Jesus. You weep because of Your compassion for these sisters who have lost a brother. The people standing around say, "See how he loved him." In all this I see You at Your most human.

Now I am about to see You at Your most divine. You are at the tomb. "Take away the stone." Martha warns: "Lord, by this time he is already decayed, for he is dead four days." You reply: "Have I not told thee that if thou believe thou shalt behold the glory of God?" What are four days of death to You who are resurrection and life!

THAT WE MAY DIE

"Lazarus, come forth!" Death obeys Life. Lazarus comes forth dressed in his burial clothes. "Unbind him and let him go," comes Your command, and it is joyfully obeyed. Then You and Your dear friends return together to their house. Where there was love before, there is greater love now. Martha and Mary make no effort to restrain their joy and gratitude. But I wonder if Lazarus is not somewhat more quiet than he has been in the past. I wonder if he does not understand life better now that he has known death. I suspect that he is sure now as he never was before that the only thing that matters in this life and the next is being with You, having You with him.

Lord, in just two weeks there is going to be another death, another tomb, and more weeping at the entrance. You will be the victim. But Thomas says to all of us: "Let us also go, that we may die with him." Dying with You is the one condition for rising with You. You will raise us up, for You are the resurrection and the life; he who believes in You, even if he die, shall live; and whoever lives and believes in You, shall never die.

The meditation of my heart is always in Your sight, O Lord, my helper and my redeemer. The meditation of my heart is the desire to follow You wherever You may lead, so long as You will be with me. I believe that You are the Christ, the Son of God, who has come into the world!

> *Prayer for the day:*
> I AM THE RESURRECTION AND THE LIFE; HE WHO BELIEVES IN ME, EVEN IF HE DIE, SHALL LIVE; AND WHOEVER LIVES AND BELIEVES IN ME, SHALL NEVER DIE.

SATURDAY, FOURTH WEEK IN LENT

> *Summary:*
> Jesus claims to be the light of the world.

NOT IN DARKNESS

Lord Jesus, You say to the Pharisees, "I am the light of the world. He who follows me does not walk in darkness, but will have the light of life." You are the light of the world. You are the light of my life. If I follow You, I will not walk in darkness, but will have the light of life.

But how can a man say that he is light, that he is the light of the world? We usually think of light as something lifeless, impersonal, cold. But You are far from being lifeless, impersonal and cold: You are far from being something. You are Person, the second Person of the Trinity, You are infinite truth and wisdom, You are God-made-man. Light is a person, and light is for persons.

When we hear of light, we automatically think of its opposite—darkness. Darkness is terrible because it is of hell. Darkness of the mind is especially terrifying. In darkness one cannot see where he is going. In darkness one is the prey of terror and groping indecision. Apart from You, without You, the world of things and of men is in darkness. But it need not be darkness; for to all of us and to the world there come Your words: "I am the Light of the world. He who follows Me does not walk in darkness."

Lord Jesus, if You are the light of the world, surely You are light for us, too. Two weeks from tonight, You are going to give us a vivid picture of this blessed truth when the Easter candle which stands for You risen from death will appear in our darkened churches. "Light of Christ!" we will hear the deacon cry out; and we will all answer with grateful hearts, "Thanks be to God." The light will go from the Easter candle to all of us in church, and soon the mass of light in church will reveal the fact of the possession of all our minds and hearts by You who are the light of our lives.

ALL THE WAY

But before we come to that blessed night, we have to follow You up a mountain called Calvary. This is the way of truth and of light. "Let us go and die with Him," Thomas said in yesterday's gospel. That is what following You means. We have to follow You all the way, trusting in Your guidance, trusting above all in Your love for us, if we are to come to a full share in You who are light.

And this is not just the two weeks of passiontide, it is all of life. There is suffering, the cross, death for me, because there is suffering, the cross, death for You, my Head. But there is also Your word: "I am the light of the world . . . I am the resurrection and the life." You are all this to me in all the sacraments, in the "sacrament" of the Church Year, in Your holy gospel, and in this and every Mass. In the midst of Your Church You are the light of our world.

Lord Jesus, I shall follow You who are light. You have become my refuge, and my deliverer: and in You I will put my trust (offertory verse). You rule me, and I shall want nothing. You have set me in a place of pasture: You have brought me up on the water of refreshment (communion verse).

Prayer for the day:
I AM THE LIGHT OF THE WORLD.

FIRST PASSION SUNDAY

Summary:

Jesus justifies Himself and claims to be God, while His enemies accuse Him of being possessed by a devil.

I AM

Lord Jesus, what has happened to these men that they should hate You so violently? I wonder if they themselves know. You try to reason with them, but hatred has closed their minds to the truth. You tell them what their trouble is: "He who is of God hears the words of God. The reason why you do not hear is that you are not of God."

Lord Jesus, if they are not of God, then of whom are they?

They persist in their insults. They call You their worst name, a Samaritan, and charge that You have a devil. You answer: "I have not a devil, but I honor my Father, and you dishonor me. Yet,

I do not seek my own glory; there is one who seeks and who judges. Amen I say to you, if anyone keep my word, he will never see death."

The accusations and answers pile up. They bring in Abraham father of their nation. You say: "Abraham your father rejoiced that he was to see my day. He saw it and was glad." They shriek at You: "Thou art not yet fifty years old, and hast thou seen Abraham?" Calmly and with deep dignity You reply: "Amen, amen I say to you, before Abraham came to be, I am."

I AM. That is what Your Father called Himself speaking to Moses from the burning bush. Those awesome words from Your mouth seem to them the height of blasphemy, for they think You are only man. They prepare to deal out the ancient punishment for blasphemy. But before they can grasp the stones with which to kill You, You hide Yourself and go out of the temple.

Lord Jesus, what are You thinking about during this encounter? The external audible conflict is painful enough; it does not conceal the inner conflict in Your mind—Your revulsion against their hatred of You, against the torture and dying that You know are inevitable —which will grow and evolve in Your mind till that moment when You will cry out: "My God, my God, why hast Thou forsaken me?"

HE WHO IS OF GOD

It is Your very nature to love and be loved. Here You feel the full force of the hatred of men. It is painful to be the recipient of hate; it is harder still for You to realize what ravages it can work in the hearts of men. For, despite all their faults, these enemies are dear to You. You love them, You are going to ask from the cross that Your Father forgive them; You are going to die for them.

Lord Jesus, it is much easier to be sympathetic with You than with Your enemies. But I recall the words You will use on the cross: "They know not what they do." They do not know You for what You are, they do not know Your resurrection and Your triumph— events that prove beyond question that before Abraham came to be *You are*.

On the other hand, I do know You. I know You as the suffering Savior who proves to be God. And with this knowledge and experience of Your special care and love for me, I still do what Your enemies did: I refuse You my love. I sin.

Now it is Passion Sunday. Your Church is going to re-enact Your passion and death. You say to all of us, to me, "If I speak to you truth, why do you not believe me? He who is of God hears the words of God."

What shall I answer, Lord Jesus? I can only say, praying that You will confirm my sincerity, "I will confess to Thee, O Lord, with my whole heart; I shall live and keep Thy words: enliven me according to Thy word, O Lord" (offertory verse). What is the word of God that You would have me hear? Here it is: "O Lord, teach me to do Thy will" (gradual). Teach me to love.

> *Prayer for the day:*
> HE WHO IS OF GOD HEARS THE WORDS OF GOD.

MONDAY OF PASSION WEEK

> *Summary:*
> Jesus proposes Himself as the fulfillment of all human desires: "If anyone thirst, let him come to me and drink."

YOU WILL SEEK

Lord Jesus, there is no doubt in Your mind about the final outcome of all this Pharisaic hatred of You. They are after Your blood, and they will get it; but You will make the sacrifice of Your own free will. "Yet a little while I am with you, and then I go to Him who sent me. You will seek me and will not find me; and where I am you cannot come."

You are thinking in Your heart: "Have mercy on me, O Lord,

for man hath trodden me under foot: all the day long he hath afflicted me, fighting against me. My enemies have trodden on me all the day long: for they are many that make war against me. Have mercy on me" (introit).

Lord Jesus, You say that they will seek You. Isn't that what man is supposed to do? But their seeking You is not the kind that You want. Instead of being full of desire for You, their seeking is inspired by hatred. It must be a terrible thing to know that men can so contaminate the deep desire that You plant in their hearts. You are the answer to humanity's longing, but these men refuse to see it, even when You stand in their midst and cry out: "If anyone thirst, let him come to me and drink. He who believes in me, as the Scripture says, 'From within him shall flow rivers of living water.'"

Lord Jesus, how deeply these words of Yours reveal Your thirst for men, for our love!

HE WHO BELIEVES

They do not know the gift of God. But how much better do I do? How strong is my thirst for You? It is a fact of life that thirst for God can be dulled by over-indulgence in thirst for sense pleasures. The Church is aware of this fact and she knows correspondingly that there is only one remedy for restoring spiritual desire to its rightful place in our life. That remedy is fasting. Fasting sharpens desire. This Lent we have been fasting, but we may have grown careless. There are only two weeks remaining. Therefore You remind us again today of our basic needs: "Sanctify our fasts, we beseech Thee, O Lord, and in Thy mercy grant us pardon for all our sins" (collect).

Lord, You say to me: "If any one thirst, let him come to me and drink. He who believes in me, from within him shall flow rivers of living water." You do not allow any doubt about what You will do for us.

On Holy Saturday night we will sing: "As the hart panteth after the fountains of water, so my soul panteth after Thee, O God. My soul hath thirsted for the living God: when shall I come and appear before the face of God?" You are the object of our thirst, You provide us the means for fulfilling it, You are our all. Lord

Jesus, may this Your word always keep me from thirsting after the wrong things. I want You, and only You.

Prayer for the day:

IF ANYONE THIRST, LET HIM COME TO ME AND DRINK.

TUESDAY OF PASSION WEEK

Summary:

Jesus goes up to Jerusalem secretly for the Feast of Tabernacles and is the object of much discussion among the people.

A GOOD MAN

Lord Jesus, I am beginning to understand better the full extent of Your passion. Next week, of course, we will see You sweating blood, cut to ribbons by soldiers' whips, bleeding from a head pierced with thorns, reigning from Your throne, the cross. The gospels of these days of Passion Week let us glimpse the building up of that inner grief that will eventually break Your heart. You say: Redeem me, O God of Israel, from all my tribulations (communion verse).

For example, today we see You talking to Your "brethren," those cousins of Yours who seem more interested in You as a possible credit to the family relationship than as savior of men. St. John observes that not even they believe in You. They want You to go to Judea to show off Your miraculous powers. "Leave here and go into Judea that thy disciples also may see the works that thou dost; for no one does a thing in secret if he wants to be publicly known."

What sadness, then, in Your words: "The world cannot hate You, but it hates me because I bear witness concerning it, that its works are evil." It is not easy for You who are ultimate truth and perfect love to be so disbelieved and hated . . . or even argued about. Who are these people who have any right to discuss You and Your qualifications? You are the Holy One, God in Person. They are men, weak men, sinful men. They are discussing You! Some say, "He is a good man." Others contradict: "No, rather he seduces the crowd." So are You tossed from mind to mind, from mouth to mouth.

ITS WORKS ARE EVIL

Lord Jesus, is not this the Passion already, this being subject to the preference of men? Is it this that Your Father asks You to bear and to accept? You do accept, but You are still human enough to rebel at the injustice of it all. "Defend my cause, O Lord; deliver me from unjust and wicked men. Send Your light and Your truth; they will guide me and conduct me to Your holy mountain" (gradual).

So do You pray, Lord Jesus. But Your Father wills that You drink the chalice of bitterness to the bottom. The unjust and wicked men will kill You. Your Father's divine light and truth will guide and conduct You to a holy hill, and there You will give up Your life. "The world cannot hate you," You say, "but it hates me because I bear witness concerning it, that its works are evil."

Calvary is a holy hill, because it is the scene of Your sacrifice. But it is not the end for You. Resurrection will be the end. But if Calvary and resurrection are the way for You, can I escape it? "Thou does not forsake them that seek Thee; seek ye the Lord, who dwelleth in Sion; for He hath not forgotten the cry of the poor" (offertory).

"May our fasts be acceptable to Thee, O Lord, and expiate our sins; may they make us worthy of Thy grace, and lead us unto life everlasting" (collect). You, O Lord, are my light and my salvation: whom shall I fear?

Prayer for the day:
HE IS A GOOD MAN.

WEDNESDAY OF PASSION WEEK

Summary:

Jesus calls Himself a shepherd and defends Himself against the attack of His enemies, claiming to be one with His Father.

MANY GOOD WORKS

Lord Jesus, You tell the Pharisees, "You do not believe me because you are not my sheep. My sheep hear my voice, and I know them and they follow me. And I give them everlasting life."

They have just demanded, with all the disdainful scorn that their hatred can sum up: "How long dost thou keep us in suspense? If thou art the Christ, tell us openly." The truth is that they don't want to know if You are the Christ: they want to hear You claim to be God so that they can accuse You of blasphemy. They will not be disappointed.

But first You tell them that You are the Good Shepherd. A good shepherd is one who knows his sheep, talks to them, leads them to pasture, gives them everlasting life. Your way of answering their question about Your messianic claims is to insist that You are a good shepherd. It goes without saying that they repudiate Your answer. They don't want to be Your sheep. But they want You to admit who You are? Well then, let them listen: "No one is able to snatch anything out of the hand of my Father. I and the Father are one."

This is what they have been waiting for: this gives them the occasion to put into execution the vengeance they have been plotting. You see the stones in their hands and ask: "Many good works have I shown you from my Father. For which of these do you stone me?" They hiss their answer: "Not for a good work do we stone thee, but for blasphemy, and because thou, being a man, makest thyself God."

THEY FOLLOW ME

So there You are, Good Shepherd, in the midst of the wolf pack, with the prayer in Your heart: "Deliver me from my enemies, O my

God: and defend me from them that rise up against me, O Lord" (offertory verse). They snarl, bite, hate. You defend and rebuke. But You are helpless to make a point with them or to put up any kind of defense: their hatred has led them beyond all reasoning.

They seek to seize You; but they must wait for that "hour" of Yours. It will not be long. But You are already entered upon Your passion; for what greater suffering is there than to be hated by those whom You have come to save, those whom You so want to love? The pain is intensified by Your certain knowledge that their hatred of You is also hatred of the Father.

Meanwhile, what about us? You say, "My sheep hear my voice, and I know them, and they follow me." To hear Your voice and to follow You wherever You desire to lead me is my test. Now, this Passiontide, is the time for me to pass the test. It means following You to Calvary and there listening to the voice of Your love drawing all things—and me—to Your heart. It means joyful acceptance in my life here and now of any pain or grief You might want to send me. Lord, Thy will be done! I hear Your voice, I want to and will follow You.

There is only one alternative to being Your sheep: it is to be one of the wolves, one of the hate-filled Pharisees. Lord Jesus, deliver me from that hell! You are indeed my deliverer from the angry nations: You wilt lift me up above them that rise up against me . . . I will love You, O Lord, my strength; You are my firmament, and my refuge, and my deliverer (introit). You will give me everlasting life.

Prayer for the day:

MY SHEEP HEAR MY VOICE, AND I KNOW THEM, AND THEY FOLLOW ME.

THURSDAY OF PASSION WEEK

Summary:

Because she has loved much, many sins are forgiven the woman who washes Jesus' feet with her tears and wipes them with her hair.

A SINFUL WOMAN

Lord Jesus, I suppose this scene must at first be rather startling to You. Startling, but surely not embarrassing, for You are pure and sinless. Only a sinner would be embarrassed at having another sinner make a fuss over him. Nor is the sinful woman embarrassed.

She is at Your feet because there is only one thing that matters to her now: the fact that she sees in a blinding flash of feminine intuition how greatly her sinful past has profaned the love that You have for her. What else can she do but weep? Tears and precious ointment poured out on Your feet manifest the grief, the regret, the repentant love she now feels for You.

Of course, it is a shameful exhibition in the sight of the pious Pharisee who has invited You to dinner—an invitation prompted by something considerably less than good hospitality. "This man, were he a prophet, would surely know what manner of woman this is who is touching him, for she is a sinner."

With a remark like that, Simon is asking for the rebuke that You deal him. To his shame, You contrast him and his conduct with that of the sinful woman. He has offered You none of the courtesies customarily offered to guests: the washing of feet, the friendly kiss of peace, the anointing of the head. In his eyes You aren't worth any such consideration. He hates You. This scarlet woman more than supplies Simon's scornful omissions.

"Dost thou see this woman?" You ask Simon. "I came into thy house; thou gavest me no water for my feet; but she has bathed my feet with tears, and has wiped them with her hair. Thou gavest me no kiss; but she, from the moment she entered, has not ceased to kiss my feet. Thou didst not anoint my head with oil; but she has anointed my feet with ointment. Wherefore I say to thee, her sins, many as they are, shall be forgiven her because she has loved much. But he to whom little is forgiven, loves little." And then You tell her, "Thy sins are forgiven . . . Thy faith has saved thee; go in peace."

MUCH LOVE

Lord Jesus, what a wonderful combination—Your forgiving heart and the sorrowful love of this woman's sinful heart. There is mutual attraction between them. And it is very mysterious, too. On the one hand, there is nothing more hideous than sin and a sin-inclined will to You who are infinitely holy. But on the other hand, once sin has been committed, there is no one more approachable than You. And when these two come together, sorrowful heart with sinful heart, anything can happen—holiness, heroism, union, martyrdom.

Lord Jesus, the ingredients for this wonderful experience are present in the lives of each of us. We have all sinned. We have violated Your love. But if there is sin, there is also the Savior, You. Like the sinful woman of this gospel, we can cast ourselves at Your feet in holy confession. And we can say, "Have mercy on me, according to the multitude of Your tender mercies."

Create a clean heart in us, O God. "All that Thou hast done to us, O Lord, Thou hast done in true judgment: because we have sinned against Thee, and have not obeyed Thy commandments: but give glory to Thy name, and deal with us according to the multitude of Thy mercy" (introit).

Lord Jesus, look on this willed expression of our sorrow as You look upon the tears of the sinful woman. We can never equal her grief, but perhaps if our desire is strong enough, true love for You coming from You in the sacrament of Penance will renew us as it did her. Lord, have mercy on us.

> Prayer for the day:
> **HER SINS . . . SHALL BE FORGIVEN HER, BECAUSE SHE HAS LOVED MUCH.**

FRIDAY OF PASSION WEEK

Summary:

The assembly of chief priests and Pharisees definitely decide to put Jesus to death.

THE HIGH PRIEST

Lord Jesus, there is a kind of desperation in the tone of the council of chief priests and Pharisees. "What are we doing? for this man is working many signs. If we let him alone as he is, all will believe in him, and the Romans will come and take away both our place and our nation."

They are speaking about You, of course, and what they say is most interesting: "If *we* let him alone . . ." Who do they think they are? As though they might prevent what You have begun, as though they might stop the visitation of God's love upon man.

Well, if the rest of them are still doubtful about saying outright what malice they have in their hearts, Caiphas, the High Priest of the year, is troubled by no hesitation. "You know nothing at all; nor do you reflect that it is expedient for us that one man die for the people, instead of the whole nation perishing." Caiphas doesn't know how right he is, how much of a prophet he is.

It is indeed expedient that one man should die for the people. You are that Man, and from Your death will come life; and, as St. John says, by Your death You will gather into one the children of God who are spread abroad. That includes us . . . and the Romans whose own country You will one day conquer through your disciples.

"Blessed art Thou, O Lord," You say to the Father. "Teach me Thy justifications; and give me not up to them that slander me: and so shall I answer them that trouble me: for unjust witnesses have risen up against me, and iniquity hath lied to itself" (offertory and communion verses).

THAT ONE MAN DIE

So, Lord, they have decided Your fate. From that day forth their plan is to put You to death, but until Your hour comes, You no longer go about openly among them. You withdraw to the district near the desert where You stay with Your disciples. Soon the prophecy that You Yourself once made will be fulfilled: "As Moses lifted up the serpent in the desert, even so must the Son of Man be lifted up that those who believe in Him may not perish, but may have life everlasting" (John 3: 14-15).

They will carry out their plan one week from today. Even though You know that plan corresponds with the will of Your Father, You anticipate it with horror and dread. The words of today's introit come straight from Your heart: "Have mercy on me, O Lord, for I am afflicted: deliver me out of the hands of my enemies, and from them that persecute me: O Lord, let me not be confounded, for I have called upon Thee. In Thee, O Lord, have I hoped, let me never be confounded: deliver me in Thy justice. Have mercy on me."

Lord Jesus, I live in the fulfillment of the prophecy of today's gospel. You have died and risen; and You have drawn me by means of baptism into Your death and resurrection. But I am far from being converted to You and as one with You as You want. Therefore, in the making-present-again of Your death and resurrection in the days ahead, "Heal me, O Lord, and I shall be healed; save me, and I shall be saved: for Thou art my praise" (epistle).

Prayer for the day:

IT IS EXPEDIENT FOR US THAT ONE MAN DIE FOR THE PEOPLE.

SATURDAY OF PASSION WEEK

Summary:

Jesus announces that He is like a grain of wheat that must die and be buried, and thus bring forth fruit.

GRAIN OF WHEAT

Lord Jesus, the chief priests are getting more and more deranged. Now they want to kill Lazarus because on his account many of the Jews are beginning to believe in You. He is living proof of Your divine power. This is pretty ironical—to want to kill a man whom You have just brought back from death! But how can one expect reasoned action and thinking from men who are so mixed up by hatred?

You are now ready to explain all the theological implications of Your coming passion and death. You have endured more than could be expected of any man. Hatred against You is building up. "Do you see that we avail nothing?" the Pharisees complain. "Behold, the entire world has gone after him."

To rub it in, certain Gentiles come and ask Philip, saying, "Sir, we wish to see Jesus." Lord, it is a holy and wonderful desire to want to see You. You answer: "The hour has come for the Son of Man to be glorified. Amen, amen, I say to you, unless the grain of wheat fall into the ground and die, it remains alone. But if it die, it brings forth much fruit."

Even in this most serious hour—perhaps because it is so serious —you talk in images. You do it because You want them and us to understand You clearly. You are describing Yourself. You are the seed. You will die at the hands of Your enemies, You will go into the ground, the tomb. But Your dying is the prelude to life for Yourself and for all of us. In death is life, without death, no life.

Of course, You are also describing the life of Your followers. "He who loves his life, loses it; and he who hates his life in this world, keeps it unto life everlasting. If anyone serve me, let him follow me; and where I am there also shall my servant be."

BY WHAT DEATH

Lord, You leave no room for escape. The passion and death rise before You inevitably. I too face them. If I am to be sincere in following You, I must go like You into the ground, I must lose my life, I must follow You along this way of the cross, rise up with You onto the cross, die and be buried. In other words, I must share Your sacrificial will and put myself wholly into the hands of Your Father. I don't like the idea any more than You do. With You I say, "Now my soul is troubled. And what shall I say? Father, save me from this hour! No, this is why I came to this hour. Father, glorify thy name!"

Your Father hears Your plea and answers: "I have glorified it, and I will glorify it again." And You go on to tell the people that the voice is not for You, but for them. And it is true, Lord Jesus. The Father's voice tells us about Your origin—what You are and where You come from. You are God, infinitely above man. You who are God come to dwell among men, You become man, You are about to die for man. Why? Is this Your answer: "And I, if I be lifted up from the earth, will draw all things to myself"?

Lord Jesus, if that is the only way to win our love (and You seem to think it is) then so be it! In Thee, O Lord have I hoped, let me never be confounded: deliver me in thy justice. Have mercy on me. In this and in every Mass, draw me to Yourself so that with You I may be taken down from the cross, placed in the tomb, and then rise with You in glorious victory. Teach me to do thy will!

> *Prayer for the day:*
> AND I, IF I BE LIFTED UP FROM THE EARTH, WILL DRAW ALL THINGS TO MYSELF.

SECOND PASSION SUNDAY or PALM SUNDAY

> *Summary:*
> Fulfilling an ancient prophecy, Jesus rides into Jerusalem in triumph, and the Jews cry out: "Blessed is he who comes in the name of the Lord."

BLESSED IS HE

Lord Jesus, You have planned well. In Your past doings with these people, You have done all things in the light of Your knowledge of human nature—especially its weaknesses. You have healed their sick, raised their dead, fed their bodies and their souls. You know how many times they have wanted to force kingship upon You. But You always escaped.

Today it seems to be different. You deliberately expose Yourself to the glorification of the crowd. You exercise Your rights as Creator-Owner of all things when You tell the apostles to borrow the ass and its colt and bring them to You.

You accept the joyous acclaim of the disciples and people. You are pleased at the way they all show their enthusiasm—spreading their garments and tree branches in Your path and shouting: "Hosanna to the Son of David! Blessed is He who comes in the name of the Lord!"

You know what they are thinking about: that they believe You have finally consented to rule their nation as a political figure and that their joy is therefore not wholly spiritual. Nevertheless, You are glad with their tribute. And You know that, if there is self-interest in the Hosannas of the grown-ups, the children's shouts rise from innocent, love-filled hearts.

Lord Jesus, You seem to want the acclaim, You rejoice in it, so much so that St. Luke even quotes Your reply to the long-faced, angry Pharisees who ask You to rebuke the people: "I tell you that if these keep silence, the stones will cry out" (Luke 19:40).

You seem to be saying that You are willing to accept ardent praise as it comes and when it comes and from no matter whom it comes—even from those who in five short days will use those same mouths to cry out again, only then for Your blood, for Your death.

ACCEPTING THE PALM

I think that this willingness of Yours to be acclaimed by the people proves truly that You are man. It proves that You are King of Kings. Above all, it proves that You are God. God hungers for human love. So it has always been in Your dealings with the likes of us, Lord Jesus. And so it will always be. Where is the mystery here? Is it in the depths of Your divine goodness that finds its joy in stimulating human hearts to their deepest fulfillment, to the love that literally makes them like unto You?

I don't know the answers, Lord. But I do know that the mystery of Palm Sunday will go on till the end of time. You will always be giving Yourself to us, to our cities, our parishes, school, convents, hoping for the adoring shouts we are capable of, knowing all the while that in our fickleness we will soon be turning away from You to other enthusiasms and in some cases even crucifying You again with our sins.

But if You give Yourself to us often enough, perhaps some day our hearts will be set, never again to be changed, where true love is to be found.

Lord Jesus, at Mass today I shall receive a palm from Your priest. I shall kiss it with reverence. In all this I shall have my share in that first Palm Sunday procession. More than that, I shall by the acceptance of the palm express my willingness to die with You.

Then I shall take the palm home with me. Will You remind me every time I look at that palm in the months ahead that I have only one vocation: to cry out with my voice and my life: "Hosanna to the Son of David!" to die with You, to rise with You, to live for You. "Glory and praise be to Thee, Redeemer blest!"

> *Prayer for the day:*
> **BLESSED IS HE WHO COMES IN THE NAME OF THE LORD!**

MONDAY OF HOLY WEEK

> *Summary:*
> **Jesus spends the day at Bethany, the home of Mary, Martha and Lazarus.**

ODOR OF OINTMENT

Lord Jesus, what a mingling of feelings there must be at this meal in Lazarus' home. There is much joy, for You are there; and You have restored Lazarus to life. But the joy is tempered with grief because of the prevailing conviction among Your friends that the hatred of Your enemies is soon to bear its fruit.

Lazarus is, of course, the center of curiosity. How does it feel, the guests ask themselves, to return to this world from another? But for the two sisters there is no doubt about who is center of attraction. They literally shower You with attentive love—and in such different ways. Martha cooks and serves a meal for You: that's what she does best; it is her way of expressing her love.

Mary is different. She has a pound of the best and costliest ointment ("genuine nard of great value," says St. John) that she has long been treasuring. She could use it on herself, in small dabs, and it would last a long time. That would be the old, selfish way of doing things. She takes her treasure and pours it over Your feet, all of it at once. But what she really pours is her love. The gesture is startling and spectacular. That's Mary's way of doing things.

But Judas doesn't think much of her way of doing things. Oh, the waste! Expensive perfume poured over a man's *feet*. That's no place for it, he thinks, even though the feet be those of the Son of God. He breathes in the odor, he swims in the air of love, but love does not touch his heart. "Why was not this ointment sold and the proceeds given to the poor?" Judas says.

You see through him, You know what is in Judas' heart, Lord Jesus. You know that he doesn't love the poor, that he doesn't love You. You know that he doesn't love anyone or anything but money . . . and himself. "Let her be," You answer Judas, "that she may keep it for the day of my burial. For the poor you have always with you; but you do not always have me."

LET HER BE

Let her be . . . You accept Mary's love with gratitude and understanding, for You know that the love she manifests enlarges her personality and perfects her. You are hurt at Judas' hardness, for You know the final outcome of one whom You have chosen and taught and loved for three years. "Let them blush and be ashamed together, who rejoice at my evils: let them be clothed with shame and fear, who speak malignant things against me" (communion verse).

Lord Jesus, here at the beginning of Holy Week I ask myself what my attitude is towards You. Is it like Martha's: am I willing enough to express my love for You by working for You? Is it like Mary's: is it the most precious thing in my life? Does love for You take precedence over all other values? Or is it like Judas' love: is it only love of self?

Lord, You know the answer to all these questions better than I do. I know one thing: You can perfect all love. Perfect and purify mine. Free it from all self-seeking. To Thee do I flee, Lord Jesus. Let the sight of pure love which You are going to show us when You sweat blood and die for us draw from all our hearts a return that at least approaches a love that is worthy of You. Teach me to do Thy will, for Thou art my God (offertory).

Prayer for the day:
MARY ANOINTED THE FEET OF JESUS, AND WITH HER HAIR WIPED HIS FEET DRY.

TUESDAY OF HOLY WEEK

Summary:
St. Mark describes the internal and external suffering of Jesus in His passion.

LOVE TO THE END

Lord Jesus, Jeremias well expresses Your mind in his epistle today: "I am as a meek lamb that is carried to be a victim: and I know that they have devised counsels against me, saying: Let us put wood on his bread and cut him off from the land of the living, and let his name be remembered no more." Surely, You fulfill this prophecy in the passion that St. Mark described so vividly.

There are all the familiar details: Your betrayal by Judas, denial by Peter, Your being scourged, Your carrying the cross, Your death. Having loved Your own who are in the world, You love them to the end.

Lord, I find myself thinking what all this can possibly mean to me. I read and hear it year after year. The panorama of divine-human pain passes before my eyes in four versions. A few minutes of more or less vivid realization, and then it is gone for another year. This is the account of Your passion, Lord Jesus. Could You do anything to make it more of a reality to me? Could I?

Obviously, I cannot know by intuition or even by imagination what a cold, black night of sorrow, terror, grief, and mental pain fills Your soul. You are You and I am I. As I cannot fully understand Your mind and truth, so I cannot begin to understand divine suffering. Perhaps I am out of my mind even to try to see into You. I should just stand and adore and love. You do want that, yet I am convinced You want more. But what?

INTO THE PASSION

Isn't it that in my *will, my intention* You desire me to accompany You into what Guardini calls "destruction and oblivion"? This is a realm of thinking and living that breathes terror into the human mind. It includes the complete emptying out of my own will; but that's just a part, perhaps just the beginning. Where I go from here is up to You. I know only one thing: I *want* to follow You into this passion, I want to belong to it, to You.

Guardini again helps to point the way. He says that to imitate You means to live in You, to learn from Your spirit to do hour by hour what is right. Living in You, adhering to You, is the one condition for having You live in me to the end that Your mind eventually absorbs me. I can help in the process by keeping in touch with You by contemplation and study. I can will to celebrate the mystery of Your passion.

In this area of liturgical celebration and human study, You can perhaps find a way into my soul so that I can finally follow Paul's request that I have Your mind as my mind.

For only in that way can I really follow his other recommendation in today's introit: that I glory in Your cross, for only in Your cross, and in the mind that willed that cross, is my salvation, my life, my resurrection.

Prayer for the day:

MY SOUL IS SAD, EVEN UNTO DEATH. WAIT HERE AND WATCH.

WEDNESDAY OF HOLY WEEK

Summary:

St. Luke describes the Passion of Jesus.

NO BEAUTY IN HIM

Lord Jesus, Your prophet Isaias sees You in a vision and describes You thus: "There is no beauty in Him, nor comeliness: and we have seen Him, and there is no sightliness, that we should be desirous of Him: despised and the most abject of men, a man of sorrows and acquainted with infirmity." Surely, Lord, that is an exact description of what You look like after the soldiers beat Your back and crown Your head with thorns. No beauty in You: just raw flesh, welts, blood.

What is behind it all? Once more Isaias tells it: "Surely He hath borne our infirmities and carried our sorrows: and we have thought Him as it were a leper, and as one struck by God and afflicted. But He was wounded for our iniquities, He was bruised for our sins . . . and by His bruises we are healed. All we like sheep have gone astray . . . and the Lord hath laid on Him the iniquity of us all. He was offered because it was His own will, and He opened not His mouth: he shall be led as a sheep to the slaughter" (epistle).

It is all there, Lord Jesus, in the vision of Your prophet. Isaias misses nothing. Seeing You as this account of the Passion shows You to me, and reading Isaias' commentary makes me see myself in all my cheapness. "For the wickedness of My people have I struck Him," Your Father says (epistle). What does the Father mean? Why should You, goodness and love incarnate, be struck and so treated because of our wickedness? Is it because You are goodness and love incarnate? Is it that our wickedness is so great that it takes God's own Son to wipe it out?

One thing is certain: this is no faked passion You are enduring. Again the psalmist's words find their full meaning on Your lips: "Turn not away Thy face from Thy servant, for I am in trouble; hear me speedily. Save me, O God, for the waters are come

125

in even unto my soul: I stick fast in the mire of the deep, and there is no sure standing" (gradual). You being perfect Man, can feel as no other human being ever could know the ultimate terror of approaching, inevitable death.

OBEDIENCE UNTO DEATH

It is this perfection of Your manhood, the intellectual keenness of Your mind making You see so clearly the malice of men and the horror of men thus treating their God that makes You cry out to the Father: "Father, if thou art willing, remove this cup from me; yet not my will but thine be done" (gospel). What You see in advance of Your passion makes You sweat blood.

"Deepen our *capacity to believe*, O almighty God, that by Thy Son's death in time, to which these holy Mysteries testify, Thou hast granted us life in eternity" (postcommunion).

Lord Jesus, Your Church gives us the right mentality on this eve of Your making-present-again of Your passion, death, and resurrection. "In the name of Jesus let every knee bow, of those that are in heaven, on earth, and under the earth; for the Lord became obedient unto death, even to the death of the cross. Therefore our Lord Jesus Christ is in the glory of God the Father" (introit). Lord, I can cast myself on my knees before Your total abasement. You must perfect the love and the obedience I there seek to express.

> Prayer for the day:
> > FATHER, INTO THY HANDS I COMMEND MY SPIRIT.

MAUNDY THURSDAY

> Summary:
> > At the Last Supper Jesus washes the feet of the apostles and tells them: You ought to wash the feet of one another . . .

WASHING THEIR FEET

Lord Jesus, at the Last Supper in Jerusalem You wash the disciples' feet, You institute the Eucharist, give them Your new commandment of love for one another, promise to send them the Holy Spirit and pray that they may all be one in You and in Your Father. Then You go out and sweat blood in the Garden of Olives. You pray Your Father not to make You drink the cup of suffering, "Yet, not as I will, but as thou willest."

All this You do at the Last Supper. May I ask, Lord Jesus, why Your Church out of all those apparently more important events chooses Your washing of the apostles' feet as the gospel for this Holy Thursday? Or why do You wash their feet in the first place? Your disciple John says that You, having loved Your own who were in the world, loved them unto the end. Could that be the answer?

You know Yourself to be the embodiment of divine Love, and You wash their feet so that they will always remember You for what You are, Love incarnate. Your Church wants us to remember that, too. And she wants us, following Your example, to be love incarnate in our surroundings.

You have always been their hero. For three years they have come to see You as the center of their lives and as their God. You have had everything under control. But here they see You doing something that only slaves do. It is incredible: You are washing their feet! The splash of the water and the rustling of the towel continues. Now You stand before Peter. As You kneel, Peter says what all have been thinking: "Lord, dost thou wash my feet? Thou shalt never wash my feet."

You look up at Peter and say these strange words: "If I do not wash thee, thou shalt have no part with me." What do You mean, Lord Jesus? I think that one of the most valuable lessons in life is to learn to accept love and love's gifts graciously. Would Peter's refusal of this humiliating action of Yours be a refusal to accept You and Your love? Would it mean further that it could be a refusal to accept Your way of life?

Peter must have got the idea; he definitely wants to have part with You: "Lord, not only my feet, but also my hands and my head."

Even in that serious moment, You must smile at this plain, good, enthusiastic man who is to be Your future vicar. You tell him: "He who has bathed needs only to wash, and he is clean all over . . ."

MASTER AND LORD

After You have made the rounds of all, including the one who is to betray You, You explain further: "Do you know what I have done for you? You call me Master and Lord, and you say well, for so I am. If, therefore, I the Lord and Master have washed your feet; you also ought to wash the feet of one another. For I have given you an example, that as I have done to you, so you also should do."

Lord, now I can understand why Your washing the apostles' feet is Your Church's choice for today's gospel. You have come not only to be a Savior, but a way of life, a way of life with but one mark: *love for one another*. In a few minutes You are going to say: "A new commandment I give you, that you love one another: that as I have loved you, you also love one another. By this will all men know that you are my disciples, if you have love for one another" (John 13:35).

Lord Jesus, wash my feet. Wash away false humility that stands opposed to Your show of love for me. Wash away that false self within that prevents my obeying You when You say to me: "I have given you an example, that as I have done to you, so you also should do." Make me see that "Where charity and love are, there (and there alone) is God" (antiphon at the washing of the feet, Holy Thursday).

> *Prayer for the day:*
> **LORD, DOST THOU WASH MY FEET?**

GOOD FRIDAY

> *Summary:*
> **Jesus is nailed to the cross, lifted up, and after three hours, dies.**

IT IS CONSUMMATED

Lord Jesus, after the Last Supper, in the garden, You pray: "Father, if it be possible, let this cup pass away from me; yet not as I will, but as Thou willest" (Matt. 26:39). As You pray a sweat of blood covers Your body and falls on the ground. The internal, life-long sacrifice of obedience and abandon to Your Father's will is becoming external, and Your blood is the visible sign.

More of that holy blood appears when the soldiers beat Your back into raw flesh and force a crown of thorns upon and into Your head. It leaves a trail of red all the way up to Calvary. It spurts from the holes the nails make in Your hands and feet.

As it drops upon the rock during those three hours of Your being lifted up, Your life slowly drains away. Internal and external sacrifice are now one. "Father, into Thy hands I commend my spirit . . . It is consummated."

What are You thinking of up there on the cross, Lord Jesus? Am I right in concluding that the words You have spoken in the past come back to You now? "My food is to do the will of Him who sent me, to accomplish His work" (John 4:34). "I have come, not to do my own will but the will of Him who sent me" (John 6:38).

You and Your Father! Once You said to the Pharisees, "I know Him . . . I do know Him, and do keep His words." At the Last Supper You told Him, "I have glorified Thee on earth; I have accomplished the work that Thou hast given me to do" (John 17:3). But there is communion between Him and You. His words spoken to the world at Your baptism are now for You alone: "Thou art my beloved Son in whom I am well pleased."

There on the cross You are also thinking of Your people, Lord Jesus. You are dying not only out of obedience of Your Father's will, but out of love for men. In the Good Friday liturgy Your Church has You expressing these thoughts, "My people, what have I done to thee? or in what have I grieved thee? I brought thee out of the land of Egypt . . . I led thee through the desert forty years: and fed thee with manna, and brought thee into a land exceedingly good, and thou hast prepared a cross for thy Savior . . . I have

exalted thee with great power; and thou hast hanged me on the
gibbet of the cross."

BEHOLD THY MOTHER

These are Your thoughts as You hang there, and You are thinking not only of Your people, the Jews. You are thinking of Your
people, the Christians. "My people, what have I done to you?"

These are Your thoughts. And mine? I hardly dare say what I
think. Let me again have recourse to Your Church. "Behold the
wood of the cross on which hung the Savior of the world." I behold
the wood. I behold You on the wood. "Come, let us adore." I don't
have to say anything particular to follow that instruction. I just
stand beneath the cross. Like Mary, Your Mother. Son, behold thy
Mother. Mary says nothing. She does nothing. She stands there looking up at You. That's all she does.

But standing there she is something. She is the perfection of
human love and human self-abandon in the presence of crucified
divine love and divine self-abandon.

Standing is the sign of expectation and hope, of willingness to
die, of desire for active participation. So it was for Mary. So it can
be for me. From now on at every Mass I shall stand at Redemption
with Mary, hoping that she will impart to me her willingness to die
with You.

Lord Jesus, You say to us, "Behold thy Mother." You say to
Mary, "Behold thy son." Your Church says to all of us: "Behold
your Savior." Lord, in this triple *Behold* is all life and all love. In
it I want to rest.

Prayer for the day:
MY PEOPLE, WHAT HAVE I DONE TO YOU?

HOLY SATURDAY

Summary:

Near dawn Mary Magdalen and the other Mary come to the sepulchre to anoint Jesus. An angel tells them not to be afraid. Jesus is risen.

LIGHT OF CHRIST

Lord Jesus, now You have been in the tomb since Friday afternoon. Meanwhile, Your Church is waiting and longing for You, and we are part of her expectation. But there is confidence in our prayer. We take it for granted that You will rise again.

We gather in our churches for the blessing of the new fire which, struck from a flint, reminds us of Your coming from Your rocky sepulchre. The flame of the Easter candle breaks through the darkness of the night. "Light of Christ!" the priest sings out; and we can hardly wait to answer: "Thanks be to God!" as we genuflect to You, our Savior and our God.

The light from the candle passes to the clergy in the procession, then to all the people, the whole parish. All are one with one another, all are one with You. It is this unity of love that You have been working for all during Lent. Now You have it. How we love this moment! Proud Mother Church with her confidence in her Spouse! And proud all of us her children with our joyous cries of gratitude to You!

Then comes the most triumphant song of the year, the Exultet. "Rejoice, you hosts of heaven, rejoice, all ministers of God! Let trumpets sound the triumph of the mighty King, for He has wrought salvation!" It is only Your resurrection that can thus turn staid clergymen into little children, fully possessed by joy. "This is the night in which Christ burst the bonds of death and came forth as conquerer from the grave . . . O wondrous condescension of thy mercy toward us! O incomprehensible goodness of love!"

WE DO BELIEVE

These are words of love, Lord Jesus. And they are ours. We go

131

on through the drama of Your rising, we hear the prophecies that foretell Your holy sacrament of Baptism, we behold the blessing of the holy font, the womb of Your Church through which all her children pass into a rebirth of divine life, we renew our baptism pledging our loyalty and love to You now as we did when we were baptised as children. "We do believe!"

And so on and on, one moment better than the last. Baptism leads to the Eucharist. At the gospel we stand with Magdalen and the other Mary at Your tomb. We hear the angel say to us: "Do not be afraid; for I know that you seek Jesus, who was crucified. He is not here. For He has risen as He said." To that we can only answer "Praise be to Thee, O Christ!"

Lord Jesus, You have indeed risen as You said You would. Grant that we may be truly risen with You; grant that being risen with You, we may seek the things that are above where You are seated at the right hand of the Father. For we have died, and our life is hidden with You in God.

Prayer for the day:
THANKS BE TO GOD! ALLELUIA, ALLELUIA!

EASTER SUNDAY

Summary:
Holy women, come to anoint Jesus in His tomb are told by an angel that Jesus is risen.

LOOKING FOR JESUS

Lord Jesus, these holy women are surely very faithful. Their affection for You does not die with Your death. They feel driven to express it in the spices they have bought for anointing Your dead body. They wish to wrap You in their love.

But how are they going to get into the tomb? That great stone that the soldiers have rolled against the entrance — what can they do about that? For ordinary women, it would be an impossible obstacle and problem, but these are not ordinary women. Perhaps they recall something You once said about having faith that could move mountains, and a stone is a very tiny mountain.

They love You, they long for You, they hurry to the tomb. But . . . the stone is gone! They enter the cave. So is Your body gone. Amazement, anger, grief possess them. Are they to be deprived of the chance to show You this last sign of their devotion?

Then they see the young man who says to them: "Do not be terrified. You are looking for Jesus of Nazareth, who was crucified. He has risen, He is not here. Behold the place where they laid Him . . ."

"You are looking for Jesus of Nazareth." Lord, what a magnificent compliment to pay to anyone: to be told that they seek You. For surely, to seek You is all that matters in life. To seek is to find. Oh, it is true; the tomb is empty: You have risen. You have risen so that You can reward their seeking. For if they had simply found a dead body there, even Your dead body, the seeking would have ended in frustration.

THE LIVING GOD

Lord Jesus, Your resurrection is the ultimate answer to the deepest desire of man. Man thirsts for the *living* God. You are the living God, Lord Jesus. Your resurrection proves it. As the deer longs for the fountains of water, so does my soul long for Thee, O God. My soul thirsts for God, for the living God: when shall I come and see the face of God (Psalm 41)?

"You are looking for Jesus of Nazareth," the angel says to me, too. And he is right. "He has risen, He is not here," the angel repeats. Again he is right. You are not in the tomb, Lord Jesus, because You have risen into the heart of Your Church whence You cry out to us: "I have risen and am still with thee, alleluia."

It is so much better having You with and in me than to have You in the grave; for now I know the end of my seeking. I know it in the joy of possession.

Your Church today is ablaze with joy and with love, like the women who go to the tomb. "We, Lord! With faithful heart and

cheerful voice, on this, Thy resurrection day, rejoice" (sequence)!
Truly, this is the day that the Lord has made, and we must rejoice
and be glad in it. We must give praise to Your Father for He is
good: for His mercy endures forever. You, Christ, our Passover,
have been sacrificed!

"Pour forth upon us, O Lord, the spirit of Thy Love, and in Thy
goodness make us to be of one mind and heart, whom Thou hast
fed with Thy Easter Sacrament" (postcommunion).

Prayer for the day:
HE IS RISEN. HE IS NOT HERE.

EASTER MONDAY

Summary:
Jesus walks and talks with two disciples on their
way to Emmaus; they recognize Him in the
breaking of bread.

BURNING HEART

Lord, Jesus, the two disciples are walking along the road to
Emmaus, reviewing the events of the past few exciting, tragic days.
Suddenly, they have a companion. It is You, but they do not immediately recognize You. You ask why they are so sad. They in
turn wonder where You have been that You should not know what
has recently transpired in Jerusalem.

You play innocent. "What has happened?" You ask. Then comes
their sorry story: the account of their life with You, "a prophet,
mighty in work and word before God and all the people," the
initial enthusiasm of Your followers, the broken hopes at Your
death, and despite the wild rumors of Your resurrection, their apparent willingness to write You off as a bad bet: "We were hoping
that it was He who should redeem Israel."

Your response to this judgment of earth-bound minds is long

overdue. "O foolish ones and slow of heart to believe in all that the prophets have spoken! Did not the Christ have to suffer these things before entering into His glory?" Then You unfold for them the plan of Your Father for the world's salvation. What a lesson in Scripture that must have been, Lord Jesus! When You have finished, they say to one another, "Was not our heart burning within us while he was speaking on the road and explaining to us the Scriptures?" That same lesson can be mine, any time, for You are always willing to show men how You dwell in holy Scripture.

GETTING TOWARD EVENING

But I am getting ahead of myself. You and they come to the village. They see that You want to go on, so they beg: "Stay with us, for it is getting towards evening, and the day is now far spent." You obey them (as You always answer this universal prayer of men for their God). At table You bless bread and give it to them, and then they see! They hold out trembling hands to touch You, but You vanish from their sight.

They forget about food. You, their Lord and Master, You have risen! They rise up immediately and rush back to Jerusalem to be greeted by news they already know: "The Lord has risen indeed, and has appeared to Simon." They tell their story, finishing off by the opening of their eyes at the table.

So, Lord Jesus, You are truly risen. Now stay with us, for it is getting towards evening, and the day is now far spent. Stay with us and teach us the essentials of life: especially that You do indeed have to suffer before entering into Your glory, and that we, Your followers, have to do the same. Yes, Lord, this Easter joy, this "heart burning within us," is the best argument for the wisdom of Your Father. Now we know the way that we have to follow. "Lord Jesus, pour forth upon us the Spirit of Thy love, that by Thy loving kindness Thou mayest make us to be of one mind, those whom Thou hast fed with these paschal sacraments" (postcommunion).

Prayer for the day:

STAY WITH US, LORD, FOR IT IS GETTING TOWARD EVENING.

EASTER TUESDAY

Summary:

Jesus appears to the eleven and proves that He has risen by eating fish and a honeycomb.

WOUNDS STILL FRESH

Lord Jesus, the two disciples whom You accompanied to Emmaus are still breathlessly describing their experience with You to the other apostles when You appear in the midst of them all. "Peace to you! It is I, do not be afraid." It is the old familiar greeting that they have so often heard You give them; but they are startled and panic-stricken, thinking You are a spirit.

Their panic is understandable, Lord, for the events of the past few days and above all the violence done to You whom they so loved have been a severe shock to them. They have seen You horribly mutilated and hung upon a cross. They have seen You die and then sealed in a tomb. And now You stand before them. Are they to believe their senses? Who has ever experienced anything like this?

Nevertheless, You ask: "Why are you disturbed, and why do doubts arise in your hearts? See my hands and feet, that it is I myself. Feel me and see; for a spirit does not have flesh and bones, as you see I have." And You show them Your hands and feet, the wounds still fresh. They are still doubtful (or are they simply mystified?), although there is a seed of joy expanding within them that is rapidly destroying the doubt.

You will fix that: You ask for food. A spirit does not eat material food. They give You fish and a honeycomb; You eat and show them the remains. Now their disbelief is transformed into love and longing.

THINGS ABOVE

They are ready for the explanation that You give: how and why it had to happen as it did. "Thus it is written; and thus the Christ should suffer, and should rise again from the dead on the third day;

136

and that repentance and remission of sins should be preached in His name to all nations, beginning from Jerusalem. And you yourselves are witnesses of these things. And I send forth upon you the promise of my Father. But wait here in the city, until you are clothed with power from on high."

Lord Jesus, this is twice now that You insist that suffering had to be Your way to glory. It must be so, and I do believe it. Suffering, sorrow, death. Resurrection, joy, love. Such is the law of life that You establish for all of us whom by Baptism You have chosen to associate with Your plan for the world. There may be grief in the suffering and dying, but death is swallowed up in victory. The joy of possessing You again, possessing You arisen in victory is a joy that surpasses limitations of time, space, environment.

This is the day which the Lord has made. Let us rejoice and be glad in it. Truly, Lord Jesus, this is a request of Your Church that it is a pleasure to obey. And having risen with You, we shall raise our desires to heaven, seeking the things that are above, relishing the things that are above. Grant, O Lord, that the virtue of the paschal sacrament which we have received may ever remain in our souls! (postcommunion).

Prayer for the day:
IT IS I, DO NOT BE AFRAID.

EASTER WEDNESDAY

Summary:
Jesus appears on the lake shore and prepares a meal for the apostles.

GOING FISHING

Lord Jesus, it isn't surprising that Peter should want to go fishing and that some of the other apostles should want to go with him. They have had strenuous experiences and there is nothing so relaxing as a few hours in a boat on the lake. And, after all, Peter is a fisherman by trade. Perhaps they do not even mind too much the lack of success during the night. Daylight finds them not too far off shore. They hear someone call out: "Any luck?"

They answer, "No, no luck." The voice comes back, "Cast the net to the right of the boat and you will find them." They follow the directions, and the net isn't big enough for the catch. There is only One who can thus reward their efforts; and it is naturally John, Your beloved disciple, who first recognizes Your miraculous "touch." "It is the Lord!" he cries out.

They cannot wait to get to You, Lord Jesus. Peter even jumps into the water and starts to swim, propelled by love and desire for You. Soon they are all with You. But what is this? They see that You have prepared breakfast for them: there is a fire ready, and a fish laid on it, and some bread. You say: "Come and breakfast." And none of them dares to ask You, "Who art thou?" knowing that it is You.

You take the bread and fish and give it to them. It is good, and they eat and are glad to be with You. Their minds go back to that other Meal, just a few day ago, when You gave them another kind of Food. At first they are shy and restrained, for they remember how You predicted at that Meal that they would abandon You, and how right You were. But You are so natural and so full of solicitude and friendliness that the old familiarity slowly returns. You have risen from the dead and are still with them. And they are glad.

SATISFYING MEN'S NEEDS

Lord Jesus, I find this close to unbelievable that You should thus prepare breakfast for these men. You have died, You spent three days in a grave, and have risen from death. No other person in all history has ever done what You have done. And here You are doing something as simple and commonplace as to broil a fish for these men who a few days before failed You in Your ordeal.

Yet, what You do here is in line with what You have been doing from the beginning: You satisfy men's needs. These apostles want fish, they are hungry. You take care of them. But more than that, they have gone through violent emotional shocks in first losing You (and in such a violent manner!) and now in finding You back with them after rising from death. You gently reestablish the old comradeship.

But what You do here is no more extraordinary than what You do for us every morning. You satisfy our needs, too. In the Old Testament, You opened the doors of heaven, and rained down manna upon the Jews to eat: You gave them the bread from heaven: man ate the bread of angels (offertory verse). Twice You have multiplied loaves for the crowds who flocked to You in the past three years. But to us You have given Your Body and Blood by which we, Your Church, are wonderfully fed and nourished (secret).

Lord Jesus, Your love and kindness know no limits. So when Your Church commands us: "Sing ye to the Lord a new canticle: sing to the Lord through the whole earth," I try to obey with full heart. Praise be to You, O Christ!

> *Prayer for the day:*
> **IT IS THE LORD!**

EASTER THURSDAY

> *Summary:*
> **Jesus appears at the tomb to Mary Magdalen and sends her to bring the news of His resurrection to the apostles.**

WEEPING AT THE TOMB

Lord Jesus, today's gospel takes us back to the early morning of Your resurrection. Mary Magdalen has made the discovery of Your empty tomb and has just returned from having summoned Peter and John. Now exhausted, she stands outside the tomb weeping. As she weeps, she stoops down and looks into the tomb. Two angels sitting there ask her, "Woman, why art thou weeping?" She answers: "Because they have taken away my Lord, and I do not know where they have laid Him."

Then she hears someone back of her. It is You, but she cannot recognize You through her tears. You ask her, "Woman, why art thou weeping? Whom dost thou seek?" Blinded with her tears and thinking You are the gardener, she cries, "Sir, if thou hast removed Him, tell me where thou hast laid Him and I will take Him away."

You say just one word, "Mary!" Her answer is as brief, "Master!" And she falls at Your feet to kiss them as she once did in the house of Simon the Leper. But You tell her, "Do not touch me, for I have not yet ascended to my Father, but go to my brethren and say to them, 'I ascend to my Father and your Father, to my God and your God.'" And obeying You rather than her feelings, Mary runs off again to announce the good news to Your apostles.

Lord, Mary has learned her lesson well. Loving You as she does, she nevertheless leaves You to go to do Your work, to be a herald of Your resurrection. Perhaps that is the very reason why she obeys You so willingly. Love for You that is genuine drives one to want to share it with others. And, undoubtedly, Mary finds that in announcing Your resurrection, she keeps You more than if she had simply wept at Your feet.

DESIRE FOR HIM

Lord Jesus, I can understand why Your Church reads Mary's mind and has her saying in one of the responses of matins: "Congratulate me, all ye who love the Lord, for He whom I sought has appeared to me, and while I was weeping at the tomb, I saw the Lord. The disciples having left, I did not depart, but afire with love for Him, I burned with desire for Him."

I don't suppose it is given to everyone to love You as Mary does. But in so many things Mary provides a pattern for us to imitate. "Whom dost thou seek?" You say to each of us. Our answer must be the same as hers: We seek You, but we seek You the risen Christ, not the dead Christ in the tomb. We can seek and desire You and give ourselves to You so that You may plant love for You within us. And we can do exactly what she does: we can go to announce to our world Your resurrection. And again, like her, in announcing your resurrection, we keep You.

You insist on Your resurrection being publicized. This is the whole idea of the light ceremony on Holy Saturday night: light comes from You, the Christ-candle, to us. The light must spread till it covers the world. And today's communion verse indicates the same idea: "People whom God has purchased, declare the virtues (perfections) of Him who has called you out of darkness into His admirable light."

> *Prayer for the day:*
> I HAVE SEEN THE LORD, AND THESE THINGS
> HE SAID TO ME.

EASTER FRIDAY

Summary:

> Jesus commissions the apostles to go into the whole world preaching and baptizing; and He will be with them all days.

ALL POWER

Lord Jesus, these Easter week gospels cover much ground and time. In today's portion, St. Matthew shows You just before Your ascension.

You have told the apostles to gather on a certain mountain in Galilee. You appear in their midst, and seeing You, they worship You, although St. Matthew says, some of them at first have some doubts. You seem to them too good to be true.

Then come Your final words to them in this world. You have come to the world that men might have life and have it more abundantly. You have brought the divine Light of Truth that men need in order to find their way in the world. You have died and risen in order that truth and life might become available to the world;

and You have instituted sacred signs called sacraments through which You might reach into the lives of all men and meet all men's needs for Truth and Life.

You are Savior of the whole world, Lord Jesus, Savior of all men of all time, not just the Palestinians of Your time. You have done everything and You have acted up to now in Your own person and with Your own physical body. Now You will begin to act through others, using men as Your hands. But it will still be You and Your work and Your salvation and truth that the world will continue to know. As the Father has sent You, You now send the apostles . . . and us.

Therefore, You command: "All power in heaven and on earth has been given to me. Go, therefore, and make disciples of all nations, baptizing them in the name of the Father, and of the Son, and of the Holy Spirit, teaching them to observe all that I have commanded you; and behold, I am with you all days, even unto the consummation of the world."

UNTO THE CONSUMMATION

Lord Jesus, they are Your Church: You are with them, You act through them, You desire to give Yourself to and to love the world through them. We are Your Church: You are with us, You wish to act through us, You wish to love our world in and through us. Light of Christ, thanks be to God!

Behold Your people, we beseech You, O Lord, and as You have vouchsafed to renew them with eternal mysteries, mercifully absolve them from temporal faults (postcommunion). Lord Jesus, You have just cleansed us of our self-centeredness in Lent and Holy Week just passed. Make us see our lives more and more as part of Your plan to give Yourself to our world. Help us to share Your missionary-mindedness, help us to fulfill Your will.

You are with us as individuals, but most of all, You rise from the dead in order to be with us as a Church. You will be and remain with us only if we are true to our vocation as members of a missionary apostolic Church. Blessed are You who come in the name of the Lord: You, Lord, are truly God, and You have shone forth unto us (gradual). Say ye among the nations that the Lord hath reigned from a tree (alleluia verse).

Lord Jesus, Light of Christ, Thanks be to God! Thanks to You for making us to be Your light and Your truth to our world.

Prayer for the day:
I AM WITH YOU ALL DAYS.

EASTER SATURDAY

Summary:
Peter and John, alerted by Mary Magdalen, run to the tomb and find it empty.

EARLY TO THE TOMB

Lord Jesus, at the end of this week of Your triumph, we are back at the beginning, back at the first Easter morning. This gospel has to do with three people whom You love very much and who in turn love You more than life. Mary's love is a woman's love: it drives her to the tomb while it is still dark. Immediately she is aware that the stone is taken away from the entrance.

When she looks inside and sees that the tomb is empty, she rushes to tell Peter and John about it. I think she knows that You would want her to do that. She cries: "They have taken the Lord from the tomb, and we do not know where they have laid Him."

They hurry off. John is younger and speedier and reaches Your tomb first. He looks in and sees the linen cloths lying there, but does not enter. Peter is Your choice as head of the apostles, a fact that John remembers even in his excitement. It is right that he should enter the tomb first. Peter finally arrives, he enters the rocky cavity and sees the linen cloths and handkerchief with which Your sacred body had been wrapped. Then John also enters and he says of himself that he sees and believes, for, as yet, they do not understand the Scripture, that You must rise from the dead.

The two disciples go back again to their home. There You will see them, and they will understand better. And as understanding grows, so will their love for You build up. Some time later, when he has lived and worked in the glow of Your resurrection as head of Your Church, Peter will write to his flock: "Lay aside, therefore, all malice, and all deceit, and pretense, and envy, and all slander. Crave, as newborn babes, pure spiritual milk, that by it you may grow to salvation; if, indeed, you have tasted that the Lord is sweet" (epistle).

GROWTH IN UNION

Lord Jesus, now at the end of this Easter week, we can look back with new appreciation on its meaning and its joy. We cannot share the initial bewilderment of the apostles and the holy women, for they have had to grow into the unheard of and absolutely new idea of the resurrection of a dead man to life again. But it is less necessary to share their bewilderment than to share their love for You and the new direction that Your resurrection gives to one's life.

The future lies ahead for us just as it did for them. It must be a future of growth in union with You. The communion verse of this Mass quotes St. Paul most fittingly: "All you who have been baptized in Christ have put on Christ." You have risen from death in order to come and dwell and grow in us. We have put You on, Lord Jesus, in our baptism, and You are more than ever at home in us now that our baptisms have been so recently renewed. But there is such a gap between Your mind, Your principles and way of life and the way You see us acting. Renewed by the gift of our redemption, we beseech You, O Lord, that by this help to eternal salvation, faith may ever increase (postcommunion). Lord Jesus, increase our faith, strengthen our love. Finish what You have begun.

Prayer for the day:

BLESSED IS HE THAT COMETH IN THE NAME OF THE LORD!

FIRST SUNDAY AFTER EASTER

Summary:

Jesus appears to the apostles, institutes the sacrament of Penance, and confronts Thomas who had doubted His resurrection.

THROUGH CLOSED DOORS

Lord Jesus, You whom they loved have returned from death. "Peace be to you!" You greet them, as You show them Your wounds. Only when I think of their years of familiar intimacy with You and then their having forsaken You in Your need can I realize how very much they must rejoice at Your return. Now, they think, they can make it up to You, they can wipe out their desertion.

You understand them now as You always have. They may have abandoned You on Friday, but they are Your men, the ones You have chosen to do Your work, and You are glad to be back with them. You will not give up on them now. "As the Father has sent me, I also send you. Receive ye the Holy Spirit; whose sins You shall forgive, they are forgiven them; whose sins You shall retain, they are retained."

To forgive sins! "Who can forgive sins, save God alone?" the Pharisees asked. Now they are to have that power. You made them priests at the Last Supper when You told them: "Do this in commemoration of me," so that they can offer Your body and blood in sacrifice. Now they can also forgive sins. All of which means that You will act in and through them until the end of time. You are thinking of us, of our need for constant forgiveness and for sacrifice.

Thomas isn't there when You appear, and You are gone by the time he returns. He refuses to accept the word of his companions. Unless he can see the hole of the nails and put his hand into Your side, he will not believe.

I can see him there all that week, holding himself aloof from their joy, his loud protests gradually giving way to the conviction

145

of the others, but still too stubbornly human to admit that he was wrong.

Now it is Sunday again. It is like last Sunday, only Thomas is present. You stand in their midst, the focus of their love-filled eyes. You give Your old greeting: "Peace be to you!" Then You turn to Thomas: "Bring here thy hand and put it into my side; and be not unbelieving, but believing."

INTO MY SIDE

It is one of the most dramatic moments in all history. "My Lord and my God!"

Surely it is also one of the most religious moments. Just five words are spoken, but they shoot forth from the depths of a man who has failed You not once, but twice . . . and bragged about it. It is a cry of grief, of sorrow, of desire, of love, as well as praise and adoration. It is the voice of Adam and Eve and all their descendants, it is the cry of mankind in the presence of the Savior of mankind: a Savior who is man, for He suffers and dies; a Savior who is God, for He rises from the dead.

You accept Thomas' gift of praise as You will later accept the pouring out of his blood of which this moment of confession is the foreshadowing. Your words to him sound a little harsh. But that's only appearance. How could You be harsh with one who will be such a "savior" to us? Thomas, the good sinner, shows all future sinners what to do: "My Lord and my God!"

"Because thou hast seen me, Thomas, thou hast believed. Blessed are they who have not seen, and yet have believed."

That's all of us, Lord Jesus. We do not see You. We just try to live Your life. And if we believe and merit Your praise, much of the credit must go to poor, more-or-less disgraced, doubting Thomas who knew enough to admit his mistake, who gives us the words that create faith, life, and love if we will only use them: My Lord and my God! A word of thanks to You . . . and to him.

Prayer for the day:
MY LORD AND MY GOD!

SECOND SUNDAY AFTER EASTER

Summary:
Jesus uses the parable of the Good Shepherd to sum up and describe what He has done for us.

GOOD SHEPHERD

Lord Jesus, You say, "I am the good shepherd. The good shepherd lays down his life for his sheep." You have proved Your claim to be a good shepherd in the best possible way: You have given Your life for us. The memory of that Friday is still alive. "Father, into Thy hands I commend my spirit," You said, and bowing Your head, You expired. The Good Shepherd lays down His life for His sheep.

There is another mark of a good shepherd: he knows each of his sheep by name, and they know him. You also make this claim: "I am the good shepherd, and I know mine and mine know me, even as the Father knows me and I know the Father."

Lord Jesus, I cannot fully understand You without a thorough knowledge of what You mean when You say, "I know." Someone has said that to know means "to understand, to have confidence in, to love, to live for." You say that You know us, Your sheep. That means that You *understand* us; You understand everything about us, our potentiality for good and for evil.

In spite of that understanding, You seem to *have confidence* in us, for You put Your shepherding into our hands. Surely You have shown that You *love* us — that is really what this image of the Shepherd means. And You wouldn't be our *Good* Shepherd if You hadn't risen *to live for* and in us.

"I know mine . . . " Now You can really fulfill Your vocation as the shepherd who gathers His flock around Him to feed them and unify them and give them a chance to know You. For is that not eternal life, to know You and Your Father?

"Mine know me . . ." We do not do nearly as well as You. I think I understand You better now that Lent and Holy Week are over; and my understanding will grow with the meditation of these gospels and the year-by-year living of Your Church Year. And nothing helps more than Easter to deepen my *confidence* in You. So also nothing helps more than the Eucharist, "Your Easter Sacrament," to increase my *love* for You. If that love is tainted with self-interest, I do want it purified.

LIVING FOR JESUS

I have gone through a kind of dying, too, during Lent and Holy Week. Of course, it wasn't very painful, but I have at least tried and wanted to share Your sacrificial will. And I have risen with You at Easter. Now only one thing remains: *to live for* You by prayer and action so that the ultimate desire of Your Good Shepherd heart may be gratified: that there may be one flock and one shepherd.

If there is anything that describes You, it is that last sentence. You are the Savior of men, of all men. You gave Your life for all. You are distressed at the vast number of pagans and still more at the division among us Christians. What You began on Calvary and Easter must continue. And You have chosen us — priests, religious *and* laity — to finish Your work.

Perhaps this is the final mark of Your love for us: Your knowing us, Your having confidence in us, Your giving us the blessed responsibility of bringing other sheep to You as tokens of our love for You.

"O God, my God, to Thee do I watch at the break of day: and in Thy Name I will lift up my hands, alleluia!"

> *Prayer for the day:*
> **I LAY DOWN MY LIFE FOR MY SHEEP.**

THIRD SUNDAY AFTER EASTER

> *Summary:*
> > Jesus tells the apostles that He is going away and that they will not see Him till after a "little while."

A LITTLE WHILE

Lord Jesus, the scene of today's gospel takes place at the Last Supper, but what You say then is made to order for us today. You tell the apostles: "A little while and you shall see me no longer; and again a little while and you shall see me, because I go to the Father."

It is a night of mystery for them, even though they have been so long with You, and these words add to their wonder. "What is this he says to us, "A little while and you shall not see me, and again a little while and you shall see me; and 'I go to the Father'?"

They ask one another these questions. You see their puzzlement and hear their ill-concealed whispers. Full of understanding as always, You explain: "You inquire about this among yourselves . . . Amen, amen I say to you, that you shall weep and lament, but the world shall rejoice; and you shall be sorrowful, but your sorrow shall be turned into joy . . . you will have sorrow now; but I will see you again, and your hearts shall rejoice, and your joy no man shall take from you."

Lord Jesus, You go out from the supper room. You go through Your passion, You die, rise from death, stay with them forty days, ascend into heaven and send them the Holy Spirit at Pentecost. Then begins their "little while." Like Your life, theirs is full of sorrow, suffering, labor, sacrifice; for they are other Christs.

But through it all, You are with and in them. All their apostolic life, they feel Your presence within, they remember and take courage from Your words here tonight; and in less than a little while their sorrow is turned into joy. They die Your death — it is liberation — they see You again, and their hearts rejoice with a joy that no one will ever take from them.

SORROW INTO JOY

Lord Jesus, to us also You say: "You will have sorrow now; but I will see you again . . ." If it is hard for me to imagine Your words as pertinent to my life, it must have been thus for the apostles, too. I can see these, our family elders at Your side now, nodding their agreement to Your words, telling us: "He was right as always."

Something has happened in my life these past weeks. Here is

the way Your Church puts this thing that has happened: "The Lord hath sent redemption to His people. Alleluia. It behooved Christ to suffer these things, and so to enter into his glory" (alleluia verse).

You have sent Your redemption to be lived and experienced in our own lives and then to be shared with others according to our state of life. Inescapably, this will entail suffering and sorrow and the cross now. But just as it behooved You—and Your apostles— to suffer these things and *so* to enter into Your glory, so must it behoove each of us to do exactly the same.

Lord, all this is nonsense to the world. It is nonsense to me also unless I believe and love. You have sent redemption to your people. Now send us the faith to see it and the love to activate it. You seem to have to do everything. But there is one thing I can do (with Your help, of course): "Praise the Lord, O my soul, in my life I will praise the Lord: I will sing to my God as long as I shall be. Alleluia" (offertory verse).

Doing Your work, praising the Father in and through You, will make my little while a short while and surely worth while. It is the only life that will guarantee my hearing Your words: "I will see *you* again, and your heart shall rejoice, and your joy no one shall take from you."

Prayer for the day:

YOU SHALL BE SORROWFUL, BUT YOUR SORROW SHALL BE TURNED INTO JOY.

FOURTH SUNDAY AFTER EASTER

Summary:

Jesus tells the apostles that it is expedient for them that He depart: for if He does not depart, the Holy Spirit will not come to them.

SPIRIT OF TRUTH

Lord Jesus, like last Sunday's gospel, this one is again taken from Your discourse at the Last Supper. In less than twenty-four hours You will be crucified, but Your thought goes beyond that particular "going away."

You are speaking of Your return to the Father in heaven: "I am going to Him who sent me . . . But because I have spoken to you these things, sadness has filled your heart. But . . . it is expedient for you that I depart. For if I do not go, the Advocate will not come to you; but if I go, I will send Him to you."

These must be strange words to Your chosen ones. They love You. They have You now. And You cannot blame them if they are saddened at hearing You say that You are about to leave them. Why should they "trade" You whom they so know and so love for an unknown "Advocate" whom they have never seen?

It isn't that they do not want the Holy Spirit. You say that He is necessary for them, and what You say must be true. But they want You, too. They do not know that in receiving Your Spirit, they will not lose, but will keep and gain. "When He, the Spirit of truth has come, He will teach you all the truth . . . He will glorify me, because He will receive of what is mine and declare it to you."

I think You are trying to convince them and us that simply to know You and to have the courage to be like unto You—and to be Your apostle—are two different things. Knowledge alone is not enough for the Christian and the Christian apostle. Love must fire the knowledge. Your Church seems to recognize this fact, for she has us pray in the secret: "O God, who, by the Holy Communion of this Sacrifice, hast made us partakers of Thy one and supreme Divine Nature, grant that *we who know Thy truth, may also follow it by a worthy life.*"

GIFT FROM ABOVE

Now I understand why You say to us: "It is expedient for you that I depart." It is expedient for the same reason: that You may be able to send us the same Holy Spirit who by enkindling the knowledge we have of You will "convince the world of sin, and of justice, and of judgment." What do You mean by these mysterious words if not that holiness (the Holy Spirit in a person) accuses and disturbs those who are worldly? You are well aware that when people are stirred up by the holiness of others, they are the best possible soil for the sowing of Your grace.

I think I understand now as I haven't before why You want to send the Holy Spirit. Without Him there is no apostolate, no continuation and completion of what You have begun.

Lord Jesus, like Advent these pre-Pentecost days are full of seeking, longing, desiring. During Advent we longed and prepared for You. Now we desire Your Spirit, the "perfect gift which is from above, coming down from the Father of Lights" (epistle). Now as then, we will receive only in proportion to our desire.

Therefore, "O God, who dost make the faithful to be of one mind and will, grant that we, Thy people, may love what Thou dost command and *desire what Thou dost promise*; so that, amid the changing things of this world, our hearts may be fixed where true joys are to be found" (collect).

Grant that we may desire what Thou dost promise. You say: If I go, I will send Him to you. To that my only answer is: come, Holy Spirit! Come and fill our hearts with the fire of Thy divine love!

> *Prayer for the day:*
> IT IS EXPEDIENT FOR YOU THAT I DEPART.

FIFTH SUNDAY AFTER EASTER

> *Summary:*
> Jesus tells the apostles to ask the Father anything in His name and it will be granted.

ANYTHING IN HIS NAME

Lord Jesus, it was towards the end of the Last Supper that in a brief sentence, You summed up all of Your life: "I came forth from the Father and have come into the world (we celebrated that coming at Christmas). Again I leave the world and go to the Father (we are about to celebrate Your Ascension, Your return to the Father now)."

After a night of bewilderment during which their human minds consistently failed to grasp the full meaning of Your divine truth, the apostles finally claim to understand You: "Behold, now thou speakest plainly and utterest no parable. Now we know that Thou knowest all things . . . For this reason we believe that Thou camest forth from God."

Since that night You have died, risen, ascended to Your Father and sent Your Holy Spirit to take possession of the Church You founded. Physically You have left the world and are with the Father. But, Lord Jesus, have You really left us? There is great power and splendid Presence in Your words to us today: "If You ask the Father anything in my name, He will give it to you."

I'll take You at Your word, Lord. You say: Ask anything. All right, I ask for You. Your Father cannot refuse that request, and You seem to have foreseen it. You give mankind a Church in which You remain till the end of time. In it You make present all that You are and have done.

In it is Your Sacrifice of Yourself and us, in it are Your sacraments in which You continue to heal and consecrate and make holy. In it is Your very own prayer, the Divine Office. In Your Church Year You re-enact Your whole life for our participation and the glory of Your Father. In it by our private prayer You make Yourself living and real to us.

FORTH FROM GOD

In Your Church we join with all the heavenly citizens, angels and saints, friends and relatives, as well as with all the members of Your family here on earth to celebrate Your having redeemed us by Your death and resurrection and now Your glorious Ascension: "Sing ye to the Lord, alleluia; sing ye to the Lord, and bless His Name; show forth His salvation from day to day, alleluia" (communion).

In all this we are certain of a magnificent truth: that Your Father loves us. He is the God from whom all good things proceed. If we ask Him anything in Your name, He will give it to us. He will give it because He loves us, but most of all because He loves You, You who are the personification of divine love for men. You assign another reason for His love for us. You say that the Father Himself loves us because we have loved You, and have believed that You came forth from God.

Well, we won't quarrel over who loves most or for what reasons. I know one thing: love can grow only if both parties want it to grow. So now I know my answer to Your invitation to ask for anything: "Do Thou, O Lord, grant unto us who have been nourished and strengthened at Thy heavenly table, both to desire what is right and to obtain what we desire" (postcommunion).

Lord Jesus, ultimately the only right thing for men to desire is love of God issuing forth in praise. *This I ask in Your name, Amen.*

> Prayer for the day:
> ASK AND YOU SHALL RECEIVE.

ROGATION DAY

Summary:
> Jesus teaches that persistent prayer is certain to be heard.

WHO SEEKS FINDS

Lord Jesus, these days before You leave us to ascend into heaven are called Rogation days. They are days of concentrated asking You for all the needs of our life. Sunday You told us that we must pray in Your name: whatever we ask the Father in Your name, He will give it to us.

Now You give us a further lesson — we are to pray with persistence and with confidence; and the device You use to bring this truth home to us is almost amusing. I am in bed and a knock comes at the door: it is a friend coming from a long journey. I want to give him something to eat, but when I go to the kitchen to look for food, I discover that there is none there.

What to do? There is my neighbor next door. I ring his door bell and wake him. "Lend me some bread," I beg, "so that I can feed a friend who has just come to visit me." He is not happy about being awakened. "Do not disturb me; the door is now shut, and my children and I are in bed; I cannot get up and give to thee." I insist that my friend is hungry. I cannot let him go to bed hungry. "Please give me some bread!"

My refusal to be put off will finally win the day. Because of my persistence my neighbor will get up and give me all that I need. So say You, Lord Jesus, and You drive the thought home for us on a spiritual level. "Ask, and it shall be given to you. For everyone who asks receives; and he who seeks finds; and to him who knocks it shall be opened."

What are You telling us, Lord Jesus? It would almost seem as though You go too far in likening Your Father in heaven to the reluctant friend who hates to be disturbed and who finally yields just to get rid of me. But I can see that really You want us to think more about constancy in prayer — about never giving up — about lasting perseverance — than about the attitude of God.

OUR FATHER

But You take care of that, too. You clinch Your argument for persistent prayer by bringing out the glorious fact that God is our Father, and that He loves and cares for us, His children. "If one of you asks his father for a loaf, will he hand him a stone? or for a fish, will he for a fish hand him a serpent? or if he asks for an egg, will he hand him a scorpion? Therefore, if you, evil as you are, know how to give good gifts to your children, how much more will your heavenly Father give the Good Spirit to those who ask Him."

Lord Jesus, You win the argument. I know now, as I never realized before, how I must pray and to Whom. It must be prayer in Your name and it must be addressed with faith, confidence and perseverance to Him whom You call Your Father and My Father.

I will love You, O Lord, my strength; You are my firmament,

my refuge, and my deliverer. I will give praise to You for You are good: for Your mercy endures forever (alleluia verse).

Prayer for the day:
ASK, AND IT SHALL BE GIVEN TO YOU.

VIGIL OF ASCENSION

Summary:
Jesus sums up His life and accomplishments in His final prayer to the Father, and He asks that the Father will now glorify Him.

THE WORK FINISHED

Lord Jesus, today's section of the gospel comes from Your final words at the Last Supper; but again they apply most appropriately to Your final hours before Your ascension into heaven.

You sum up what You have done and what You hope will result from Your work, You ask the Father that He will glorify You so that You might glorify Him, even as He has given You power over all flesh in order that all to whom He has given You might have everlasting life.

And this is everlasting life — that men may know the Father the only true God, and You whom the Father has sent. You have glorified Him on earth, You have finished the work the Father has given You to do. Now You ask the Father to glorify You with Himself, with the glory You have had with Him before the world existed.

You have manifested the Father's name to the apostles. They were the Father's and He has given them to You, and they have kept the Father's word. They have learned that whatever the Father has given You is from Him; because the words the Father has given You, You have given to them. And the apostles have received these words and have known that You have come forth from the

Father, and they have believed that You have been sent by the Father.

You pray for the apostles . . . and for all those whom the Father has given You, because they really are the Father's, and all things that are Yours are His, and His are Yours, and You are glorified in them. And You are no longer in the world, but these men are in the world, and You are coming to the Father.

COMING TO THEE

Yes, Lord Jesus, You are indeed going to the Father. But You remain with Your Church, which continues to do what You have begun. You continue now to grant eternal life through the sacraments. You continue to reveal the Father's word to men so that they can know You and the Father and thus share the secrets of the heart of God and possess eternal life.

Lord Jesus, help us to be worthy of the word that You give to us. Inspire us to long for it, to make ourselves ready to receive it and allow it to grow in us. Then we will do what You and the Father desire: we will *will* to be saved. We will continue Your glorification of the Father and we will truly rejoice. We will do what You ask the Father to do — we will glorify You as You deserve to be glorified.

Lord Jesus, draw from us all singly and as a holy community the resolution to be what You pray we should be when You say to the Father: "I pray for them; not for the world do I pray, but for those whom Thou has given me, because they are Thine; and all things that are mine are Thine, and Thine are mine . . . *grant that all may be one, even as Thou, Father, in me, and I in Thee; that they also may be one in us."*

It is only in oneness with one another and with You that we can ultimately do Your will, Lord Jesus. O bless the Lord our God, ye peoples, and make the voice of His praise to be heard: who hath set my soul to live. Blessed be the Lord, who hath not turned away my prayer, nor His mercy from me (offertory verse).

> #### Prayer for the day:
>
> #### THIS IS ETERNAL LIFE, THAT THEY MAY KNOW THEE.

ASCENSION DAY

Summary:

Jesus gives a final command to the apostles to preach the gospel in the whole world; then He ascends into heaven.

TAKEN INTO HEAVEN

Lord Jesus, we have experienced wonderful things since we began to pray last Advent: "Come, Lord Jesus! Come and do not delay. To Thee have I lifted up my soul." You have come to live with us, You have instructed us by word and by Your holy example. You have loved us to the end of dying and rising for us.

Now today You appear to us while we are at the table of the Eucharist. As You scolded the apostles, so do You also upbraid us for our lack of faith and our hardness of heart in that we have not effectively believed those (Your evangelists) who have seen You after You arose, and because we have not acted as risen men. Then You say to us: "Go into the whole world and preach the gospel to every creature. He who believes and is baptized shall be saved, but he who does not believe shall be condemned."

Then after You have finished speaking to us about our duties as Your co-workers, You are taken up into heaven where You abide at the right hand of Your Father. We, like the apostles, must go forth and by word and example bring You and Your ideals to our world, sure of Your promise that You will be with us and will confirm everything that we do.

Lord Jesus, it has been a half-year of desiring, seeking and finding. Must we now give You up? You are going from us physically, but You did promise to be with Your Church all days, did You not? You are going to send us the Holy Spirit in ten days to be the bond of life and love between You and us. Come, Holy Spirit!

You are with us always in Your Mass and in the holy Scriptures. And You are with us in the work of the apostolate that we do in Your name. In the apostolate You want to live and act in and through us, using us as Your instruments in order to bring others

158

to Your love. I am struck by the fact that Your last words on earth deal with the apostolate, but why not? It has been Your life. Your ambition. It must go on!

KING OF GLORY

This seems to be implied also in the words of the Angels who interrupt the rapt gaze of the apostles following You into heaven. "Why do you stand looking up to heaven? This Jesus who has been taken up from you into heaven, will come in the same way as you have seen Him going up to heaven." The best way for us to be prepared for that second coming is to be what You have been: "saviors" who give our lives for the salvation of many.

But surely, Lord Jesus, it will be all right if, while doing Your work, we "dwell in heavenly places" (collect) with You, longing for greater union with You, lifting up our hearts to You. The Christian should be the complete man: like You he seeks to perfect and consecrate the world to Your Father, but he knows that his true home is finally with You in heaven. Perhaps one of the most valuable apostolic lessons we can give our world is that of our life oriented towards the heights where You reign in glory.

But all that is for tomorrow and thereafter. Today is for rejoicing in Your triumph. "Sing ye to the Lord, who mounteth above the heaven of heavens to the east. Alleluia" (communion verse). "O King of glory, Lord of hosts, who hast this day mounted in triumph above all heavens, leave us not orphans; but send unto us the Promise of the Father, the Spirit of truth, alleluia" (magnificat antiphon)!

> "Thou guide to heaven, and Thou the way!
> Be Thou the goal where our hearts tend;
> Be Thou our joy mid tears, we pray;
> Be Thou our life's sweet prize and end."
> (vespers hymn).

Prayer for the day:
HE WHO BELIEVES SHALL BE SAVED.

SUNDAY AFTER ASCENSION

Summary:

Jesus promises to send the Holy Spirit to the apostles and predicts future persecution for His followers.

SEEKING HIS FACE

Lord Jesus, after You ascend from the midst of the apostles, they return to the upper room to wait in prayer and longing for the fulfillment of Your promise to send Your Holy Spirit: We share in their warm desire both for You and for the Spirit. "Hear O Lord, my voice with which I have cried to Thee: my heart hath said to Thee, I have sought Thy face. Thy face, O Lord, I will seek" (introit).

You have known how we would feel at being momentarily deprived of Your presence. It was with this in mind that You spoke to the apostles and to us: "When the Advocate has come, whom I will send you from the Father, the Spirit of truth who proceeds from the Father, He will bear witness concerning me."

Lord Jesus, You promise, we pray. Come, Holy Spirit! Come so that we may not fail You in Your prophecy: "You also will bear witness, because from the beginning you are with me. These things I have spoken to you that you may not be scandalized . . . The hour is coming for everyone who kills you to think he is offering worship to God . . . But these things I have spoken to you, that when the time for them has come you may remember that I told you."

Lord Jesus, Your prophecy to the apostles has been fulfilled. They, indeed, bore witness to You with their blood. They were faithful, and their bloody deaths were the guarantee of their fidelity. But was not their victory simply the victory of Your Spirit within them?

If this prophecy of Yours has me in mind (and I have no reason to doubt that) then I can only repeat: Come, Holy Spirit! You seem to expect so very much from us who are so very human. You expect

160

my life. It isn't much, but it's all I have. This would be an impossible hope on Your part unless You provide the heart within that will inspire my giving. Therefore, I have confidence in Your promise: "I will not leave you orphans; I go away and I am coming to you, and your heart shall rejoice."

FIRE OF LOVE

Lord Jesus, there is so much fear in and around us. Come, Holy Spirit. There is so much hatred. Come, Holy Spirit. There is so much materialism. Come, Holy Spirit. There is so much selfishness and individualism, so much despair. Come, Holy Spirit, fill the hearts of Thy faithful: and kindle in them the fire of Thy love.

All these vices are in our world, in our Church, in us. We need the fulfillment of Your promise. You must not fail us. "Hear, O Lord, my voice with which I have cried to Thee, alleluia: my heart hath said to Thee, I have sought Thy face; Thy face, O Lord, I will seek: turn not away Thy face from me, alleluia, alleluia. The Lord is my light and my salvation: whom shall I fear?"

But Yours is the best prayer of all: "Father, while I was with them, I kept them whom Thou has given Me; but now I am coming to Thee; I do not pray that Thou take them out of the world, but that Thou keep them from evil" (communion verse).

Our answer to that can only be, "Amen."

Prayer for the day:
FROM THE BEGINNING YOU ARE WITH ME.

VIGIL OF PENTECOST

Summary:
Jesus promises to send the Advocate, the Holy Spirit, to those who love Him and do His word.

SPIRIT OF FAITH

Lord Jesus, You tell us that the way to prove our love for You is to keep Your commandments, and You promise to send us the Advocate who will dwell with us forever. He is the Spirit of truth whom the world cannot receive, because it neither sees Him nor knows Him. But, You say, we will know Him, because He will dwell in us, and be in us.

You promise not to leave us orphans; You will come to us. Yet a little while and the world sees You no longer, but we will see You, for You live and we shall live. In that day we will know that You are in Your Father, and we in You, and You in us. He who has Your commandments and keeps them, he it is who loves You. But he who loves You will be loved by Your Father, and You will love him and will manifest Yourself to him.

Lord Jesus, You have originally spoken these words to Your apostles; today You talk to us. You speak to us about doing Your will, about proving our love by deed. You promise us the Holy Spirit for our needs here and now in our world. Send forth Thy Spirit, and we shall be made a new creation, and Thou shalt renew the face of the earth. May Thy glory endure forever (offertory verse).

Lord, You know our needs better than we do ourselves . . . and You know the needs of our world. Hearts grow cold only too easily, and cold hearts never inspire any one to the kind of apostolic action that You know is necessary to win our world to You.

Lord Jesus, send forth Your Spirit! Send Him to us so that we may truly be the Church that is worthy to continue Your salvation for and in our world. You say You will not leave us orphans. Lord Jesus, we long for the fulfillment of Your promise.

COME, HOLY SPIRIT

Grant, we beseech Thee, almighty God, that the brightness of Thy glory may shine forth upon us; and the light of Thy light by the illumination of the Holy Spirit, may confirm the hearts of those who have been born again by Thy grace (collect).

Lord, Your Church in this collect shows her great wisdom. She is the Church that came forth from Your side on the cross — the Church that You showed forth to the world so gloriously on that first Pentecost. She knows that if she is to fulfill her mission in our world, she still needs the Holy Spirit.

May He confirm the *hearts* of those who have been born again by Your grace. Lord, You have instructed our minds. Now give us the Spirit who will instruct our hearts. Give us the Holy Spirit who will teach us to love as You love. Give us the Holy Spirit so that we can praise the Father with all the power that is in Your Church. Come, Holy Spirit.

I shall bless the Lord at all times; His praise shall be always in my mouth (introit).

> Prayer for the day:
> **IF YOU LOVE ME, KEEP MY COMMANDMENTS.**

PENTECOST

Summary:

Jesus at the Last Supper promises to send the Holy Spirit and indicates the work the Spirit will do in the Church.

BLESSED LIGHT DIVINE

Lord Jesus, it is now ten days since You left the apostles and ascended to Your Father. It is close to nine o'clock in the morning; they feel the hour of the fulfillment of Your promise is at hand. They have been waiting, hoping, fearing, desiring.

As they wait, snatches of Your prediction run through their minds. They recall Your saying: "The Advocate, the Holy Spirit, whom the Father will send in my name, He will teach you all things and bring to your mind whatever I have said to you."

Suddenly there is a sound from heaven, as of a violent wind, and it fills the whole house where they are sitting. But this sound is nothing compared to the divine invasion of their beings. Light, courage, joy, enthusiasm and love possess them as individuals and as a body, showing on their foreheads as fiery tongues. You have told them: "If any man love me, he will keep my word, and my Father will love him, and we will come to him and make our abode with him."

This is not one man loving You, Lord Jesus. It is a community, it is Your Church, Your Mystical Body. They love You. And as they love You, Your Father loves them, and You and He and the Holy Spirit come to them and make Your abode in them. That abiding is forever, Lord Jesus. You have never forsaken Your Church.

Their fear, their jealousy, their lack of understanding, their selfishness all vanish before the Light and the Love which is Your Spirit. This is goodness that they cannot possibly retain for themselves. They rush out into the hostile city and begin to act according to what they now are. They begin to be and to do as Your apostles, full of You and the Spirit, fired with but one desire, to increase love for You by telling the whole world about Your goodness and desirability.

FIRE OF LOVE

So this is what You have been talking about and aiming at all Your life, Lord Jesus. And especially what You have been talking about at the Last Supper. Now I can see how right You have been and had to be. Now I can see what I have to be: the dwelling place of divine Love and the channel of that Love among men.

You have never abandoned Your Church, Lord Jesus, but we, members of Your Church, can and do grow cold. We need this Feast and the Holy Spirit that the Feast bears within it just as much as the apostles needed it. And our world needs it, too. Lord Jesus, send forth Thy Spirit and we shall be created: and Thou shalt renew the face of the earth!

We need light, strength, courage. Come, Holy Spirit! We are afraid, divided, full of envy. We are dried up spiritually, blinded by material values. Come, Holy Spirit. "May the outpouring of the Holy Spirit purify our hearts, O Lord, and so sprinkle them with the dew of His interior grace that they may be fruitful in good works" (postcommunion).

"Come, O Holy Spirit, fill the hearts of Thy faithful: and kindle in them the fire of Thy love."

Prayer for the day:

WE WILL COME TO HIM AND MAKE OUR ABODE WITH HIM.

PENTECOST MONDAY

Summary:

God has loved the world so much that He sent His Son to save the world; but the world will not be saved if it refuses to believe in the Son.

PROOF OF LOVE

Lord Jesus, the commentators tell us that the verses of today's gospel most probably belong to St. John himself, that they are his loving and appreciative reaction to what You have been saying to Nicodemus.

He takes us back into the everlastingness of eternity and tells us that it is the Father's love for the world that prompts Him to give You, His divine Son, to save the world, that those who believe in You might not perish but might have life everlasting. For God has not sent You into the world to judge the world but that the world might be saved through You. He who believes in You is not judged; he who does not believe is already judged.

John goes on to say that the light (he means You) has come into the world, yet men have loved the darkness rather than the light, for their works are evil. Everyone who does evil hates the light, and he avoids the light that his deeds may not be exposed. But he who does the truth comes to the light that his deeds may be made manifest, for they have been performed in God.

Lord Jesus, the learned men who study the heart of man tell us that the greatest need of that heart is to know that it is loved. And it is all to the good when the one who loves is God Himself.

How wonderful it is to know that God loves us! You are the living proof. You belong to us! And not being satisfied with such an evidence of the Father's love, both You and He send us Your Holy Spirit. "O how good and sweet is Thy Spirit, O Lord, within us" (alleluia verse, Pentecost Friday). You have literally flooded us with divine love.

But humanity has always been reluctant to receive its God. You are light in the world, but what if men do not believe You, if they love the darkness more than the light, if they even hate the light? What if they refuse to believe that You have loved them? We have to believe in You, accept You, love You, give our lives to You. This is our coming-together-with-You, it is our response to Your love, but it is a human response that can only be accomplished by the working of Your Holy Spirit in us. Come, Holy Spirit, inflame the hearts of Thy faithful . . . !

HEARTS THAT HOPE

This is a point I have brought up before: the fact that all Your teaching, all Your light and truth must remain fruitless in me unless I welcome You and Your truth with loving desire and the willingness to have You grow in me. It is only Your Holy Spirit who can bring me to express this willingness. Come, Holy Spirit.

Your work must go on in our world, and You have made us part of it, carrying out what You so gloriously began. Truth must find a welcome in human hearts, and Pentecost, more than any other feast, can both inflame our hearts and give zest to the truth.

Therefore, "O blessed light of life Thou art, fill with Thy light the inmost hearts of those that hope in Thee. Lord, wash our sinful stains away, water from heaven our barren clay, our wounds and bruises heal. To Thy sweet yoke our stiff necks bow, warm with Thy love our hearts of snow, our wandering feet recall. Grant to Thy faithful, dearest Lord, whose only hope is in Thy word, Thy sevenfold gift of grace" (sequence).

Prayer for the day:

GOD SO LOVED THE WORLD THAT HE GAVE HIS ONLY-BEGOTTEN SON.

PENTECOST TUESDAY

Summary:

Jesus claims to be the door of the sheepfold, the shepherd, the one who has come that we might have life and have it more abundantly.

MORE ABUNDANT LIFE

Lord Jesus, if You love to come back again and again to the image of the good shepherd, it must be because by it You best express Yourself — Your inner being, activity, and purpose. You say that he who does not enter the sheepfold by the door, but climbs up another way, is a thief and robber. But he who enters by the door is the shepherd of the sheep. The doorkeeper opens up to him, and the sheep hear his voice, he calls them by name and leads them out, going before them as a true shepherd-leader should. The sheep follow him because they know his voice.

Now You make Your claim: You say that You are the door of the sheepfold: by You, if any man enters in, he shall be saved. If anyone enter by You he shall be safe, and shall go in and out, and shall find pastures. You end by leaving the speech of imagery and coming out plainly: "I came that they might have life and have it more abundantly."

Lord Jesus, I must try to see how Your being a good shepherd is related to Your sending the Holy Spirit on Pentecost to us again this year. Would the connection be love? He who is love in person, the Holy Spirit, is the one who inspired You to become man in the first place, to become our good shepherd, to found the Church which is the sheepfold into which Your love has gathered us.

We enter it by entering through You, by being baptized into You. You are the door. By being grafted into Your sacred humanity we enter into salvation.

LAW OF LOVE

In this Church You continue to feed us by means of Your sacraments with the very Life that You have in Yourself so abundantly.

167

And if You give us a sharing in Your Life, You also share with us the love that binds You and the Father and the Holy Spirit into one. You filled Your Church with the Spirit of love that first Pentecost. Now You again send Him to us so that we may become more and more one with one another and with You; and above all so that He will inspire us to be both doors and shepherds to our world even as You and Your apostles have been.

It is from the midst of Your Church that You now say to our world: "I am the door . . . I am the good shepherd . . . I have come that *you* might have life, and have it more abundantly." But our world will hear Your voice only if we who are already in the sheepfold will give this world an example of genuine love for one another and then lend You our hearts and beings so that You can love through us.

And as You speak to the world from the midst of the Church, so You also have a message for us: Receive the most sweet gift which shall be your glory, alleluia: giving thanks to God, alleluia, who hath called you to the heavenly kingdom (introit).

Lord Jesus, this most sweet gift is Your Spirit of love. Make us open up to His dynamic activity in us as individuals and as a Church so that we may obey You as You command us: Attend, O my people, to my law: incline your ears to the words of my mouth (introit). And the law that is Yours? It is the law of love, the law of the Spirit of love, the Spirit who impels men to give themselves for love of men.

Prayer for the day:
> I CAME THAT THEY MAY HAVE LIFE, AND HAVE IT MORE ABUNDANTLY.

PENTECOST WEDNESDAY

Summary:
> Jesus teaches that no one can come to Him unless the Father draws him; and He promises to give His flesh as bread for the life of the world.

BEING DRAWN TO GOD

Lord Jesus, today You speak of that mysterious activity called grace whereby Your Father draws us to Himself by drawing us to You. You say that no one can come to You unless the Father who sends You draws him. Everyone who has listened to the Father and has learned, comes to You: he who believes in You has life everlasting.

Lord, in His mercy the Father has drawn me to You. The very fact that I am reading this gospel and trying to understand it as the expression of Your divine mind would seem to indicate that His grace and His and Your Holy Spirit is active in me.

You have been teaching me divine truth even as You used to teach the apostles, and Your Holy Spirit has been teaching my heart to become what my mind has apprehended — giving me that "inner sense of truth and energy of love" (Vann) that make me want to become Your witness in our world.

May the Holy Comforter who proceedeth from Thee, enlighten our minds, we beseech Thee, O Lord, and lead us into all truth, even as Thy Son has promised (collect). I will meditate on Thy commandments, which I have loved much; and I will lift up my hands to Thy commandments, which I have loved (offertory verse).

Lord Jesus, Your Holy Spirit is active in us when the Father is drawing us to You. He is also active in every celebration of Your Holy Eucharist and in all the carrying-out of its effects in our lives. You say that You are the bread of life . . . the bread that comes down from heaven, so that if anyone eat of it he will not die. You are the living bread that has come down from heaven. If anyone eat of this bread, he shall live forever; and the bread that You will give is Your flesh for the life of the world.

FILL OUR HEARTS

This is Your word. You have given and You continue to give us this bread day after day. Divine drawing by the Father, divine truth and food given to us by You the Son — such is the manifestation of Your love in our regard. Lord Jesus, give us the Spirit so that we will *know* in our hearts as well as in our minds what we are and who is loving us and what is being done in and for us. Give Him to us more and more so that we can make the proper response of loving gratitude that all Your divine action deserves. Accept, we beseech Thee, O Lord, the oblation of our gift; and grant that we may realize by a devout life what we celebrate in these mysteries (secret prayer).

Lord Jesus, come, fill our hearts with love.

Prayer for the day:
> THE BREAD THAT I WILL GIVE IS MY FLESH FOR THE LIFE OF THE WORLD.

PENTECOST THURSDAY

Summary:
> Jesus sends the apostles to preach the kingdom of God, to heal the sick and to drive out devils.

PREVIEW OF PENTECOST

Lord Jesus, the events of this section of the gospel take place in the course of Your public life. You have been teaching the apostles for some time, preparing them to be Your mouthpieces, and now You feel they are ready for their baptism of fire. First, You give them power and authority over all the devils and the power to cure diseases.

Then You tell them: "Take nothing for your journey, neither staff, nor wallet, nor bread, nor money; neither have two tunics. And whatever house you enter, stay there, and do not leave the place. And whoever does not receive you — go forth from that town, and shake off even the dust from your feet for a witness against them."

And going forth, they go about from village to village, preaching the gospel and working cures everywhere.

Lord Jesus, this is kind of a preview of Pentecost — not nearly so spectacular, of course, but the idea is there. And the apostles must be very happy indeed to be thus appointed Your messengers to the people. They are not altogether ready for the apostolate in all its fullness: they are still very human and faulty both in their ideas and intentions. But You send them, You give them power over the evil spirits, it is Your work they are doing, and they go about it with all the enthusiasm of youth.

Do they remember this first experience later on when they have received Your Holy Spirit and really realize the potential that has been in them? Probably they do, and if they are more sensational at Pentecost, in the fullness of their divine enlightenment, they know that they simply continue what they began on the day described by this gospel.

They know that they are dealing with truth, then and now, and that You are the one whose mission they are fulfilling. And so, too, the enemy is the same — the devil, the spirit of ignorance and evil, against whom all Your being and activity are directed.

TRUTH ALWAYS ESSENTIAL

Would that be the reason why You inspire Your Church to choose this gospel for the Thursday after Pentecost? For You truth is always important, always essential, for all men of all times. You want Your Church to be as concerned about conveying truth as You were in Your public life; for the world cannot live without it.

And yet, You will not force Your truth on anyone. "Whoever does not receive you — go forth from that town, and shake off even the dust from your feet for a witness against them."

Lord Jesus, the commission You give the apostles is ours now, or rather, Yours and ours together. You tell us to take nothing for our journey, neither staff, nor wallet, nor bread, nor money. In other words, You want us to have some confidence in You and to appreciate our dependence on You. You have never yet let any of your representatives down. "May the outpouring of the Holy Spirit purify our hearts, O Lord, and by the inward sprinkling of His heavenly dew may they be made fruitful" (postcommunion).

Prayer for the day:
THE SPIRIT OF THE LORD HATH FILLED THE WHOLE WORLD.

PENTECOST FRIDAY

Summary:

Jesus proves His power to forgive sins by healing a paralytic.

WONDERFUL THINGS

Lord Jesus, the men carrying the paralytic must be credited with foresight as well as persistence. They cannot get to You through the crowd surrounding You; so they go up to the roof, remove the tiles, and lower the man at Your feet. Touched both by his and their faith, You say: "Man, thy sins are forgiven thee."

It is a strange thing to say, Lord; at least so think the Pharisees. Not only strange, but shocking and scandalous. They begin to murmur: "Who is this man who speaks blasphemies? Who can forgive sins, but God only?"

That is a good question, and how true it is! Only God *can* forgive sins. They aren't the only ones who know that fact: You above all are aware of it.

That is why You read their thoughts and say to them, "Why are you arguing in your hearts? Which is easier, to say 'Thy sins are forgiven thee,' or to say, 'Arise and walk'? But that you may know that the Son of Man has power on earth to forgive sins" — You say to the paralytic — "I say to thee, arise, take up thy pallet and go to thy house."

And immediately he rises, takes up his cot, and goes away to his house, glorifying God. An astonishment seizes on them all, and they glorify God and are filled with fear, saying, "We have seen wonderful things today." Wonderful things indeed! They have seen the living proof that You who are man are also God.

Lord Jesus, this paralytic is all of us together and each of us individually. He is humanity and man within humanity. What You have done to him here today, You have done to each of us not once but time and time again. You take away his paralysis, give him new health even as You take away his sins. Simultaneously filled with new physical life and new spiritual life of grace, he glorifies God. And so must we . . . always. "Praise the Lord, O my soul!"

REMISSION OF SINS

Again I ask, Lord, why Your Church picks this gospel for today? What is the connection between Your healing and forgiving the paralytic and the celebration of Pentecost? Is it that the life of grace that results from Your forgiveness now in the sacrament of Penance is essentially the indwelling of the Holy Spirit? The postcommunion of the Mass of Pentecost Tuesday calls the Holy Spirit the "remission of all sins." He is purity and love personified. Sin cannot co-exist in the same soul with Him. "O how good and sweet is Thy Spirit, O Lord, within us" (alleluia verse)!

Not only is the Holy Spirit the remission of sins; in some mysterious way He is associated with You in forgiving them. The sacraments are Your personal activities, Lord Jesus: they are the glorious extension of Your humanity and Your healing heart and hands.

But You, Yourself, in instituting the sacrament of Penance, say: *Receive ye the Holy Spirit,* whose sins you shall forgive, they are forgiven. The Holy Spirit hovers over the confessionals in Your Church, enlightening the minds and filling with Your love the hearts of Your priests whom You have empowered to continue what You began on earth.

And once the words of Your forgiving absolution are pronounced, it is the Holy Spirit who floods hearts and souls with love and life that are divine. Praise the Lord, O my soul: in my life I will praise the Lord: I will sing to my God as long as I shall be (offertory verse)!

Prayer for the day:
WE HAVE SEEN WONDERFUL THINGS TODAY.

PENTECOST SATURDAY

Summary:
Jesus spends an evening healing the sick and driving out devils.

HEALING ALL

You have been in the synagogue at Capharnaum teaching truth with authority and working miracles. Now You are tired, so You depart for Simon Peter's house. When You get there, You find Peter's mother-in-law ill with a terrible fever. Naturally they beg You to heal her. You stand at her bed, look at her suffering and command the fever to depart. Your word is enough. She gets up, and shows her gratitude to You by doing what she does best: cooking and preparing a meal for You and the rest of the guests.

But the word of Your whereabouts has spread. Evening has come, but there is no rest for You who so love those who suffer. The house is full of sick with various diseases. You place Your hands on each of them — each one is a person to You — and You heal them all.

There are some possessed persons there, too. They are the ones who are really ill. You command the devils even as You commanded the fever in Peter's mother-in-law. They know You better than the people who only gradually come to know You as God, and they cry out: "Thou art the Son of God." What good teachers they are, without wanting to be!

You labor all through the night. There hasn't been much rest for You. When it is daylight, You go out and depart into a desert place. Even there the crowds come seeking You, begging You not to depart from them. But You say to them, "To the other towns also I must proclaim the kingdom of God, for this is why I have been sent." And You are preaching in the synagogues of Galilee.

Lord Jesus, You are the Son of God! You have come into Peter's house, that is to say, You have come into the Church — our house. There are many of us invalids in the house. You have healed us all You have taken away sin over and over again. It is especially in Lent and Easter that You have renewed us and made us whole. And now You have filled us with Your Holy Spirit. "The charity of God is poured forth in our hearts by His Spirit dwelling in us. Bless the Lord O my soul: and let all that is within me bless His holy name" (introit). "Blessed art Thou, O Lord the God of our fathers, and worthy to be praised forever" (alleluia verse).

HIS MERCY CONFIRMED

Now it is time for us to imitate Peter's mother-in-law and to rise up and begin to wait on You. Our waiting on You is not only by the tasks of our daily life, doing them as well as possible and thus worshipping the Father through You; our waiting on You is not only loving You with all our hearts and souls: it is also helping You to proclaim the kingdom of God.

This is why You send us. If we ever forget about the kingdom of God, or lose interest in its advance, or fail to do our part in that advance, we miss the whole point of why the Father has sent You. Temporary relief from illness is important: You have surely shown us that. Your heart has constantly gone out to the poor, the sick, the unfortunate.

But ultimately, the important thing in Your thinking is the glory of Your Father to be accomplished by the ever increasing concentration of the love of as many as possible of the beings to whom You give souls capable of love. Lord Jesus, help us always to see our lives in relation to this purpose.

O praise the Lord, all ye nations: and praise Him together, all ye people. For His mercy is confirmed upon us: and the truth of the Lord remaineth forever (tract).

Prayer for the day:
THOU ART THE SON OF GOD.

TRINITY SUNDAY

Summary:

Jesus commands the apostles to go out and teach and baptize all nations in the name of the Father, and of the Son, and of the Holy Spirit.

THREE PERSONS—ONE GOD

O Lord, our Lord, how wonderful is Thy name in all the earth! Lord Jesus, just before You return to the Father, You command

Your apostles to go out into the whole world and to teach all nations, baptizing them in the name of the Father, and of the Son, and of the Holy Spirit.

Thus do You fit into one concise sentence all Your teaching about the trinity of three divine Persons in one supreme Godhead. And thus do You command that the apostles bequeath that teaching to the world, to us.

Many times You have spoken to us about Your Father, of Your desire to do His will. Your passion for His glory has dominated Your life, as the events of the past half-year have proved. You are perfect Son of the perfect Father. But You have taught us more about the Father (and Your relation to Him) by being a Son than by Your words. Nor have You neglected the latter.

You have told us, "Thus shalt thou pray: Our Father, who art in heaven, hallowed by Thy name, Thy kingdom come, Thy will be done . . ." You have lived that prayer even as You have prayed it. It rises up out of the fullness of Your being. You are a true Son of the Father, You trust in Him, You give Yourself to Him in love. So must we.

You have promised to send the Holy Spirit to us, and He came in a blaze of glory last Sunday to possess us all and fire us with His love and His desire to bear witness to You. Come, Holy Spirit!

But You Yourself have dwelt among us. You who are God, Second Person of the Trinity, equal to the Father and the Holy Spirit — You have become man, one of us. God so loved the world as to give His only-begotten Son. In You the invisible, supreme, almighty God becomes flesh. You are divine Love made visible. You are our way, our truth, our life. Praise be to Thee, O Christ!

READY HEARTS

If You are the proof of the love of God, You have taught us how to love. Love reaches its perfection and completion in worship. You have commanded all men to be baptized in the name of the Father, in Your name, and in the name of the Holy Spirit. And so we have been baptized. And being baptized, we have been made members of a worshipping Church, Your own Mystical Body. We bless the

God of heaven, and before all living we will praise Him; because He has shown His mercy to us (communion verse).

In worship we are best fitted to fulfill the destiny You have marked out for us: we are most dear children of the Father, we are sharers in Your praise as the Son, we are aflame with the love of the Spirit. Our hearts are ready, O God, our hearts are ready! Lord Jesus, grant that the worship we share in now may perfect itself day by day, year by year unto the final blossoming out into the heavenly worship that will never end.

Blessed art Thou, O Lord, the God of our Fathers, and worthy to be praised forever. Alleluia (alleluia verse).

Prayer for the day:
I AM WITH YOU ALL DAYS.

CORPUS CHRISTI

Summary:
Jesus tells the Jews that He will give the world His flesh to eat and His blood to drink.

O SACRED BANQUET

Lord Jesus, man's bodily hungers and thirsts reveal to him the thirsts and hungers of his spirit. Man's body requires food. He eats and is filled, but his satisfaction is only momentary. Soon he is hungry again. And if it is so with the body and its food, it is all the more true of the heart of man.

Man thirsts for food that will keep his longing heart forever satisfied. As You put it so well in this same sixth chapter of St. John's gospel from which today's verses are taken: "Do not labor for the food that perishes, but for that which endures unto life everlasting, which the Son of Man will give you."

We ourselves recognize our basic needs, Lord Jesus. Your psalmist puts these words in our mouth today: "The eyes of all hope in

Thee, O Lord, and Thou givest them meat in due season. Thou openest Thy hand, and fillest every living creature with blessing" (gradual). We hope in You. Body and soul we hope in You. And You do not fail us. "I am the bread of life. He who comes to me shall not hunger, and he who believes in me shall never thirst . . . My flesh is food indeed, and my blood is drink indeed."

Lord, You are speaking to the Jews, but Your promise is fulfilled in and for us. You give Yourself to us to satisfy all our deepest hungers. You are the "Living Bread" that we need "or else we die." O sacred banquet!

Ordinary food I take into my body and assimilate it to myself. On it I grow and mature. But You, Your body and blood, have an opposite effect. You assimilate me to Yourself. I am made one with You according to Your own word: "He who eats my flesh and drinks my blood, *abides in me, and I in him*." But I am still myself, even though I am one with You in this holy sacrament. How could I love You as a person if I did not retain my own personality? But feeding me as You do, You help me to be more myself than ever, more a complete and full human being.

WHO EATS THIS BREAD

Yes, Lord, I am still myself, and that is the difficulty. I am a person who is free to think and love and choose, but I am also a person who is free to grow cold and lax and forgetful and blind to the realities of the spirit. You say that when I receive Communion, You abide in me, and I in You. You who are God, You dwell in me. You are more one with me than a husband is one with his wife or a mother with the child she carries in her womb. But I am so busy thinking about other things that this wondrous fact leaves me cold. And so I go on longing, hungering, and desiring in the midst of plenty.

Lord Jesus, much as we need to eat Your flesh and drink Your blood, just as much and more do we need this great celebration of Corpus Christi, with all its praise and joyous gratitude, to sharpen our thirst and stimulate our hearty thanks.

We need this feast to bring us to see and know what You have wanted to do in and for us. Above all, we need it to remind us that communion with You is communion with You as the divine Victim of Calvary. As often as we eat this bread and drink the cup, we proclaim Your death until You return at time's end.

I eat Your flesh, I abide in You, You the Victim. I am thus one with You in Your offering of Yourself to the Father, in Your praise and worship of the Father. I am part of Your obedience to His Holy will, of Your surrender of self for men and for love of men. This is all good theory, it is what can happen.

But there has to be a change deep within me. You can do it, Lord Jesus. If You can change bread and wine into Your body and blood, You can also change me into a person who sees as never before that You are the only answer to all hunger and all desires and who freely, lovingly wills the change that You so desire. "In Thy mercy, compel our rebellious wills to turn unto Thee" (secret, 4th Sunday after Pentecost).

> Prayer for the day:
> MY FLESH IS FOOD INDEED.

SECOND SUNDAY AFTER PENTECOST

> Summary:
> Jesus tells the parable about the great supper to which many are invited but then refuse to attend.

A GREAT SUPPER

Lord Jesus, it is Your Father who gives this great supper, to which so many guests are invited. A banquet is a joyous and glorious occasion: why is it that so many are so hesitant about accepting the invitation? Is it that they fear the consequences of being counted among Your friends?

In any case, You are trying to tell the Pharisees that their excuses for refusing to accept You are quite absurd and really insulting: and that, if they will not take advantage of Your Incarnation and redemption, You know of others who will.

Through Your mysterious goodness, it is evident that because of our Baptism we are among those Gentiles who in this moment of history have been invited by Your Father to the banquet of membership in Your holy Church. We are the "poor and the crippled, and the blind, and the lame." "The Lord became my protector, and He brought me forth into a large place. He saved me because He was well pleased with me" (introit).

Lord Jesus, few of your parables bring out as forcefully as this one Your *insistence* on Your holy Incarnation. Once You decide to become man, You let nothing stand in Your way, either in becoming man to the utter limits of identification with our misery, or in bringing men into union with Your divinity through making them members of Your humanity. You want to give Yourself to us. "In this we have known the charity of God, because He hath laid down His life for us" (epistle).

Not only have You laid down Your life for us, made us members of Your Church, protected us, loved us, You have also given us Your body and blood as our food. Your flesh is meat indeed, Your blood is drink indeed. The memory of the Feast of Your Body and Blood is still with us. When I think of it, our attitude to Your self-giving is just as reluctant as that of the people of Your story. We resist the divine, we resist You, we resist love.

STILL THERE IS ROOM

I know how many times I have refrained from joining myself to Your Sacrifice and receiving You in holy Communion. You invite, I refuse. Or perhaps my fault is not so much in staying away from the banquet as becoming too used to it, too indifferent to its reality, taking You too much for granted. I should know better than the Pharisees. I should know that it is above all through Your Eucharist that You continue to draw men to Yourself, that You continue Your Incarnation by transforming us into Yourself.

I should know that this is the Food You provide for the all-essential task You give us of bringing men into Your membership today. And I should remember finally that unless I do my part in extending and consolidating Your Incarnation by personal action, prayer and sacrifice, I might well find myself in the position of the man at the wedding feast who refuses to wear a wedding garment.

Lord Jesus, I do give thanks to You for Your Incarnation, for having brought me into it, for Your Eucharist, for all Your protective love. You have invited me both to Your Church and to Your Eucharist. I can have but one response to all that You have done for me: "I will love Thee, O Lord, my strength: the Lord is my firmament, and my refuge, and my deliverer" (introit).

Prayer for the day:

O LORD, MY GOD, IN THEE HAVE I PUT MY TRUST.

FEAST OF THE SACRED HEART

Summary:

One of the soldiers opens Jesus' side with a lance, and there comes out blood and water.

BLOOD AND WATER

Lord Jesus, the soldier hardly knows what an instrument of God he really is. He opens Your side with his lance, and Your heart is laid bare to the elements and the gaze of Your friends and Your enemies. They can see that You are dead. Your heart has stopped working in Your body.

You have been saying that You are the Good Shepherd, that the good shepherd lays down his life for his sheep. You have laid down Your life for us: Your pierced heart is the evidence.

But life springs from death. You die, Your Church is born. St. Augustine is perhaps the first one to notice the beautiful parallel between You and Adam, the first man, the first father of the human race. Eve, "mother of all the living," comes into the world when Your Father casts Adam into a deep sleep and takes part of his side and with this builds up the first woman. Now from Your side, You the second Adam, sleeping the sleep of death on the cross, there comes forth the second Eve, Your Spouse the Church, the new mother of all the living.

As Your spouse, the Church knows all the secrets of Your Sacred Heart. She shares Your love for all of us her children; she shares Your utter dedication to Your Father, Your desire to glorify Him in all things.

This beginning of the Church is "the mystery which has been hidden from all the eternity in God" (epistle) revealed now for the first time. This is the thought of Your heart which will last forever, delivering our souls from death and in famine feeding us with Your own body and blood (introit).

Lord Jesus, Your pierced, broken heart tells us these things better than words. No one can now miss the conclusion that You have loved us to the end and that Your love has driven You to sacrificial heights up to now undreamed of in our world. Greater love than this no man could possibly have.

GIVE YOUR HEART

But this pierced heart sings another song, one that is seldom thought of or heard by men: it sings of Your utter, all-embracing love for Your Father and Your total dedication to His holy will. "Behold I come," You say in holy prophecy through the Psalmist, "In the head of the book it is written of me, that I should do Thy will: O my God, I have desired it, and Thy law in the midst of my heart" (offertory verse).

Lord Jesus, I know for sure that all my love for You, all my gratitude is lacking in true sincerity if I do not share this essential love and dedication and abandonment to the will of Your Father that You hold out to me as the best grace of this feast. You say to me: "Son, give me your heart." Your Father has first said that to You, and You granted His request. Now You ask me for the same selfgiving. You ask for my heart, my whole life, now and to come.

Well, here it is, this heart that is mine. It is still too much attached to its own will rather than Yours. But perhaps if I stand often enough with Your Mother and the other holy women beneath

Your cross made present on our altars, looking up at You who are dedication and love personified, You will give me the grace to be one with You in fact as well as in desire.

Teach me what true love is. I can ask this because You have said: "Come to me, all you that labor and are burdened, and I will refresh you" (vespers antiphon). With You there is merciful forgiveness, and plenteous redemption.

> **Prayer for the day:**
> THEY SHALL LOOK UPON HIM WHOM THEY HAVE PIERCED.

THIRD SUNDAY AFTER PENTECOST

Summary:

Jesus tells us that, being a good shepherd, He is necessarily interested in sinners: there is joy in heaven over one sinner who repents.

A MAN IN LOVE

Lord Jesus, You never tire of giving us signs of Your love for us. A few days ago You showed us Your heart pierced for love of the Father and us, and now today the image of the Good Shepherd tells us the same story. "This man welcomes sinners and eats with them," the Pharisees complain about You, little knowing what a magnificent tribute they pay You, and never knowing, as we have, how true the reality has been. Thou hast not forsaken them that seek Thee: sing ye to the Lord . . . for He has not forgotten the cry of the poor (offertory).

Your opened heart and the image of the good shepherd going out to look for lost sheep tell us in unforgettable terms that You, Lord Jesus, while on earth are a man in love. You are in love with each of us and with all Your flock.

As Your Church has it so beautifully in the Vespers antiphon of the Feast of the Sacred Heart: "With a perpetual love God has loved us, because, being lifted up from earth, He has mercifully drawn us to His heart." And You have loved Your Father even more: "In the head of the book it is written of me, that I should do Thy will: O my God, I have desired it, and Thy law in the midst of my heart" (Paschaltide offertory verse of Feast of Sacred Heart).

This being in love, this complete self-dedication to the Father's will, is Your inner life, Lord Jesus, as Priest and as Savior. It is the soul of Your worship. All Your thinking and doing are centered on the Father, springing from Your heart on fire with love for Him and for us.

Where can I find You today? I believe that I can find You — You, the God-Man, still in love with the Father and with each of us — in the Liturgy of Your Church. I believe that in the Liturgy I can find You showing the Father Your love and abandonment, and not only Yours, but ours, too.

WELCOMING SINNERS

Lord Jesus, we use the word "liturgical" rather loosely at times. We talk about certain activities, such as chant, dialogue Masses, altars, vestments, art and architecture as being liturgical. And considering the way You have made us — with bodies and souls and with our bodily senses the avenues through which You approach our souls and again by which we express our love outwardly — all these things are important to us. They are to be correctly esteemed.

But I must always remember that behind these externals are You, Lord Jesus, You the Man-God still in love with the Father, still welcoming sinners, eating with them, going out to find those who are lost. To Thee, O Lord, have I lifted up my soul: in Thee, my God, I put my trust (introit).

In today's Mass and that of the Feast of the Sacred Heart You call out to each of us: "My son, give me your heart." Not only do You ask us thus for our free gift of self to You, You show us how to enter through the door of word, song, symbol into Your heart, still open to receive us.

Through active and loving participation in Your public prayer

I can identify myself with You, with Your love. There I can make Your prayer my own: Behold *I* come. In the head of the book it is written of me, that *I* should do Thy will: O my God, I have desired it, and Thy law in the midst of my heart.

Prayer for the day:
THIS MAN WELCOMES SINNERS AND EATS WITH THEM.

FOURTH SUNDAY AFTER PENTECOST

Summary:
Jesus teaches the multitudes from Peter's ship and then arranges that the disciples should catch a great multitude of fishes.

PRESSING UPON JESUS

Lord Jesus, it is a lovely picture of You that St. Luke shows us today. He says that the crowds press upon You to hear the word of God. It is a very significant phrase. You will not disappoint them, but first You must find a convenient pulpit. There are two boats moored by the lake. You deliberately choose the one that is Peter's, You put out a little from the land and begin to teach the crowds from the boat.

You who are Truth in Person, You teach from Peter's ship: You give Yourself to them — to their eyes, their ears, their hearts. You still do the same thing from out of Peter's ship, Your Church!

Why do You teach, Lord Jesus? I suppose You teach for many reasons, but mostly because teaching is part of Your work as Savior of the world. I also think You teach because You love people, and teaching truth is one of the best ways of showing Your love. You know that to thirst for knowledge is really to thirst for God; You know, therefore, that the need to know truth is one of the deep necessities of the heart of man. They *press* upon You to hear the word of God. You know their need and You satisfy it . . . and all because You love them.

Your love manifesting itself in teaching truth goes on, Lord Jesus, in Your Church today. You teach primarily through Your Vicar, our Holy Father, through Your bishops when they preach and write pastoral letters, through Your priests when they preach and teach in classrooms and the parish Church. And may we not also say that You continue to teach through Your chosen brides, the Sisters, in parochial schools? And how about fathers and mothers teaching their little ones at home? Are You not helping and guiding them in conveying truth, in doing Your work in our world?

AT THY WORD

But it is above all at Your Mass that You make Yourself available to us—all of You: truth, grace, love, mercy, friendship, joy and peace. Here we press around You to hear You. In the Mass of the Catechumens You teach us truth in the epistle and gospel. Then in the Mass of the Faithful You tell us to launch out into the deep and lower our nets for a catch.

We may have been working all night, all day, all week — it doesn't matter — but *at Your word* we will lower the nets of our minds and hearts, full of longing desire as they are. We will lower them into the sea of Your love and You will fill them with a multitude of fishes. Lord Jesus, You fill our nets with Yourself. It is no accident that the fish is pictured in the catacombs as the symbol of Your holy name.

Perhaps if we lower our nets into Your love often enough, we will eventually find ourselves alongside of Peter at Your knees, saying, "Depart from me, for I am a sinful man, O Lord." But just as surely Your voice will come to us: "Do not be afraid; henceforth thou shalt catch men."

And we, again like the apostles, will leave all things and follow You . . . not half-heartedly and reluctantly and imperfectly as in the past, but with all our power, all our love. Then we will know that "The Lord is my light and my salvation; whom shall I fear" (introit)? The Lord is my firmament, my refuge, and my deliverer; my God is my helper (communion verse).

> *Prayer for the day:*
> ## AT THY WORD I WILL LOWER THE NET.

FIFTH SUNDAY AFTER PENTECOST

Summary:
> Jesus insists that the practice of loving forgive-
> ness towards neighbors is an essential quality
> of fruitful worship of God.

LEAVE THY GIFT

Lord Jesus, You almost go to extremes to show us how much we need to be charitable. I must recall the background of Your words to the disciples: You are speaking to Jews, to men who have a vital sense of the divine demand that man's first duty is to worship and sacrifice to the Supreme Being. How often have they heard: "Hear, O Israel, the Lord thy God is one God . . . I am the Lord, thy God. Thou shalt not have strange gods before Me"? To adore this God is man's first need and greatest privilege.

And here You are telling them that worship of God must be held up, put off, if there is division between the hearts of the worshipping community occasioned by hatred or any ill-will. "Leave thy gift before the altar and go first to be reconciled to thy brother, and then come and offer thy gift."

Lord, this is extraordinary doctrine You are teaching. It isn't that You want Your Father to go without worship or that You want to diminish the importance of worship or that You would want to make love of neighbor take precedence over love of God. It is rather that You love both the Father and man, and You want the best for both.

First of all, You want the best for the Father: the fullest worship, the greatest amount of love. He deserves it, He is God our Father. The fullest and best worship of the Father can only come from You, Lord Jesus, for You are His Son. But You are incomplete, as it were, without us, our Church, Your Mystical Body. It seems to me that whenever You talk about charity, about love of neighbor, You touch on the very heart of Your life and work and the effect You want to achieve. You seem to say that if we fail to love one another we fail You, we defeat You, make You seem superfluous and unnecessary.

This is a terrible thing to consider, but then lack of love *is* terrible. To be at odds with one's neighbor, to refuse forgiveness — and deliberately to will that condition, doing nothing to remedy it — means to destroy Your community of love and thereby to diminish the fullness of worship that You will to give to the Father *together with all of us*. So You say: "Go first to be reconciled and then come and offer thy gift."

ABOVE ALL THINGS

There is another reason why You so insist on charity and forgiveness: if lack of it destroys the unity in the community and thus diminishes worship of Your Father, it also destroys the unity within the single human heart. The heart of man is made by You for You, it is made for love both for You and for fellow-man. A heart made for You but which tries to live without You and without love is doomed . . . We have all endured the tragic experience that hatred and an unforgiving spirit injure the one who hates more than it injures the victim of the hate.

Lord Jesus, You want the best for the Father, the best for us. These two goods go together, flowing one from the other. The best for the Father will result from Catholic hearts functioning at their highest capacity within the framework of Your Mystical Body. Hearts functioning thus can only be those that love.

Lord, grant us the courage and desire always to forgive. Grant us the will to love You in all things and above all things (collect) so that filled with love for You we may be channels of Your love into our world. "Hear, O Lord, my voice with which I have cried to Thee: be Thou my helper, forsake me not, nor do Thou despise me,

O God my Savior: the Lord is my light and my salvation: whom shall I fear" (introit)?

Prayer for the day:
GO FIRST AND BE RECONCILED

SIXTH SUNDAY AFTER PENTECOST

Summary:
Jesus shows His compassion on a group of four thousand by feeding them with loaves and fishes miraculously multiplied.

HOW MANY LOAVES

Lord Jesus, maybe I shouldn't be this way, but the first thing that strikes me about this gospel is not Your miraculous power but the fact that so large a crowd becomes so absorbed in You that they lack food without seeming to miss it!

What hold do You have on them? Others preach, and the best of them are able to hold an audience for half an hour, or at most, an hour. Undoubtedly, You do more than preach to these thousands: You walk among them, listen to their personal problems, You give Yourself to them. And they forget their bodily hunger. Their physical "emptiness" vanishes in the vivid realization that they have You, the complete answer to their *hearts'* desire.

But if they momentarily forget that they are human beings, with souls and bodies, You remember. "I have compassion on the crowd," You say, "for behold, they have now been with me three days, and have nothing to eat; and if I send them away to their homes fasting, they will faint on the way." This presents a problem to the disciples: "How will anyone be able to satisfy these with bread, here in a desert?" You answer with another question: "How many loaves have you?" They say, "Seven," hoping, I suppose, that You won't ask them to give up the loaves.

You will not ask them to give up the bread. You only want them to share it. You have compassion on the people and therefore You feed them with Your word, Your truth, the love of Your Sacred Heart. That same compassion now takes care of their physical needs. Bread and fishes for a few are placed in Your hands; but after You give thanks and bless them, they become bread and fishes for a multitude, so that all have more than they want! You have fed them with truth and with bread; You have fed their souls and their bodies; You have fed them as men. And all because You love them.

IN OUR MIDST

Lord Jesus, "In Thee have I hoped, let me never be confounded: deliver me in Thy justice and release me; bow down Thy ear to me, make haste to deliver me" (alleluia verse).

I am glad You use the present tense: "I *have* compassion on the crowd." You who are man know mankind's needs. You know how much man needs to learn truth and to experience love. You who are God know how to satisfy all our needs. Because You are what You are, God and man, You are able to perpetuate Your compassion, making it available to all the world. You still say today from the heart of Your Church, Your Mystical Body: "I have compassion on the crowd." We experience that mercy today just as vividly as those 4000 experienced it then.

You are in our midst now. Your love and Your truth reach us through Your holy gospels and above all the sacrament of the Eucharist.

Lord Jesus, I do thank You for Your compassion, for Your words of life and wisdom, for Your Body and Blood, and for Your Church in which You and all Your possessions dwell. I am grateful to You, too, humbly grateful, for Your example. Perhaps if I experience Your object lesson on mercy for the needy often enough, some of Your compassion will rub off onto me to the end that I may contribute my share to Your work of satisfying the hunger of man, all of it: that of the mind, of the heart, of the body.

"Perfect, Thou, my goings in Thy paths . . . show forth Thy wonderful mercies, Thou who savest them that trust in Thee, O Lord" (offertory verse).

Prayer for the day:
I HAVE COMPASSION ON THE CROWD.

SEVENTH SUNDAY AFTER PENTECOST

Summary:
Not by words only will man be saved, but by doing the will of the Father.

BY THEIR FRUITS

Lord Jesus, I see often that there are meanings upon meanings in Your words. You begin this gospel with a sure test for falsity or genuineness in those who claim to lead men. Look at their fruits, their works, You say. "A good tree cannot bear bad fruit, nor can a bad tree bear good fruit." This is good plain common sense.

The real test for one who would direct others is his sacrificial spirit, his doing of the Father's will. You tell us that the prophet, the man of God, must truly be God's man, that is to say, his whole life must be given into God's hands, he must want to be possessed by God. As Peguy puts it, he must want to be like a staff in the hands of the Father in heaven.

You are talking about me, about every one of us, Your followers. I am one of the trees in Your garden. If I do not bear good fruit, I shall be cut down and cast into the fire of hell. Mere loveless words and bare routine performance of the externals of religion will not bring me heaven or peace or joy. I must do the Father's will.

But this is hard doctrine, Lord Jesus, very hard to accept and to practice. As one of Your good friends, Fr. Vincent McNabb, O.P., once said, "It is consummate perfection when a person really desires to do God's will. We mean it up to a point; but it takes a lifetime to make it a full truth. It is a desire which we shirk" (*Of His Fulness,* by Gerald Vann, O.P., p. 49). Yes, we shirk the desire, mostly I suppose, because we are afraid of You and of the Father, afraid that if we really make the gift of all our life into Your hands, You might make it too hard on us.

LOVE CONSUMES FEAR

But if we are afraid of Your will, it is mostly because we do not know You or the Father. We forget Your words about the Father Himself loving us because He is our Father. We do not know how to estimate correctly all those eventualities that seem so distasteful to us now. We have to learn to love the Father (You'll have to help us there, too), for love alone can consume fear, replacing it with trust. "So let our sacrifice be made in Thy sight this day, that it may please Thee: *for there is no confusion to them that trust in Thee, O Lord*" (offertory verse).

And above all, we have to look at the results: at Your saints, at Mary Your Mother. They did the Father's will all the way, and they didn't do so badly, it seems. Surely, by their fruits they are well known. They stood the test.

As for me, I've still got a lot to do. I simply must want to do Your and the Father's will. I cannot risk not being a good tree. Just two verses further than the end of today's gospel, You say: "Many will say to me in that day, 'Lord, Lord did we not prophesy in Thy name, and cast out devils in Thy name, and work many miracles in Thy name?' And then I will declare to them, 'I never knew you. Depart from me, you workers of iniquity!'"

Lord Jesus, casting out devils, working miracles, prophesying in Your name — great as these works may be — can never substitute for self-abandon to You. "I never knew you. Depart from me, you workers of iniquity." There is only one way of having You know me. That is by opening up my life to You and accepting Your will as my very own.

Lord, help me to be sincere when I say, "Thy will be done on earth as it is in heaven." I want to be a staff in Your Father's hand.

I want to be a good tree in His garden, bearing good fruit. Be it done to me according to Thy word!

Prayer for the day:

HE WHO DOES THE WILL OF MY FATHER IN HEAVEN SHALL ENTER THE KINGDOM OF HEAVEN.

EIGHTH SUNDAY AFTER PENTECOST

Summary:

Christ tells a parable about a rich man who demands an accounting of his unfaithful servant . . . and draws a lesson for our life from the servant's action.

MAKE AN ACCOUNTING

Lord Jesus, Your parables are supposed to be teaching devices; but sometimes they are not so easy to understand. Or is it that You just want us to do some thinking? That we can always try.

First of all, the certain rich man is surely Your Father, and I am the steward who has been accused (and rightly so) of having wasted His goods. All my life I have received graces from Him. I have been in charge of certain responsibilities for Him in the Church and in society, according to my vocation; and I have not done so well. The time is inevitably coming when I shall hear Him say to me: "Make an accounting of thy stewardship, for thou canst be steward no longer."

(Somehow or other, I find it hard to imagine God saying that to me, and I suppose others feel the same way. We just can't get it into our heads that we won't live forever. And so we go on and on, wasting the Lord's goods, more or less concerned about spiritual realities, mostly less. But it is inevitable: that day of giving an account. What if I am not ready!)

When the unjust steward in Your parable hears that command, he shrewdly and dishonestly manages to protect himself and his future. He ingratiates himself with his master's debtors so that they will take him in when he loses his position. "And the master commended the unjust steward, in that he had acted prudently; for the children of this world are in relation to their own generation more prudent than the children of light."

Surely, You are not praising dishonesty, Lord Jesus. But are You not telling us that we should stop being superficial and careless about things that matter most? The "children of this world," You say, are not superficial about costs, stocks, bonds, financial gain. Look at their dedication, You are saying to us. See how carefully they plan and scheme to get ahead. If they are so devoted to these passing values, how can you be so careless about preparing for that day of judgment when there will be no more turning back, no more subterfuge, no falsifying the record? Is this what You want to tell us?

FIDELITY

So, You are telling us, not to be careless and shallow about spiritual realities, about union with Your Father, about our vocation, our being in charge of a particular task in Your Church. You warn us to be at least as serious and thorough about these things as the materialists are in their pursuits.

I think I can see another ray into the parable, Lord Jesus. It is the fact of being a steward, of being in charge of Your property. The unjust steward could have continued in his position if he had been faithful. He was judged as a steward, not by any other standards. And as a steward he failed. So will it be with me.

I shall be judged according to the standards of my vocation. It is my vocation, then, that makes or breaks me. It is my vocation that makes me a saint or sends me to hell. No, that is not quite exact. The vocation is always holy: it is my fidelity to it that matters.

The unjust steward was faithless to his vocation. He just tried to get by. He is not a very attractive figure; but if I can just learn from him that I must deepen my concepts about duty and fidelity to the responsibilities You give me and resolve to do something more than just get by, then I must ever be grateful to You for having shown him to me. "Taste and see that the Lord is sweet: blessed is the man that hopeth in Him" (communion verse).

Fidelity to my vocation must bring me to that experience. Help me to taste and to see and to hope!

> Prayer for the day:
>> MAKE AN ACCOUNTING OF THY STEWARD-SHIP.

NINTH SUNDAY AFTER PENTECOST

> Summary:
>> Jesus weeps over Jerusalem, foretells its destruction, and drives the money-changers out of the temple.

HOUSE OF PRAYER

Lord Jesus, You talk to Jerusalem as You would to a person, to one who is very dear to You. "If thou hadst known, in this thy day, the things that are to thy peace." You talk to Jerusalem, and You weep over her.

Why do You weep, Lord Jesus? Because Jerusalem has ignored You? or because, when she does consider You, she will crucify You? That would make You and Your feelings the measure of Your emotion. I cannot believe that Your tears spring from hurt feelings. I think they come rather because Jerusalem, whom You truly love, refuses You and thus hurts herself. And the net result is that the Father is deprived of a great fund of love which would have been given Him if the city had listened to You.

Definitely, the Father is in Your mind. You can stand insult, neglect, ignoring; but when His rights and honor are attacked, You go into action. They are turning away the Father's love by scorning You, His messenger, and they are using His house as a place of business. You throw them out: "It is written, 'My house is a house of prayer,' but you have made it a den of thieves."

Lord, now that I think of it, I wonder if there is any good reason why our cities and this Jerusalem which is our 20th Century culture should be spared the destruction You predict for the Holy City of Your time. To be sure, we have not known Your physical presence; but there is more than one way in which You can walk in our midst. We have the fullness of Your truth, we have Your constant presence in Your Church, we have Your vital activity in all Your sacraments, we have the proof of Your final, glorious victory over death. What is the difference between rejecting You and rejecting Your principles?

One thing is certain: You are warning us just as surely as You warned Jerusalem . . . and for the same reasons: for our materialism, our scorn of You and of all spiritual values. And You warn with love: "If thou hadst known, in this thy day, even thou, the things that are for thy peace!"

ADMIRABLE IS THY NAME

Lord, where am I in this drama of Your tears? Do You weep over me? I can hear Your answer: You tell me to look into my heart. If I ignore You consistently, refuse You entrance into my thinking and living, if I use this temple (which I am) as a place of business rather than a house of prayer, then You weep over me. And if I continue in this way, I will be destroyed as utterly as Jerusalem.

Usually, when we see a beloved one weeping, we want — and try — to console him. I don't suppose that is possible in Your case; nor do You want it. You are beyond consolation. But You are still You, You still work in and upon us by Your word and Your inspirations. You are not beyond the thirst for our love and the desire for true conversions on our part. And surely, You will always will the glory of the Father of which we are capable.

Therefore, "Deliver me from my enemies, O my God: and defend me from them that rise up against me" (alleluia verse). That is, deliver me from thoughtlessness, from blindness to Your presence, from forgetfulness of Your love for me. And open me up to my vocation to praise so that now and always I may truly be Your

Father's house. "O Lord, our Lord, how admirable is Thy Name in the whole earth! For Thy magnificence is elevated above the heavens" (gradual).

> **Prayer for the day:**
> **MY HOUSE IS A HOUSE OF PRAYER.**

TENTH SUNDAY AFTER PENTECOST

> **Summary:**
> In the parable about the Pharisee and the pub-
> lican, Jesus teaches the necessity of humility.

TWO MEN

Lord Jesus, to Thee do I lift up my soul: in Thee, O my God, I put my trust, let me not be ashamed (offertory verse). This is a fitting prayer to go with Your story about the Pharisee and the publican.

You undoubtedly have a good crowd gathered about You as You tell the parable, many of them trusting in themselves as being just and despising others. The contrasts between the two men could hardly be more perfectly depicted. There is the Pharisee, undoubtedly close to the front of the temple, praying within himself: "O God, I thank Thee that I am not like the rest of men, robbers, dishonest, adulterers, or even like this publican. I fast twice a week; I pay tithes of all that I possess."

Lord, in examining this parable, I must be careful to keep down any such thoughts as, "I thank God I am not like the Pharisee." But it seems to me that the prayer of the Pharisee is not a prayer at all. He does address the Father and thanks Him, but there is no acknowledgment of any kind of dependence on Him—or need for Him — but rather a proud catalog of his achievements.

It must be admitted that his accomplishments aren't bad at all.

There is nothing wrong with fasting from food and paying a good percentage of one's income to the Temple. But it is clear that he has been doing these things, not for love of the Father, but for love of himself. He has been feeding his own ego. His god is not Your Father in heaven, it is himself.

God cannot penetrate into a heart so surrounded by pride and self-love. If He could, He wouldn't be recognized. The man has no needs, he has everything under control.

TO ME A SINNER

The publican is someone else again. He doesn't dare approach the sanctuary but stands far off, eyes cast down and strikes his breast in the original gesture of sorrow while saying: "O God, be merciful to me the sinner!" It is a beautiful prayer, a perfect prayer; for it gushes forth from the depths of a man who, knowing God and knowing himself draws the inevitable conclusion — that, having betrayed God's love so often, his only recourse is to God's mercy.

The sincerity of his admission brings this judgment from Your holy lips: "This man went back to his home justified rather than the other; for everyone who exalts himself shall be humbled, and he who humbles himself shall be exalted." Unlike the condition of the Pharisee, there is no barrier in him to Your Father's all-pervading love. Holiness is now possible to him.

Lord Jesus, be merciful to me the sinner. Be merciful to me in this Mass. What failing is more common to us than that of trusting in ourselves as being just and despising others? Pharisaic pride makes no sense at all. As You show so vividly, it makes fools of us and can well destroy us; yet, we go on and on indulging it. All of which drives me to the inevitable conclusion that we are totally dependent on You for everything, even for the recognition of our need of You.

All we can do is to lift up our soul to You. In You, O my God, I put my trust. That I do, willingly, hopefully, longingly, in this and in every Mass. I think if I do this lifting up often enough, You will in the end make me see divine goodness in its perfection, and then there will be no choice for me but to be a publican all the way.

In the meantime, keep me, O Lord, as the apple of Thy eye: protect me under the shadow of Thy wings (gradual).

Prayer for the day:

O GOD, BE MERCIFUL TO ME THE SINNER!

ELEVENTH SUNDAY AFTER PENTECOST

Summary:

Jesus touches the ears and the tongue of a deaf-mute and heals him.

BE THOU OPENED

Lord Jesus, few of us realize what it means to be deaf and dumb till we reflect that it almost implies living death. Man is made to hear divine truth — he can hardly live as man without it, since it is communication with Your divine mind — and then to respond to that truth with word and song expressing his praiseful love.

You know this all too well; so there is no hesitation about Your answer to the people who bring the deaf-mute to you. You take hold of the man and separate him from the crowd. You put Your fingers into his ears, You spit and touch his tongue. Looking up to heaven, You sigh, and then say to him, "Ephpheta," that is, "Be thou opened."

And divine healing flows along Your fingers and obeys Your word. The man's ears are opened and the bond of his tongue is loosed, and he begins to speak correctly. It is fitting that the first word he should hear should be from Your lips and that his first words should be "correct" words, that is, words of gratitude to You. The people "wonder" (that's a good expression; it means that they are amazed, delighted and more than a little awe-inspired) so that they cry out with full hearts: "He has done all things well. He has made both the deaf to hear and the dumb to speak."

Lord Jesus, how perfectly do these people characterize You and all Your compassionate influence in our lives! You do more for us than for the deaf-mute. In Baptism You give us *faith*, that glorious virtue that enables us to hear You and to see You. More than that, in Baptism You loose our tongues so that with all members of Your Church everywhere on earth and in heaven we can praise You and Your Father through You.

It is You who speak to us through the "sacrament" of the world of creative beauty. You seek entrance into our minds and hearts through the word of Your gospel that we read or hear in this and every Mass. It is You who enter into our inner being along the channels of all the sacraments, especially the Blessed Eucharist.

TOUCH OUR TONGUES

I will extol Thee, O Lord, for Thou hast upheld me; and hast not made my enemies to rejoice over me: O Lord, I have cried to Thee, and Thou hast heard me (offertory verse).

Lord Jesus, You have given us faith with which we see and hear You and so enter into the divine world of Your mind. But faith can grow dim through our neglect to exercise it and with the dimming a corresponding lack of enthusiasm in our response to Your love. Therefore, in Your blessed laying on of hands in this Mass, put Your fingers into our ears, touch our tongues and say to us: "Be thou opened."

Above all, touch our hearts so that we can cry out of the fullness of those hearts: In God has my heart confided, and I have been helped; and my flesh has flourished again; and with my will I will give praise to Him. Unto Thee will I cry, O Lord; O my God, be not Thou silent; depart not from me. Rejoice to God our helper; sing aloud to the God of Jacob: take a pleasant psalm with the harp (gradual and alleluia verses).

"By the reception of Thy sacrament, we beseech Thee, O Lord, may we feel a support of mind and body, that, saved in both, we may glory in the fullness of the heavenly remedy" (postcommunion prayer).

Prayer for the day:
HE HAS DONE ALL THINGS WELL.

TWELFTH SUNDAY AFTER PENTECOST

Summary:

To be saved we must love God above all things and our neighbor as ourselves. Jesus teaches who our neighbor is.

DO THIS AND LIVE

Lord Jesus, You say, "Blessed are the eyes that see what you see!" You are speaking to a group of Your disciples: and indeed eyes that see You in the flesh are blessed, whether they know it or not. But there is a lawyer present who is not sure he is blessed seeing and hearing You. He wants to test You, so he asks, "Master, what must I do to gain eternal life?"

You make him answer the question himself, making him repeat the blessed scriptural words: "Thou shalt love the Lord thy God with thy whole heart, and with thy whole soul, and with thy whole strength, and with thy whole mind; and thy neighbor as thyself." You say, "Thou hast answered rightly; do this and thou shalt live."

It is very simple . . . or is it? But the lawyer is not satisfied. Apparently he wants something involved and difficult; so he asks You, "And who is my neighbor?" You answer with a story.

A man is robbed and beaten and left dying in a ditch. Members of the clergy pass by — a priest and a Levite. They look at the sorry victim and go on their way. Then a member of the outcast, despised Samaritan nation comes along. He sees the wounded Jew and moved with compassion, he gives him first aid and puts him on his donkey and takes him to an inn for further care, He even opens his purse and gives the innkeeper money saying, "Take care of him; and whatever more thou spendest, I, on my way back, will repay thee."

Then You ask the lawyer, "Which of these three, in thy opinion, proved himself neighbor to him who fell among the robbers?" What can he answer? He hates to give any credit to a despised Samaritan; but he has to admit, "He who took pity on him." You drive the point home: "Go and do thou also in like manner."

SAMARITANS ALL

Lord Jesus, You are the merciful Samaritan and we who make up humanity are the victim. You go out of Your way to give first aid (without You we would surely have died eternally); and then You bring us to the Inn which is Your Church where You restore us to health completely by Your sacraments. Many prophets and kings have desired to see what we see, and to hear what we hear, and they have not heard it. Praise and thanks be to You, O Christ!

But I suspect that You want us to do more than review our beginnings as Your followers. You want us to love God according to the ancient formula, with our whole heart and soul and strength and mind. You want us to love our neighbor, whether he be of the same religion or not. You want us to love as the Samaritan loves, as You do: *all* neighbors. Anything short of that love is unworthy of those whom You have chosen to do Your loving for You in our world.

We must be Samaritans, all. But how can we? To love that way is a divine work: it is possible only with Your heart. But if You demand it of us, Lord Jesus, You will not refuse the means. O God, incline unto my aid: O Lord, make haste to help me (introit). Help us also, like the Samaritan — and above all like You — to see in our neighbors not nationality, nor age, nor sex, nor color, nor religion but *persons,* created by You, loved and redeemed by You.

Help us to see that this kind of love makes us not only human, but divine. For it makes us one with You. And it is to that condition that You call us. Therefore, I will bless the Lord at all times; His praise shall always be in my mouth. In the Lord shall my soul be praised: let the meek hear and rejoice (gradual). Lord, come to us in this Mass and fill us with Yourself, with love.

Prayer for the day:
GO AND DO THOU ALSO IN LIKE MANNER.

THIRTEENTH SUNDAY AFTER PENTECOST

Summary:

Jesus heals ten lepers but only one returns to thank Him.

SHOW YOURSELVES

Lord Jesus, it is probably very difficult for us who have never had a deadly disease to realize the anguish and pleading in the cry of the ten lepers, "Jesus, Master, have pity on us!" As usual the cry pierces Your heart. There is no hesitation in Your answer: "Go, show yourselves to the priests."

They start off. And never has there been a cure like this one. As their leprosy has been a progress towards death, so now their way to the priests in the temple becomes a progress towards life. The despair and terror of five minutes ago gives way to elation. They shout, dance, slap one another on the back. But they do not turn or even look back at You, the cause of all their joy. They run off instead in all directions, spreading the good news.

Lord, I can see You standing there watching them. But the smile of joy on Your face at having relieved suffering is tempered with a wisp of disappointment at their thoughtless lack of gratitude. Are You thinking that so it would be always down through the ages with those whom You would choose to help and save and cure?

But wait. One of the ex-lepers stops in his tracks. He turns around and sees You standing there waiting. He rushes back and throws himself at Your feet, his loud shouts telling eloquently the gratitude in his heart. Then You speak. "Were not ten made clean? But where are the nine?" You are not speaking to the poor fellow at Your feet: Your words go out to mankind, to us. They reveal how very human You are, for who, whether he be God or man or both, is not hurt at ingratitude?

A WAY OF LIFE

But You are also divine. You know the weakness of men. And so You know, too, the greatness of which man is capable. Would it be using my imagination too much, Lord Jesus, to say that the gratitude of the Samaritan, the thankful one among the ten, and the love that prompted him to return to You far outweighed the neglect of the nine? I hope so. Because then gratitude and reparation can become a way of life for me.

But I'd better start realizing that Your love for me in choosing me to be a member of Your Church, feeding me with Your body and blood, repeatedly forgiving the leprosy of my sins is as great a sign of love as that which You have for the lepers. And yet what place has gratitude so far played in my life? I take You and everything You do so much for granted. All my life I have been one of the nine. Now I see, because I know You and Your desire for gratitude. Maybe from now on I can make up not only for my own past ingratitude but for that of so many others who do not even realize that they are indebted to you.

In Thee, O Lord, have I hoped: I said, Thou art my God, my times are in Thy hands (offertory verse). One thing I can be sure of: my mentality will always be right, it will always be a thankful mentality, if I allow myself to be trained and possessed by gratitude itself, Your blessed Eucharist.

"Thou hast given us, O Lord, bread from heaven, having in it all that is delicious, and the sweetness of every taste (communion verse). It is fitting indeed and just, right and helpful unto salvation, for us always and everywhere to give thanks to Thee, holy Lord, Father Almighty, Eternal God, through Christ our Lord."

Prayer for the day:
JESUS, MASTER, HAVE MERCY ON US.

FOURTEENTH SUNDAY AFTER PENTECOST

Summary:
If we seek first the kingdom of heaven and trust in the Father, He will take care of all our needs.

DO NOT BE ANXIOUS

Lord Jesus, You argue and plead with us a bit today: "You cannot serve God and mammon." God and mammon (wealth, riches) tend to demand of us the fullest possible love, with no half-way compromising. Each is a master over thinking and doing, and "No man can serve two masters." It is a hard lesson to get across to men, but You spare no effort, loving us as You do, and knowing how essential to our final happiness this teaching is.

You say that we cannot serve God and mammon at one and the same time, and immediately You draw a conclusion that seems almost as though You leave out one of the steps in the argument: "Therefore I say to you, do not be anxious for your life, what you shall eat; nor yet for your body, what you shall put on." And then You go on to drive home the point with the lovely examples of Your Father's care for the birds of the air and the lilies of the field. He feeds the birds and clothes the lilies. Therefore, You say to us, will He not see to our needs too? Are we not of much more value than birds and flowers?

It is a positive and workable lesson in living, that You give us, Lord Jesus. It is trust, love, gift of self to the Father with that childlike confidence that knows no doubt, no hesitation. It is worship, the kind of service that the Father deeply desires from His children. And if we have this trust as the abiding, permanent directing ideal for our life in this world, then we will be at peace and will never fall victims of any false ideas about the deification of worldly riches and security.

TASTE AND SEE

You must admit that this is not a very easy ideal for us to put into practice, faced as we are with uncertain futures filled with inevitable sickness, grief, possible loss of all things, and death. You have made us body-spirit beings with human needs and affections which are very real to us. Are we to deny this nature?

I know the answer. You do not want us to deny our nature at all, but rather to safeguard it and bring it to full development by submitting it to a higher law—the law of Your love and of the

Father's love for us. "It is good to have confidence in the Lord, rather than to have confidence in man. It is good to trust in the Lord, rather than to trust in princes. Come, let us praise the Lord with joy" (gradual and alleluia verses).

Lord, when You say to us, "Your Father knows that you have need of all these things," You speak from personal experience of Your Father's love. These are the key words in Your whole argument: The Father has known and chosen and loved us from all eternity. He will not abandon those He loves.

I believe You, Lord Jesus, not only because You say those things but most of all because You and Your Mother Mary have lived them. Help my unbelief, help me to seek first Your kingdom and Your justice always, not so much that I may achieve all those things that the world prizes, but that I may more and more become worthy of Your and the Father's love. Only thus can I "taste and see that the Lord is sweet" (offertory verse).

> *Prayer for the day:*
> **SEEK FIRST THE KINGDOM OF GOD.**

FIFTEENTH SUNDAY AFTER PENTECOST

Summary:
> Touched with compassion for the widow of Naim, Jesus restores life to her son.

DO NOT WEEP

Lord Jesus, You do manage always to be in the right place at the right time. It is easy to picture this scene: the two crowds approaching one another—You who are Life, the focus of the one going towards the city; and the widow's son who is dead, the center of the other, leaving it. At the gate the two groups become one; and You stand face to face with the widow, both of you looking down at the dead boy.

You look at her, too, You know her life, her suffering, the loss of her husband. You know the daily work and worry, the poverty, the difficult task of raising a child all by herself. Most men have no idea what an only child can mean to a mother. But You know, You who made the human heart.

I find myself wondering, Lord, if this scene doesn't make You look months ahead into the future. Can it be that You see in this widow Your own Mother looking at her only Son, You, dead in her arms? As You would want men to have compassion on Your Mother, so now You give the example. Filled with compassion on her, You say to her, "Do not weep." Then You address the dead body: "Young man, I say to thee, arise." He opens his eyes. Sitting up he begins to speak. And You give him to his mother.

You can do these things, Lord Jesus, because life and death are in Your hands, You being God. You have given the boy to her in the first place, and now You give him back. All because You have compassion on her and are touched by her sorrow.

The attitude of the crowd is most interesting. St. Luke says: "Fear seized upon all, and they began to glorify God, saying, 'A great prophet has risen among us, and God has visited His people.'" Lord, why are they afraid? How can they be afraid of One who is so capable of sympathy and mercy? Is it awe rising from the momentary glimpse of Your being God as well as man?

COMPASSION

Well, whatever may have prompted their fear, they react correctly: *they glorify God,* saying, "A great prophet has risen among us, and God has visited His people." To glorify God: that is what we can always do all our lives in this world and the next . . . because of the compassion You show us each time You raise us from death by Your holy absolution and by the Life You give us in all Your sacraments.

I would like to make one more observation, Lord Jesus. It is about this compassion. It is so much a part of You, all Your life. As a matter of fact, You are compassion incarnate. We are supposed to be other Christs; we must become compassion incarnate now. Lord, grant us this gift. Help us to be more compassionate to all unfortunate persons — to widows, the sick, the poor, the homeless, the imprisoned.

We cannot raise to life as You have done. We cannot be God as You are. But by being compassionate, we can be God-*like*. We can be more human. We can suffer with the unfortunate. We can give them our heart, our mercy, our love. And as we grow in compassion, You grow in us. And what matters more than that?

"It is good to give praise to the Lord: and to sing to Thy Name, O most High. To show forth Thy mercy in the morning, and Thy truth in the night. Alleluia, Alleluia. For the Lord is a great God, and a great King above all the earth" (gradual and alleluia verses).

> **Prayer for the day:**
> I SAY TO THEE, ARISE.

SIXTEENTH SUNDAY AFTER PENTECOST

Summary:

Jesus heals a man sick of the dropsy on the Sabbath day and rebukes the Pharisees for seeking always the first places at table.

WATCHING JESUS

Why does the ruler of the Pharisees invite You to a meal, Lord Jesus? Out of a sense of hospitality? It seems unlikely. St. Luke says that they are watching You. There are, of course, different ways of "watching" You. Some can watch You with indifference; others can look at You with suspicion and hate; and others again with love and longing. The Pharisees definitely do not fall in the latter class.

In the room there is a visibly sick man. He is watching You, too, with hope and desire. Maybe the Pharisees have invited him there for their own purposes. You have healed on the Sabbath before; You might do it again; and that will strengthen their case against You, or so they think. There You go: You fall for their trap, asking, "Is it lawful to cure on the Sabbath?" They are silent. What answer could they give that would not expose their hatred and envy? You have a choice—to relieve the sick man of his suffering or to refrain from offending hyprocrites. There is no doubt about Your decision. You heal.

Then You give Your reasons. "Which of you shall have an ass or an ox fall into a pit, and will not immediately draw him up on the Sabbath?" They should be able to figure out the implications to Your question. The Sabbath day is indeed for God's glory. But it is inconceivable that there be any conflict between God's glory and a sick man being made whole. The fact is that they are not much interested in God, nor in the Sabbath, nor in beasts, or men; but only in the gratification of their hatred of You. What a terrible way for anyone to live!

But You are not through with them. You find other evidence of their self-seeking: You note particularly their preference for prominent places at table, and You read them a lesson in courtesy that is simultaneously a solid directive for spiritual development.

Do not go putting yourself right away in the first places at table, You tell them. You might get replaced by someone with more rank, and then you'll be shamed in the sight of all. But rather take the lowest place so that the master of the house can say, "'Friend, go up higher.' Then thou wilt be honored in the presence of all who are at table with thee. For everyone who exalts himself shall be humbled, and he who humbles himself shall be exalted."

BE OUR HUMILITY

How well You know men and all their petty weaknesses and ambitions! To be at the head of the table, what an ambition! It would seem that feeding one's vanity is more important than feeding the body. But that's the way we are, all of us (not just the Pharisees), in spite of Your word and example and the truth of Your word which we so often learn by sad experience.

Lord Jesus, the Pharisees never seem to profit much from Your corrections. But we are not any more successful. Is it that we do not take You seriously? You tell us that humility is a fundamental virtue for our happiness and our spiritual growth. You are humble.

Your Mother Mary is humble. All the Saints have been humble: there is no holiness without it. We must be humble.

What can we do about our lack of success in being what You are? I have read somewhere that St. Teresa of the Child Jesus used to ask You to practice charity in her since she was having so much trouble being charitable with her sisters. Lord Jesus, if it is so with charity, why not also with humility? Will You please be humble in us? You are our life and our hope. Be also our love and our humility.

"Have mercy on me, O Lord, for I have cried to Thee all the day; for Thou, O Lord, art sweet and mild, and plenteous in mercy to all that call on Thee. Bow down Thy ear to me, O Lord, and hear me, for I am needy and poor" (introit).

> *Prayer for the day:*
> HE WHO HUMBLES HIMSELF SHALL BE EX-
> ALTED.

SEVENTEENTH SUNDAY AFTER PENTECOST

Summary:
> Jesus says that the whole law is summed up in love of God and love of neighbor. He claims to be more than a descendant of David: He is God's Son.

GREAT COMMANDMENT

Lord Jesus, I wonder what kind of answer the Pharisee expects when he asks You what is the great commandment of the Law. Does he think You will have another answer than that in the Law itself? "Thou shalt love the Lord thy God with thy whole heart, and with thy whole soul, and with thy whole mind." These are Your Father's words to us, His command. But Lord, how can You *command* love?

Doesn't love have to be freely given? Isn't that the way You want it? I recall the wonderful words that Peguy puts into the mouth of the Father: "When once you have known what it is to be loved freely, the submission no longer has any relish. All the prostrations in the world are not worth the beautiful upright attitude of a free man as he kneels. All the submission, all the dejection in the world are not equal in value to the soaring up point, the beautiful straight soaring up of one single invocation from a love that is free" (*Basic Verities*, p. 207). No one wants to be loved by slaves, You and Your Father least of all.

Would this great commandment be then not so much a command as a plea, Lord Jesus? Your Father doesn't need to be loved, He desires our love. He desires it because loving us as He does, He knows that we can best achieve our happiness by loving Him. And by loving Him above all else, with all the love of which we are capable.

And You say that we must love our neighbor as much as we love ourselves. That's quite a love, Lord. Would this also be a plea? or a plea *and* a command? As You want freely given love, so do we humans. To love one another will make us whole. By love we become more than we were. Without love we are just ourselves, and that's not very much. We are even less if we allow any kind of hatred or bitterness or scorn towards our fellowmen to poison the source of our love, our human hearts. Hatred and uncharity hurt the one who hates much more than the one against whom hatred is directed. There is only one proper activity of the human heart and that is love, sympathy, self-donation.

And so, Lord Jesus, love for Your Father, for You, and for one another can also be considered a command. We must love because the Creator, knowing the heart of man, knows that without love that heart can never be one with Your heart. It can only be alone and lonely, and that is hell.

BE OUR LOVE

But what is love, Lord Jesus? You have told us, You have shown us that love is not emotional feeling nor mere sentimental attraction to others. It is rather gift of self. It is living for others, dying for them if necessary. It is openness to receive them; it is sympathy, compassion, mercy. Love is willing the good of men and proving our sincerity in willing that good by going out of our way to do good for them.

Love is one, is it not, Lord? The love that we have for men is not different than the love we have for You and for the Father. To give oneself to Your little ones, to Your poor and sick is to give oneself to You. You have told us that many times. This simplifies life and religion, too. God is love, You say through St. John. Religion is love. We are made for love because we are made for God.

Lord Jesus, increase our love always. Perfect it. Above all, purify it of self-love. But since I seem so incapable of fulfilling this greatest of Your commandments, and since it is a commandment that is so essential, I feel I can fulfill it only on one condition. As last Sunday I asked You to be humble in me, so now I pray: *Be* my love. Make use of my heart, my will, my whole being to love Your Father and my brethren. "Look down, O Lord, to help me!"

Prayer for the day:
LOVE THE LORD WITH THY WHOLE HEART.

EMBER WEDNESDAY IN SEPTEMBER

Summary:
Jesus casts out a dumb spirit from a boy, telling the people that prayer and fasting are necessary if they are to cast out certain evil spirits.

HELP MY UNBELIEF

Lord Jesus, in anguish the boy's father comes to You. "Master, I have brought to Thee my son, who has a dumb spirit; and wherever it seizes him it throws him down, and he foams and grinds his teeth; and he is wasting away. And I told Your disciples to cast it out, but they could not."

Your answer is not too reassuring; it implies a rebuke either for the man or for Your disciples, or for the people as a whole: "O un-believing generation, how long shall I be with you? How long shall I put up with you? Bring him to Me."

As they obey You, the evil spirit possessing the boy seeing You throws the boy into convulsions. It is a pitiful sight. You ask the father, "How long is it since this has come upon him?" The father replies: "From his infancy. Often times it has thrown him into the fire and into the waters to destroy him. But if Thou canst do any-thing, have compassion on us and save us."

Now You are genuinely moved . . . both by the condition of the boy and the terrible suffering of the father. But before acting, You must require one condition: "If thou canst believe, all things are possible to him who believes." The boy's father cries out, saying with tears: "I do believe; help Thou my unbelief."

The man's confession of his desire to believe together with his grief unlocks Your compassion. You rebuke the unclean spirit, say-ing to it, "Thou deaf and dumb spirit, I command thee, go out of him and enter him no more." And crying out and violently con-vulsing him, the spirit leaves him, and the boy becomes like one dead, so that many say, "He is dead." But You know differently. You take him by the hand, raise him and he stands up.

And it isn't hard to imagine the great joy and gratitude both of the child and the father. "Who is as the Lord our God, who dwells on high; and looks down on the low things in heaven and on earth? Raising up the needy from the earth; and lifting up the poor out of the dunghill" (gradual).

PRAYER AND FASTING

Now You are alone in the house with the disciples. And out comes the question that has been bothering them since they have seen You in action: "Why could not we cast it out?" You have, of course, commissioned them to do this very thing, and apparently they have been quite successful up to now. Your answer is not only for them, it is for all Your disciples through the ages, for us today: "This kind can be cast out in no way except by prayer and fasting."

Lord Jesus, I have no son, but I am myself, and there are plenty of ambitious spirits around seeking to gain control over me. I can cast myself on Your mercy, entreating You to free me and keep me immune from evil. You continue to lay down Your condition, "If you can believe, all things are possible to him who believes." Believing in You is essential. Faith is a trigger releasing Your mercy. But prayer and fasting are just as essential. They make us more and more worthy of Your healing. And keeping faith strong and bright with the vision of You, prayer and fasting prevent evil's return.

"Grant, we beseech Thee, O Lord, to Thy suppliant children, that, as they abstain from bodily food, they may likewise refrain their mind from vice (prayer). Lord Jesus, always will I lift up my hands to Thy commandments which I have loved" (offertory verse).

Prayer for the day:
LORD, I DO BELIEVE, HELP MY UNBELIEF.

EMBER FRIDAY IN AUTUMN

Summary:

A woman of the city washes Jesus' feet with her tears and wipes them with her hair and anoints them with precious ointment.

SINFUL WOMAN

Lord Jesus, in this scene in the Pharisee's house with the sinful woman of the city, You are at Your best. You must admit that the event is rather sensational; but You do not in the least seem embarrassed by her outburst of love. I suspect that it is only those who do not know what love is who are embarrassed by it.

You and she are central. The Pharisee is only a foil, but a necessary one for the full point of the incident. She has sinned . . . and it isn't necessary to go into details. Probably she has never known up to her meeting You that she had sinned. Perhaps she has only been seeking to fill up her heart with the love for which You Yourself have made it. False love on first sight often looks like the real thing.

Now she sees You who are Love personified, and at once she sees where she has been wrong all those years. She knows what it means to be loved, and she is vaguely beginning to see what it means to love. Violent as her sins have been, and perhaps as shameless, so now is her repentance. She weeps, she wipes Your feet with her hair, she kisses them. You sit there, smiling at her. You accept her gift, her tears, her kisses and all the love that they manifest. Praise be to You, O Christ, for this picture of Yourself!

The Pharisee doesn't like it. He thinks the whole affair is pretty disgraceful. He thinks it shows You up as a fake. (If he only knew how it really does show You up!) He says to himself, "This man, were He a prophet, would surely know who and what manner of woman this is who is touching Him, for she is a sinner." You read his mind and put him to the test. You ask him which debtor loves the money-lender most, the one who is released from paying a debt of 500 denarii, or another who is excused from paying 50 denarii?

MUCH LOVE

The Pharisee must admit it himself: he who has the biggest debt must love most if it is forgiven. He has no love for You, he shows You no respect, no regard whatsoever, he just wants to use You. He sees nothing in You; and so there is no exchange between him and You. He is in no way bettered by knowing You. But not so with the woman. If she has offended You in the past with much sin, now she loves.

And You see her love, forgive all the sins, and so she is better by far than the Pharisee, holy as he may look from the outside. You say to her and to all her sisters down through the ages: "Many sins are forgiven her because she has loved much."

Lord Jesus, this incident shows You to be more divine and more human than almost any other in Your public life. Among all the beautiful things You have ever said, Your words to this sinful woman are what we need most. She is each one of us. We all sin. Then You cross our path, You draw forth love from our hearts by showing us how You love us. And then the exchange takes place and we no longer belong to ourselves but to You.

Your words to the sinful woman do not encourage sinning, as

some might think. They rather encourage love for You. And love destroys sin and is the best preventive against falling again. Thank You, Lord Jesus, for this gospel evidence of that fact. Bless the Lord, O my soul, and never forget all that He has done for thee: and thy youth shall be renewed like an eagle's (offertory verse).

> Prayer for the day:
>> MANY SINS ARE FORGIVEN HER BECAUSE SHE LOVES MUCH.

EMBER SATURDAY IN AUTUMN

> Summary:
>> Jesus cures a woman who had been bent over double for eighteen years.

THOU ART DELIVERED

Lord Jesus, a person bent double is obviously, helplessly sick. She says nothing to You; it isn't necessary. You look at her and Your mind is made up. "Woman, thou art delivered from thy infirmity." You lay Your hands on her, and immediately she straightens up and for the first time in all those years looks a man in the eye.

You are that man, You her deliverer. Undoubtedly she thinks that it is worth eighteen years of looking at the ground just to look You in the face in the end. O praise the Lord, all ye nations: and praise Him together, all ye people. For His mercy is confirmed upon us (tract).

But the ruler of the synagogue doesn't seem to share her joy . . . or Your satisfaction at a work well done. He is indignant that You have healed on the Sabbath. "There are six days in which one ought to work," he complains, "on these days therefore come and be cured, and not on the Sabbath." What work have You done, Lord? Or has she worked either in being in Your presence or in standing straight after so many years?

It is evident that he is not thinking about the holiness of the Sabbath or the honor due to the heavenly Father from its careful observance. Under the cloak of a holy law, he is expressing his jealous hatred of You. He hides his real feelings under the falsity of concern for God's honor.

More than any sin of weakness (which, of course, You never approve) deliberate insincerity always stirs Your just anger. You blast him and everyone of his kind: "You hyprocrites! does not each one of you on the Sabbath loose his ox or ass from the manger, and lead it forth to water? And this woman, daughter of Abraham as she is, whom Satan has bound, lo, for eighteen years, ought not she too be loosed from this bond on the Sabbath?"

GLORIOUS THINGS

Here it is again, Lord Jesus—that loving respect for persons that so sets You apart from the Pharisees. Dumb animals would seem to mean more to hate-blinded leaders than people. I can see Your adversaries flushing and turning away, seeking to hide in the crowd. But surely there they feel ill at ease, for St. Luke says that the entire crowd rejoices at all the glorious things that are being done by You.

Lord Jesus, again I should like to join with those people and especially with the happy ex-invalid in their and her rejoicing and gratitude. Come, let us praise the Lord with joy: let us joyfully sing to God our Savior (introit). You still do glorious things for us, for me. Satan has bound her with bodily illness. I have been bound by sin, which is much worse. You touch me, speak to me, heal me, not once but again and again.

Lord, as I thank You now, I beg You to straighten me up once and for always so that I may look at You and You at me. Because to look at You is enough. To look at You is to know that You respect and love me (undeserving though I am) and that I have to love You. It is love and love alone that keeps us straight. Let my prayer be directed as incense in Thy sight, O Lord. The lifting up of my hands as evening sacrifice (gradual).

Prayer for the day:

THEY REJOICED AT THE GLORIOUS THINGS DONE BY HIM.

EIGHTEENTH SUNDAY AFTER PENTECOST

Summary:

Jesus forgives the sins of a paralytic and proves His power to forgive sin (and therefore His divinity) by curing the man of his paralysis.

WHICH IS EASIER

Lord Jesus, as soon as You step out of the boat at Your town, You see some of Your friends bringing a poor paralytic to You. Your sympathy immediately goes out to the sick man. But what strange words are You saying to him, "Take courage, son, thy sins are forgiven thee"? He is crippled, he can hardly move. He wants relief and health, and You tell him his sins are forgiven. I wonder if he wasn't perhaps a little disappointed at Your greeting.

You will come back to him. But first You look into the minds of the bystanders to see how they receive Your words. In all the minds You see perplexity; in some You also see hatred, jealousy, and the unspoken judgment: "This man blasphemes."

The Jewish People have engrained in them a very strong sense of the holiness of God and the consequent hideousness of sin. They know instinctively that sin as an offense against the majesty and holiness of God can be forgiven only by Him. They would be the last ones in the world to consider that sin is unimportant or trivial. But these Scribes and Pharisees so often fail to see sin in themselves, in their attitudes. Hatred and jealousy of You, for example, seem perfectly lawful to them.

Their great blindness, of course, is in refusing to believe that You are God and that You therefore have divine power to forgive. Your argument with them is conclusive: "Why do you harbor evil thoughts in your hearts? For which is easier, to say, 'Thy sins are forgiven thee,' or to say, 'Arise, and walk'?"

It is a question they have to answer, there is no choice, and in their hearts they know the answer even before You phrase it. "That you may know that the Son of Man has power on earth to forgive sins," then You say to the paralytic, "Arise, take up thy pallet and go into thy house."

SINS FORGIVEN

The syllogism is complete: Only God can forgive sin; You prove You are God by healing the paralytic; therefore You can forgive sin. And I might add, therefore You can pass on to men that same power to forgive sin. For here You are definitely thinking of more than this paralytic; and Your words are certainly meant for more than the Scribes who accuse You of blasphemy. You are answering all the objections that men down through the ages will make against the sacrament of Penance.

To these men and maybe even to us You address Your question: "Why do you think evil in your hearts?" If we give way to despair at the enormity of our sins, thinking that You will not forgive us, we think evil. If at the other extreme we think we can do or say anything we want and be free of sin, we think evil. If we refuse to consider that You have passed on Your power to forgive sin, we think evil.

Lord Jesus, in everything we have been enriched in You (epistle). How many times have I heard Your loving words: "Take courage, son, thy sins are forgiven thee." One of Your priests hears sins and absolves; it is You who hear and absolve. You want to forgive us our sins. Your sacrament of penance is very dear to You: it is one of the most striking signs of Your mercy.

But surely, Lord, You do not want us to sin just so that You can exercise forgiveness. You want us to learn to love You so much that sin will disappear from our lives. Lord, by means of Your forgiveness in the sacrament of Penance, and especially by means of communion in the adorable sacrifice of the Mass, You make us partakers in Your supreme Godhead. Grant, we pray You, that since we know Your truth, we may live up to it by a worthy life (secret). The only life worthy of You is a life of deepest love for You. Pour it forth into all our hearts!

Prayer for the day:

TAKE COURAGE, SON, THY SINS ARE FOR-GIVEN.

NINETEENTH SUNDAY AFTER PENTECOST

Summary:

Jesus tells a parable about the resistance of invited guests to the wedding feast of the king's
son, their subsequent punishment, and that of a
guest who enters without a wedding garment.

MANY ARE CALLED

Lord Jesus, You are the King's Son. The wedding feast is membership in Your Church and sharing Your salvation. The people of
Palestine in Your time are the first invited guests to turn down Your
loving invitation. Since then there have been many others whose
excuses sound as absurd as the ones in this parable.

It is hard to understand their way of thinking, Lord Jesus. Why
are these people so opposed to joining Your kingdom? Why are people in our day so hard to convince? It is resistance to divine love,
resistance to the *spiritual*. Farming, trading, business—all seem more
preferable than associating with You and developing a relationship
of intimacy with You.

This blindness is not reasonable or logical, Lord Jesus, but it is
more or less understandable. For it points out the age-old difficulty
about this human nature of ours: that, while we are made for You
and we know in our hearts that You only can give true and permanent joy, nevertheless we do have bodies with desires and urges that
usually seem much more attractive than those that are spiritual.

You know better than we do what is good for us. That is why
You so insist on getting people to the banquet. Your love for us will
not be denied.

But You indicate that along with Your desire for men to be
one with You in Your Church, You also want them to appreciate
what they possess as Your members. I am referring to the incident
of the wedding garment. The man in the parable who doesn't have
on a wedding garment more than lacks courtesy. He is careless and
disrespectful. Actually he scorns and despises the king and the king's
son. He might be there for want of something better to do. He receives his just reward.

220

Lord Jesus, we know that the wedding garment is the symbol of that inner transformation that membership in You aims to produce in us. At the end of time (or at the end of our life) You are going to enter the banquet hall. If I have not put You on, if I do not have Your mind, Your vision of life, Your love for the Father and for my brethren, then I too will hear those words: "Cast him out into the exterior darkness."

THEIR LORD FOREVER

Lord Jesus, the wedding garment is then the whole point of this parable. I will have it or I will not have it. And You are the garment. I must possess You and be possessed by You. There is no other choice. Your words, "Many are called, but few are chosen" are terrifying, especially in the light of all Your love for us.

You do almost everything. You invite us into Your Church, You feed us at the banquet of the Eucharist, You overwhelm us with evident signs of Your desire for us. As You Yourself put it in the introit: "I am the salvation of the people: in whatever tribulation they shall cry to Me, I will hear them, and I will be their Lord forever." You *are* what You say You are, our salvation.

But You also say in the same introit: "Attend, O My people, to My law; incline your ears to the words of My mouth." If I have failed in enthusiasm for You in the past, perhaps there is the cause: I have not sufficiently attended to the words of Your mouth coming to me through Your Scriptures nor the love of Your heart coming to me in the Eucharist.

"If I shall walk in the midst of tribulation, Thou wilt quicken me, O Lord; and Thou wilt stretch forth Thy hand against the wrath of my enemies; and Thy right hand will save me" (offertory verse). Lord Jesus, I cry out to You to help me in my need, to make me know the danger of over-confidence as well as that of carelessness about the words of Your mouth.

You are my salvation. Continue to be my salvation so that You will then be my Lord forever.

Prayer for the day:
THE MARRIAGE FEAST INDEED IS READY.

TWENTIETH SUNDAY AFTER PENTECOST

Summary:

At a distance Jesus cures the dying son of a certain royal official who would not take No for an answer.

GO THY WAY

Lord Jesus, rich man or poor, ruler or ruled, when a man has a sick child he is only a father. A father can be sick himself, and he won't worry too much. But let his young son begin to get seriously ill, and he looks around for someone or something to hold onto.

Your arrival in Galilee coincides with the sickness of the ruler's son. He has heard about Your merciful kindness to children and to the sick. He is sure You will grant his request: "Come down before my child dies."

Lord, You have Your own reasons for at first refusing him. "Unless you see signs and wonders, you do not believe," You tell him. Have You perhaps heard him in better days brush You aside as a quack healer? Or are You simply complaining about people in general being attracted to You more by what You can do for them than by Your inner worth?

But the royal official who is a father is in no mood to argue. He may have been guilty of lack of faith or of selfishness in the past. But now his son is sick and dying, and he believes that You can heal the child. He therefore pleads again: "Lord, come down before my child dies." The father's grief and fear move You. Above all, You see his faith—his firm conviction that You will not fail him in his need. Quietly and with a smile You say to him: "Go thy way, thy son lives."

Your words are enough. The man turns away and heads for Capharnaum . . . and his boy. You see him go, You see into his mind. No longer is he afraid, for he believes. True faith in You (like love for You) casts out fear.

Meanwhile, things have been happening back home in Capharnaum. The child has been getting worse. The doctors are consulting together with growing apprehension. Already the atmosphere of death is gathering. Then suddenly at the seventh hour the boy's fever eases away. He looks about, sits up, and asks for something to eat. He is well again just like that.

THY SON LIVES

The joyous servants' first thought is of the father. Someone must go and tell the father. They go, they meet. "He is alive!" they cry out even before they come together. "When did he get better?" the father asks. "Yesterday at the seventh hour the fever left him." The royal official smiles. He knows it must be so. For "Yesterday at the seventh hour" is Your hour, Lord Jesus.

They all hurry home, and there is much joyous celebrating for a while. But the father does not forget You, the cause of all the joy. Already a bond of gratitude and faith is forming that will tie him and his household to You as long as they live. The son is thenceforth the token and sign of Your love for them and of the love and gratitude they must ever have for You.

Lord Jesus, the royal official is the symbol of us all, surrounded as we are by sickness and fear, and inevitably confronted by death and judgment. Before I know it, I shall meet You as my Judge. But here You still are, the merciful Healer. This son of mine, this being which I am, is sick. I have done so little, I have loved so imperfectly, I have been so terribly self-centered. And now I am afraid.

Lord, You alone can destroy my fear. You do it by filling me with faith, by *being* my faith. Lord, come to me before my soul dies. The eyes of all hope in Thee. My heart is ready, O God, my heart is ready: I will sing, and will give praise to Thee, my glory (gradual and alleluia verses).

Prayer for the day:
COME DOWN BEFORE MY SON DIES.

FEAST OF CHRIST THE KING

Summary:

In answer to Pilate's question, Jesus claims to be King, but His kingdom is not of this world.

EVERLASTING POWER

Lord Jesus, the prophets have long ago foretold Your Kingship in both its extent and its duration: "He shall rule from *sea to sea*, and from the river to the ends of the earth. And all kings shall adore Him, and all nations shall serve Him" (gradual). "His power shall be an everlasting power, which shall not be taken away; and His Kingdom a kingdom that shall not decay" (alleluia verse).

This is very fine. But how do we see You fulfilling that prophecy? You are standing there before Pilate, and it is this very matter of Your kingship that is being discussed. Pilate has probably never heard of the prophecies, but there have been rumors about Your royalty. Yet here You are before him—beaten, bound, disgraced. Can You blame Pilate for the unbelief in his question: "Are *you* the King of the Jews?" Kings do not ordinarily allow themselves to be so treated.

But You are no ordinary King, Lord Jesus. "My kingdom is not of this world." It is not a political kingdom, You tell Pilate. But You insist that You are a king. "Thou sayest it: I am a king. This is why I was born, and why I have come into the world, to bear witness to the truth."

So there seems to be no doubt about the fact of Your kingship and Your desire to be king. You couldn't give away Your power if You wanted to. Being king is essential to Your *being* as Creator and Savior. This is the truth to which You must necessarily bear witness—the fact that You are the Lord God, King of the world, and that You therefore have a right to the service and worship and adoration of all men and all things in the world. "Ask of Me," the Father tells You from all eternity, "and I will give Thee the Gentiles for Thy inheritance, and the utmost parts of the earth for Thy possession" (offertory verse).

In a few hours You are going to mount a throne from which You will rule Your kingdom. But what a throne! You are nailed to a cross. Your arms are stretched out to embrace Your kingdom. "God has reigned from a tree." My Kingdom is not of this world. All power has been given to Me in heaven and on earth.

RULE BY LOVE

There is another truth to which You bear witness, Lord Jesus. King though You are, with every right of our worship, You do not ever force Yourself upon us or require us to give You that worship. You have made us free, and You want us to serve You willingly and freely. Ruling from the cross, You rule by love. That is, You reveal Your great love for us by dying for us; and it is that kind of love that pleads for a return from us. "The Lamb that was slain is worthy to receive power and divinity and wisdom and strength and honor; to Him be glory and empire for ever and ever" (introit).

Lord Jesus, Your throne now is the altar of our church. There You rule. There You are lifted up to draw all things and all hearts to Yourself. But the altar is more than Your throne: it is also the bridge over which I can climb up to You; it is the holy place where I can make that free and loving gift of myself to You. It is the meeting-place of Your divine heart and our human ones.

Lord, it is the altar of sacrifice that separates true love from sentimentality. This feast of Your kingship and this altar accuse and challenge my mediocrity. Believe me when I say that I want to give You entire dominion over my being and my life to dispose of as You will and when You will. And accept this promise: that I shall pray and I shall work with all my strength so that Your kingdom may grow in extent and in depth in this our world. You, Lord Jesus, are a king. This is why You have been born, this is why You have come into the world. To You be glory and dominion forever and ever!

Prayer for the day:

THOU SAYEST IT: I AM A KING.

TWENTY-FIRST SUNDAY AFTER PENTECOST

Summary:

Jesus' parable tells of the need for us to forgive our neighbor's offenses against us if we expect God to forgive our offenses against Him.

FORGIVE YOUR BROTHERS

Lord Jesus, Your parable today gets to the heart of our relations with one another and therefore with You and Your Father. The servant's debt is vast. To save himself, he begs the master for more time. The master, moved with compassion, does not only grant time, he forgives the whole debt. The servant then meets one of his fellow servants who owes him a very insignificant sum. He throttles the poor man, refuses to listen to his plea for patience, and casts him into prison.

The other servants hear of his action and report him to the master. The latter calls him and says: "Wicked servant! I forgave thee all the debt, because thou didst entreat me. Shouldst not thou also have had pity on thy fellow-servant, even as I had pity on thee?" And the master, being angry, hands him over to the torturers until he should pay all that was due him.

Then, Lord, You make the application to us: "So also my heavenly Father will do to you, if you do not each forgive your brothers from your hearts."

You purposely make the wicked servant's actions ridiculous. There is first of all the contrast between what he owes (ten thousand talents) and what his fellow-servant owes (a hundred denarii). Great mercy has been shown him: he refuses small mercy. We are inclined to despise the wicked servant until the thought strikes home: I am the wicked servant. What he does, I do repeatedly.

Again and again Your Father forgives us the sins we commit against Him. Every time we beseech Him, He releases us from the payment we owe. Then we run into someone who has offended us, and we refuse the forgiveness that compassion and our vocation as Your followers dictate that we grant. Our conduct is even more des-

226

picable than that of the wicked servant; for owing money can never compare with sins against Divine Majesty; and besides, the wicked servant was unforgiving only once. The Father always forgives us: we often, over and over, refuse to forgive.

HAVE PATIENCE

But I think You want to do more than point out the inconsistency of our conduct and make us ashamed of ourselves. You want to warn us now while there is still time that an unforgiving attitude towards our neighbor can slowly destroy our peace of mind now and our life with You in eternity. No one can enter heaven without having learned to forgive. Unless we learn charity, we will inevitably hear Your words: "So also my heavenly Father will do to you, if you do not each forgive your brothers from your hearts."

Lord Jesus, failure to forgive, it seems to me, is not a sign of weakness of our nature so much as other sins might be. It is usually deliberate and cultivated, springing from hurt feelings and wounded pride. It means that we haven't quite grown up into adult maturity as Your followers. It means that we are still far from having You as the single inspiration of our life. But "Lord, Thou hast been our refuge from generation to generation" (gradual).

You say I must be forgiving. I know in my heart that I must be forgiving. But in practice I go on as before. I do not ask that You take away my freedom so as to force me to be merciful and forgiving. But "Have patience with me." Open my eyes to the glory of a forgiving heart, for then I shall be like unto You who prayed from the cross: "Father, forgive them, for they know not what they do." "My soul is in Thy salvation, and in Thy word have I hoped . . . Help me, O Lord, my God" (communion verse).

Prayer for the day:
SO WILL MY HEAVENLY FATHER DO TO YOU.

TWENTY-SECOND SUNDAY AFTER PENTECOST

Summary:

Render to Caesar the things that are Caesar's and to God the things that are God's.

THINGS THAT ARE GOD'S

Lord Jesus, some of the finest compliments ever paid You have come from Your enemies. Today's gospel shows us the Pharisees trying to trap You in Your talk. This is their approach: "Master, we know that Thou art truthful, and that Thou teachest the way of God in truth, and that Thou carest naught for any man."

Unfortunately, the spokesman does not mean it: it is just flattery which he thinks might trick You into committing Yourself on a political issue: Is it lawful to pay tribute to Caesar, or not? No matter what Your answer, it would make You enemies, either Jewish or Roman. If You say it is lawful to pay tribute, You will antagonize the Jews. If You say it is unlawful, the Romans will be displeased.

Lord, Your answer is divine, more because of its content than its cleverness. You ask whose image is on the coin of the tribute. It is Caesar's, they reply. Then You say: "Render to Caesar the things that are Caesar's and to God the things that are God's." You are telling them (and all of us, too) to be good citizens, men and women with a sense of responsibility to the nation. Political and social life would be renewed if we took Your word seriously.

But Your answer is divine mainly because of the second half of Your statement: Render to God the things that are God's. This is altogether in line with Your constant thinking: it is what You have been doing all Your life. No one could ever accuse You of being a careless citizen. You pay Your taxes, even working a miracle so that Peter could have the wherewithal to pay.

But You are at Your best at rendering to God the things that are God's. That means Yourself, first of all. You give Yourself to Him from the beginning and all the way through. Your meat is to do the will of Your Father in heaven: whatsoever pleases Him, that You do. On the threshold of Your public life, Satan tempts You to adore him. You cry out to him and to the world: "Begone, Satan! The Lord thy God shalt thou worship and Him only shalt thou serve." And at the end of Your life You are going to render Yourself to God in a display of loving self-oblation that will outweigh in value all the other sacrifices ever made, and then some, for Your sacrifice is of infinite worth. Truly, Master, You *are* truthful. You do teach the way of God in truth.

A GOOD WORK

I have cried, for Thou hast heard me, O God: incline Thy ear, and hear my words. Lord Jesus, I am in great need of a more vivid appreciation of this truth that I must render to God His things, that I must render myself to Him. Above all, I must learn to put my heart in my worship.

You have come to be our Savior. You have died for that end. Salvation for me has resulted from Your having rendered Yourself to Your Father. But have You not also come to show me the way by which You could best bring me the fruits of that salvation? Have You not given me the Mass, which contains You in the very act of rendering Yourself to the Father, as the perfect way whereby I may join myself intimately to Your sacrifice, making it my own?

Lord Jesus, why do I not see that worship is its own best reward: that in giving myself I receive You. You cannot give Yourself to me unless I offer my heart to You, so that You may imprint Your beloved face upon it. But it is not too late. If Thou, O Lord, wilt mark iniquities, Lord, who shall stand it? For with Thee is propitiation, O God of Israel. Out of the depths I have cried to Thee, O Lord: Lord, hear my voice (introit). Lord Jesus, You have begun a good work in me. In this Mass and in all that follow all my life, bring that work to completion until the day of Christ Jesus (epistle).

Prayer for the day:

RENDER TO GOD THE THINGS THAT ARE GOD'S.

TWENTY-THIRD SUNDAY AFTER PENTECOST

Summary:

A woman touches Jesus' coat and is cured of a hemorrhage. Jesus restores life to a young girl who has died.

A GIRL ASLEEP

Lord Jesus, the bare words of the gospel seldom reveal the grief with which they were originally spoken. A man's daughter has just died. Your evangelist simply reports his coming to You and saying: "Lord, my daughter has just now died; but come and lay thy hand upon her, and she will return to life." A woman who is physically and financially exhausted after twelve years of hemorrhaging says to herself: "If I touch but his cloak, I shall be saved."

There is a sea of sorrow into which a person can be submerged by the misfortunes of life. "From the depths I have cried out to Thee, O Lord; Lord, hear my prayer; from the depths I have cried out to Thee." How well do these words of today's offertory fit in the mouths of the stricken father and the poor sick woman!

You are never very successful in resisting such prayers, Lord. The woman reaches out to touch Your garment. Immediately she is healthy again. After twelve years! She will never forget Your words: "Take courage, daughter; thy faith has saved thee." Yes, her faith has indeed saved her; and the rest of her life her restored health will remind her of the abundant gratitude she owes You for Your mercy to her. Ever after You will be present to her.

But here You are at the ruler's house. The hired mourners are in the midst of their concert of sorrow when You enter. It is all an act. Falseness never has appealed to You. You tell them: "Begone, the girl is asleep, not dead." They laugh scornfully, they know better: she is dead, and they are earning their fee. Then the ruler, the girl's father, takes over and throws them out. You are with him, and in his heart he knows that they are useless; for he has faith in You who are Life that does away with the need for paid mourners who thrive on death.

230

THOUGHTS OF PEACE

You are standing at the girl's bed looking down at her body. You take her by the hand and lift her to Yourself. She comes along with Your drawing. She is alive!

"And the report of this spread throughout all the district," says St. Matthew. I am sure that the restored woman, the joyous father, and the little girl who has tasted death have more than a little to do with spreading that report. Gratitude such as they have never vanishes.

Lord Jesus, in today's introit You say: "I think thoughts of peace, and not of affliction: you shall call upon Me, and I will hear you." All right, then, I do call upon You. Out of the depths I cry to You. Lord, hear my prayer. Do I have to have a dead daughter or a twelve-year hemorrhage to know my sorry condition and my utter need for Your help? Isn't it enough to be a weak sinner, wounded by mediocrity; and faced with the inevitable prospect of meeting You soon (I do not know when, You do) as my Judge? "O Lord, grant that we may be delivered *from the bonds of sins*, which by our frailty we have committed" (collect).

Lord, open my eyes, increase my faith so that with the sick woman I may cry out to You present to me in Your sacraments and so willing to cure me: "If I touch but his cloak, I shall be saved." You are the Master of life and death, of sickness and of health, now as You are in the scene of today's gospel. Lay Your hand upon me, and I shall live. Lord, hear my prayer!

Prayer for the day:
TAKE COURAGE, THY FAITH HAS SAVED THEE.

FIFTH SUNDAY AFTER EPIPHANY

Summary:
Jesus tells the parable about the weeds growing alongside the good grain till the harvest.

GOOD SEED AND BAD

Lord Jesus, You say that the kingdom of heaven is like a man who sows good seed in his field. Then while the men are asleep, the owner's enemy comes and sows weeds among the wheat and goes away. When the seed springs up and brings forth fruit, the weeds also appear.

The servants ask the owner: "Sir, didn't you sow good seed in your field? How then does it have weeds?" He answers: "An enemy has done this." They ask, "Do you want us to pick the weeds?" "No," he says, "lest in gathering the weeds you root up the wheat along with them. Let both grow together until the harvest; and at the harvest time I will say to the reapers: gather up the weeds first, and bind them in bundles to burn; but gather the wheat into my barn."

Lord Jesus, it isn't hard to identify the various personages in the parable. The kingdom of heaven is Your Church, and in likening it to a field, You indicate that Your Church is a living, growing organism (in the epistle today, St. Paul calls it a living *body* to which we are all called). It is growing towards the harvest when the good grain will be gathered up into the barns and the bad weeds thrown into the fire and burned.

In Your Church there are good Catholics and bad. It has not always been so—the initial planting was good—but then the enemy, Satan, comes and sows the bad seed, to say nothing of corrupting the good. You do not wish the weeds to be gathered up immediately perhaps for two reasons: the good wheat might be injured in such a rooting out, and secondly, because Your grace can always change the bad grain into good. You will never force men to convert to You, but as long as they still live, there is always a chance that they will respond to Your love and yet be saved.

UNTIL HARVEST

Such is Your Church, Lord Jesus—good grain and bad weeds. It sometimes shocks a lot of people who do not understand Your gift of human freedom, but it is the kind of Church in which You find Yourself best at home, having come, as You admit, not to save the just but the sinners. We offer unto Thee, O Lord, sacrifices of propitiation; that taking compassion on us, Thou mayest both absolve us from our sins, and guide our inconstant hearts (secret).

As for me, all I know is that You have planted me in the field of Your Church and that harvest is coming. You know my condition much better than I do. Desire is mine, desire to have You work Your will in me, desire to bring forth good fruit; but I recall Your words about not he who says Lord, Lord, shall enter the kingdom of heaven, but he only who does the will of Your Father. Wishful thinking does not produce much genuine spirituality.

Lord Jesus, protect and guard us all unto the end. Let Your word dwell in us abundantly, let it take root and bear fruit in more and more perfect union of Your mind and ours. Above all, in this and all following Masses, let Your word inspire us to that total gift of self that alone guarantees a good harvest both for the individual soul and for the Church as a whole. Lord, grant that whatever we do in word or in work, we may do all in Your holy Name, giving thanks to God the Father through You (epistle).

> *Prayer for the day:*
> GATHER THE WHEAT INTO MY BARN.

SIXTH SUNDAY AFTER EPIPHANY

> *Summary:*
> Jesus compares His kingdom to a mustard seed —a small seed but it grows into a great tree— and to yeast that causes the mass of dough to rise.

GROWING CHURCH

Lord Jesus, You say that Your Kingdom is like a grain of mustard seed which a man takes and sows in his field. A mustard seed is the least of all the seeds, but when it is grown up, it is greater than all the herbs so that the birds of the air come and dwell in it.

The idea You want to convey is that Your Kingdom, Your Church, is a growing Church that is destined to fill the world. Surely history has borne out Your prediction, Lord. From that little seed that takes root in Palestine, watered by Your blood and that of Your martyrs, Your Church has grown into a giant tree with branches reaching into every corner of the globe.

There is tremendous energy and potentiality in this seed, Lord Jesus, and the reason is that *You are the seed*. You are one with Your Church; and there is no more holding back Your advance into the world than there is keeping You in Your tomb that first Easter morning. You are the divine seed that has been planted in the soil of the world and is now a great tree that is on its way to filling the earth.

You are also divine yeast. Yeast in bread dough penetrates the whole mass and makes the dough rise so that when baked it is light and pleasant to taste. A small bit of yeast quickly transforms a large mass of dough. So do You want to penetrate and transform all men so that it is no longer we who live, but You who live and work in us.

The trouble is that most of us are not exactly eager to have You transform us. For there is another leaven at work in us, a different kind of "yeast" with ambitions nearly as forceful as Yours. It is the leaven of worldliness and self-seeking, and it has all the advantages of modern propaganda on its side (not to mention our own fallen nature which relishes its own gratification more than the moderation and mortification that following You requires).

CHRIST IN US

What are we to do in the face of Your truth? We have to decide which leaven is to form us—You or worldliness.

In my mind I know that the yeast of worldliness can destroy me, that its pleasures are of short endurance; but I still continue to will a hazy kind of compromise between You and the world. In his fine book about You called "The Lord," Romano Guardini touches on this problem. He speaks of Your demand that we not only consent intellectually to the correctness of Your teaching, but that we feel with heart and soul and with every cell of our being the claim of that truth upon *us*.

This implies a realization of what we are as created beings who are "continuously receiving ourselves from Your divine hands" (p. 294), and it implies also and as a result that we yearn for that trust in You that will throw out fear—fear of the consequences of the decision that imposes itself on our sincerity: the decision to give in to the demands of Your love on us and to return that love with the only gift worthy of You—our lives now and in the future with all their heartbreak, prayer, pain, illness and apostolic labor.

Lord Jesus, You are the Seed, You are the Yeast. You are in me. Think and will in me; grow in me, permeate me and consume the hesitancy and self-will that retard my transformation into You. We beseech Thee, O Lord, that we may ever hunger after those things by which we truly live (postcommunion).

> Prayer for the day:
> THE KINGDOM OF HEAVEN IS LIKE LEAVEN.

LAST SUNDAY AFTER PENTECOST

Summary:
Jesus describes the events of the end of the world and His second coming in glory.

THE SIGNS IN HEAVEN

Lord Jesus, You started us off last Advent with a description of Your coming in judgment at the end of time; and now we end the year meditating on the same thing. You must think the Last Judgment an important idea for us to consider. "Then will appear the sign of the Son of Man in heaven . . . they will see the Son of Man coming upon the clouds of heaven with great power and majesty." You are this Son of Man. You who are my Savior will be my Judge.

We began last Advent by crying out, "Come, Lord Jesus." You

have come, and we have seen Your glory in Your birth, Your manifestation to the Magi, Your miracles, Your death, resurrection, and ascension. St. Paul sums up the results of Your coming in today's epistle when he says that Your Father "has rescued us from the power of darkness and transferred us into the kingdom of His beloved Son, in whom we have our redemption, through His blood, the remission of sins." You have shown us how to live and, more than that, in Your Mass and Your sacraments You have given us the power to make those lessons effective in our life.

Year's end is always a good time for self-examination. I am a year closer to meeting You in death and judgment. Am I closer to You in my inner being? Do I seem more like You to others? Can they see You—Your thinking, Your attitudes, Your patience and charity and mercy—in me? Am I more and more aware of Your presence in me? The Christian life is supposed to be a slow invasion of You, Lord Jesus, into all aspects of my daily thinking and living. Now another year has passed. There seems to have been so little progress. I find myself wondering . . .

And here You are saying that I had better wonder. You are telling me that death and judgment could happen to me at any moment. I could go to bed tonight and wake up in Your presence. It is a matter of eternal life or eternal death. You have died for me, and You do not want to lose me. You want me with You forever, and if it is necessary to scare me into being prepared for Your coming in judgment, then let it be fear. But most of all, You want me to long for You and to love You and so to make myself ready to be judged by You.

DESIRABLE ONE

Remember how we started last Advent with talk about desiring and seeking You as the essential vocation of the Christian? Now that the year is over, I know how true it is. The Saints and Your blessed Mother have taught me that, to say nothing of my own heart. The Saints are the really down-to-earth people, who see only what is basic and essential. They desire You so intensely that they seem unable to wait. Death, judgment hold no terrors for them.

They literally burn with desire to see Your face and be finally one with You.

Lord Jesus, I do not yet have that desire. But desire, like love, depends on acquaintance. I do think that by meditating on Your holy words, You have become more real to me. You have revealed to me Your passion for the Father's will and His glory, Your all-embracing love for the poor, the diseased and the down-trodden. You have shown Yourself to me as the completely desirable One in my life.

In the last analysis, I know that You are everything. But my desire for You is still so fickle and so in danger of being swallowed up by taste for the fleeting and the unworthy; so I pray with all my heart: "Convert the hearts of all of us to Thyself, so that being set free from the greed of earthly pleasures, we may pass on to the *desire of heavenly treasures*" (secret).

You are this treasure. My last word is this: I know now that without You I can do nothing—nothing, that is, except to follow Your Church's urging. "From the depths I cry to Thee, O Lord: Lord, hear my prayer." Come, Lord Jesus, for Thou art my God!

Prayer for the day:
MY WORDS WILL NOT PASS AWAY.

Common Gospels of the Saints

NO. 1 COMMON OF THE BLESSED VIRGIN MARY

Summary:

Blessed even more than being physical mother of Jesus is it to do and keep His will.

BLESSED

Lord Jesus, this is one of the shortest but most beautiful and fruitful of the gospel selections. This nameless lady has heard You confound Your enemies; she has seen You work a miracle; she has listened to Your words of life; and she cannot contain her sentiments towards You: "Blessed is the womb that bore Thee and the breasts that nursed Thee!"

(Incidentally, isn't this an almost perfect example of what mental prayer should be—to hear and behold You and then to react to You with love?)

Obviously, this lady is of the opinion that You are wonderful beyond comparison. And she has no hesitation in telling the world how she feels about You . . . and in terms that only a woman and a mother would use. She thinks to herself and says aloud: if only I could have borne in my womb and brought forth such a son as Jesus, the Son of Mary!

There seems to be a kind of envy of Mary in her voice. But it's a holy envy and understandable. What mother wouldn't want You for a son! Your Church has always taken the woman's words as a tribute, not only to You, but to Your Mother, and she uses the words whenever possible in the Liturgy so that now all of us can make the words our own.

But what strange reply do You make to the woman's outburst of admiration? "Rather, blessed are they who hear the word of God and keep it." Surely, You do not want to take any credit away from Your Mother. You are saying that to hear God's word, to receive it eagerly so that it forms our lives, is to do the Father's will: it is to put one's whole life into the Father's hands. And this perfect hearing and doing of the Father's will, this complete trust in Him, is an even greater privilege than being Your physical mother.

241

WHO HEAR THE WORD

Mary Your Mother has done both. She is really the one who has heard the word of God and kept it. She perfectly fulfills Your standard for being blessed, for no one has ever done the will of the Father as completely as she has done. "Be it done to me according to thy word," she said when the angel announced that she was to be Your Mother. And it is this total gift of herself rather than her physical motherhood that makes her truly great and blessed.

So I think You mean the last words of the gospel mainly for us. No one can ever again be Your Mother in the way Mary was. But all of us can hear the word and do the will of God. And so in us Your saying can be fulfilled, "Blessed are they who hear the word of God and keep it."

Lord Jesus, there seems to be no limit to the possibility of holiness and glory that You and Your Mother open up to us by Your word and example. And not only by Your word and example, but by the power of fulfillment that You offer to us in this and every Mass.

For here we hear Your word, here we can make Your will our own, here we receive You into our bodies as the Food that makes saints. Indeed, we are the ones who should never cease crying out: "Blessed is the womb that bore Thee, Lord Jesus, and the breasts that nursed Thee!"

> Prayer for the day:
>
> BLESSED ARE THEY WHO HEAR THE WORD OF GOD AND KEEP IT.

NO. 2 COMMON OF ONE OR MORE SUPREME PONTIFFS

> Summary:
>
> Peter confesses that Jesus is the Son of the living God, and Jesus appoints him as head of His church.

THOU ART THE CHRIST

You are walking along the dusty road with Your apostles. They are probably talking about the way You just cured the blind man; they wonder about the weather; they watch You. Suddenly You stop. Your question is sudden and rather unexpected: "Who do men say that the Son of Man is?" You know, of course, better than they who men say that You are. Their answer is matter-of-fact: "Some say You are John the Baptist; and others, Elias; and others, Jeremias, or one of the prophets."

Then straight and sharp comes Your next question: "But who do you say that I am?" There isn't one of them who wouldn't like to answer that question; but instinctively they recognize that this is an historic moment that requires an historic answer from the man You have chosen for an historic destiny. All turn to Peter. His words ring out today as clearly as on that day so many years ago: "Thou art the Christ, the Son of the living God!" Conviction, deepest love, complete self-dedication give urgency to his voice.

And You meet him more than half way: "Blessed art thou, Simon Bar-Jona, for flesh and blood has not revealed this to thee, but My Father in heaven. And I say to thee, thou art Peter, and upon this rock I will build my Church: and the gates of hell shall not prevail against it. And I will give thee the keys of the kingdom of heaven; and whatever thou shalt bind on earth shall be bound in heaven, and whatever thou shalt loose on earth shall be loosed in heaven."

So do You found Your Church—on the man Peter, the man who believes and confesses that You are the Son of God. There have been many Peters since that time, many Holy Fathers, to each of whom You say: "Thou art Peter, thou art the rock, and on this rock I will build my Church and keep it built, so that the gates of hell shall not prevail against it." And when these modern Peters believe strongly enough that You are the Christ, the Son of the living God, not only do You make them strong foundations for Your Church, but You also make them saints.

THOU ART PETER

But I must not feel that all this has no relation to my life, here and now. I shall never be Pope. But it was to all the apostles that You addressed Your first question: "Who do men say that I am?" You want an answer to that question from each one of us.

Here is my answer: "Lord Jesus, You are the Christ, the Son of the living God!" I believe that with all the strength of my soul. I cannot have Peter's conviction, much as I want it; for Your Father, You remember, had something to do with his being informed on the subject. But I can have the will to believe and the power to repeat my convictions and the desire to grow in faith and in love. And perhaps if I say often enough that You are the Christ, the Son of the living God, I too can help the living Peter to extend and establish Your Church.

I will extoll Thee, O Lord, for Thou hast upheld me: and hast not made my enemies to rejoice over me (introit).

Thou art the Christ, the Son of the living God!

Thou art Peter, and upon this rock I will build.

> Prayer for the day:
> WHO DO YOU SAY THAT I AM?

NO. 3 COMMON OF A MARTYR-BISHOP (STATUIT)

> Summary:
> Jesus demands whole-hearted service from those who would be His disciples.

EVEN HIS OWN LIFE

Lord Jesus, Your words are surely very startling: If any one comes after You and does not hate his father and mother, and wife and children, and brothers and sisters, yes, even his own life, he cannot be Your disciple. And he who does not carry his cross and follow You, cannot be Your disciple.

I do not believe You actually mean that we must *hate* anyone who stands in the way to being Your disciple, for that would seem to go against all Your strong teaching about loving one another as You have loved us. The ordinary meaning of the word "hate" implies ill-will towards a person. Surely You do not want us to will evil to anyone—relative, friend, or enemy.

The commentary in my New Testament says that the word "hate" here means to "love less," and that makes sense. We must keep our values straight: no human attachment to people or things or self can stand in the way of following You and doing Your apostolic work, once You have chosen us for that work.

This means total dedication to You even as You have been totally dedicated to the Father and what He wants done in the world. Once more, it is the supremacy of God that is at issue. Once I see that one vital fact, all human objections fade to their proper stature of the important-but-not-the-essential.

In other words, this life that You have given me is not mine exclusively. It implies an obligation and a responsibility to You, to the Church, to the saving of souls, to the glory of the Father. It is only in *selfless* living for You and Your cause that I will be saved and the world made holier. And any kind of interference to this selflessness from family, friends, possessions, and above all from my own comfort and convenience must be put in its proper place. This is not easy doctrine, but Your cross has no mattress on it.

MY DISCIPLE

Lord Jesus, the inescapable lesson that You and all Your martyrs teach us is that suffering and death are the only facts that promise true growth for Your Church. There is none of us who does not have to face suffering and dying in our everyday life; but too often we fail to relate our daily martyrdom to You and to the extension of Christianity.

When we can come to see our life as time that You lend us for progressive growth in awareness of You living and suffering in us; and when we come to see the contents of those days—joys, grief, work, sickness, death—as constant incentives to love You more and more, then we will be carrying Your cross and will truly be Your disciples.

Lord Jesus, make me Your martyr. Help me to see what matters in life. Give me the strength to bear witness to the glory of the Father. Make me a true channel of Your sacrificial love into our world.

Prayer for the day:

HE WHO DOES NOT CARRY HIS CROSS AND FOLLOW ME, CANNOT BE MY DISCIPLE.

NO. 4 COMMON OF A MARTYR-BISHOP (SACERDOTES DEI)

Summary:

Jesus tells us that the best way to save our souls is to lose them for His sake.

WHAT PROFIT

Lord Jesus, You tell us that if we wish to come after You, we must deny ourselves and take up our cross and follow You. You say that losing and spending our lives for Your sake is the best way to be saved. "For what does it profit a man," You ask, "if he gain the whole world, but suffer the loss of his own soul? Or what will a man give in exchange for his soul? For the Son of Man is come with His angels in the glory of His Father, and then He will render to everyone according to his conduct."

Lord Jesus, in the past I have always thought of Your words here apart from any context. They stood by themselves: What does it profit a man to have as much as he desires of everything that this world prizes if in the end he loses his soul and is separated from You forever and eternity? Now I see the context . . . and the contrast.

It isn't merely a question of losing one's soul by going off after wrong values, for example, making riches and wealth one's god. It is mainly a question of *preferring* these wrong values to taking up our cross and following You and being Your apostles.

I don't want to overdraw the situation, but it does seem to me that—according to Your word—there is no middle ground between being Your apostle and true follower on the one hand and being headed straight to hell on the other. "For he who would save his life will lose it; but he who loses his life for My sake will find it." At the end of our life You will come with Your angels in the glory of the Father, and then You will render to each of us according to our conduct; that is, according to our fidelity to Your cross and to *everything* that the cross and following You implies.

WHAT EXCHANGE

The frightening inevitability of this word of Yours forces me to examine my own position, Lord Jesus. I do want to come after You and be Your follower, but I am afraid there is more wishful thinking in my profession of Faith than true and real determination to follow You as honesty demands that I follow You. Oh, there is a certain amount of self-denial in my life according to the season of the year. And the cross, well, I haven't exactly dodged whatever there has been of it.

But there is mediocrity, reluctance, joylessness in my following You. I blush when I think of the difference between my life and that of the martyr whose feast we celebrate today . . . or between my life and that of a Catholic behind the Iron Curtain . . . or a prisoner in a jail or an invalid doomed to die. What end will this mediocrity bring me to? If I want to save my life, I *must* lose it.

Lord Jesus, You always have been, and still are, the inspiration and the strength of the martyrs. St. Paul puts it so well in today's epistle: For as the sufferings of Christ abound in us, so also through Christ our comfort abounds. I am not asking for martyrdom: I fear being too afraid of it.

All I'm asking for is the courage to be sincere and honest in carrying out my profession as Your dedicated follower: I'm asking that You fill me with the love for You that will inspire me to deny myself, and take up Your cross and follow You. But if love for You doesn't bring me to my senses before it is too late, then make me see clearly without any rose-coloring the dreadful consequences for me in Your words: "What will a man give in exchange for his soul?"

Prayer for the day:

HE WHO LOSES HIS LIFE FOR MY SAKE WILL FIND IT.

NO. 5 COMMON OF A MARTYR NOT A BISHOP (IN VIRTUE)

Summary:

Jesus gives the requirements for following Him: He is to be preferred to all other goods.

A SWORD NOT PEACE

Lord Jesus, sometimes Your words are very strange. You say in today's gospel that You have not come to send peace upon the earth, that You have come to bring a sword, not peace. You have come to set a man at variance with his father, and a daughter with her mother, and a daughter-in-law with her mother-in-law; and a man's enemies will be those of his own household. All this seems very harsh and unlike You and so many other sentiments of Yours. How am I to understand You?

When You speak of peace, do You mean what we mean today—absence of bother and even discussion, passivity, or perhaps even stagnation? I have come to bring a sword, not peace, not passivity or indifference to truth, You say. You surely have not come to relieve us of the necessity to think and discuss and learn truth. And if arriving at Your truth means antagonizing others within the household or without, then we must put first things first. You are first now and always. You alone matter, Lord Jesus.

Therefore, You tell us that if we love father or mother or daughter or son more than You, we are not worthy of You. You can say this, of course, because of what and who You are: God's only Son. It is the old story of the relationship between creatures and God, a relationship that meditating these gospels brings out again and again and more and more.

There is a mysterious divine truth that challenges our minds here. Its full meaning is not too readily apparent. To choose You in preference to dear ones and their opinions on a human level ordinarily brings pain both to oneself and to them. But that is the mystery of being Your follower, that is the cross that You constantly speak about and hold up to our contemplation. He who does not take up his cross and follow You, is not worthy of You. He who finds his life shall lose it, and he who loses his life for Your sake, will find it.

JUST MAN'S REWARD

Yes, Lord Jesus, he who loses his life for Your sake will find it; and more than that, those who at first oppose You and seek to keep You out of their life inevitably find peace and life and truth through the sacrifice of Your witness, Your follower, Your martyr. So it has always been.

Lord Jesus, I mentioned something at the beginning about Your sounding harsh. Now it comes out just the opposite. All good things come to men and the world through You, through choosing You and going along with You all the way, not taking into account the *momentary* grief of those who do not understand divine depths of truth. Here as in everything, the more God's values are safeguarded, the more good comes to men, and more love expands over the world.

Lord Jesus, now that I have figured out all this, please help me to put it into practice whenever the occasion arises. Most of us do not have to oppose those near and dear to us in order to follow You. The conflict is usually within our inner beings—between Your demands and our lack of courage. You constantly accuse and shock us, saying: "He who does not take up his cross and follow me, is not worthy of me." But in Thy strength, O Lord, the just man shall joy: and in Thy salvation he shall rejoice exceedingly: Thou hast given him his heart's desire (introit).

Prayer for the day:
HE WHO LOSES HIS LIFE FOR MY SAKE, WILL FIND IT.

NO. 6 COMMON OF A MARTYR NOT A BISHOP (LAETABITUR)

Summary:

Everyone who acknowledges Jesus before men, him will Christ acknowledge before the Father in heaven.

DO NOT BE AFRAID

Lord Jesus, You say that there is nothing concealed that will not be disclosed, and nothing hidden that will not be made known. What You tell us in darkness, we are to speak in the light; and what we hear whispered, we are to preach on the housetops. This is good advice for our life as Your followers in the world.

Then You go on. "Do not be afraid," You say, "of those who kill the body but cannot kill the soul. But rather be afraid of him who is able to destroy both soul and body in hell." You are talking about the devil, of course. It is perfectly normal for us to be afraid of storms, people, heavy traffic and war. These things can take away our bodily life and send us to an early grave. But sometimes we fear these things more than we fear Satan who is able to destroy both our body and our soul in hell.

Satan works through visible things, even as You do through the sacraments and through the visible beauty of earthly creation. But unlike You, he makes visible things a means of damnation rather than of salvation. It is especially by worldliness that the devil would destroy both my soul and my body, making me feel that things are ends in themselves rather than means to You.

The best remedy against worldliness and all its effects is a firm trust in the paternal love of Your Father. You go on to say: "Are not two sparrows sold for a farthing? And yet not one of them will fall to the ground without your Father's leave. But as for you, the very hairs of your head are all numbered. Therefore do not be afraid: you are of more value than many sparrows. Therefore, everyone who acknowledges Me before men, I also will acknowledge him before My Father in heaven."

BEFORE MY FATHER

Why do I not take Your word in these things, Lord Jesus? Your heavenly Father is *infinite* wisdom: there is nothing He does not know—the hairs of our heads, the grains of sand on the seashores, the feathers on all the birds. And the fact that all these things (and we) exist means also that the Father loves all of us. And loving us, He watches over us. We are better than many sparrows, for being made in Your image and likeness, we may share divine knowledge by seeking truth, and we may become one with divine love by loving You and loving one another. Above all, we are better than many sparrows because You have died to save us.

Fear not, You say. I'll try to do better from now on in obeying this command, Lord Jesus. If I have been slow to believe and to trust in the past, it is mainly because I have not known You and the Father as You are. I have judged worldly strength and people and security more worthy of trust.

But henceforth I shall believe, and I shall take You at Your word. This will be the best way for me to confess You before men, to bear witness to my love for You. And if I try my best to do that, then You will confess me before Your Father in heaven. "Here he is," You will say to the Father. "He trusted in You, put his life in Your hands. Now You'll have to take him." And I believe the Father will. I have Your word for it, Lord Jesus.

> *Prayer for the day:*
> **THEREFORE DO NOT BE AFRAID.**

NO. 7 COMMON OF TWO OR MORE MARTYRS (INTRET)

Summary:

Jesus foretells the persecution that will befall His followers; but He abandons no one.

YOUR BEARING WITNESS

Lord Jesus, this is a terrifying catastrophe that You describe—this prelude to the end of the world: the wars, earthquakes, pestilences and famines, the terrors and great signs from heaven. I suppose that when the apostles first hear You speaking in this manner, they hardly know what You are talking about.

Then You become more personal—*they* will be persecuted, cast into prison, dragged before kings for Your name's sake, betrayed by parents and brothers, relatives and friends; and some will be put to death. And it will be because of their relation to You that they will be hated by everyone. Yet not a hair of their heads shall perish. By their patience they will save their souls.

Lord Jesus, how many times has Your prophecy been fulfilled since You first spoke! The apostles were the first of a long line of Christians who will continue to the end of time to bear witness to You by their blood. We have the Faith today because it has been won for us by the love of martyrs for You, by their preferring You to any and all earthly possessions. And Your prophecy is being fulfilled today. You are still inspiring martyrs to give their lives so that they may win more love for You and the Father.

All this seems so far away from me both in time, distance, and the possibility of its ever happening to me or to anyone close to me. It isn't good that I should feel so detached from the martyrs, Lord Jesus. Surely, You are not detached from them: they are very dear to You, and You Yourself are their courage. Glorious is God in His saints, marvelous in majesty, doing wonders (gradual). Let the sighing of the prisoners come in before Thee, O Lord (introit).

BY YOUR PATIENCE

Meanwhile, here I am, living my own little life, looking for the easy way, concerned over-much with creature comforts and the pleasure of the moment. Lord Jesus, the blood of martyrs is the seed of Christians. The blood of martyrs also accuses us Christians of our mental separation from suffering and martyrdom everywhere; it accuses us of our unmartyr-like lives, so centered on the care of the body and so unmindful of the demands of the spirit; it accuses us of mediocrity, lukewarmness and cowardice.

But perhaps there was a time in their lives when they were just as small and self-centered as I am now. It could be that Your love and the blood of other martyrs won their grace for them. And if that is the case then, why not now? For all I know, it might very well be the blood of a modern martyr in China that prompts me to say to You now: Here I am, Lord Jesus. Do with me as You will.

Prayer for the day:
BY YOUR PATIENCE YOU WILL WIN YOUR SOUL.

NO. 8 ANOTHER MASS OF TWO OR MORE MARTYRS (SAPIENTIAM)

Summary:
Jesus stands in the midst of the crowds and teaches the beatitudes.

POWER WENT FORTH

Lord Jesus, it is easy to picture this scene: the level stretch of land filled with the great multitude of the sick, the lame, blind, the possessed and the merely curious; all of them are trying to touch You, for power goes out from You and heals all. This isn't the first time Your evangelist mentions this manner of Your healing, Lord Jesus. Your sacred humanity becomes an instrument for the healing of all troubles, all sicknesses. To touch You is enough to make people whole again.

But men need more than bodily healing, important as that is in Your merciful eyes. There will be other crowds in other centuries whose need for You will be as great as these whom You look on today. Very few of the world's sick, starving and persecuted people will be able to touch You as these do in today's gospel. You want them to know that they, too, are precious to You and Your total apostolic work of saving the world.

Therefore, You speak to all who are in any distress whatsoever: Blessed are you poor . . . Blessed are you who hunger now . . . Blessed are you who weep . . . Blessed shall you be when men hate you, and when they shut you out, and reproach you, and reject your name as evil, because of the Son of Man. Rejoice in that day and exult, for behold your reward is great in heaven.

Lord Jesus, there is a type of thinking that would seek to discredit all social reform on the basis of Your words here about the reward of all these misfortunes being great in heaven. But I don't believe You mean it that way. If so, why all Your life do You heal men's bodies? why do You feed them? why do You bring them back to life after they have died? Why do You not just tell them to be patient and resigned and after a few short years of suffering, they will be more than amply rewarded in heaven?

REJOICE AND EXULT

What You do here is most instructive: You do all within Your power to take care of their bodily needs; and *then* You speak the healing, consoling words that give courage and meaning to the lives of all those whom Your Father wills not to heal, but rather to share the passion and cross with You.

You alone know the vast multitudes down the ages who have reached out to touch You in their pain and sickness and have received healing for their bodies from You. You also know the much greater number whom You have not healed, but who have thrilled at Your words, "Blessed are you . . . rejoice and exult, for behold your reward is great in heaven." And not only in heaven, even in this life they feel blessed, for they have already experienced the fulfillment of Your promise which far exceeds in worth the temporary health that could come to them.

Lord Jesus, I marvel at Your understanding of man — the whole man and all of his needs — and above all I rejoice at Your all-embracing compassion and mercy. You do more than speak consoling words that bolster our necessary self-esteem. You make present Your own passion and death, Your own martyrdom, in this and all Masses so that we can join our martyrdom to it. Against the background of Calvary, we can all see ourselves as we really are — as being loved by You, Lord Jesus, with a love that surpasses the understanding of the heart of man. Praise be to Thee, O Christ!

Prayer for the day:
> POWER WENT FORTH FROM HIM AND HEALED ALL.

NO. 9 THIRD MASS OF TWO OR MORE MARTYRS (SALUS AUTEM)

Summary:
> Jesus tells us not to be afraid of those who kill the body but rather of those who are able to cast both soul and body into hell.

THAN MANY SPARROWS

Lord Jesus, You tell the disciples (and us) to beware of the leaven of the Pharisees, which is hypocrisy. Leaven or yeast is a penetrating influence in a mass of bread dough. You are telling us not to allow ourselves to be influenced by Pharisaic hypocrisy. You say: don't be insincere or dishonest or false: don't be fakers or pretenders to what you are not. In a word, don't try to deceive anyone — especially not God — because it won't do you any good. Face to face with Your God, "There is nothing concealed that will not be disclosed, and nothing hidden that will not be made known."

You ask us not to be afraid of persecutors of our body, but to fear only those who have power to cast both body and soul into hell. Better a million times to have one's earthly life cut off a bit prematurely than to spend eternity in hell separated from You.

Not that the prospect of martyrdom is to be lightly considered by anyone. It is a terrifying thing to be killed. But You remind us again that, no matter what happens, the Father who knows all things and who protects those whom He loves will not let us be panic-stricken in the pinch. "Do not be afraid," You say, "you are of more value than many sparrows. And I say to you, everyone who acknowledges Me before men, him will the Son of Man also acknowledge before the angels of God."

Lord Jesus, at first it is hard to see the connection between martyrdom and Your warning against insincerity. Is it that hypocrisy destroys the will to belong to *You*? The only cause a hypocrite believes in is himself, and even that cause will find him backing down when it is a question of shedding his blood. The opposite of hypocrisy is sincerity, honesty with oneself and with others.

BEFORE THE ANGELS

Essentially, a martyr is a person who is utterly sincere about himself, about his beliefs, and the life those beliefs dictate, even though that life will lead him to the loss of his reputation and to his death. There is no making himself out to be anything other than what he is: a Christian, Your follower, a man dedicated to the proposition that — because You say so — the Father loves him and will take care of him. In his sincerity, he does his best to acknowledge You before men, to bear witness to his full faith and trust in You, convinced in his heart that You in turn will bear witness to him before the angels of God.

Indeed, "The souls of the just are in the hand of God, and the torment of death shall not touch them: in the sight of the unwise they seemed to die, but they are in peace" (offertory verse). The martyr believes this with all his heart.

Lord Jesus, I see more and more how much You and Your grace figure in all that makes a saint to be a saint. Grace is everything it seems. As the introit of today's Mass so well says it, "The salvation of the just is from the Lord: and He is their protector in the time of trouble."

But grace is not quite everything. Our sincerity and our honesty is our personal response to You, to Your love and Your grace. But even here, I feel dependent on You. You, by Your divine word and above all by Your sacramental action, can make me more and more sincere. That is to say, You can make me more and more a martyr, more and more a person who bears witness to You everywhere and at all times, not counting the cost in blood, reputation, effort, or possessions. Lord Jesus, teach me to be sincere.

> Prayer for the day:
> DO NOT BE AFRAID.

NO. 10 COMMON OF ONE MARTYR IN PASCHAL TIME (PROTEXISTI)

> Summary:
> Jesus is the vine, the Father is the vine-dresser, we are the branches.

TRUE VINE

Lord Jesus, You could hardly have chosen a more striking or perfect symbol to bring out the relationship You wish to maintain between Yourself and us. What can be closer to the trunk of the tree than the branch that grows out of it? As branch and trunk are one, so are You one with us, so do You share the divine Life that You have in abundance with us, Your members.

You and we together are like a single tree. Tree and branches belong together; the same sap that is in the trunk (You) is in the branches (us): the divine Life that You have as Son of God is now our life too. And the Father is the vine-dresser. His task is to prune the branches so that Your divine Life, Your divine ideas and principles, may have fuller sway in our life and that we may bear more and better fruit. This pruning is the suffering in our life, which, endured in union with You and with love for You, will surely bring forth more and more abundant fruit.

You ask us to abide in You, so that You can abide in us. As the branch cannot bear fruit of itself unless it remain in the vine, so neither can we unless we abide in You. You are the vine, we are the branches. He who abides in You so that You can abide in him

257

will bear much fruit; for without You we can do nothing. If anyone does not abide in You, he shall be cast outside as a branch and wither; and they shall gather them up and cast them into the fire and they shall burn. If we abide in You, and if Your words abide in us, then whatever we ask of You, You will grant it to us.

ABIDE IN ME

Lord Jesus, there is a threat here: dead branches are useless except for providing food for a fire. And it is very possible, You say, for us to become dead to You by our mortal sins. The warning is sharp and unmistakable. But what You want us to meditate on is the positive lesson, the oneness we have with You — more and more intimacy, more and more loving union with You. You want us to grow in vivid awareness of our life-relationship with You so that we may bring forth fruit of personal holiness and thus become Your instruments for attracting others to Your love.

You ask us to abide in You, Lord Jesus. You imply that our consent and desire is the necessary condition for Your abiding and growing in us. Lord, I do desire this union. This is new life in me, Your life in me. You say: "If you abide in Me, and if My words abide in you, ask whatever you will and it shall be done to you."

All right, I'll take You at Your word. Whatever I ask, You will give it to me. I want to abide in You more and more. And Your words are coming to me more and more and are staying with and in me. So I am entitled to ask You for whatever I will and it shall be done to me. What do I ask? Hallowed be Thy name, Thy will be done on earth as it is in heaven. Lord, teach me to do Thy will. Make me a fruitful branch on You the vine.

Prayer for the day:
I AM THE VINE, YOU ARE THE BRANCHES.

NO. 11 COMMON OF TWO OR MORE MARTYRS IN PASCHAL TIME (SANCTI TUI)

Summary:

Since we are branches on Christ the Vine, He expects us to bring forth much fruit.

BRINGING FORTH FRUIT

Lord Jesus, You are the vine and we who are baptized are the branches growing out of You, filled with Your Life, called to the vocation of bringing forth the fruit of sanctity in and according to the demands of the vocation to which You have called each of us. You tell us that in this is Your Father glorified: that we may bear very much fruit and become Your disciples. As the Father has loved You, You also have loved us.

"Abide in My love," You plead with us. And then You go on to explain how we are to abide in Your love: "If you keep My commandments you will abide in My love, as I also have kept My Father's commandments, and abide in His love." You speak constantly about bringing forth fruit by abiding in You. Is there any difference between abiding in You and abiding in Your love? To be in You, to grow out of You, is to be filled with Your life and Your love: it is to be encompassed by You, to be possessed and inspired by You.

But all this seems somewhat mysterious and vague. Abiding in You . . . abiding in Your love: how can I get my mind around that concept? Maybe I am sticking too closely to the image of the tree and branch — trying to imagine what it feels like to be a branch on a tree — and forgetting that once we arrive at the basic truth You are trying to teach, we can forget about the image.

The basic truth is that You want the *objective reality of a union of life between You and Your members to become a vivid and conscious awareness on our part.* As the beloved is constantly in the mind of the lover, so do You want us to have You in mind. This is abiding in Your love.

259

FULL JOY

We must think of You, talk to You, listen to You. Then You will grow in us and teach us to become more and more aware of You. But above all, we must keep Your commandments. The only way to grow in love for You is to do what You want us to do. It is to will what You will. It is to will what Your Father wills. It is the old, old story about total abandon and the gift of self to the Father. You have gone before us and showed us the way. Then Your apostles have come after You . . . and then all the martyrs through the ages. They have followed Your directions, abiding in You and in Your love. Therefore they have brought forth much fruit, and in this has Your Father been glorified.

Lord Jesus, all this sounds less mysterious and vague now. But it is still a bit misty, mostly because of my material-mindedness. But maybe the material-mindedness will fall away with growth in awareness and union.

To have Your life in us, that is great. To have Your love in us and to abide in that love, that is better. But, Lord Jesus, there seems to be no limit to Your lavish mercy towards us. "These things I have spoken to you *that My joy may be in you,* and that your joy may be full."

Lord Jesus, my gratitude will last as long as I exist. "I will extol Thee, O God, my King; and I will bless Thy name forever. Yea, forever and ever" (introit).

Prayer for the day:

AS THE FATHER HAS LOVED ME, I ALSO HAVE LOVED YOU.

NO. 12 COMMON OF A CONFESSOR-BISHOP (STATUIT EI)

Summary:

Jesus tells a parable about the uses to which three men put the talents given them by the master . . . and the manner in which each is rewarded.

A MAN HANDS OVER GOODS

Lord Jesus, You say that the kingdom of heaven is like a man going abroad who calls his servants and gives them a share in his wealth, to each according to his particular ability. To one he gives five talents, to another, two, and to the third, one. The man with five talents trades and makes five more; so also does the man with two talents double his money; but the man with one talent buries the money in the ground where he judges it will be safe. Upon his return the master commends the two industrious servants: "Well done, good and faithful servant; because thou hast been faithful over a few things, I will set thee over many; enter into the joy of thy master."

Lord Jesus, the word *talent* here means a certain amount of money according to the custom of Your time. But I have also thought of the word in its modern sense, as when we say of a man: "He has great (or limited) talent." You give to each of us the amount of talent You think we should have; and if we develop this talent and use it according to the vocation to which You call us, we can become saints. The important thing — I have always felt — is work and sincere fidelity to all the demands of the vocation, great or small, the fidelity being motivated, of course, by love for the Master who watches over all.

But St. Jerome has another interpretation. According to him, the talents represent the divine word which You confide to the apostles and their successors so that they might make it bear fruit. It makes sense, Lord Jesus. You give us Your word — not just to bury in the recesses of our mind close to the realm of forgetfulness

261

(and above all, not to be allowed to lie unused in the pages of a book) — but You give it to us to turn over in our minds, to apply to our life, to pray with and pray over, and to pass on to others. You give this divine word to each of us according to our capacity, and if we use it, it will sanctify us.

WELL DONE

Surely, Lord Jesus, the saint whose feast we celebrate today was one who received Your word and made it bear fruit in his own life and in the lives of all with whom he came into contact. For I am convinced that there is no saint who became holy without devotion to Your word, and without wanting to communicate it to others. "Behold a great priest, who in his days, pleased God. There was not one found the like to him, who kept the law of the Most High" (gradual).

Lord Jesus, the men of business concentrate on their negotiations, their investments — some of them too exclusively. With them the investments become the food for their "contemplation."

Your investment in our hands is You, Your divine grace, and Your sacred word. You want me to grow in this grace and You want me to feed my whole being on Your truth so that I may (as Fr. Bernard Meyer, M.M. indicates) become a living, walking gospel that others may read and from which they can take inspiration.

When You and Your word become the center of my life, then once again Your Church might be able to sing: "Blessed is the man who fears the Lord: He shall delight exceedingly in His commandments. His seed shall be mighty upon earth: the generation of the righteous shall be blessed. Glory and wealth shall be in his house: and his justice remains forever and ever" (tract).

Lord Jesus, make me see that there is no more fruitful source both for You and for Your word than the holy Sacrifice of the Mass.

Prayer for the day:
BECAUSE THOU HAST BEEN FAITHFUL OVER A FEW THINGS, I WILL SET THEE OVER MANY.

NO. 13 COMMON OF A CONFESSOR-BISHOP (SACERDOTES TUI)

Summary:

Jesus tells His disciples always to be prepared for judgment, for they never know when the Lord will come.

WATCH

Lord Jesus, You tell us to be watchful, for we know not the day nor the hour of Your coming in judgment to us. Being watchful means being ready for that unexpected hour when You, the Son of Man, will come.

The Saint whose feast we celebrate today is a bishop who became a saint because he was a good bishop. The word bishop (episcopus) means *watcher*. A bishop fulfills his duty and is true to his high vocation when he watches over his flock — guarding, protecting, guiding his flock (as You did, Lord Jesus) — feeding them with Your divine truth and life so that each of the flock will be ready for Your return in judgment.

You put it so well Yourself: "Who, dost thou think, is the faithful and prudent servant whom his master has set over his household to give them food in due time? Blessed is that servant whom his master, when he comes, shall find doing so. Amen I say to you, he will set him over all his goods."

So You stress the word and the idea of watching. And I have no doubt that for You the idea of watching implies more than merely being ready and in the state of grace in order to escape hell. Is it not also a question of mental orientation? Don't You mean that, in addition to being free from mortal sin, we are to be *watchfully eager* for Your coming and overflowing with desire for You. I don't see how even You could make a man a saint without this desire for You.

OVER ALL HIS GOODS

So a bishop is above all a watcher. But his watching over his flock should be more than mere protective watching, important and

263

essential as that is. He watches best who imparts to his flock his own eagerness and desire for final union with You, so that his people are motivated not by fear of hell but rather by loving longing for You. Clearly, today's Saint did his watching very well. He was true to his vocation. You in turn have loved him and adorned him; You clothed him with a robe of glory (alleluia verse).

Lord Jesus, most of us are not bishops in the strict sense; but every one of us must be watchers over our own lives and over whatever little or big flock You place us. I do not know at what hour You will come to take me out of this life. I don't believe I even want to know that hour. But one thing I do want: I want to be prepared.

But more than the minimum of being without mortal sin, I want to be filled with Your truth and Your grace; for then I know I will also be filled with desire and love for You. This blessed state will be impossible to me unless I begin now to feed on Your truth and then to grow and become enlarged with love.

My truth and My mercy shall be with him: and in My name shall his horn be exalted (offertory verse).

Lord Jesus, You who are infinite truth, truth made flesh, make me good soil for Your truth. Make this truth bud forth and grow in me so that all my life in this world and the next I may desire and love You with all my heart.

Prayer for the day:

WATCH, THEREFORE, FOR YOU DO NOT KNOW AT WHAT HOUR YOUR LORD IS TO COME.

NO. 14 COMMON OF A DOCTOR OF THE CHURCH (IN MEDIO)

Summary:

Jesus gives His disciples the responsibility of being "salt of the earth" and "light of the world."

SALT OF THE EARTH

Lord Jesus, examination and thought bring out of these gospels a freshness of content that constant repetition may have concealed for long years. Today You call Your disciples "salt." How can men be salt? What is salt used for? It adds to the fulness of food, making the food more tasty and desirable. But if the salt lose its inner powers to elevate the food, then both salt and food might as well never come together: there is no exchange between them.

How can men be salt? Men are salt by their inner being, their conception of life, the sharpness of their convictions and judgments — all of which come from their constant gazing upon You, Lord Jesus. You who are infinite freshness and infinite love.

What do men salt? By being amidst other men, they can add to the wholeness and all around goodness of those with whom they associate. They can stimulate men to become curious themselves about divine truth and above all to be full of desire for You.

It is a terrible thing for men called to be instruments of Your divine love to fail You: "If the salt loses its strength, what shall it be salted with? It is no longer of any use but to be thrown out and trodden under foot by men."

LIGHT OF THE WORLD

You also tell us that we are the light of the world. Light is brilliance, by its nature it wants to be seen; it dispels darkness and points the way to the goal. You say to us: "You are the light of the world . . . let your light shine before men, in order that they may see your good works and give glory to your Father in heaven."

Again, how can we be light, Lord Jesus? You are the light of the world. By baptism we share in Your life, in Your light (I remember the lighted Easter Candle on Holy Saturday night and the glorious words: "Light of Christ . . . Thanks be to God!" And then there is the lighted candle given to us at our Baptism indicating also what we are).

If we allow You to invade our lives, invite You to sweep away our faults, will what You will and love what You love; in short, if we allow You to take full possession of our thinking, our willing and our acting, then Your words will be true of us: "*You* are the light of the world." And our presence in the midst of men will be a presence of light for men. But, of course, it will not be we who are the light, but You in us. Then, too, they will want to come to You and be carriers of Your light themselves.

Lord Jesus, You have called me to be Your salt, Your light. Forgive my having failed You up to now. I have surely not been equal to the vocation to which You have called me; and if anyone has been stimulated to a better, fuller, more Christian life because of me, it has hardly been my doing.

And as for being light, showing the way to others, I'm afraid there has been too much thought of walking alone and in solitude, without wanting to be bothered with the masses. But now I want to take You seriously. You command that I be salt and light. All You have to do in this and all Masses is to fill me with the steadfast desire and determination to make Your command a reality.

Lord Jesus, I *want* to do what You want, be what You will me to be, think what You think, love what You love. Come, Lord Jesus!

Prayer for the day:
> YOU ARE THE SALT OF THE EARTH . . . YOU
> ARE THE LIGHT OF THE WORLD.

NO. 15 MASS OF A CONFESSOR NOT A BISHOP (OS JUSTI)

Summary:
> Jesus tells the disciples that they must be prepared for the coming of the Master, for no one knows the day nor the hour of His coming.

YOUR LAMPS BURNING

Lord Jesus, Your images are proper to Palestine and somewhat strange to us, but not if we think a little. You tell us to be dressed and ready for Your coming so that when You knock we may straightway open to You. "Blessed are those servants whom the master, on his return, shall find watching. Amen I say to you, he will gird himself and will make them recline at table, and will come and serve them . . . You also must be ready, because at an hour that you do not expect, the Son of Man is coming."

I must be ready, You tell me, because I do not and cannot know when You will come to me as my Judge at the moment of death.

Your Church uses Your imagery to describe a special kind of saint, a confessor who has not had the responsibility of shepherding a diocesan flock. The Saint whose feast we celebrate today is one who has meditated wisdom and whose tongue speaks judgment: "The law of his God is in his heart" (introit). I think there is a very close connection between being prepared for death and having the law of God in the midst of one's heart.

What is this "law of God" that Your Church speaks about? You give a hint when You say "My truth and My mercy shall be with him: and in My name shall his horn be exalted" (offertory verse). Law is the expression of someone's will. To have the law of God in one's heart means to be fully and completely united to the Father's will (as You were), so that one chooses always in the light of divine principles what he will do and think and say and live by.

BE READY

But it is not a cold, joyless, merely intellectual union based only on fear of judgment; it is rather a doing of Your Father's will that comes from recognition of His tender goodness and love for and providential care for us: "My truth and My *mercy* shall be with him." It is delighting in Your commandments, as the psalmist puts it. Today's Saint became a saint, I am sure, not primarily because of fear of judgment (important as that is for us), but mostly because he was a "watcher," a man whose mind and heart were so fired up with Your divine truth that he could hardly wait till he saw You face to face.

Lord Jesus, I'm afraid that if I died at the present moment, I would hardly be eligible for this Mass of a Common of a Confessor Not a Bishop. One always hopes he is in the state of grace, but that is just the minimum. The minimum — just getting by — never made a saint of anyone. You have offered Your truth and Your mercy to me in Your scriptures and in all manner of approaches to me; but I have not so far delighted in Your commandments.

But by Your mercy You can set afoot the beginning of desire for You and for final union. You can also prosper that longing. Help me to meditate wisdom, to fill my heart as well as my mind with Your law. I don't know when You will come and knock, but with Your law filling me with longing desire, it doesn't matter. One filled with Your law leaves such things up to You. That is the ultimate test of love.

> *Prayer for the day:*
> YOU MUST BE READY, BECAUSE AT AN HOUR THAT YOU DO NOT EXPECT, THE SON OF MAN IS COMING.

NO. 16 ANOTHER MASS OF A CONFESSOR NOT A BISHOP (JUSTUS UT PALMA)

> *Summary:*
> Jesus tells His disciples of the great need they have to give alms and to be unattached to worldly pleasures.

LITTLE FLOCK

These are strange words, again, Lord Jesus, or are they strange only because we have so far departed from the spirit of Your gospel (and therefore from sanctity)? You ask us not to be afraid, for it has pleased the Father to give us the kingdom. We are to sell what we have and give alms, to make for ourselves purses that do not grow old, a treasure unfailing in heaven, where neither thief draws near nor moth destroys. For where our treasure is, there also will our heart be.

Lord, You tell us not to be afraid (of the future? of life? of eternity?) because our Father will give us the kingdom. Obviously, You are speaking here, not of one of this world's kingdoms but of a possession that You consider our highest good, a possession that can satisfy us forever and never endanger our souls' salvation.

And our Father will give it to us. A Father looks after and protects his children. The great, majestic, awe-inspiring God of the ages is our Father, You tell us confidently, He interests Himself in each of us, His children, and He will give us a kingdom that no kind of natural catastrophe can destroy. Therefore, away with financial fears, fears of the future! As a matter of fact, You tell us even to sell what we have and give alms. The more we give, the more a fortune will be built up for us in heaven "where neither thief draws near nor moth destroys."

This sounds beautiful, Lord Jesus, but how practical is it: for the parents of a family, the pastor of a parish, a student, or a monk or nun? Monks and nuns have the vow of poverty, which means that they have only the use of money and property and have to give an account of what they spend and give. This does not automatically prevent their violating the spirit of Your teaching here.

Fathers of families usually have little to spare for savings, and if they have families, Your Popes teach that they have a right to a living wage in order to provide for their families' sustenance, education, and for their own old age. And every pastor knows that no parish ever has enough for all the demands upon it.

WHERE YOUR TREASURE IS

Are You telling us, Lord Jesus, that this is all a matter of detachment and attachment — a matter of whether we trust money in the hand (or in the bank) or the loving care of Your and our Father? Those who trust partially, half in Your Father and half in the bank might do all right as ordinary Christians: they will probably never be saints. The saint is the one whose trust knows no bounds or qualifications. He is *detached* from worldly possessions — doesn't make them a goal or a god — and He is *attached* to the providential will of the Father, in whom he trusts without hesitation or dilution.

His treasure is Your Father's mercy and that's where his heart is. Lord Jesus, I believe that the test for us is clear consciousness. If we are more vividly aware of our possessions (or lack of them) than we are of the love of the Father, we are far from the condition You want us to be in.

Vivid awareness of wealth and meditating on how to increase it might very well bring more wealth (every cent of which we leave behind when we leave this world). But vivid awareness of and meditation on You who are God's Wisdom and Truth in person, destroys fear, gives joy, stimulates longing for the Kingdom that eternity itself will never exhaust.

Lord Jesus, it sounds nice but it's just about Your hardest truth. Grant us the grace to understand it and to live it. And start us off with the meditation that will bring wisdom.

Prayer for the day:
FOR WHERE YOUR TREASURE IS, THERE ALSO WILL YOUR HEART BE.

NO. 17 COMMON OF AN ABBOT (OS JUSTI MEDITABITUR)

Summary:
Jesus promises a hundredfold reward to all those who have truly left all things to follow Him.

WHO FOLLOW CHRIST

Lord Jesus, if Peter is not direct and outspoken, no one is. What is in his mind has no difficulty finding a way out. He has been thinking of his life as Your apostle, and suddenly he asks You: "Behold, we have left all and followed Thee; what then shall we have?" Most of us who have gone through the motions of leaving all things have probably thought the same way: we have not asked You Peter's question outright, perhaps because we are afraid in our hearts that we haven't really left all things . . . yet. I suspect that You are more pleased with Peter's directness than with our half-hearted indecisiveness.

You answer Peter in a way he doesn't quite expect at his present stage of spiritual progress: "Amen I say to you, that you who have followed Me, in the regeneration when the Son of Man shall sit on the throne of His glory, shall also sit on twelve thrones, judging the twelve tribes of Israel." It is a promise of spiritual, rather than temporal or human, reward; and I imagine that it is better capable of being understood by these men of Palestine than by us.

But then You lift up Your eyes to the future centuries, and You see us and others who have desired to be Your followers in more than an ordinary way. You speak now to us: "Everyone who has left house, or brothers, or sisters, or father, or mother, or wife, or children, or lands, for My name's sake, shall receive a hundredfold, and shall possess life everlasting." We hear the promise so often that its glory seldom reaches into the inner room of our awareness.

Your Church applies this promise to abbots who have succeeded in fulfilling its conditions and have become saints. Because an abbot is thought to take Your place in a monastery, he must truly leave all things, since any kind of unworthy attachment makes it very difficult, if not impossible, to serve Your flock. And it is in serving his flock — in giving himself to his flock (as You have done) that he fulfills his vocation as abbot and becomes a saint.

FOR HIS NAME'S SAKE

But You want the lesson of this gospel to apply to everyone who is called to the religious life. The hundredfold reward of life everlasting depends on two conditions: that we really leave all things and persons and that we do it for Your Name's sake.

Lord Jesus, human love is a good and wonderful thing: it is also a permanent bond that attaches members of families to one another. I don't believe You want us to cease to love our relatives, and surely You don't want us to hate those who are near and dear to us.

What You mean is that we must prevent any person's standing in the way of that total attachment of self to You that You require of those who freely choose to be Your special followers. The secret is *in loving people in You*, which means loving You so much that our love bursts out of our hearts and overflows to those whom You have related to us by ties of blood or friendship.

The second condition is that we do all that You desire *for Your Name's sake*. That means love again, doing these things because we want to please You. Any other motive would make the leave-taking from family and friends a mere exercise in stoicism or selfish pride. One of Your saints once said that to pick up a pin out of love for You could save a soul. In other words, it is not so much the thing done as the intensity of love for You that counts. If that is the case, what unlimited possibilities of saving souls and promoting Your Father's glory are contained in the millions of Your chosen friends throughout the world who truly leave all things for love of You!

Lord Jesus, help us all to leave all things according to our vocation; above all, give us the grace to do this leaving out of love for You. Or just give the love, and then let all things follow in their appointed course.

> *Prayer for the day:*
> BEHOLD, WE HAVE LEFT ALL AND FOLLOWED THEE.

NO. 18 COMMON OF A VIRGIN-MARTYR (LOQUEBAR)

> *Summary:*
> Jesus' parable about the wise and foolish virgins reminds us that we must always be prepared for His coming, for we know not the day nor the hour.

FOOLISH VIRGINS

Lord Jesus, the five foolish virgins are foolish because they forget to take extra oil for their lamps with them. Wisdom for the wise ones consists in their farseeing and careful preparations for whatever might happen.

All watch and wait for the coming of the bridegroom, all get drowsy and fall asleep; but when the bridegroom arrives and the call comes to the virgins to go forth with their lamps to meet him, the foolish ones have no oil and their lamps have gone out. They try to borrow oil from the wise ones, but that would exhaust their supply too. So they have to rush off to the market to buy oil. When they return, the door to the marriage feast is shut. They cry out: "Sir, sir, open the door for us!" But he answers and says, "Amen, I say to you, I do not know you." And You add the moral: "Watch, therefore, for you know neither the day nor the hour."

Lord Jesus, this parable of Yours has been the guide and inspiration for ever so much holiness. Since You are speaking of virgins, we usually apply the parable only to those who have pledged themselves to You by vows of poverty, chastity and obedience; and it is so used in this Common Mass of a Virgin-Martyr.

But I wonder if Your original meaning is not broader, and Your lesson intended for every one of us? You would be the Bridegroom, of course, and we Christian souls are the virgins — some of us wise, some foolish. The coming of the Bridegroom is the moment of judgment, either at the end of our particular lives or the end of time. Going forth to meet the Bridegroom and the bride is the period of our life in this world. We carry lamps in our hands, and it is the responsibility of each to see to it that the oil never runs short.

OPEN THE DOOR

What is this oil, Lord Jesus? For the whole parable turns on the meaning of the oil? I have always thought that it means divine Life, the life of grace, and more specifically it seems to me that it means charity. If charity, love for You and for our neighbor, fills our whole being, then we'll be more than ready to go forth to meet You at the final wedding feast of death.

Charity, love, is a possession we cannot trifle with. It is not a matter of trying to get by with the bare minimum of love, for such an attitude runs the risk of being caught short and indicates that we undervalue it, that we weigh it against other values and (at times) consider it of lesser importance.

Charity, love, implies that there is a lover and a beloved. They want to be together, want to be fulfilled in one another. The Christian soul, then, especially the one dedicated to virginity according to Your special invitation, is one who awaits Your coming with longing. The more she awaits, the greater is her expectation and desire, for she feels that she is an emptiness that only You can complete. And there is no authentic waiting and longing if her love for You is half-hearted and secondary to other goods.

Lord, if full union comes only at the moment of Your return, there can always be anticipated union with You in this life. It depends on our inner communication with You, our absorbing of Your word so that it will spring forth in love. Without our thinking about You and desiring You now, we may well run the risk of hearing You say when we knock on the door of eternity: "Amen, I say to you, I do not know you."

Lord Jesus, blessed are the undefiled in the way: who walk in the law of the Lord. Inspire me to meditate on Your commandments, help me to love them exceedingly (introit) for then I will be filled with hunger for You, burning with desire for final union . . . and ready to give You the final, all-out bestowal of a heart made only for You.

Prayer for the day:

WATCH THEREFORE, FOR YOU KNOW NEI-THER THE DAY NOR THE HOUR.

NO. 19a COMMON OF A VIRGIN-MARTYR (ME EXSPECTAVERUNT)

Summary:

Jesus compares the kingdom of heaven to a treasure hidden in a field, or to a pearl of great price or to a net gathering in all manner of fishes.

KINGDOM OF HEAVEN

Lord Jesus, You surely use all manner of images to bring out the great truth, riches, preciousness and possibilities of the kingdom of heaven. It is not Your fault if we fail to grasp its desirability. Today You say that the kingdom of heaven is like a treasure hidden in a field: the finder hides it and in his joy sells all that he has to get money to buy the field. Or the kingdom of heaven is like a merchant who seeks fine pearls. He finds a very precious pearl and goes and sells all that he has to buy it.

Or again, the kingdom is like a net that gathers out of the sea fish of every kind. When it is filled, they haul it out, and sitting down on the beach, they gather the good fish into vessels, but throw away the bad. So will it be at the end of the world. The angels will separate the wicked from the just, and will cast them into the furnace of fire, where there will be weeping and gnashing of teeth. But to return to the first two images . . .

I think it would warm our hearts a little if we saw this treasure in the field and the pearl of great price as not something, but *Someone*; namely, You, Lord Jesus. Compared to possessing You and having You as the center of one's life, no earthly goods, things, or persons have any proportionate value. There can be no comparison at all between possessing wealth or jewels (and being lorded over by them) on the one hand and possessing You and being possessed by You on the other.

Lord Jesus, I notice that both of the men in Your parable are seeking: the one seeks and finds in a field; the other, at the seashore (or wherever it is that men look for pearls). So must we seek You; if we seek, we find. In both cases the preciousness of the discovery dictates the appropriate action — to give up all and everything that stands in the way to full possession of Your love.

TRUE VIRGINITY

We are celebrating the feast of one of Your chosen brides, a virgin who manifested her love for You by giving her life. She is one who sought and found and who knew in the end that the bargain she acquired was worth all that You said it would be and more.

She is one who learned that true virginity is not a sad and joyless repression of her deep instinctive desires for human love, but rather the total gift of herself to You in love that brought about the highest fulfillment of all her hopes.

To possess You and be possessed by You resulted in a condition or state between You and her that was well worth selling all that she possessed — giving up the very best that the human heart is capable of — to buy the pearl, the treasure, You. You and she now know that the transaction can never be improved on forever. Her life itself was not too much to pay for what You have given her in return.

Lord Jesus, this is all very well for her and others like her; but surely You do not intend that all should be virgins and martyrs. What is there in this parable for ordinary people with less spectacular ambitions? I can hear You say: Married or single, man or woman, young or old, you can all seek and hope. And above all, you can keep your values straight in life, realizing that to possess all the wealth in the world, but not Me, is to be a fool, a top candidate for the furnace of fire where there will be the weeping and the gnashing of teeth.

But even to seek sincerely implies the stirring of Your grace in us. Your Church sings of this Saint, Lord Jesus: "God will help her with His countenance: God is in the midst of her, she shall not be moved" (gradual). To be helped by Your countenance, to have You in one's midst was a fact for her. Lord Jesus, make it a fact for us. Help us to be undefiled in the way: help us to walk in the law of the Lord.

> **Prayer for the day:**
> WHEN HE FINDS A PEARL OF GREAT PRICE, HE GOES AND SELLS ALL THAT HE HAS AND BUYS IT.

NO. 19b ALTERNATE GOSPEL FOR THE FEAST OF A VIRGIN-MARTYR

Summary:

Jesus delivers His teaching on the indissolubility of marriage and the difficulty of the life of virginity.

MALE AND FEMALE

Lord Jesus, Your enemies are always trying to catch You teaching otherwise than Moses taught. This time they want to know about marriage and divorce, and in answering them, You give us a beautiful lesson on Christian marriage and virginity. They ask: "Is it lawful for a man to put away his wife for any cause?"

Your answer is in the form of a question: "Have you not read that the Creator, from the beginning, made them male and female, and said, 'For this cause a man shall leave his father and mother, and cleave to his wife, and the two shall become one flesh'? Therefore now they are no longer two, but one flesh. What therefore God has joined together, let no man put asunder."

On this teaching is based all the beauty and grandeur of Your divine doctrine on marriage — doctrine that will reach its highest point of mysterious goodness when Your apostle Paul compares the union of man and wife to the union between You and Your Bride, the Church. Man and wife are two in one flesh: two wills, two minds, two bodies, two personalities whom You join together to the end that, becoming more and more one with one another, they become the providential creative instruments for the propagation of Your life and Your love in the world.

But the Pharisees are unhappy with Your teaching. They bring up Moses' leniency in regard to divorce. You make short work of this objection: "I say to you, that whoever puts away his wife, except for immorality, and marries another, commits adultery; and he who marries a woman who has been put away commits adultery."

ACCEPT IT WHO CAN

Your teaching causes this comment from the disciples: "If the

277

case of a man with his wife is so, it is not expedient to marry." And You answer: "Not all can accept this teaching; but those to whom it has been given. For there are eunuchs who were born so from their mother's womb; and there are eunuchs who were made so by men; and there are eunuchs who have made themselves so for the kingdom of heaven's sake. Let him accept it who can."

Your words are plain, Lord Jesus. You speak of the various ways of renouncing the joys of marriage. There are some men and women who have no interest in the joys of marriage, who might even despise, or be ashamed of, those joys. You are not concerned with them. You are thinking and speaking only of those who freely give up those joys for the sake of the kingdom of heaven, that is, out of love for You. These are the blessed ones about whom Your Church sings: "Oh, how beautiful is the chaste generation with glory" (alleluia verse).

Lord, how wonderful that You should speak about this kind of renouncement in connection with Your Father's teaching on marriage! For virginity is marriage. It is union with You, springing from total gift of self and abandon of one's whole life to You. And it is a free gift. "Let him accept it who can."

Lord Jesus, whoever we are — married or single, with vow of virginity or without — help us to be true to our vocation. If we are married, help us to be truly one with one another on all the levels of our being. If we are virgins, help us to make our gift more and more perfect and exhaustive. And help us to live this vocation always for love of You. You and You alone are the secret of happiness in marriage. You and You alone are the secret of a perfected virginity: of its constancy, its fruitfulness, its final and total joy.

Prayer for the day:
LET HIM ACCEPT IT WHO CAN.

NO. 20 COMMON OF THE DEDICATION OF A CHURCH

Summary:

Zacchaeus climbs a tree to see Jesus and thus by his eagerness wins an invitation to entertain Jesus in his house.

MAN IN A TREE

Lord Jesus, Zacchaeus is apparently not a very popular man in Jericho: tax collectors rarely are, in any land, at any time. But Zacchaeus has his own ideas about life and what is important in life. He hears that You are passing through town, and naturally he wants to see You (and judging by the events that follow, I don't think it is mere curiosity).

But because of the large crowd surrounding You and his own small size, he has to resort to extraordinary means. Like a little boy, he climbs up a sycamore tree and waits for You to pass below. There is the rich tax collector in his expensive clothing up in the tree, eagerly waiting for You to come his way. He is prepared.

But he is hardly prepared for what happens now. You look up and see him, and surely You are delighted with the sight. Without ever having seen him before, You know his name. Above all, You know his heart and his desire. You say: "Zacchaeus, make haste and come down; for I must stay in thy house today." The little tax collector hurries down and welcomes You joyfully to his home.

This scandalizes the proud Pharisees (and probably a few others) who murmur, "He has gone to be the guest of a man who is a sinner." Zacchaeus has a good defense — the very best, according to Your own standards: "Behold, Lord, I give one-half of my possessions to the poor, and if I have defrauded anyone of anything, I restore it four-fold." That's enough for You, as if You do not already know, and You say: "Today salvation has come to this house, since he, too, is a son of Abraham. For the Son of Man came to seek and to save what was lost."

HOUSE OF GOD

Lord Jesus, there doesn't seem to be much connection between this gospel and the idea of a dedication of a church. But we can see. A church is a house of God, the dwelling place of the Most High Lord. As such it should inspire awe and trembling, as the first part of the introit has it: "Terrible (that is, frightening, awe-inspiring) is this place: it is the house of God, and the gate of heaven." But a church also inspires longing desire for heaven, as the second part of the introit so well shows: "How lovely are Thy tabernacles, O Lord of Hosts! My soul longs and faints for the courts of the Lord."

You have entered Zacchaeus' home; and that makes it the house of God, too. Your presence there makes him aware of his sinfulness, and undoubtedly he is considerably awe-struck at Your holiness, but above all he experiences the blessedness of Your presence and wishes You would stay forever.

But there is another connection, and it is to be found in Your words: "Today salvation has come to this house . . . for the Son of Man came to seek and to save what was lost." Your Church is more than a building, Lord Jesus. It is an organism, a living body, of which You are the Head and we the members.

You have come to save us sinners, that is, to make us living members of Your Body so that we are in You and You in us (even more intimately than You are in Zacchaeus' house and he in Your presence). So sinners, through Your loving kindness, can become one with You in Your all-embracing mission of worshipping the Father — the primary purpose of any House of God.

Lord Jesus, I have always smiled at Zacchaeus. But he is the one who is smart and deep and wise about the things that matter most. Give me his eagerness to see and welcome You, his sense of unworthiness, his charity. And whenever I enter one of Your houses, help me to realize more and more that it is not only an awe-inspiring place, but that it is also a holy of holies reminding me of heaven after which my soul should always aspire. You are there. How lovely are Your tabernacles! My soul longeth and panteth for the courts of the Lord, for You, Lord Jesus.

Prayer for the day:

TODAY SALVATION HAS COME TO THIS HOUSE.

MASS OF THE BLESSED VIRGIN ON SATURDAY (DURING ADVENT)

Summary:

Mary consents to become the Mother of God; and the Word takes flesh in her womb.

HAIL, FULL OF GRACE

Lord Jesus, I imagine that this section of the sacred writings must be among Your favorites. Mary is praying there in Nazareth. She does not know anything about her great destiny. All she knows is that God is good, and she loves Him very much, and she is telling Him so. But now is the time. The Father sends His Angel Gabriel who greets Mary very mysteriously: "Hail, full of grace, the Lord is with thee. Blessed art thou among women."

She is puzzled, and Gabriel sees it in her face. "Do not be afraid, Mary, for thou hast found grace with God. And behold, thou shalt conceive in thy womb and shalt bring forth a son; and thou shalt call His name Jesus. He shall be great and shall be called the Son of the Most High; and the Lord God will give Him the throne of David His father, and He shall be king over the house of Jacob forever; and of His kingdom there shall be no end."

But Mary has made a vow of virginity. The sacrifice of motherhood — woman's most precious privilege — is her gift to God. Such is her love for God. But Gabriel goes on to explain: for the first and only time in history a woman shall be a mother and shall retain her virginity; and this is how it will be: "The Holy Spirit shall come upon thee and the power of the Most High shall overshadow thee; and therefore the Holy One to be born shall be called the Son of God."

This is all she needs to know. She has long since given herself and her future to her God, and He has accepted her gift in a most marvelous way. He accepts her and gives her back His most precious possession, You, His Son.

Mary consents to be the most glorious instrument of Your Father's will: "Behold the handmaid of the Lord; be it done to me according to thy word." At that moment, by the power of the Most High and the overshadowing of the Holy Spirit, You, Lord Jesus, become man. You the Word, the Second Person of the Godhead, born before all ages, equal to the Father and the Holy Spirit in all things, God of God, Light of Light — You wed Yourself to humanity, You take a human body from the pure body of Your Mother Mary. And she is now Your Mother forever and forever.

THE LORD WITH THEE

Hail, Mary, full of grace; the Lord is with thee; blessed art thou among women, and blessed is the fruit of thy womb. Lord Jesus, You are the fruit of her womb. Blessed are You!

This, of course, is only the beginning — for You, for Mary, for us. You will live and develop in her womb for nine months, and then she will bring You forth into the world. You will continue to live with her for thirty years, and then she will give You to the world, to death, to Your redeeming work. "Pour forth, we beseech Thee, O Lord, Thy grace into our hearts, that we, to whom the Incarnation of Christ, Thy Son, was made known by the message of an angel, may by His passion and cross be brought to the glory of His resurrection" (postcommunion).

Birth, life, death, resurrection for You are indicated in this gospel; and so the same for her. All because both You and she know only one desire: to do the will of the Father. David prophesied of You: "Behold I come; in the book it is written of me: To do thy will, O my God, is my delight, and thy law is in my very heart" (Psalm 39:8-9). And now Mary echoes Your words: "Behold the handmaid of the Lord; be it done to me according to thy word."

Lord Jesus, I want to be part of this event. I want You to become more and more incarnate in me so that I too can have Mary for my mother. And then grant that like her I may live for and center my life on You. Come, Lord Jesus!

> *Prayer for the day:*
>> BEHOLD THE HANDMAID OF THE LORD: BE IT DONE TO ME ACCORDING TO THY WORD.

MASS OF THE BLESSED VIRGIN ON SATURDAY (FROM CHRISTMAS TO THE FEAST OF THE PURIFICATION)

> *Summary:*
>> The shepherds decide to go to Bethlehem, and there they find Mary and Joseph and Jesus.

OVER TO BETHLEHEM

Now we are back, Lord Jesus, in the night when You are born. The angels have just appeared to the shepherds to announce Your birth to them. As soon as they recover from the shock of such a heavenly visitation, they say: "Let us go over to Bethlehem and see this thing that has come to pass."

So they hurry along the hilly paths, and soon they are at the door of Your palace, the stable, where You have just been born. They enter, and sure enough, the angels were right! There You are lying in the wooden manger, wrapped in swaddling clothes, watched over by Your Mother and Joseph and the cattle.

Now they understand what the angels have told them. They gaze on You, fall on their knees and worship You. And then, being filled with the vision of You, they rush out — the very first apostles, they might be called — to spread the good tidings around the countryside.

And all who hear marvel at the things told them by the shepherds, but I suspect that the shepherds do not stir up too many people that night, Lord Jesus. The people are all tired and sleepy, and there are so many other more important things to do than to listen to simple shepherds. But that's all right with the shepherds. They have seen and loved You, the Son of God, the Messias, the Savior of the world. And they have announced the good news abroad; now they can go back to their shepherding, back to their vocation.

But henceforth their work will have a different meaning for them: it will be part of their praising and glorifying of Your Father; and they will always be grateful for having been chosen by Your Father to be shepherds; for they are the first, apart from Mary and Joseph, to have seen their God!

WORDS IN HER HEART

But Mary Your Mother keeps in mind all the words and all the actions of the shepherds and the angels, pondering them in her heart. That means, she does the pondering with love. She is, of course, used to pondering divine words and events in her heart: that's the way she has arrived at this night of glory. Most of all, she is used to pondering You, the *Word,* in her heart. And as she looks at You, she admires, abandons herself, rejoices in You, loves You with all the power of her perfect, pure and powerful heart.

"For thou art happy, O holy Virgin Mary, and most worthy of all praise: because from thee arose the sun of justice, Christ our Lord" (offertory).

Lord Jesus, there is much for me in the actions both of the shepherds and Mary. Help me more and more to ponder You and Your words, not only in my mind, but above all in my heart; for the more pondering there is, the more You will come to me and make me like unto You; and then the more I will want to rush abroad like the shepherds to tell everyone about You.

And telling about You will make me more and more enthusiastic about Your Mother, whose fruitful virginity the Church will never cease to praise. Blessed is the womb of the Virgin Mary, that bore the Son of the Eternal Father! Thou, Lord Jesus, art beautiful above the sons of men: grace is poured abroad in Thy lips (gradual).

Prayer for the day:

THEY FOUND MARY AND JOSEPH, AND THE BABE LYING IN A MANGER.

MASS OF THE BLESSED VIRGIN ON SATURDAY (FROM PURIFICATION TO THE SATURDAY AFTER SEXAGESIMA SUNDAY)

Gospel for the Common of the Blessed Virgin Mary, No. 1 page 241.

MASS OF THE BLESSED VIRGIN ON SATURDAY (DURING PASCHAL TIME)

Summary:

> From the cross, Jesus gives His Mother to John and John to her.

BEHOLD THY SON

Lord Jesus, You are up there on the cross, nailed to it hand and foot, Your whole being flooded with agony both physical and mental. And Your Mother is at the foot of the cross looking up at You. She is suffering every moment and all the intensity of Your pain with You. With her is her sister, Mary of Cleophas, Mary Magdalen, and John, the disciple You love. I don't suppose there has ever been such a collectivity of love on one mountain top before or since.

You know the outcome, not only of this dying You are going through, but of the excitement of the next weeks: how You will die, rise, and then ascend into heaven. You know that Your Mother would have good care from any of Your followers, and she could even look after herself. But You have special reasons for Your next words. You say to her: "Woman, behold thy son." You cannot point, You just look, and following Your look, she sees John, Your beloved disciple. Then You say to John: "Behold thy mother."

And so the exchange is made. So a new kind of motherhood and sonship is established, and a very real relationship it is, too. Now the words of St. Luke describing Your birth make even more sense. He says that Mary "brought forth her *firstborn* Son," referring directly to You. Mary now has another son direct from the hands of God Himself, from You; and of course, John is just the first of a long, innumerable line of sons and daughters. That's the way You want it; that's the way it always will be.

BEHOLD THY MOTHER

It is really very wonderful being part of Your plan of accepting Mary as our Mother and being accepted by her as her children. Only You in Your infinite wisdom could have thought of it, Lord Jesus. It is a great joy to have her as a Mother to whom we can go in all our needs and with all our hopes and prayers.

It is also marvelous accepting her into our care. This I haven't thought of much before — that we can continue John's work of taking Mary into our homes and looking after her. Of course, we cannot do it quite as literally as John, but when we look after and give our hearts to others of her children who are homeless, ill, suffering in any way, poor and dying, we surely do look after her. If You could say that whatever is done to the least of Your brethren is done to You, may we not also say that it is done to her who is so one with You?

So Mary is ours and we are hers; but both she and we are Yours, Lord Jesus. You are still the center of our life, of all life; for You being lifted up onto the cross continue to draw all things to Yourself. Lord, never allow us to forget that there is only one essential place for those who want to love You: it is beneath the cross looking up at You, dying with You.

Mary and John stand at Redemption beneath the cross. We all stand at Redemption at every Holy Mass. Make us realize more and more vividly that at every Mass we do exactly what these holy ones do on Calvary — we stand looking up to You, to Your sacrifice, to Your love for the Father and the world. We share in the desire to sacrifice herself that Mary has in her heart; and wonder of wonders, in proportion to our love and self-sacrificing will, we share in the love that You have for her and for John.

Lord Jesus, thank You for giving us Your Mother, and make us worthy of being her true sons and daughters.

Prayer for the day:

> WOMAN, BEHOLD THY SON. SON, BEHOLD THY MOTHER.

MASS OF THE BLESSED VIRGIN ON SATURDAY (AFTER PENTECOST TO THE FIRST SUNDAY OF ADVENT)

Gospel for the Common of the Blessed Virgin, No. 1, page 241.

DAILY MASS FOR THE DEAD

Summary:

> Jesus promises bread that will make those who eat it live forever; and the bread that He will give is His flesh for the life of the world.

IF ANYONE EAT

Lord Jesus, usually our thinking about death is hesitant, reluctant, and incomplete. We see it all around us, but seldom do we think of ourselves as proximate prospects for experiencing it. You who are the Lord of Life have known death; but You have also known resurrection from the dead, both of which facts would make You more qualified than anyone else to talk about death.

According to You, the only way to talk about death is to talk about life. And so You do. You call Yourself the Bread of Life. "If anyone eat of this bread he shall *live forever*; and the bread that I will give is My flesh for the life of the world."

Obviously, You are playing here on the words and the idea of life and death. Each and every one of us is going to die. Our life principle, our soul, is going to separate from the body. The body will be put into a grave, and the soul will go into eternity. Will it go into life everlasting? Will it really live with You forever in peace and joy? That depends on the way we conduct ourselves in this world, and above all on the use we make of the means of life, Your body and blood.

I have an idea, Lord Jesus, that we don't really know what it is to live. To live, to be alive, means to have all our powers and faculties working at their fullest capacity. It means above all *to know* and *to love* to the very best of our power to know and to love.

You say, "He who eats My flesh and drinks My blood has life everlasting and I will raise him up on the last day." The Eucharist, then, is life-giving because it gives You who are boundless Life; and it gives You to us so that You can prepare us more and more not merely to do the minimum in order to escape hell but really to *live*. Feeding us with Your body and blood, You want to draw out the best possibilities of our mind and heart to the end that both in this life and the next we may know and love God to our fullest capacity.

THE LAST DAY

You say to the Jews: "Your fathers ate the manna in the desert, and have died. This is the bread that comes down from heaven, so that if anyone eat of it he will not die. I am the living bread that has come down from heaven. If anyone eat of this bread he shall live forever; and the bread that I will give is My flesh for the life of the world" (John 6:48-52).

Lord Jesus, the manna from heaven was food for the Jews traveling in the desert to the Promised Land. But there was a lot of death along that way. The manna did not confer immortality. No earthly food can give immortality; that is Your privilege alone.

Your body and blood are another kind of manna, a true Viaticum, a life-giving food for the way which leads to the promised land of heaven, but which already in this world helps us to live as we ought, to live at our highest point of development, that is, to live in You.

Lord Jesus, open our eyes to the reality of death, not only the reality of physical death, but above all the real horror of being forever separated from and dead to You (which death can well come from the neglect or misuse of the Eucharist). Above all, open our eyes to the reality of life and the means of life. As long as I live, I want to eat Your flesh and drink Your blood so that You can raise me up on the last day.

> *Prayer for the day:*
>> THE BREAD THAT I WILL GIVE IS MY FLESH FOR THE LIFE OF THE WORLD.

MASS ON THE DAY OF DEATH OR BURIAL, OR FOR THE THIRD, SEVENTH, OR THIRTIETH DAY AFTER DEATH

> **Summary:**
>> Jesus tells Martha that He is the resurrection and the life; he who believes in Him shall never die.

RESURRECTION AND LIFE

Lord Jesus, Your friend Lazarus has been in the tomb for four days. His sister Martha greets You with the words, "Lord, if Thou hadst been here my brother would not have died. But even now I know that whatever Thou shalt ask of God, God will give it to Thee." It is a beautiful tribute of faith and love from a good woman who has come to know that anything merciful can happen when You are around. She knows what You have done for the son of the widow of Naim and the daughter of Jairus. Surely, she thinks, You might very well do the same for Your friend.

Your answer is not wholly satisfactory to her: "Thy brother shall rise." She replies, "I know that he will rise at the resurrection, on the last day." But she wants him back right now, as You can plainly see, even though she doesn't tell You outright. She will get him back, but thinking of other bereaved followers of Yours down through history, You first say to her: "I am the resurrection and the life; he who believes in Me, even if he dies, shall live; and whoever lives and believes in me, shall never die. Dost thou believe this?" She answers: "Yes, Lord, I believe that Thou art the Christ, the Son of God, who hast come into the world."

It is a glorious profession of faith that wins from You one of Your greatest miracles: Lazarus, dead four days, comes back into the land of the living at Your command. You want him and his sisters, Martha and Mary, to live longer in this world so that they might give us an example of Christian living that would help to prepare others for resurrection on the last day. They have You in their midst, they believe in You, they love You, they love one another.

WHOEVER LIVES AND BELIEVES

But You are not thinking only of the sorrow of Martha and Mary. You have in mind here all the grief of all Your friends to come who are faced with the death of a loved one. Death is a terrible and terrifying experience in any family. You Yourself weep at Lazarus' tomb, and he is not even related to You. Your Mother weeps at Your cross.

The separation from loved ones may be only temporary, and we may very well believe that the loved one is happy with the God who made him or her for Himself; nevertheless, we are human, and there is a finality about the separation that temporarily floods us with anguish. Grief is not evil. The only grief that is unworthy of the Christian is the kind that we refuse to offer with love as part of Your sorrow, Your Cross.

Grief joined to faith in You and motivated by love for You (as it was with Your own Mother and with Martha and Mary) can bring life and salvation into our world. It can be part of Your own redeeming cross. If there is anything that can give a sense of being worthwhile to our lives, it should be this conviction that our pain, mental or physical, continues what You have begun.

But there is another secret here, Lord Jesus. You say: "Whoever lives and believes in Me, shall never die." The greater our faith in You and the more intense our love for You, the more vividly You live in us. I believe that this departed one who has died in You, lives in You and has his life now from You; therefore he lives for me, too. You are the bond between us; in You we still communicate together; in You is our love solidified.

Lord Jesus, increase my faith in You, intensify my love. And special thanks to Martha for having won from Your compassionate heart not only a glorious miracle, but these words that give and maintain life!

Prayer for the day:
I AM THE RESURRECTION AND THE LIFE.

MASS ON THE ANNIVERSARY OF THE DEATH OR BURIAL

Summary:
Jesus says that it is the will of the Father that He should lose nothing of what the Father has given Him, but that He should raise it up on the last day.

THE FATHER'S WILL

Lord Jesus, You say that all that the Father gives You will come to You, and him who comes to You, You will not cast out. You go on to say that You have come down from heaven, not to do Your own will, but the will of Him who sent You. And the will of Him who sent You is that You should lose nothing of what He has given to You, but that You should raise it up on the last day. For this is the will of Your Father who sent You, that whoever beholds You, and believes in You, shall have everlasting life, and You will raise him up on the last day.

Lord Jesus, out of all this mysterious talk of Yours, there is one idea that stands out: Your love and hunger for souls. During Your life You speak again and again of doing the Father's will, and I have always understood this attachment to the Father's will as the interior immolation of Yourself that motivated Your life-long redeeming work. It is the Father's will that You should be obedient unto death, even the death of the cross.

But here You indicate another aspect of that will—that You should lose nothing of what the Father has given You, but that You should raise it up on the last day. Further, that it is the will of the Father that whoever beholds You, His Son, and believes in You, shall have everlasting life so that You will raise him up on the last day.

According to Your word, then, the Father puts the responsibility of losing nothing that He gives You on Your shoulders, Lord. Not only does He want You to suffer, die, and rise for men to save them for eternal life with You and Him and the Holy Spirit, but He wants You to see to it that they remain saved.

EVERLASTING LIFE

Now I can understand better all that You have done to project Your saving sacrifice into future centuries by instituting Your Church and the life-giving sacraments in Your Church. I can understand better Your Church Year which makes present for us the entire life that You have lived on earth so that we can come to You and live with You and not be cast out. I can understand all the impulses of grace, the sudden inspirations whereby You urge me to do good or avoid evil. You do everything for us that is consistent with our free will.

Lord Jesus, it is now a year (several years) since the soul whose anniversary day we are keeping has been with You. We have had this time in which to grow in awareness of Your will for us, which has included the death of this loved one. We now see more plainly than we did during those days of grief and feeling of loss how our life here is related to Your redemption.

We are grateful to You for having drawn us to Yourself, for the privilege of sharing in Your work, for the love You give us. Above all, we thank You for this new awareness of the universality of the working of Your will in us. Now help us to behold You, to believe in You, so that we, too, may have everlasting life and be raised up on the last day.

Prayer for the day:
>> HIM WHO COMES TO ME I WILL NOT CAST OUT.

VOTIVE MASSES

Monday: VOTIVE MASS OF THE MOST HOLY TRINITY

Summary:
>> When the Holy Spirit, whom Jesus will send from the Father, comes, He will bear witness concerning Jesus.

THREE DIVINE PERSONS

Lord Jesus, it is at the Last Supper that You teach Your clearest doctrine about the Blessed Trinity. You say that when the Advocate (Your special name for the Holy Spirit) comes whom You will send from the Father, the Spirit of truth who proceeds from the Father, He will bear witness concerning You. And the apostles, too, will bear witness to You and to Your doctrine of Three Persons in one God.

You tell them that they will be expelled from the synagogues. Yes, the hour is coming for everyone who kills them to think that he is offering worship to God. And these things the persecutors will do because they have not known the Father nor You. But these things You speak to the apostles that when the time for the persecution comes, they may remember that You have told them.

Lord Jesus, persecutors persecute because they do not know the Father nor You. And of course, not knowing You two, they do not know the Holy Spirit either. We are made to know God, that is, to know You and the Father and the Holy Spirit. You give us minds which make us like unto You and enable us to know truth and to plunge into the meanings of things. And when our plunging reaches the boundaries of the Mystery which You three Persons are, You also provide us with the virtue of Faith whereby we may share in the very vision of God.

Being made in Your image, we also have wills: we can love as You can love. We can love one another according to Your divine command. Best of all, You give us the divine virtue of Charity so that we may share in the love that You and Your Father have for one another. And we know that that Love is Love personified, Your and the Father's Holy Spirit.

ONE GOD

Lord Jesus, most of us seem afraid, or at least neglectful of Your doctrine of the Blessed Trinity. Yet You have become man in order to bring the doctrine to us. You want us to know it. As You say in this gospel, those who do not know You nor the Father become persecutors, they become less than men.

We always come back to this: we must be human, that is, we must make use of our minds and our wills, we must know and love. I remember Your words, "If anyone love Me, he will keep My word, and My Father will love him, and We will come to him and make our abode with him" (John 14:23). *We* will come, You say. That means all three of You; and You want to make Yourselves at home in us. You want to be our guests. But if You are our guests, we must talk to You, confide in You, love You.

Thus, and only thus, will we come to know You as Persons, as the most Blessed Trinity. And when we get tired of talking, or more exactly, if we run out of our own words, there is always the Prayer of Your Church that eagerly awaits our voices. "With our whole heart and voice we acknowledge Thee, we praise Thee, we bless Thee, God the Father unbegotten, Thee, the Only-begotten Son, Thee, the Holy Spirit, the Paraclete, the holy and undivided Trinity.

For Thou art great, and dost wonderful things: Thou alone art God.
To Thee be praise, to Thee glory, to Thee thanksgiving forever and
ever, O Blessed Trinity" (tract)!

Praying like that makes us know You, it expands the abysses of
our hearts so that You can come and fill them with Yourself, O
Blessed Trinity.

Prayer for the day:
> YOU WILL BEAR WITNESS, BECAUSE FROM
> THE BEGINNING YOU ARE WITH ME.

Tuesday: VOTIVE MASS OF THE HOLY ANGELS

Summary:
> Jesus promises Nathanael that He will see the
> heavens opened, and the angels of God as-
> cending and descending upon the Son of Man.

ANGELS OF GOD

Lord Jesus, it is early in Your public life, and You are in the act
of choosing Your apostles. You see a man coming towards You:
You decide on the spot that he has the qualifications You want. You
say to him, "Behold a true Israelite in whom there is no guile!"
Nathanael is his name, and he is a little startled at Your words. He
says: "Whence knowest Thou me?"

You answer "Before Philip called thee, when thou wast under
the fig tree, I saw thee." Your words drive away any doubt Nathanael might have had about any good coming out of Nazareth, as he
has slightingly remarked to Philip. "Rabbi," he exclaims, "Thou art
the Son of God, Thou art King of Israel." You reply: "Because I
said to thee that I saw thee under the fig tree, thou dost believe.
Greater things than these shalt thou see."

And then You add the words that make Your Church choose

this section of the gospel for Its Votive Mass of the Holy Angels: "Amen, amen, I say to you, you shall see heaven opened, and the angels of God ascending and descending upon the Son of Man."

Lord Jesus, You speak familiarly about angels because You know them as we never can; You know how You have used them from the beginning of history to manifest Your will to men. An angel announces Your birth to Your Mother, and multitudes of them rejoice at that birth on the hillsides of Bethlehem. They minister to You after Satan tempts You in the desert; they announce Your resurrection and are present at Your ascension.

And now, according to St. John, they surround Your heavenly throne, crying out with a loud voice: "Worthy is the Lamb who was slain to receive power and divinity and wisdom and strength and honor and glory and blessing" (epistle).

ASCENDING AND DESCENDING

Lord Jesus, with these facts facing us, it is not right that we should be so unfamiliar and even somewhat stand-offish with Your angels. Being so close to You in Your redeeming work all Your life, they must share Your love for us, they must (like you) want to be known and esteemed by us. They must want to be part of our religion, our life- and love-relationship with You.

What can we do to become more familiar with them? There is, of course, the tried and true method of talking to them as we do with You (although most of us will first have to introduce ourselves). Then we can grow in awareness of our common vocation as Your members; namely, our dedication to the work of praise of God. "I will sing praise to Thee in the sight of the angels: I will worship towards Thy holy temple, and I will give glory to Thy name" (alleluia verse).

Lord Jesus, You can help this awareness within us. You can do it at this very Mass. "We offer Thee, O Lord, a sacrifice of praise, and humbly beseech Thee that, *through the prayers of the angels pleading for us*, Thou wouldst be pleased to accept it, and grant that it may avail us unto salvation" (secret).

Holy, Holy, Holy, Lord God of Hosts. Heaven and earth are filled with Thy glory. Hosanna in the highest. Blessed is He Who comes in the name of the Lord. Hosanna in the highest. So sing the angels in heaven. So sing we with them at every holy Mass. You are the cause of their joy, as of ours. In You we, angels and men, are one.

Prayer for the day:

YOU SHALL SEE HEAVEN OPENED, AND THE ANGELS OF GOD ASCENDING AND DE-SCENDING UPON THE SON OF MAN.

VOTIVE MASS OF ST. JOSEPH

Summary:

At the age of thirty, Jesus is baptized by John, being (as it was supposed) the son of Joseph.

GOOD FATHER

Lord Jesus, it is a decisive moment in Your life, this day of Your baptism by John. For thirty years You have been living a quiet, studious, prayerful and strenuous life as a carpenter in Nazareth. It is taken for granted that You are the son of Mary and Joseph; and that is all right with You (as it surely must be with them). These have been thirty years of work in the midst of a family: above all, thirty years of love. Now You are ready for Your active life in the world.

To that active life the man Joseph has contributed much. He has not given You physical life as human fathers give to their sons. But he has given You a large part of himself. He has helped to educate You: has taught You the goodness of wood and iron, the usefulness of tools, the preciousness of a well-planned and honestly-executed cabinet or table or chair. There is something of Joseph in You, Lord Jesus, something You would not have had were it not for him.

So maybe we ought not feel so "sorry" for Joseph as we some-times do. You are You, You are the Man, Christ Jesus, carpenter and

Savior of the world, because (at least to a certain degree) Joseph has done his duty by You as a good father.

BELOVED SON

Joseph is probably not at the Jordan today for Your baptism by John. He is not yet in heaven, for You have not yet opened heaven to all the souls of the Old Testament just. But wherever he is, he sees the Holy Spirit descend upon You in bodily form as a dove, he hears the voice of Your heavenly Father saying to all the world, us included: "Thou art my beloved Son, in thee I am well pleased."

And Joseph rejoices in those words as few mortals can possibly rejoice. That is exactly what he has been saying all his life. He cannot say it as Your real Father can. But if a foster father cannot give life, he can give love and education. And the resulting relationship is very wonderful indeed.

Lord Jesus, You always reward well those who give You love. Joseph, Your foster-father, is no exception. You reward him, this strong, honest worker, by giving him the responsibility of caring for, protecting and leading to You a countless multitude of sons and daughters.

He gives us what he has given to You—the lesson of reverence for matter as having come from Your creative hands, the dignity of creative work, the necessity of doing to the best of one's ability that which has to be done.

Above all, he gives us the example of living for You, of centering our lives on You. Lord Jesus, grant us all the grace to be worthy of such a father! And to take his example to heart!

Prayer for the day:

THOU ART MY BELOVED SON, IN THEE I AM WELL PLEASED.

Wednesday: VOTIVE MASS OF THE HOLY APOSTLES PETER AND PAUL

Summary:

Jesus promises a hundredfold reward to all those who have truly left all things to follow Him.

WHO FOLLOW CHRIST

Lord Jesus, if Peter is not direct and outspoken, no one is. What is in his mind has no difficulty finding a way out. He has been thinking of his life as Your apostle, and suddenly he asks You: "Behold, we have left all and followed Thee; what then shall we have?" Most of us who have gone through the motions of leaving all things have probably thought the same way: we have not asked You Peter's question outright, perhaps because we are afraid in our hearts that we haven't really left all things . . . yet. I suspect that You are more pleased with Peter's directness than with our half-hearted indecisiveness.

You answer Peter in a way he doesn't quite expect at his present stage of spiritual progress: "Amen I say to you, that you who have followed Me, in the regeneration when the Son of Man shall sit on the throne of His glory, shall also sit on twelve thrones, judging the twelve tribes of Israel." It is a promise of spiritual, rather than temporal or human, reward; and I imagine that it is better understood by Peter and his companions than by us.

But then You lift up Your eyes to the future centuries, and You see us and others who have desired to be Your followers in more than an ordinary way. You speak to us now: "Everyone who has left house, or brothers, or sisters, or father, or mother, or wife, or children, or lands, for My Name's sake, shall receive a hundredfold, and shall possess life everlasting." We hear the promise so often that its glory seldom reaches into the inner room of our awareness.

FOR HIS NAME'S SAKE

Lord Jesus, I believe that You want to apply the lesson of this gospel to everyone whom You call to the religious life. The hundred-

299

fold reward of life everlasting depends on two conditions: that we really leave all things and persons and that we do it for Your Name's sake.

Lord, human love is a good and wonderful thing: it is also a permanent bond that attaches members of families one to another. I don't believe that You want us to cease to love our relatives, and surely You don't want us to hate those who are near and dear to us.

What You mean is that we must prevent any person's standing in the way to that total attachment and gift of self to You that You require of those who freely choose to be Your special followers. The secret is *in loving people in You*, which means loving You so much that our love bursts out of our hearts and overflows to those whom You have related to us by ties of blood or friendship. This is exactly what the apostles did, and it accounts for their great zeal.

The second condition is that we do all that You desire *for Your Name's sake*. That means love again, doing these things because we want to please You. Any other motive would make the leave-taking from family and friends a mere exercise in stoicism or selfish pride. Here again the apostles show us the way. Their sound went forth into all the earth: and their words to the ends of the world (offertory verse), because they wanted what You wanted.

Lord Jesus, help us all to leave all things according to our vocation. Help us to carry on the work of the apostles. Above all, give us the grace to follow in their footsteps out of love for You. Or just give the love, and then let all things follow in their appointed course.

Prayer for the day:

  BEHOLD, WE HAVE LEFT ALL AND FOLLOWED THEE.

Thursday: VOTIVE MASS OF THE ETERNAL PRIESTHOOD OF OUR LORD JESUS CHRIST

Summary:

At the Last Supper Jesus changes bread into His body and wine into His blood and commissions the apostles to do the same.

GREAT DESIRE

Lord Jesus, it is at the Last Supper, and You are speaking to the twelve apostles reclining around You at table: "I have greatly desired to eat this passover with you before I suffer; for I say to you that I will eat of it no more, until it has been fulfilled in the kingdom of God."

Then having taken a cup, You give thanks and say: "Take this and share it among you; for I say to you that I will not drink of the fruit of the vine, until the kingdom of God comes." And having taken bread, You give thanks and break and give it to them, saying: "This is My body, which is being given for you; *do this in remembrance of Me*." In like manner, You take also the cup after the supper, saying: "This cup is the new covenant in My blood, which shall be shed for you."

Lord Jesus, we see You acting here as high priest. You have a great desire to be in the midst of the apostles, and from their midst You offer Yourself in sacrifice to the Father even as You give Yourself as food to them. You fulfill the two purposes of Your coming into the world: You glorify the Father with the gift-offering of Your whole being as Man—an offering that You will make the next day in a bloody manner on Calvary—and You sanctify and unify men, giving them Your body and blood as their food. You the one Christ to all the twelve.

Here is fulfilled the ancient prophecy of the Psalmist: "The Lord has sworn and will not repent: *Thou art a priest forever* according to the order of Melchisedech" (introit). You, priest according to the order of Melchisedech, offer the sacrifice of bread and wine, but bread and wine become Your body and blood.

301

Lord Jesus, because You continue forever, You have an everlasting priesthood (alleluia verse). Your priesthood is active and is fulfilling itself today and will continue to do so until the end . . . and all because You say to the apostles as You institute the Eucharist, "Do this in remembrance of Me." Your priesthood continues because Your original intention of glorifying the Father by sanctifying and unifying men goes on.

PRIEST AND VICTIM

And everything is centered in the Mass. Being at holy Mass, we are at the Last Supper, gathered around You and hearing You say to us: "I have greatly desired to eat this passover with you before I suffer." At holy Mass the other and equally important aspect of Your priesthood, referred to twice in this Votive Mass, is fulfilled: For here in the epistle and gospel You bring good news to the poor, to us; You bring Your word of life, and here You heal the contrite of heart (gradual).

Lord Jesus, through Your mercy You have made some of us priests, giving us the same power over Your body and blood that You have given here to the apostles. We do what You have done, and so we show forth Your death until You return. But if not all have that privilege of changing bread into Your body and wine into Your blood, no Christian, ordained or not, is denied the glory of sharing in Your *priestly, sacrificial will*, that will whereby You give Yourself to the Father with all the love of Your Sacred Heart as the Lamb of God, the supreme Victim for the sins of the world. Praise be to Thee, O Christ!

"We beseech Thee, O Lord, that the Divine Victim which we have offered and received, may give us life, so that united with Thee in enduring bonds of love, we may bring forth everlasting fruit" (post-communion).

Lord Jesus, perfect us ever more and more as co-victims with You in Your sacrifice.

Prayer for the day:
I HAVE GREATLY DESIRED TO EAT THIS PASS-
OVER WITH YOU BEFORE I SUFFER.

Thursday: VOTIVE MASS OF THE HOLY SPIRIT

Gospel same as on Feast of Pentecost, page 163.

Thursday: VOTIVE MASS OF THE BLESSED SACRAMENT

Gospel same as for Feast of Corpus Christi, page 177.

Friday: MASS OF THE HOLY CROSS

Summary:

Jesus predicts that He will be crucified and put to death, but the third day He will rise again.

UP TO JERUSALEM

Lord Jesus, You have been with the apostles now for nearly three years. You have tried to form them according to Your mind and Your set of values. But it has been hard; for they have had so much to unlearn and learn.

So they scarcely understand when You say to them: "Behold, we are going up to Jerusalem, and the Son of Man will be betrayed to the chief priests and the Scribes; and they will condemn Him to death, and will deliver Him to the Gentiles to be mocked and scourged and crucified; and on the third day He will rise again."

It is easier for us, looking back from here. We can see the fulfillment of Your prophecy on the cross on Calvary. Every detail that You here mention is filled in by Your enemies. You become obedient for us to death, even to death on a cross. But death is swallowed up in victory. The third day You rise again. Therefore God also has exalted You and has bestowed upon You the Name that is above every name (gradual).

"Say ye among the Gentiles, that the Lord has reigned from the wood. Alleluia. Sweet the wood, sweet the nails, sweet the load that hangs thereon: to bear up the King and Lord of heaven, no tree was worthy, save thou, O Holy Cross" (alleluia verse).

Yes, Lord Jesus, we can look back to Calvary—it is always a good thing to do. And we can share Your Church's lyrical and childlike joy as she magnifies Your holy Cross, almost giving it a personality. "O blessed Cross, which alone was worthy to bear the King of heaven and the Lord" (tract). We can even adore the Cross, bending our knee before it: "We adore Thy Cross, O Lord, we commemorate Thy glorious Passion: have mercy on us, Thou who didst suffer for us" (tract).

SCOURGED AND CRUCIFIED

But better than looking back, we can be with You now on Your Cross, in Your sacrifice made present in our midst. Each Mass we share in plunges us more and more into that sacrificial mind that motivated Your words in today's gospel: "Behold, we are going up to Jerusalem . . ." Each Mass can make us more and more obedient unto death, even to death on a cross. Our growing sacrificial mindedness in each Mass is our answer to Your demand of us: "Unless you take up *your* cross and follow after Me, you cannot be My disciple."

Lord Jesus, the world is full of pain and sorrow and suffering— physical and mental. Your life, death, and resurrection have not eliminated that. But You show us a way that illuminates and glorifies human pain, making it divine and redemptive: making it, in short, Your very own. You give us Your cross.

Your cross is now a bed of sickness, a desk, a kitchen sink, a counter, a truck, a barred cell. No matter what the shape, it is Your cross and ours. It has its roots in Your altar, and Your altar is Calvary. We adore Thee, O Christ, and we bless Thee: because by Thy Cross Thou hast redeemed the world (tract). We adore Thee, O Christ, and we bless Thee: because by this present cross and our love, You continue to redeem the world.

Lord Jesus, now I believe as never before that "It behooves us to glory in the Cross of our Lord Jesus Christ: in whom is our salvation, life and resurrection: by whom we are saved and delivered" (introit).

Prayer for the day:
BEHOLD, WE ARE GOING UP TO JERUSALEM.

Friday: VOTIVE MASS OF THE PASSION OF OUR LORD

Summary:
Bowing His head, Jesus gives up His spirit.

IT IS CONSUMMATED

Lord Jesus, knowing that all things are now accomplished, that the Scripture might be fulfilled, You say, "I thirst." Now there is standing there a vessel full of common wine; and having put a sponge soaked with the wine on a stalk of hyssop, they put it to Your mouth. When You take the wine, You say, "It is consummated." And bowing Your head, You give up Your spirit.

Your enemies do not want Your body to remain on the cross on the Sabbath, so they ask Pilate to have Your legs broken. The soldiers do break the legs of the two thieves who are crucified with You, but when they come to You, and see that You are already dead, they do not break Your legs; but one of the soldiers opens Your side with a lance, and immediately there comes out blood and water. You are dead. There is no doubt about it. It is consummated.

So this is the Passion, this the fulfillment of the prophecies. "They have pierced My hands and My feet: they have numbered all My bones" (communion verse). "My heart has expected reproach and misery: and I looked for one who would grieve together with Me, and there was none: They gave Me gall for My food, and in My thirst they gave Me vinegar to drink" (gradual).

The Prophets can prophesy, and the Evangelists can describe, and we may gaze upon You up there on the Cross; but who dares to enter into Your mind at this moment, Lord Jesus? For an ordinary human being to endure what You have endured is horrible to contemplate. But You are the most perfect of men. No one has ever been so sensitive to pain as You; and worst of all, no one has ever experienced the dread torture of human hatred as have You, nor the pain of loss, of being abandoned even by Your Father.

"My God, my God, why hast thou forsaken Me? Thou art far from the prayers, from the words of my cry . . . But I am a worm and not a man, the scorn of men and despised of the people . . . They divide my garments among them, and for my vesture they cast lots" (Psalm 21).

BLOOD AND WATER

Lord, I can't say what I feel. Let me borrow from the great theologian Guardini: "Christ on the cross! Inconceivable what He went through as He hung there. In the degree that we are Christian and have learned to love the Lord, we begin to sense something of that mystery of utter helplessness, hopelessness. This then the end of all effort and struggle! Everything, without reserve—body, heart, and spirit given over to the illimitable flame of omnipresent agony, to the terrible judgment of assumed world-sin that none can alleviate and whose horror only death can end" (*The Lord,* p. 399).

Lord Jesus, a Christian is supposed to be a man of the resurrection; but how can we ever understand Your rising unless again and again we stand under Your cross and at least try to comprehend the depths to which Your love for us plunges You?

Lord Jesus, having thought about this gospel, I think I do understand more what holy Mass means, for nowhere is there a better description of the Mass. I think I am more ready to make Your passion my own and to want to be a victim with You. One thing I do know: I love You more, I want to praise and thank You now and always.

"Hail, Thou our King: Thou alone hast had compassion on our errors: obedient to the Father, Thou wert led to be crucified like a meek lamb to the slaughter. To Thee be glory, hosanna: to Thee be triumph and victory: to Thee a crown of highest praise and honor" (alleluia verses).

Prayer for the day:
IT IS CONSUMMATED.

Friday:
VOTIVE MASS OF THE SACRED HEART

Gospel same as on Feast of the Sacred Heart, page 181.

VOTIVE MASS OF THE BRIDEGROOM AND BRIDE

Summary:
Jesus teaches the indissolubility of marriage.

MALE AND FEMALE

Lord Jesus, whenever the Pharisees ask You any questions, the last thing they want to hear is truth. They simply want to trick You into saying something that will discredit You. But You who are Truth in person, can never think or say or do anything but the truth.

So today the Pharisees come to You and ask, "Is it lawful for a man to put away his wife for any cause?" You answer them with a question of Your own: "Have you not read that the Creator, from the beginning, made them male and female, and said, 'For this cause a man shall leave his father and mother, and cleave to his wife, and the two shall become one flesh'? Therefore now they are no longer two, but one flesh. What therefore God has joined together, let no man put asunder."

"What God has joined together . . . ." Lord Jesus, I believe that God joins man and wife together in order that they may accomplish His purposes. Usually we think of His purposes primarily as the continuation of the human race, and surely this is a most worthy end both for God and for man and wife. But marriage also serves Your Father's other purpose—the beginning, growth, development and perfection of *love*.

I needn't tell You, Lord Jesus, that You, God, are not only life, but also love. It is Your divine life and love that You choose to give to husband and wife, to put in trust with them in marriage so that they may grow in life and love themselves; and thus by their loving, mutual self-giving, they become Your instruments for the creation of new souls likewise capable of continuing the stream of love that flows from the heart of the Trinity into the world and then returns swollen with new love to its source.

TWO BECOME ONE

Lord Jesus, isn't this union of husband and wife in love exactly what You Yourself do in becoming man? In the Incarnation You wed our human nature and the resulting union between You and our nature has been infinite superabundance of divine life and divine love for all of the human race.

This sounds very mystical and mysterious, but St. Paul is not afraid of it, and he wants Christian husbands and wives to think about it, too. "Just as the Church is subject to Christ, so also let wives be to their husbands in all things. Husbands, love your wives, just as Christ also loved the Church, and delivered Himself up for her, that He might sanctify her, cleansing her in the bath of water by means of the word; in order that He might present to Himself the

Church in all her glory . . . This is a great mystery—I mean in reference to Christ and to the Church" (epistle).

It seems then, Lord Jesus, that each Christian marriage reproduces Your own wedding with Your Church. Therefore their life together must also conform to Your life with Your Church: Obedience, based on respect, for the wife; delivering himself up for his wife on the part of the husband; and the whole wonderful relationship one of mutual self-giving held up by sacrificial, reverent love.

Lord Jesus, help us all, married and single, to grow in understanding appreciation of what holy Matrimony really is; for there are few of Your creations that can make us realize more how wonderful You are. And bless this couple as You alone are capable of blessing them. Just as Your union with Your Bride the Church is made present in every Mass, let them see more and more that each time they offer themselves at holy Mass, they renew their own marriage at its most abundant source. Let their constant prayer be: "In Thee, O Lord, have I put my trust; I said, Thou art my God; my times are in Thy hands" (offertory).

Prayer for the day:

WHAT THEREFORE GOD HAS JOINED TO-GETHER, LET NO MAN PUT ASUNDER.

Proper Gospels of the Saints

November 30, St. Andrew the Apostle

Summary:

Jesus invites Peter and Andrew and John to follow Him and He will make them fishers of men.

COME, FOLLOW ME

Lord Jesus, You know whom You are looking for, and You know where to find them. As God You have known these future apostles from all eternity; now is the moment in time to make Your choice official. "Come, follow Me," You say, "and I will make you fishers of men." And at once they leave their nets and take off after You. Farther on there is another pair of brothers, James and John, in a boat with their father Zebedee, mending their nets. You call them, and immediately they leave their father and the nets and follow You.

These are the facts. Nothing is revealed of the mysterious exchange that takes place between You and them: on Your part the respect that You have for each one as a person, together with the willingness to trust Your entire work into their care; and on their part the intuitive recognition that they are wanted and needed by One who seems more lovable than any other Man they've ever met.

You are a stranger who comes to them without reputation, with nothing but an invitation and the power of Your personality. The invitation is addressed to them as *men*. They give up their life work, their relatives, to follow You. They start a journey that will bring them the most terrifying of heartaches. They will experience excitement, hatred, love, death. They will give their lives as Your witnesses; but they will also experience the resurrection, Yours and their own.

"Thou shalt make them princes over all the earth: they shall remember Thy name, O Lord" (gradual). "To me Thy friends, O God, are made exceedingly honorable; their principality is exceedingly strengthened" (offertory).

313

FISHERS OF MEN

Lord Jesus, what is St. Andrew to me or I to St. Andrew? Well, since he is with You now, and since he gave his blood for the privilege of sharing You with souls, I am sure that we mean more to Andrew than he to us. But if we meditate these gospels more and more deeply, You will reveal Yourself to us as You did to him, You will teach us how dependent You have made Yourself on men, especially these apostles; and then they will become very dear to us as our ancestors in the Faith, as men who have given an example of true love and the kind of generosity that draws forth new grace from the heart of God.

"How beautiful are the feet of those who preach the gospel of peace; of those who bring glad tidings of good things! . . . Faith depends on hearing and hearing on the word of Christ" (epistle).

Lord Jesus, to every one of us who is baptized You have said: "Come, follow Me." And You say it with the same degree of respect and esteem that You had for the apostles. This invitation to follow You and to share in Your redeeming work is perhaps not going to be as thrilling as it was for Andrew; nor will it be as bloody in the end. But You issue the invitation.

Lord, strengthen my will to accept the invitation and to follow it through. Help me to see the holy Masses of this year—with the epistle, gospel, offertory, consecration and communion—as Your personal word and work preparing me to be in this world what Andrew and the other apostles were in Palestine: a follower of Yours, a witness to You, an apostle for You, and—if You so will it—a martyr. Praise be to Thee, O Christ!

Prayer for the day:

COME, FOLLOW ME, AND I WILL MAKE YOU FISHERS OF MEN.

FEASTS OF DECEMBER

* December 1, Mass of the Preceding Sunday

* December 2, Mass of the Preceding Sunday

December 3, St. Francis Xavier, Confessor

Summary:

Jesus sends the apostles into the whole world to preach the gospel and to baptize, promising that great miracles will accompany their preaching.

PREACH THE GOSPEL

Lord Jesus, You are about to ascend into heaven after Your thirty-three years of redeeming activity in our world. You have lived, preached, suffered, died, risen from the dead; and in instituting Your Church with her life-giving sacraments, You have assured that all that You are and have done and hope for will be made available for the ages to come. But this Church and all her riches must be spread by human means, by men, in accordance with Your own manner of being and acting.

Therefore, You stand before these men whom You have chosen to carry out Your commission: "Go into the whole world, and preach the gospel to every creature . . . And these signs shall attend those who believe: in My name they shall cast out devils; they shall speak in new tongues; they shall take up serpents; and if they drink any deadly thing, it shall not hurt them; they shall lay hands upon the sick and they shall get well."

The apostles hear You and accept the charge. They go out into

NOTE: An asterisk (*) in front of a date in the Proper of the Saints indicates that the Mass of the Saint may be said, or the Mass of the preceding Sunday, or a votive Mass, or a Requiem Mass at the choice of the celebrant.

315

the world they know, carrying You to unknown peoples, planting Your Church. Your promises accompany them: in Your name they cast out devils and perform healing miracles. After they have done their work (which is Yours), You call them to Yourself. But the work must go on, for You are Savior of the whole world. And it must go on through men. "My truth and My mercy shall be with him: and in My name shall his horn be exalted" (offertory).

MEDITATE HIS COMMANDMENTS

Fifteen hundred years after Your first commission to the apostles, Francis Xavier hears and heeds You. He goes into the world that is India and Japan, preaching You, casting out devils, healing the sick. His success is incredible, beyond human powers of conceiving or ambition. He works for You without any regard for himself. And the secret of all his effort and success?

You know it well. The introit puts these words in his mouth: "I meditated on Thy commandments, which I loved exceedingly." Meditating on Your commandments, contemplating You, he is compelled to the apostolate by love for You, by the desire to make You more and more loved. He has no choice but to go into the world and to cry out to men: "Praise the Lord, all ye nations, and praise Him, all ye people: because His mercy is confirmed upon us, and the truth of the Lord remaineth forever" (introit).

"O God, Who, by the preaching and miracles of Blessed Francis, was pleased to gather into Thy church the nations of the Indies, mercifully grant that we who venerate his glorious merits, *may also imitate the example of his virtues*" (collect). Lord Jesus, the great missionaries know who they are and whose work they do. This gospel tells them, and they believe it.

But if the missionaries know who is behind them and their vocation, do we? Or do we live in a world apart from them . . . and from You? Lord Jesus, this gospel is not merely a picture of Your sending forth the apostles—glorious as that is—and of the intention You have in mind. In it You want to prepare me to offer this Mass. And so it does prepare me: it arouses my desire to offer this Mass for all Your missionaries all over the world—and to offer myself, my will, with the offering You make of Your will. It helps me to see that my life must necessarily be sacrificial; because the success of the commission that You gave then and continue now depends on sacrifice, Yours and mine.

Lord Jesus, make us all Christ-minded; that is, make us all missionary-minded.

> *Prayer for the day:*
>> GO INTO THE WHOLE WORLD AND PREACH THE GOSPEL TO EVERY CREATURE.

December 4, St. Peter Chrysologus, Bishop and Confessor

Gospel No. 14, page 264.

* December 5, Mass of Preceding Sunday

December 6, St. Nicholas, Bishop and Confessor

Gospel No. 12, page 261.

December 7, St. Ambrose, Bishop and Confessor

Gospel No. 14, page 264.

December 8, Immaculate Conception of the Blessed Virgin Mary

> *Summary:*
>> God sends His angel Gabriel to Mary, to tell her He wants her to be the Mother of His Son, whom she is to name Jesus.

THE ANGEL'S MESSAGE

Lord Jesus, You are not yet man when this scene takes place. It's hard for me to think here in time—and in time's terms—about You there in the NOW of eternity, but how else can one think? You are looking down upon this young virgin. From the beginning You have known her, You have loved and chosen her to be Your Mother.

You have also formed and prepared her. That is what this feast and this gospel is all about. "Thou art all fair, O Mary, and there is in thee no stain of original sin" (alleluia verse), so sings Your Church with great and childlike gladness. And she can sing thus because it was Your idea first. Not for a split moment did You allow Satan to have any power over her. All other souls You create apart from You, without Your divine Life in them. But not Your Mother's. Nine months before her birth, at her conception in her mother's womb, she is heaven on earth, the holy of holies in which God Himself dwells.

And then she is born. She grows up and becomes a young woman. I don't suppose she was aware of her blessed condition of sinlessness. But there was no doubt about her being in Your presence always by her love and desire for You. She attracts the attention of a suitor whose name is Joseph (didn't You arrange that, too?) and accepts his proposal. It is while preparing for the wedding that the event of today's gospel occurs.

BLESSED AMONG WOMEN

You are looking down on her, and You hear Gabriel's greeting (I suspect You were responsible for that, too). "Hail, full of grace, the Lord is with thee!" Full of grace. Full of God. Full of God's Life, full of God's Love. The Lord is with her. The Lord is in her. Not Satan, but the Lord. You, Christ, You Lord God of heaven and earth, You are in her by grace before You are in her by flesh, before she gives You that pure body in which You are to dwell among us. The Lord is with her, and therefore blessed is she among all women. Hail, Mary, full of grace!

There will be many gospels in the year ahead that will give me a chance to admire Mary's understanding of You, dear Lord. But today I want to marvel at Your love for her . . . and for me. You who are mighty have done great things to and for Mary, and You will do some of the same great things to me. Your desire to sanctify her is the very same desire that You have to sanctify me. You have willed Mary's sinlessness and mine for all eternity. Now in me You aim to destroy sin, that living death which excludes Your presence. And here at this beginning of a new Church Year, You show us the beauty, loveliness, and desirability of Mary, Your pure Mother as Your greatest achievement. You made her what she was. You will not be as successful with me. But I shall do better this year with her help.

I do want what Mary, Your and my Mother, wants for me—holiness, oneness with You now and forever. "Grant that through her intercession we may be cleansed from sin and come with pure hearts to Thee" (collect).

Prayer for the day:
> HAIL, FULL OF GRACE, THE LORD IS WITH THEE.

* December 9, Mass of Preceding Sunday

* December 10, Mass of Preceding Sunday

* December 11, Mass of Preceding Sunday

* December 12, Mass of Preceding Sunday

December 13, St. Lucy, Virgin and Martyr

Gospel No. 19a, page 274.

* December 14, Mass of Preceding Sunday

* December 15, Mass of Preceding Sunday

* December 16, Mass of Preceding Sunday

*December 17, Mass of Preceding Sunday

* December 18, Mass of Preceding Sunday

* December 19, Mass of Preceding Sunday

* December 20, Mass of Preceding Sunday

NOTE: The Advent Ember Days fall on Wednesday, Friday and Saturday during the week after the Third Sunday of Advent. Those gospels can be found in the Proper of the Season.

December 21, St. Thomas, the Apostle

Summary:

Jesus appears to the doubtful Thomas after His resurrection and wins from him an unforgettable profession of Faith: "My Lord and My God!"

I WILL NOT BELIEVE

Lord, on that day of Your first appearance to Your apostles, Thomas is not with them. They joyously report to him: "We have seen the Lord!" It is hard to know the reason for his answer: "Unless I see in His hands the print of the nails, and put my finger into the place of the nails, and put my hands into His side, I will not believe." Well, at least Thomas remembers Your wounds, Lord Jesus, and he probably still hears the dull pounding of the hammer that sends the nails through Your hands and feet. He sees You hanging there on the cross and follows Your painful writhings into death.

Your wounds were the proof of Your death. Now he wants to use those same wounds as the criterion of Your resurrection. He wants to put his hands into them and to feel the warm blood of Your sacred heart. Poor Thomas. It must be a tough week for him, those eight days between Your appearances. I'm sure his doubt does not really last all eight days. Perhaps it was gone in a matter of minutes, for how could doubt have prevented the joy and convinced exulting that must charge the upper room as the others discuss Your arising? But he must keep up his pose: he has committed himself to doubt; and he is human and weak and feels he has to go through with it.

Now You are there again. The doors are locked, but that makes no difference. "Peace be to you!" You say. It is Your old familiar greeting. They look at You, hearts burning with love. You look at them one by one, and You love them, too. Finally Your glance rests on Thomas. He is not looking at You. It isn't doubt that keeps his eyes cast down, but shame, regret and grief. You have chosen him and made him one of the pillars of Your Church, You have instructed Him for three years, You made him a priest and empowered him to offer Your own sacrifice. And he has denied You, doubted Your power over death! How can he look at You now?

BRING HERE THY FINGER

There is no harshness in Your voice as You say to him: "Bring here thy finger, and see My hands; and bring here thy hand, and put it into My side; and be not unbelieving, but believing." He recognizes his own words, the blustery childish exclamation of the previous week. Has the world ever heard a more soul-scraping cry than now comes from his heart? "My Lord and my God!"

Doubt is gone in his perfect profession of faith. Doubt that has separated him from union with his fellow apostles helps him to utter words that liberate him from himself and literally enfold him into

Your sacred heart. Now come Your words, addressed to Thomas, yes, but intended perhaps most of all for all of us: "Because thou hast seen me, thou hast believed. Blessed are they who have not seen, and yet have believed."

You can be sure of Thomas from now on, Lord. He will keep his words in his heart the rest of his life. They will sustain him always, for they are a glorious prayer, and it is his prayer, wrung from his heart. The words will lead him on through a life of work and suffering in the apostolate. Finally he will die his death, following You now unafraid. And what will be his first words when he greets You in paradise? "My Lord and my God!"

Lord Jesus, in this and every Mass You stand before me just as really as You stand before Thomas in the Upper Room. *You* speak to me in the gospel: *My Lord and my God! You* make present the Last Supper and Calvary: *My Lord and my God!* You give Yourself to me in Holy Communion: *My Lord and my God!*

Prayer for the day:
>BLESSED ARE THEY WHO HAVE NOT SEEN, AND YET HAVE BELIEVED.

December 22, St. Francis Xavier Cabrini, Virgin

Gospel of Mass of St. Matthias, February 24, page 340.

December 23, Mass of Preceding Sunday

December 24, Vigil of Christmas

See Proper of the Season, page 15.

NOTE: All Masses from December 24 to January 2 inclusive, are to be found in the Proper of the Season.

FEASTS OF JANUARY

January 3, Mass of the Circumcision,
page 28.

January 4, Mass of the Circumcision,
page 28.

January 5, Mass of the Circumcision,
page 28 or Gospel No. 2, page 242.

January 6, Feast of the Epiphany,
Proper of the Season, page 31.

January 7 to 12, Gospel of Feast of the Epiphany,
page 31.

January 13,
Commemoration of the Baptism of Our Lord,
page 35.

January 14, St. Hilary, Bishop and Confessor
Gospel No. 14, page 264.

January 15, St. Paul, The First Hermit, Confessor
Gospel of St. Matthias, February 24, page 340.

323

* January 16, St. Marcellus, Pope and Martyr

Gospel No. 2, page 242.

January 17, St. Anthony, Abbot

Gospel No. 17, page 270.

January 18, St. Peter's Chair at Rome

Gospel of Sts. Peter and Paul, June 29, page 389.

* January 19,
Sts. Marius and Companions, Martyrs

Summary:

Jesus predicts the signs that will immediately precede the end of the world.

SIGNS OF THE END

Lord Jesus, it is near the end of Your life, and You have been speaking to the apostles about the end of the world. Now they come to You privately, asking You: "Tell us, when are these things to happen, and what will be the sign of Thy coming and of the end of the world?"

In answer You say to them: "Take care that no one leads You astray. For many will come in My name, saying, 'I am the Christ,' and they will lead many astray. For you shall hear of wars and rumors of wars. Take care that you do not be alarmed, for these things must come to pass, but the end is not yet. For nation will rise against nation, and kingdom against kingdom; and there will be pestilences and famines and earthquakes in various places. But all these things are the beginning of sorrows. Then they will deliver you up to tribulation, and will put you to death; and you will be hated by all nations for My Name's sake . . . And because iniquity will abound, the charity of the many will grow cold. But whoever perseveres to the end, he shall be saved."

Lord Jesus, Your predictions of the end of time and Your second coming will inevitably come true. Meanwhile the predictions are verified in the individual lives of each one of Your followers, especially Your beloved martyrs.

Martyrs are people who do not let themselves be led astray by false prophets. They do not despair at the ever-present threat of war, famine, earthquake, or other of nature's disturbances; and when ill-will and hatred fix upon them personally and deliver them up to torture and death—strong in love for and faith in You—they say: "Our soul has been delivered as a sparrow out of the snare of the fowlers: the snare is broken, and we are delivered" (offertory verse).

WHOEVER PRESEVERES

Lord Jesus, it cannot be said too often that the martyrs are Your finest achievement. "Our God is wonderful in His saints" (alleluia verse). But it seems to me that this point can be a little over-stressed. What I mean is that the martyrs are wonderful, not only for shedding their blood, but also in their cooperation with Your grace, their response to Your love. Maybe we can settle for the conclusion that martyrdom is the finest achievement known to the world on the part of Your grace and man's response to that grace *taken together*.

And that brings us into the picture. Your grace and love are always present to us in every Mass, and each of Your gospels seeks to draw a response from us. Your truth, Your grace, Your love are available to us in quantities as great as to any martyr in times past.

Lord Jesus, open our eyes to see You, open our hearts to receive You so that—constantly drawing strength from Your own martyrdom made present in daily Mass—You and we together may accomplish the Father's will wherever we may be.

Prayer for the day:

WHOEVER PERSEVERES TO THE END, HE SHALL BE SAVED.

January 20, Sts. Fabian and Sebastian, Martyrs

Gospel No. 8, page 253.

January 21, St. Agnes, Virgin and Martyr

Gospel No. 18, page 272.

* January 22,
Sts. Vincent and Anastasius, Martyrs

Gospel No. 7, page 251.

* January 23,
St. Raymond of Pennafort, Confessor

Gospel No. 15, page 266.

* January 23, St. Emerentiana, Virgin and Martyr

Gospel No. 19a, page 274.

January 24, St. Timothy, Bishop and Martyr

Gospel No. 3, page 244.

January 25, The Conversion of St. Paul

Summary:

Jesus promises a hundredfold reward to all those who have truly left all things to follow Him.

WHO FOLLOW CHRIST

Lord Jesus, you have just expressed yourself very strongly on the subject of the danger of riches; and You have no sooner finished stating Your point of view when Peter speaks up: "Behold, we have left all and followed Thee; what then shall we have?"

You answer: "Amen I say to you that you who have followed Me, in the regeneration when the Son of Man shall sit on the throne of His glory, shall also sit on twelve thrones, judging the twelve tribes of Israel. And everyone who has left house, or brothers, or sisters, or father, or mother, or wife, or children, or lands, for My Name's sake, shall receive a hundredfold, and shall possess life everlasting.

Lord Jesus, St. Paul is not there at this moment to hear You. It will be only after Your death and ascension that You will give him his call to the apostolate. The scene is memorable. He is riding along plotting how he can discover Your followers in Damascus when suddenly a light shines round him. As he falls to the ground, You speak to him: "Saul, Saul, why dost thou persecute Me?" "Who art Thou, Lord?" he asks, and You answer him in a way he never will forget: "I am Jesus, whom thou art persecuting."

The rest of the story is familiar. How You must rejoice at his first words when he knows it is You who speak to him: "Lord, what wilt Thou have me do?" This question of Paul's will characterize and determine his whole life. No more will he think of personal ambitions or convenience or national honor or anything. Only one thing will concern him—Your will, what You want him to do.

CHOSEN VESSEL

You know all of Paul's potentiality for zeal and love and power for good even before You knock him off his horse. As You put it so well to Your disciples in Damascus who are afraid to have anything to do with him: "Go, for this man is a chosen vessel to Me, to carry My name among nations and kings and the children of Israel. For I will show him how much he must suffer for My name."

So this is what You will have him do. He will leave all things and will carry Your name into the whole world. His epistles are a touching record of how he fulfills Your prophecy. For Your name he suffers heart-break, defeat of his projects, betrayal, shipwreck, imprisonment, death. But the vision of You on the Damascus road never leaves him; and love for You drives him on to fill up Your Mystical Body with new members.

"O God, Who hast taught the whole world by the preaching of Blessed Paul the Apostle, grant, we beseech Thee, that we who today celebrate his conversion, may, through his example draw nearer unto Thee" (collect).

Lord Jesus, You who appeared to St. Paul on the way to Damascus appear to us in every Mass. Lord, what wilt Thou have me do? The answer to that question is in Your hands. I am confident of one thing: whatever You decide for me, I know that You will grant the grace to carry it through. With Paul I can say: "I know Whom I have believed, and I am certain that He is able to guard the trust committed to me, against that day, being a just Judge" (introit).

Prayer for the day:
WHO ART THOU LORD? I AM JESUS, WHOM THOU ART PERSECUTING.

January 26, St. Polycarp, Bishop and Martyr

Gospel No. 6, page 250.

January 27, St. John Chrysostom, Bishop and Confessor

Gospel No. 14, page 264.

January 28, St. Peter Nolasco, Confessor

Gospel No. 16, page 268.

January 29, St. Francis of Sales, Bishop and Confessor

Gospel No. 14, page 264.

* January 30, St. Martina, Virgin and Martyr

Gospel No. 18, page 272.

January 31, St. John Bosco, Confessor

Summary:

Jesus teaches that the greatest in the kingdom
of heaven is the one who humbles himself like
a child: whoever receives a child for His sake,
receives Him.

LIKE LITTLE CHILDREN

Lord Jesus, the disciples must be arguing again about degrees of
rank in the kingdom of heaven. Of course, in any such argument
there is only One who has the final word, so to You they come:
"Who then is greatest in the kingdom of heaven?"

You answer by calling for a little child. It isn't hard to find one,
for they love being around You. There is a certain amount of ceremony about Your request this time and about the way in which You
set the child in their midst; for You have a very important life-
lesson to drive home to them and us.

When You are ready and all are quiet, You say: "Amen I say
to you, unless you turn and become like little children, you will not
enter the kingdom of heaven. Whoever, therefore, humbles himself
as this little child, he is the greatest in the kingdom of heaven. And
whoever receives one such little child for My sake, receives Me."

So they have their answer. They are discussing first places in
heaven, and You tell them they won't even get into the kingdom
unless they change their thinking and become like little children.
And then You explain what it means to become like a child. A child
humbles himself. What do You mean by that, Lord?

It seems to me that a child knows that he is important, and he
takes himself very seriously: there is no harm in that. But he knows
that others are so much more important, especially his father and
mother. And so the child makes a practice of trusting utterly in
father and mother. When away from them, the child might become

terror-stricken; but once his hand is in the big hand of the father, fear vanishes. Above all, *a child instinctively wants to be loved and protected*. That is what being a child really means: knowing he is loved.

RECEIVING LITTLE CHILDREN

So You tell us that we too must humble ourselves like little children: we must take ourselves seriously, to be sure, but we must be convinced that You and Your Father love us and will therefore never fail to protect us. And if we feel a strong enough desire to be loved by the Father, he will satisfy that desire. This is really what following You means: giving self over to the love of God.

But You go one step further: whoever receives one such little child for Your sake, receives You. That is what today's Saint has done, and it is receiving little children for Your sake that has made him a Saint. He took You at Your word. But I have an idea that he arrived at his feeling for little children first by being one himself, by applying Your formula in this gospel. Knowing himself to be loved by the Father, he was necessarily driven to be the Father's channel of love into the lives of as many little ones as You led to him.

Lord Jesus, You are wonderful in Your word, wonderful in the Saints Your word has produced, wonderful in the possibilities that this word can still bring about in the lives of all of us: parents, teachers, religious, priests, Sisters, Bishops—anyone but, again, especially parents and teachers. Whoever receives one little child for Your sake receives You. Therefore, we can all receive You again and again.

Help us all to believe that very firmly. But in all the Masses we offer, help us first to put our lives into Your hands, to trust You, and to allow You to carry our whole being into the heart of the heavenly Father. Then we too can be channels of His love into the lives of as many little ones as You lead to us.

Prayer for the day:
WHOEVER RECEIVES ONE SUCH LITTLE CHILD
FOR MY SAKE, RECEIVES ME.

FEASTS OF FEBRUARY

February 1, St. Ignatius, Bishop and Martyr

Summary:

> Jesus says that the grain of wheat must go into
> the ground and die if it is to bring forth fruit.

WHO LOVES HIS LIFE

Lord Jesus, a grain of wheat by itself is a good thing. It can be ground into flour, but not much flour results from one grain of wheat. Another possibility is that it can be planted in the ground; and from the mysterious combining of the inner power within the seed with the warmth of the sun and the moisture in the ground, new life springs forth, so that the original grain of wheat multiplies itself over and over again.

You use this fact of nature to describe a fact of Christianity—the manner of its spread from the beginning and down through the ages, yes, even in our own day. A Christian is a very important person. He or she can do much good by being a channel of Your truth and Your love in a particular environment. You always have and You always will raise up strong and fearless souls whom You use as Your powerful instruments.

This is so in our time as well as in the infancy of Your Church, the so-called age of the martyrs. A man might seem altogether essential to Your work in the Church: he has limitless capacity, achieves excellent success, is looked up to as a vast force for good. Then suddenly You take him away by an accident, or a disease; or the enemies of the Faith do it for You. Or missions are burned, generations of labor are wiped out, priests and Sisters are driven out or killed, and Christianity has to go underground as when Communists capture the government in a country.

Why does God allow such things? The plaintive question makes the rounds. Here is Your answer to the question: unless the grain of wheat falls into the ground and dies, it remains alone. But if it dies, it brings forth much fruit. He who loves his life, loses it; and

331

he who hates his life in this world, keeps it unto life everlasting. If anyone serves You, let him follow You; and where You are, there also shall Your servant be. And if anyone serves You, Your Father will honor him.

SEED OF CHRISTIANS

The human work of men is very necessary in accomplishing Your redemption; but there generally comes a moment in Your over-all plan when results have to be bought by something more precious than labor: they have to be bought by blood. The martyrs are the first ones to recognize this truth. They see their death as the perfection of their love for You and rejoice in Your choosing them for this final glory.

Thus St. Paul cries out: "With Christ I am nailed to the cross: it is now no longer I that live, but Christ in me" (Gal. 2:19-20). And St. Ignatius Martyr says: "I am the wheat of Christ; may I be ground by the teeth of beasts, that I may be found pure bread." And St. Lawrence jokes with his executioners as he lies on the gridiron.

The victory of failure is no idle idea—not since the Victory of Failure that took place on Calvary, reached its climax on Easter Sunday and is now reproduced in the life of this Saint.

Lord Jesus, in the Mass Your sacrificial will to fall into the ground and to die so as to bring forth the fruit of world-redemption is ever present, crying out to us to make it our own will. Lord, train us through the Mass to be ready for life, for death, for anything, just so it means serving and following You.

Prayer for the day:
        IF IT DIES, IT BRINGS FORTH MUCH FRUIT.

February 2,
The Purification of the Blessed Virgin Mary

Summary:

When the days of her purification are accomplished, Mary and Joseph present Jesus in the Temple.

HOLY TO THE LORD

Lord Jesus, although above the Law of Moses (for You are its Author), You freely obey it . . . as does also Your Mother Mary. When the days of her purification are fulfilled, they take You up to Jerusalem to present You to the Lord and to offer a sacrifice according to what is said in the Law of the Lord, "Every male that opens the womb shall be called holy to the Lord."

In Jerusalem there is a just and devout man named Simeon, who for many years has been waiting for the Messias. Your Holy Spirit has revealed to him that he will not die until he beholds You. So, when Mary and Joseph carry You into the Temple, Simeon takes You into his arms and blesses God, saying: "Now Thou dost dismiss Thy servant, O Lord, according to Thy word, in peace; because my eyes have seen Thy salvation, which Thou hast prepared before the face of all peoples: a light of revelation to the Gentiles, and a glory of Thy people Israel."

Lord Jesus, this is the Offertory of Your great Mass of Redemption. In Your name Mary and Joseph present You to the Father. What a serious and solemn moment for You is this first official and external act of obedience to Your Father's will! What love and dedication in Your heart! "Burnt-offering and sin-offering Thou didst not require," You are saying to the Father, "Then I said: Behold I come; in the book it is written of me: To do Thy will, O my God, is my delight, and Thy law is in my very heart" (Psalm 39:8-9).

Here You are then, priest and victim, though but a child. The consecration of this Mass of Redemption is actually thirty-three years in the future. But Your sacrificial will is already set for that moment when You will say: "This is My body which is being given for you . . . This cup is the new covenant in My blood, which shall be shed for you" (Luke 22:19-20).

LIGHT AND GLORY

Every Mass rejoices in co-offerers; and Yours has the best of all. Mary and Joseph bring You to the Temple: theirs is active participation at its peak. They also buy the turtle doves with which to redeem You from the Temple so that they can have You with them in the midst of their family at Nazareth.

And there is Simeon. He has been longing for You to come. You offer Yourself to God, and then (as at our Mass) You give Yourself in "communion" to this man of God. The chasm of infinite longing desire in him is filled. This is heaven for him: "Now Thou dost dismiss Thy servant, O Lord, according to Thy word, in peace; because my eyes have seen Thy salvation."

Then he gives You up again, he restores You to Mary so that she in turn may on the appointed day and year offer You to the fulfillment of Your work of being the salvation which Your Father has prepared before the face of *all* peoples: a light of revelation to the Gentiles, and a glory for Thy people Israel.

Lord Jesus, here we are at the fulfillment that Simeon glimpsed. We come to Your temple with Mary and Joseph, bringing our hearts and our gifts. We stand at Your redemption as You offer Yourself anew in the Consecration; and then we receive You—not into our arms only—but into our bodies, our hearts, our lives. Lord, we have indeed received Your mercy in the midst of Your temple: Great is the Lord, and exceedingly to be praised (introit)!

Now Thou dost dismiss Thy servant, O Lord, according to Thy word, in peace; because my eyes have seen Thy salvation. Praise be to Thee, O Christ!

Prayer for the day:

A LIGHT OF REVELATION TO THE GENTILES, AND A GLORY FOR THY PEOPLE ISRAEL.

* February 3, St. Blaise, Bishop and Martyr

Gospel No. 4, page 246.

February 4, St. Andrew Corsini, Bishop and Confessor

Gospel No. 12, page 261.

February 5, St. Agatha, Virgin and Martyr

Gospel No. 19b, page 277.

February 6, St. Titus, Confessor and Bishop

Summary:
> Jesus appoints seventy-two disciples and sends them out two by two to cure the sick and to announce the kingdom of God.

THE HARVEST GREAT

Lord Jesus, I imagine that Your twelve apostles have helped You to choose these seventy-two disciples. They are to go out in pairs into every town and place where You Yourself are to come. Now they stand before You for final instructions.

First of all, let them know that the work to be done—the souls to be prepared for receiving Your saving word—is greater than their number and their capacity of achievement. As they go out, then, let them at the same time pray that God will prepare and send other laborers worthy of being His representatives and precursors. Thus at the very beginning, You point out to Your disciples that the apostolate is God's work and theirs together—that they must therefore be confident and gratified at being chosen for this work.

Then You point out the difficulty they will run into: first of all, the difficulty within, in the hearts of men. Men resist the spiritual, especially Your brand of teaching on the spiritual, and they resent any attempt to change their thinking on this subject. The disciples, therefore, are being sent as lambs in the midst of wolves. They might very well be eaten up. The risk is theirs to consider and then to accept freely.

But they are men, they are workers for the people, and the worker deserves a living wage. So they will remain in the house of their choice, eating and drinking what the owner puts before them. And whatever town they enter, and into which they are received, they should eat what is set before them, and cure the sick who are there. Above all they are to announce: "The kingdom of God is at hand for you."

THE LABORERS FEW

Lord Jesus, a few verses further on, St. Luke reports on the joy that fills the disciples on their return. "Lord," they cry out as soon as they see You, "even the devils are subject to us in Thy name." You are pleased with their enthusiasm. But You feel it necessary to straighten out their thinking: they are not to rejoice in this that the spirits are subject to them, but rather in the fact that their names are written in heaven. This is the lot of all who do Your work in the apostolate: being associated with You in Your work on earth, they deserve to be associated with You in glory.

Lord, Your commission holds today. The harvest is still great— there is always more work than men. There is still resistance, even more perhaps, and the same temptations nag Your contemporary apostles. But You still expect us to go before You to announce Your Kingdom either as officially commissioned successors of the disciples —Bishops, pastors, missionaries—as lay apostles in their environments, or as religious who by prayer and suffering are able to win from Your Father more laborers for the harvest and spiritual success for those that are there. It cannot be insisted on too much that You depend on men to do Your work for You, whether it be by an active apostolate or by sickness, age and suffering joined to Your cross by strings of love.

Lord Jesus, we will all see our vocation in the right light and will possess the determination to fulfill it if we draw constantly on the wealth of inspiration and love and courage that You hold out to us in every Mass. *Ite, Missa est*—Go, the Mass is ended, You tell us. Go, and do My work; carry Me into your community, your world, your school. What shall we answer? *Deo gratias*—Thanks be to God.

Prayer for the day:

THE HARVEST INDEED IS GREAT, BUT THE LABORERS ARE FEW.

February 7, St. Romuald, Abbot

Gospel No. 17, page 270.

February 8, St. John of Matha, Confessor

Gospel No. 15, page 266.

February 9, St. Cyril of Alexandria, Bishop and Confessor

Gospel No. 14, page 264.

February 10, St. Scholastica, Virgin

Gospel No. 18, page 272.

February 11, The Apparition of Our Lady of Lourdes

Summary:

God sends His angel Gabriel to Mary, to ask her consent to becoming Mother of His Son.

THE VIRGIN'S NAME

Lord Jesus, millions of human beings have waited with great desire for the moment described in this gospel, and hundreds of millions have since warmed their hearts at the sight here pictured. But how quietly and simply it is stated.

A young woman is going about her work in her home in Nazareth. She is a virgin, espoused to a man called Joseph, of the house of David; and her name is Mary. Suddenly she feels that she is no longer alone. And her visitor is not like anyone she has ever seen before. But what are these strange words he speaks: "Hail, full of grace, the Lord is with thee. Blessed art thou among women"?

It is no wonder that she is troubled and that she wonders why he addresses her thus. How should she know that she has been conceived without original sin . . . or that she is full of grace? Why should she be blessed among women? What strange talk from so strange a person!

The angel spares her any lengthy pondering. He speaks again: "Do not be afraid, Mary, for thou has found grace with God. Behold thou shalt conceive in thy womb and shalt bring forth a son; and thou shalt call His name Jesus."

So ends the gospel of today's feast. We know how the evangelist goes on to describe Mary's consent to the plan of God—consent that results in Your taking flesh in her womb. And we know the line of glorious events that follow Your birth.

THOU ART ALL FAIR

But I want to go back to the angel's greeting to Mary: "Hail, full of grace, the Lord is with thee." Your Church has always taken these words as the scriptural backing for her teaching that Mary was immaculately conceived in her mother's womb without any kind of sin.

Many hundreds of years later another young girl is playing and praying near a cave at Lourdes, France. Suddenly she feels that she is not alone. Someone speaks to her. It is Your Mother, and she treats the girl Bernadette with the same gentle kindness that the angel showed to her in Nazareth. She too asks for trust, obedience, and a great act of faith.

Bernadette believes and the Lady, Your Mother, tells her: "I am the Immaculate Conception." And thereafter that cave becomes alive with a mysterious and holy presence.

Ever since, the faithful have flocked by the millions to Mary's shrine at Lourdes, all repeating the angel's greeting: "Hail, Mary, full of grace, the Lord is with thee . . ." But Mary leads them to You, as she always has and always will do. There is much pain and disease there, there are very few healing miracles; but invariably Mary sees to it that the invalids gain sufficient love to turn their suffering into Your redeeming cross.

Lord Jesus, not everyone can go to Lourdes; but we can all go to holy Mass. Holy Mass celebrates and makes present all Your mysteries, including the one described in today's gospel. Here at Mass *You* appear to us, You speak to us, You join us to Your sacrifice, You give us Your flesh to eat and Your blood to drink. What more can anyone desire? Lord, increase our faith!

Lord Jesus, "let the right hand of Thy Immaculate Mother uplift us whom Thou hast fed with this heavenly food, that by her help we may deserve to come to our everlasting home" (postcommunion).

> *Prayer for the day:*
> HAIL, FULL OF GRACE, THE LORD IS WITH THEE.

February 12,
The Seven Holy Founders of the Servites

Gospel No. 17, page 270.

* February 13, Mass of the Preceding Sunday

* February 14, St. Valentine, Priest and Martyr

Gospel No. 5, page 248.

* February 15-17, Mass of the Preceding Sunday

February 18,
St. Marie Bernadette Soubirous, Virgin

Gospel No. 19a, page 274.

* February 19-21, Mass of the Preceding Sunday

February 22, St. Peter's Chair at Antioch

Gospel of Feast of Sts. Peter and Paul, June 29, page 389.

February 23, St. Peter Damian

Gospel No. 14, page 264.

NOTE: During Lent the priest has a choice between the daily Lenten
Mass and the Mass of a Saint when the latter Mass is of double
rank or over.

February 24,
St. Matthias, Apostle (In Leap Year, February 25)

Summary:

No one knows the Son except the Father, and
no one knows the Father but the Son and him
to whom the Son chooses to reveal Him.

REVEALING TO LITTLE ONES

Lord Jesus, those rare occasions when You speak directly to Your
heavenly Father are most precious to us; for You always speak to
Him out of the fullness of Your knowledge and love of Him, as well
as from Your awareness of what we need to hear about Him. You
say to the Father: "I praise Thee, Father, Lord of heaven and earth,
that Thou didst hide these things from the wise and prudent, and
didst reveal them to little ones. Yes, Father, for such was Thy good
pleasure."

I find this remarkable, Lord Jesus—and wonderful, too—that the
Father's revealing of His truth to little ones should cause You to
burst forth in praise of Him. For us to reach out for and to receive
divine truth and revelation from Your Father must be a very glorious thing. I have realized that somewhat before, but never so clearly
as now. But you insist that the motive for praise is to reveal divine
things to little ones and to conceal them from the proud.

Therefore, knowledge of divine things alone is not cause for rejoicing. You are thrilled when this knowledge joins itself to a humble mind. In all this, I do not think You mean to praise ignorance, or an unwillingness to learn theology. But You do want to insist that theology blooms into love and holiness only in a humble mind that is filled with desire for You.

Now You go on to explain the manner in which communication between men and Your Father best takes place. It is through You. "All things have been delivered to Me by My Father; and no one knows the Son except the Father; nor does anyone know the Father except the Son, and him to whom the Son chooses to reveal Him."

LEARN FROM CHRIST

Lord Jesus, Your Church uses this gospel for the feasts of a variety of Your saints. Mother Cabrini was one of the busiest and most active of women; and the first Hermit, St. Paul, withdrew altogether from the world to be alone with You. Others lived out Your will in any number of vocations. The one thing common to all these saintly lives is that *they look at You.* We can do that, too. The more we look at You with love, the more we will know, not only about You, but about the Father. And not only will we know about You, we will know You, You Yourself being the teacher. Nothing matters more than that.

And this knowing You is more than mental deepening. You invite us: "Come to Me, all you who labor and are burdened, and I will give you rest. Take My yoke upon you, and learn from Me, for I am meek and humble of heart; and you will find rest for your souls. For My yoke is easy, and My burden light." You really promise everything, Lord Jesus: rest in our labor and relief from our pain.

But there is that one condition: We have to come to You and take Your yoke upon us. That would be Your cross, Your will. That would be putting our whole life in Your hands; it would be trusting abandon of all our hopes and projects into Your care, expecting You to look after them *because they are Yours,* as we are.

But it is the only way into Your mind and heart: it is the only way to become one of those "little ones," to whom Your Father reveals the fullness of truth which alone can give rest to our souls. Why do we hesitate?

Lord Jesus, You say: "Come to Me." You say it from out of Your presence in this Mass. Well, here we are — not yet very little or humble, but at least suspicious now of pride and over-confidence in self, and full of desire for You. Lord Jesus, teach us to *want* to do Your will. Make us meek and humble of heart.

Prayer for the day:
LEARN FROM ME, FOR I AM MEEK AND HUMBLE OF HEART.

February 25-26, Mass of the Season

February 27,
St. Gabriel of Our Lady of Sorrows, Confessor
(In Leap Year, February 28)

Summary:
Jesus blesses little children and invites a young man to give up all his possessions to come and follow Him.

OF SUCH IS THE KINGDOM

Lord Jesus, St. Mark tells us that when You find out that the disciples rebuke those who are bringing the little children to You so that You may touch them, You are indignant. "Let the little children come to Me," You say to them (and to everyone everywhere), "And do not hinder them, for of such is the kingdom of God. Amen I say to you, whoever does not accept the kingdom of God as a little child will not enter into it." And You put Your arms about the children, and laying Your hands on them, bless them.

Lord Jesus, You cannot help loving these little ones. You are drawn to them and they to You in an intuitive friendship that You insist may not be interrupted. I suspect that You so love them because of their holiness, their innocence unspoiled by worldliness.

You love childlikeness because that is what Christianity is, and no one is a better apostle of Your basic truths than a child.

And the disciples had better take the preaching of these children to heart. Whoever does not accept the kingdom of God as a little child, will not enter in. In other words, whoever does not want to be in their presence and who does not trust in Your Father as a little child trusts his father, will have a hard time getting into the kingdom. And if he should get in, he might not know how to act there; because heaven is a place for little ones.

This is important doctrine; and now comes more of the same. A certain man comes up running, falls on his knees before You, and asks: "Good Master, what shall I do to gain eternal life?" You say, "Why dost thou call Me good? No one is good but only God. Thou knowest the commandments: Thou shalt not commit adultery. Thou shalt not kill. Thou shalt not steal. Thou shalt not bear false witness. Thou shalt not defraud. Honor thy father and mother."

ONE THING LACKING

And the man answers: "Master, all these I have kept ever since I was a child." That is good: You love him for his fidelity to Your law and will. But You hope he will go on from there and choose heroism: "One thing is lacking to thee; go, sell whatever thou hast, and give to the poor, and thou shalt have treasure in heaven; and come, follow Me." St. Mark tells us then that the man's face falls, and he goes away sad, for he has great possessions.

Lord Jesus, You invite both the children and the man to come to You: You really want both them and him. The children accept Your invitation, and their joy in Your presence now is a foretaste of eternity. But when a child grows up, more is expected of him. He has to remain a child, trustful and loving, and then besides he has to be able to act maturely in keeping human values in their correct scale of importance.

You invite the man to go all the way with You. He doesn't really have to. This is a counsel of perfection that You do not even expect all men to accept. This man thinks of his great possessions, he makes his judgment, and goes away sad. His wealth stands between him and You. He leaves You and Your invitation, and You alone know the final outcome of his decision.

Lord Jesus, today's Saint makes up for the failure of the man with the great possessions. He becomes childlike and grows in childlikeness until he reaches the ultimate degree of childlikeness and leaves all things to follow You. Now he is with You forever.

Lord Jesus, in every Mass You invite us to come to You. In the Mass You put Your arms around us and laying hands on us, You bless us. Help us always to see the Mass as the one force that can make and keep us children, that can help us to make judgments that will always keep You in the first place in our lives.

Prayer for the day:
COME, FOLLOW ME.

FEASTS OF MARCH

March 1, 2, 3, 4, 5, Daily Lenten Mass

March 6, Sts. Perpetua and Felicitas, Martyrs

Gospel No. 19a, page 274.

March 7,
St. Thomas Aquinas, Confessor and Doctor

Gospel No. 14, page 264.

March 8, St. John of God, Confessor

Gospel of Mass of 17th Sunday after Pentecost, page 210.

March 9, St. Francis of Rome, Widow

Gospel No. 19a, page 274.

March 10, Daily Lenten Mass

March 11, Daily Lenten Mass

March 12, St. Gregory The Great, Pope

Gospel No. 2, page 242.

March 13-16, Daily Lenten Mass

March 17, St. Patrick, Bishop and Confessor

Summary:

Jesus tells the parable of the talents — the uses to which men put the gifts the master gives them and the manner in which they are rewarded.

A MAN GOING ABROAD

Lord Jesus, You say that the kingdom of heaven is like a man who, before going abroad, hands over his goods to his servants. To one he gives five talents, to another, two, to another, one; to each according to his particular ability.

The five-talent man trades and gains five more; the one with two talents likewise doubles his. But the one who has received one talent digs a hole and buries his master's money, fearing he might lose it. Conservative!

Then after a long time the master returns to settle accounts with the servants. He who has received five talents comes with his gain, saying: "Master, thou didst hand over to me five talents; behold, I have gained five others in addition." The master is pleased: "Well done, good and faithful servant; because thou hast been faithful over a few things, I will set thee over many; enter into the joy of thy master."

And there is a similar expression of satisfaction for the one to whom but two talents are given. The account-rendering of the third man does not belong to this particular selection of the gospel, but we know how displeased the master is with him. What Your Church wants to emphasize today is the positive.

FAITHFUL SERVANT

Lord Jesus, in the fourth century You grant the talents of the Faith to a man named Patrick. That faith is his delight, for it is a personal relationship of love, knowledge and life with You. You see his potentiality for generous self-sacrifice and have him consecrated a bishop by St. Germain of Auxerre in France in 432. Now he is ready for his (and Your) work.

He goes off to Ireland with You in his heart and mind. He loves You, believes in You, wants others to share his love for You. (Willingness to share You is always the true test of the genuineness of faith and love for You). He spends himself for thirty-three years in preaching, teaching, praying, forming communities of Christians until he succeeds in converting the whole land.

When You call to settle accounts with him, he says to You: "Master, Thou didst hand over to me five talents; behold, I have gained five others in addition." (It's kind of an understatement, isn't it, Lord?) And ever since, You have been saying to him as You continue to gather to Yourself the fruits of his evangelizing: "Well done, good and faithful servant; because thou hast been faithful over a few things, I will set thee over many; enter into the joy of the master."

Lord Jesus, St. Patrick shared his faith so completely in his lifetime that no persecution has been able to destroy it. And Patrick lives not only in the hearts of his followers down through time but also in their will to share by their own missionary effort the same faith that he left with them. This is his great glory . . . and Yours. You are indeed wonderful in Your saints.

"O God, Who didst vouchsafe to send Blessed Patrick, Thy confessor and bishop, to preach Thy glory to the Gentiles, grant by his merits and intercession that those things which Thou commandest us to do, we may be enabled to accomplish by Thy mercy" (collect).

Lord Jesus, through the intercession of this Saint, inspire in all of us the determination to share our faith, our love for You.

> *Prayer for the day:*
> WELL DONE, GOOD AND FAITHFUL SERVANT.

March 18,
St. Cyril of Jerusalem, Bishop and Confessor

Summary:
Jesus tells His disciples to expect persecution, but the only ones they are to fear are those who can destroy both soul and body in hell.

DO NOT BE AFRAID

Lord Jesus, sometimes Your teaching on the difficulties that will come to Your followers seems harsh. But far from being harsh or cruel, Your teaching constantly reveals Your love for them. It might have been cruel not to have given it.

The disciples probably understand that fact better after a few years of being Christians than when You first speak to them today: "When they persecute you in one town, flee to another." As Your followers they are to expect persecution, for no disciple is above his teacher, nor is the servant above his master . . . If they have called the master of the house Beelzebub, how much more those of his household. Therefore, do not be afraid of them.

Do not be afraid, You say, but rather go on with the work. For there is nothing concealed that will not be disclosed, and nothing hidden that will not be made known. What You tell them in the darkness, they are to speak in the light; and what they hear whispered, they should preach on the housetops. "And do not be afraid of those who kill the body but cannot kill the soul. But rather be afraid of him who is able to destroy both soul and body in hell."

Lord Jesus, You know the power and extent of the resistance of evil to You and Your teaching. There is no hatred like Satan's, and no limits to the efforts he puts forth to counteract You, Your truth, and the work You will to accomplish for men and for the Father. The disciples must know that in freely enlisting in Your forces, they expose themselves to a considerable amount of attention from Your enemy.

They are, then, to expect persecution and opposition, both from within themselves and from without, from Satan and the world. They might even wonder about their effectiveness as Your disciples if opposition passes them over. The greater the opposition, the closer they are to You, and the more convinced they can be that their efforts are hurting the cause of the opposition.

BODY AND SOUL

Lord, Jesus, You are speaking to all of us. And what amplitude and glory You give to the lives of the least important of us! The one thing necessary is the certitude that You are using us. This certitude of being like You and one with You in the work and in the love and dedication to the Father's will that You communicate to Your followers, is the best preventive against the worst obstacles of all: despair at the enormity of the work, and fear — fear of being thought a fool, fear of failure, fear of personal attack on the part of Satan.

The Work has to go on; the Word has to be preached; the Cross has to fill the world. This is the will of the Father — He will not be denied — and there is no greater honor than to be associated in carrying out that will in any age, in any country.

Lord Jesus, there are few gospels that prepare us to offer Holy Mass as perfectly as this one. Your disciple is at his best as Your true follower when — realizing his own weakness and utter dependence on You — he casts himself into Your Sacred Heart, trusting in the promises You make to him. This we can do at every Mass.

In the Mass, You strengthen our resolution, You give light that renews our vision of life, You identify our martyrdom with Your own, You give Yourself as the guarantee of our final victory in and through You. Praise be to Thee, O Christ!

Prayer for the day:

DO NOT BE AFRAID OF THOSE WHO KILL THE BODY BUT CANNOT KILL THE SOUL.

March 19,
St. Joseph, Spouse of the Blessed Virgin Mary

Summary:

In his sleep Joseph is told that the child whom Mary will bring forth is "of the Holy Spirit."

BETROTHED TO JOSEPH

Lord Jesus, Joseph must be the happiest man in all Israel during those months when he prepares himself and his home for the wife whom he will soon install as queen of that home. He knows the kind of woman Mary is: her simplicity, beauty, and all-around goodness. Joseph is a man's man, a working-man, with a deep capacity for appreciating values. And when a man like that falls in love with a woman like that, he falls all the way so that love literally owns him.

What a shock it must be for him, then, when he learns that Mary is with child. He has never heard of the Holy Spirit before; he knows nothing about that miraculous visit that Mary has had from the Angel Gabriel. He can only conclude either that she has deceived him or that (what is more likely) someone has deceived and taken advantage of her.

In either case, he doesn't feel that he can accept a wife who is carrying another's child; so with a broken heart he plans to put her away and end their betrothal. But it will be privately done, for he is just, and besides he still loves Mary and doesn't want to hurt her by publicly exposing her to common scorn.

It is about time for the Father to step in, Lord Jesus, if He wants Joseph for Your foster father and teacher in all manly virtues. And so He does. He sends His angel to Joseph as the just man lies in his troubled sleep. The angel says to him: "Do not be afraid, Joseph, son of David, to take to thee Mary thy wife, for that which is begotten in her is of the Holy Spirit. And she shall bring forth a Son, and thou shalt call His name Jesus; for He shall save His people from their sins."

JUST MAN

Joseph takes the angel's word: he believes, and his faith carries him off into the stream of the supernatural and the divine that has already swept away Zachary, Elizabeth and Mary. (Faith does things like that.) He rises from sleep, goes over to Mary's house and tells her to get ready for the wedding. And the Father says: "My truth and My mercy shall be with him: and in My name shall his horn be exalted" (offertory verse).

"The just man shall flourish like the palm tree: he shall grow up like the cedar of Libanus: planted in the house of the Lord, in the courts of the house of our God" (introit).

Joseph's house will be truly the house of the Lord; and in that house You will be well off. With Mary and Joseph there will be mutual learning — You from them and they from You. There will be mutual love, prayer, joy, work. And Joseph will not take a back seat. He is the husband of Mary, head of this family, its provider and protector. It is he who will give You Your name Jesus, he who will teach You — You who are His Creator and the Creator of the world — how to make things with Your hands.

"Blessed is the man who fears the Lord: he shall delight exceedingly in His commandments. His seed shall be mighty on earth: the generation of the righteous shall be blessed. Glory and wealth shall be in his house: and his justice remains forever and ever" (tract).

Lord, it is pleasant to evaluate Your admiration for this man. Love reveals itself in trusting, sharing of responsibility with the one loved. You love Joseph so much that You now share the protection of Your Church and of us Your brothers with Joseph. He will do more than his duty by us. "It is good to give praise to the Lord: and to sing to Thy name, O most High" (introit) for having given us such a guide and protector.

Lord Jesus, train us in and through the Mass to conform our wills more and more to Yours so that we may be worthy to share Joseph with You and Your Mother Mary.

> *Prayer for the day:*
> SHE SHALL BRING FORTH A SON, AND THOU SHALT CALL HIS NAME JESUS.

March 20, Daily Lenten Mass

March 21, St. Benedict, Abbot

> *Summary:*
> Jesus promises a hundredfold reward to all those who truly leave all things to follow Him.

WHO FOLLOW CHRIST

Lord Jesus, Peter asks You: "Behold, we have left all and followed Thee; what then shall we have?" Most of us who have gone through the motions of leaving all things have probably thought the same way: we have not asked You Peter's question outright — perhaps because we are afraid in our hearts that we haven't really left all things . . . yet. I suspect that You are more pleased with Peter's directness than with our half-hearted indecisiveness.

You answer Peter: "Amen I say to you, that you who have followed Me, in the regeneration when the Son of Man shall sit on the throne of His glory, shall also sit on twelve thrones, judging the twelve tribes of Israel." I don't know how this strikes Peter. To sit on twelve thrones, judging the twelve tribes of Israel might seem like an important reward to these Jewish pillars of Your Church. We are not impressed.

Then You lift up Your eyes to the future centuries, and You see us and others who have desired to be Your followers in more than an ordinary way. You speak now to us: "Everyone who has left house, or brothers, or sisters, or father, or mother, or wife, or children, or lands, for My Name's sake, shall receive a hundredfold, and shall possess life everlasting."

Your Church applies this promise to abbots who have succeeded in fulfilling its conditions and have therefore become saints. Because an abbot is thought to take Your place in a monastery, he must truly leave all things, since any kind of unworthy attachment makes it very difficult, if not impossible, to serve Your flock. And it is in giving himself to his flock that he fulfills his vocation. There are few who have so perfectly satisfied Your conditions as has St. Benedict.

FOR HIS NAME'S SAKE

In writing his Rule he establishes the criterion of the genuineness of a man's vocation to the monastic life as follows: "Does he truly seek God?" If he truly seeks You, then he belongs, and he is on his way to holiness himself. If he truly seeks and desires You as the most precious value in life, then he will see earthly things in their true light. He will know that these are all good, they have a deep and holy value, but only in relation to You. If the religious gives them up, let him really give them up—not because they are evil—but precisely because they are good, they are the very best gifts to be offered to One whom we seek and desire and love above all things.

This gospel asks all of us some serious questions, whether we be religious or laymen in the world. Laymen, too, must seek God; and they must love things lawful to them *in* God, never permitting these things to become obstacles to union with God.

As for us who are religious, You want us to look into our hearts with the light thrown by St. Benedict's glory. Have we truly sought God up to now? Have we really left all things to follow You alone? Or has the leave-taking been only on paper, as it were, an external wearing of the religious habit that conceals a heart still attached to things and people, making us self- rather than God-centered? I am almost afraid to answer these questions, Lord Jesus, for I know how you despise hypocrisy and any kind of falsification.

Lord Jesus, help us all to leave all things according to our vocation; above all, give us the grace to do this leaving out of love for You. Help us to seek You — not because of the hundredfold (we don't really know what that is) — but because You are *You*.

> *Prayer for the day:*
> BEHOLD, WE HAVE LEFT ALL AND FOLLOWED THEE.

March 22, St. Isidore, the Farm-Laborer, Confessor

Summary:
Jesus is the vine in whom all must abide if they are to bring forth fruit.

TRUE VINE

Lord Jesus, You are at the Last Supper with Your apostles, loving and teaching them to the end. But what is this strange language for such a solemn hour! "I am the true vine, and My Father is the vine-dresser," You say. "Every branch in Me that bears no fruit he will take away; and every branch that bears fruit he will cleanse, that it may bear more fruit."

The apostles may not immediately understand what You are driving at, but, fishermen though most of them are, they are close enough to the soil to know that a fruit tree, or a vine, has to be pruned with a knife, and fruitless branches and suckers have to be cut off so that the whole vine or tree will be healthier. And when the time comes for their own martyrdom, they will remember Your words about the Father cleansing the branches so that they may bear more fruit. They are the branches: their suffering and death will bring strength and fertility to You the vine, You the Church.

You go on to ask them to abide in You. As the branch cannot

bear fruit unless it remain on the vine, so neither can they unless they abide in You. You are the vine, they are the branches. He who abides in You and You in him, he bears much fruit; for without You they can do nothing.

If anyone does not abide in You, he shall be cast outside as the branch and wither; and You shall gather him up and cast him into the fire and he shall burn. If men abide in You, and if Your words abide in them, they are to ask whatever they will, and it shall be done to them.

FRUITFUL BRANCH

Lord Jesus, it is all here in this unforgettable image of the vine and branches: suffering unto spiritual growth, union with You through love and identification of will, the life-relationship between branches, the absolute need that all have of Your grace, the awful destiny of those who cut themselves off from You by serious sin.

You are describing the life and development of Your Church, Your union with all of us who are members of Your Church and our basic relationship to You.

Today we celebrate the feast of a man who becomes a Saint because he takes this word of Yours seriously. Isidore is a farm laborer — to some people not a very impressive profession. But through fidelity to his vocation and the perfect performance of all its duties, big and little, he remains a vital branch on You the vine, abiding in You and You in him so that he finally brings forth fruit of holiness for himself and of inspiring example for all future men and women whom You have called to the dignity of living on the land.

He remains in You and You in him. This is the essential thing. But I like to think that his closeness to the soil and the things that grow from the soil remind him daily of the deep spiritual truth contained in Your words about the vine and the branches.

Speaking to him through the good things of Your creation, You win his gratitude and love. The mouth of the just one meditates the wisdom You put in the world with the result that the law of his God is in his heart (gradual).

Lord Jesus, the same way to holiness is open to all of us. Open our eyes and ears that we may see and hear You speaking to us from the pulpit of Your wonderful creation. And may St. Isidore obtain for us the grace to listen, to respond with love and humility.

Prayer for the day:

HE WHO ABIDES IN ME, AND I IN HIM, HE BEARS MUCH FRUIT.

March 23, Daily Lenten Mass

March 24, St. Gabriel, Archangel

Gospel of Ember Wednesday in Advent, page 8.

March 25,
The Annunciation of the Blessed Virgin Mary

Gospel of the Mass of the Blessed Virgin on Saturday (in Advent), page 281.

March 26, Daily Lenten Mass

March 27, St. John Damascene

Summary:

To the great displeasure of the Pharisees, Jesus on the Sabbath day heals a man with a withered hand.

HAND WITHERED

You are sitting there teaching, Lord Jesus, when suddenly You see the man's hand. The Scribes and Pharisees also see him: it could be that they have even pushed the man to the front so that they can tempt You with him. They want to see if You will cure on the Sabbath, so that they might accuse You. In their eyes it is a very serious thing for You to say a healing word on the Sabbath day or for a diseased body to respond to that healing word and return to wholeness.

You know their thoughts: You say to the man with the withered hand, "Arise and stand forth in the midst." You want everyone to see what his condition is before Your "treatment" and after. It is a tense moment, everyone sensing that they are about to witness a stupendous and extraordinary event. But first You have a question to put to them: "I ask you, is it lawful on the Sabbath to do good, or to do evil; to save life, or to destroy it?"

The answer to Your question should be self-evident. The Sabbath is the Lord's day, the day of honor and worship and sacrifice to Your Father. Not by any abuse of the imagination can there be any conflict between those holy tasks and doing good by saving life and restoring men to health. And the Pharisees know it in their hearts; yet, rather than tell the truth and knowing that falsifying the truth would expose them to ridicule and loss of face with the people, they remain silent.

You look around upon them all waiting for the answer You know will not come. Their silence manifests their thinking. You say to the man: "Stretch forth thy hand." He obeys, and everyone can see what has happened. He now has two whole and good hands; and I wonder if his first act isn't to go to You and touch You with that hand — the hand itself now an instrument of his love and gratitude.

HAND RESTORED

And how do the Pharisees and Scribes react? They should be overjoyed at what they have seen, at the manifestation of divine creative power You have shown to them, or at least they should rejoice at the good fortune of one of their countrymen. But instead they are filled with fury, and begin to discuss among themselves what they should do to You.

Lord Jesus, it could be a ripe subject for reflection, but what would I gain by trying to analyze the crippled mentality of the

Scribes and Pharisees? Except to point out that I have undoubtedly done things just as illogical (and thought similarly), it is much more profitable to concentrate my attention on Your merciful and compassionate heart. That heart is still very busy, the channel of its compassion today being for the most part the Sacraments You have instituted.

In every Mass and in every absolution from sin given by You through Your priests, You say to us: Arise and stand forth in the midst . . . Stretch forth your hand . . . Hold out Your soul to Me. And when we obey, You make us spiritually whole again, working within us a miracle of healing that overshadows by far the miracle we have just seen You perform in the synagogue.

Lord Jesus, may we, recognizing our withered souls, hold them out with longing hope and ever-growing desire for You. Praise and glory and honor and thanks be to You, O Christ!

Prayer for the day:
ARISE AND STAND FORTH IN THE MIDST.

March 28-31, Daily Lenten Mass

FEASTS OF APRIL

April 1, Mass of the Season

April 2, St. Francis of Paula, Confessor

Gospel No. 16, page 268.

April 3, Mass of the Season

April 4, St. Isidore, Bishop and Confessor

Gospel No. 14, page 264.

April 5, St. Vincent Ferrer, Confessor

Gospel No. 15, page 266.

April 6-10, Mass of the Season

April 11, St. Leo the Great, Pope and Confessor

Gospel No. 2, page 242.

April 12, Mass of the Season

* April 13, St. Hermenegild, Martyr

Gospel No. 10, page 257.

April 14, St. Justin, Martyr

Summary:

> Jesus tells us not to be afraid of those who kill the body, but rather of those who are able to cast both soul and body into hell.

THAN MANY SPARROWS

You have been warning Your disciples against the insincerity and hypocrisy of the Pharisees. You do not want Your followers to be insincere or dishonest or false. Don't be fake pretenders to what you are not, You say. In a word, don't try to deceive anyone, least of all your God. Face to face with Him, "There is nothing that will not be disclosed, and nothing hidden that will not be made known."

Then You go on to tell us not to be afraid of persecutors of our body, but to fear only those who have power to cast both body and soul into hell. Better a million times to have one's earthly life cut off a bit prematurely than to spend eternity separated from You in hell.

Not that the prospect of martyrdom is to be lightly considered by anyone. It is a terrifying thing to be killed, as You Yourself well know. But You remind us again that, no matter what happens, the Father who knows all things and who protects those whom He loves will not let us be swept away by panic in the pinch. "Do not be afraid," You say, "you are of much more value than many sparrows. And I say to you, everyone who acknowledges Me before men, him will the Son of Man also acknowledge before the angels of God."

Lord Jesus, at first it is hard to see the connection between martyrdom and Your warning against insincerity. Is it that hypocrisy destroys the will to belong to *You*? The only cause a hypocrite believes in is himself, and even that cause will find him backing down when it is a question of shedding his blood. The opposite of hypocrisy is sincerity, honesty with oneself and with others.

BEFORE THE ANGELS

Essentially a martyr is a person who is utterly sincere about himself, about his beliefs, and the life those beliefs dictate, even though that life will lead him to the loss of his reputation and possibly even his head. There is no making himself out to be anything other than what he is: a Christian, Your follower, a man dedicated to the truth that — because You say so — the Father loves him and will take care of him. In his sincerity, he does his best to acknowledge You before men, to bear witness to His full faith and trust in You, convinced in his heart that You in turn will bear witness to him before the angels of God.

Lord Jesus, I see more and more how much You and Your grace figure in all that makes a saint to be a saint. Grace is everything. As the Psalmist says: "The salvation of the just is from the Lord; He is their refuge in time of trouble" (Psalm 36:39).

But grace is not quite everything. Our sincerity and our honesty is our personal response to You, to Your love and Your grace. But even here, I feel dependent on You. You, by Your divine word and above all by Your sacramental action, can make me more and more sincere. That is to say, You can make me more and more a martyr, more and more a person who bears witness to You everywhere and at all times, not counting the cost in blood, reputation, effort, or possessions. Lord Jesus, teach me to be sincere.

Prayer for the day:
DO NOT BE AFRAID, YOU ARE OF MUCH
MORE VALUE THAN MANY SPARROWS.

* April 15-16, Mass of the Preceding Sunday

* April 17, St. Anicetus, Pope and Martyr

Gospel No. 2, page 242.

* April 18-20, Mass of the Preceding Sunday

April 21, St. Anselm, Bishop and Confessor

Gospel No. 14, page 264.

* April 22,
Sts. Soter and Caius, Popes and Martyrs

Gospel No. 2, page 242.

* April 23, St. George, Martyr

Gospel No. 10, page 257.

April 24, St. Fidelis of Sigmaringen, Martyr

Gospel No. 10, page 257.

April 25, The Greater Litanies

Gospel of Rogation Mass, Page 154. Also

St. Mark, Evangelist

Gospel of Mass of February 6, page 335.

* April 26,
Sts. Cletus and Marcellinus, Popes and Martyrs

Gospel No. 2, page 242.

April 27, St. Peter Canisius, Confessor and Doctor

Gospel No. 14, page 264.

April 28, St. Paul of the Cross, Confessor

Gospel of Mass of February 6, page 335.

April 29, St. Peter of Verona, Martyr

Gospel No. 10, page 257.

April 30, St. Catherine of Siena, Virgin

Gospel No. 18, page 272.

FEASTS OF MAY

May 1, Feast of St. Joseph the Worker

Summary:

> Jesus visits His home town and the people ask where He gets all His wisdom and miracles: Is not this the carpenter's son?

HIS OWN COUNTRY

Lord Jesus, You have been acquiring a great reputation throughout the nation for Your teaching and miracles. You return to Your native countryside. You accept the people's invitation to preach in the synagogues so that they can see for themselves that Your reputation is well founded.

In their astonishment they ask one another: "Where did He get this wisdom and these miracles? Is not this the carpenter's son? Is not his mother called Mary, and his brethren James and Joseph and Simon and Jude? Then where did he get all this?"

The initial doubt in the first of these questions expands rapidly so that in a few minutes it all but destroys the strong evidence of Your teaching and miracles. They say to themselves: this cannot be, not from one of our own. They take offense at You, as You immediately notice with the sad words: "A prophet is not without honor except in his own house." And because of their unbelief, You do not work many miracles there.

Lord Jesus, today we are celebrating the Feast of St. Joseph the Worker; and the Church undoubtedly picks this gospel because of that phrase: "Is not this the carpenter's son?"

It is a good and proper question. Not knowing Your divine origin, they can hardly conclude otherwise. Joseph is a carpenter; they have seen You working in Joseph's shop as other sons have worked in their fathers' shops and stores; so their conclusion is logical. Whether they know it or not, they give You a title that You are proud of.

I don't know if they feel that there is any incompatibility be-

362

tween being a carpenter's son and a great teacher full of wisdom and miraculous power. It would almost seem so. And such an opinion would not be out of the ordinary. Too many people feel that manual labor is a lowly occupation, not quite up to the level of other less smelly and grimy professions.

It is precisely this opinion — still current after all these years — that You and Your Church want to overthrow with this Feast.

You want all of us to realize that laboring men are people, human beings — not numbers or impersonal "hands" — and that what they do has all the honorable dignity of creation itself.

In Nazareth You—who in the beginning created the world out of nothing — now learn from Joseph how to make things out of something; and You don't in the least feel that thereby You have lost any of Your divine stature.

Your example and that of St. Joseph teaches us that You want people to work, to make things with their hands; for this too is part of Your redemption. Man himself is more and more "redeemed" when he makes things, because in making he exercises and perfects his faculties of mind and body, his whole being and personality. Moreover, making things is part of that process of subduing, tilling, and dressing the earth that You began when You first put Adam in Paradise.

This is St. Joseph's Feast, Joseph the Worker. As usual I have concentrated on You, rather than on him; but I'm sure that's all right with Joseph. He doesn't come off so badly himself. What greater compliment could be paid to any man than to have people think and say that *You*, Lord Jesus, Creator, Savior, Worker, are his son. "Is not this the carpenter's son?"

Lord Jesus, by Joseph's intercession and example and Your grace, help us *all* to live up to our dignity as workers in Joseph's tradition.

Prayer for the day:
IS NOT THIS THE CARPENTER'S SON?

May 2, St. Athanasius, Bishop and Doctor

Gospel of March 18, page 347.

May 3, The Finding of the Holy Cross

Summary:

Jesus tells Nicodemus that the Son of Man must be lifted up so that those who believe in Him may not perish, but may have life everlasting.

WATER AND SPIRIT

Lord Jesus, Nicodemus is interested in You, but fearful of being known as Your follower; so he comes to see You at night. "Rabbi, we know that Thou hast come a teacher from God, for no one can do these signs that Thou workest unless God be with him." Nicodemus never spoke truer words. But he isn't quite up to Your answer—Your statement that a man must be born again in order to enter the kingdom of God. How can a man be born again?

You insist on the necessity of rebirth: "Amen, amen, I say to thee, unless a man be born again of water and the Spirit, he cannot enter into the kingdom of God. That which is born of the flesh is flesh; and that which is born of the Spirit is spirit. Do not wonder that I said to thee, 'You must be born again.' The wind blows where it will, and thou hearest its sound but dost not know where it comes or goes. So is everyone who is born of the Spirit."

It is all beyond Nicodemus: "How can these things be?" Then You indicate that as a teacher in Israel and therefore an expert in the Scriptures, he should be aware of meanings beyond meanings in those Scriptures which would make Your present teaching more apparent to him: "Thou art a teacher in Israel and dost not know these things?" You ask.

Well, I am the last one in the world to be critical of Nicodemus and his insensitivity to some of the most mysterious words You have ever spoken. Looking back from here, I can know that You are talking about Baptism's deep effects in the soul — effects so deep-seated that it is like being born again, so that a man lives no longer simply as a man, on a purely natural level, but as one who is dwelled in by Your Holy Spirit. This re-birth is absolutely essential for getting to heaven and knowing how to live when once there. That is why You say, "Unless a man be born again, he cannot see the kingdom of God."

LIFE EVERLASTING

And how does this new life come to us? Not by any power of our own. God alone can share His inner nature, His own divine life. And the way decreed by Your Father for that sharing is through Your Cross. So You say: "As Moses lifted up the serpent in the desert, even so must the Son of Man be lifted up, that those who believe in Him may not perish, but may have life everlasting."

In the Old Testament, those bitten by serpents are healed by looking at a serpent of brass hung upon a cross. Now it is You who hang upon a cross. You become Life to those who come into contact with You by Baptism and faith. We who are baptized and who believe in You will not perish, but will have life everlasting.

Lord Jesus, this is the Feast of the Finding of Your Holy Cross, a day of great rejoicing for us all. "It behooves us to glory in the Cross of our Lord Jesus Christ: in whom is our salvation, life and resurrection: by whom we are saved, and delivered" (introit). It behooves us also to have in ourselves the mind that was in You: You who humbled Yourself and became obedient unto death, even the death of the cross (epistle).

We can do our glorying, our thanking, and we can exercise ourselves in Your mind at holy Mass. As Moses lifted up the serpent in the desert, as You, Son of Man, are lifted up on Calvary, so are You now lifted up on our altars. Lord Jesus, I believe in *You*. Increase my faith so that I may not perish but that, loving You with my whole heart, I may have life everlasting.

Prayer for the day:
THE SON OF MAN MUST BE LIFTED UP.

May 4, St. Monica, Widow

Gospel No. 19a, page 274.

May 5, St. Pius V, Pope and Confessor

Gospel No. 2, page 242.

May 6, St. John Before the Latin Gate

Summary:

Jesus promises suffering rather than political glory to John and James, sons of Zebedee.

A MOTHER'S REQUEST

Lord Jesus, I don't know whose idea it is first — the mother's or the sons'. Like a good mother, she undoubtedly knows their ambitions, and if they are a little shy and hesitant about speaking to You themselves, she's not afraid. So she leads them to You—they, just a little ashamed and wishing they could restrain her.

You know what is in her mind even before You ask: "What dost thou want?" She comes straight to the point: "Command that these my two sons may sit, one at Thy right hand and one at Thy left hand, in Thy kingdom." She has done her part.

But You do not look at her. You turn to them and observe: "You do not know what you are asking for. Can you drink of the cup of which I am about to drink?" You are right: they do not know what they are asking for, at least, not fully. Your idea of the kingdom is not theirs. Yours will be a spiritual kingdom, and preferment in it must be bought with the price of blood. Can they drink the cup that You will drink? Maybe they understand, probably they don't. But they are young and generous. They can have only one answer: "We can."

Your reply is both an acceptance and a prophecy: "Of My cup you shall indeed drink; but as for sitting at My right hand and at My left, that is not mine to give you, but it belongs to those for whom it has been prepared by My Father." James will fulfill the promise literally, entering into Your passion and dying with You as a martyr.

You have other plans for John. He has signified his will to die with and for You and never takes it back; but in Your own mysterious designs, You want him to remain in the world till he is a very old man, turning over in his mind and heart the experiences he has had with You and the words You have spoken and summing up both experiences and words in the phrase: "In this has the love of

God been shown in our case, that God has sent His only-begotten Son into the world that we may live through Him" (I John 4:9).

BURNING OIL

Lord Jesus, today we celebrate the feast of this same John Before The Latin Gate. He has been brought to Rome and condemned to death by being boiled in oil. There is probably no apostle who so wants to die for You. Now, he thinks, is the moment of final union with You. He remembers Your words on this occasion and his answer: "Can you drink of the cup of which I am about to drink?" Over and over again he now repeats, "We can." Then they throw him into the boiling oil, and nothing happens! A miracle saves him.

I wouldn't be surprised if he isn't pretty disappointed, Lord Jesus. But then he remembers Your other words: To sit at My right hand and at My left, that is not Mine to give you, but it belongs to those for whom it has been prepared by My Father. You have taught him and he has learned well. The Father knows best, the Father knows when, the Father knows how. So off he goes into exile at Patmos, off to his visions, to his sacred compositions and his love.

Lord Jesus, in this Mass our Mother the Church brings us, her sons, to You. There are no longer any requests for political advancement, but only for full participation in You and Your sacrifice. You ask us: "Can you drink of the cup of which I am about to drink?" There can be only one answer: We can. Or we hope that the intercession of John, his inspired words and example, and our own constant practice may add sincerity, conviction and eventual perfection to our drinking of Your Chalice.

> *Prayer for the day:*
> OF MY CUP YOU SHALL INDEED DRINK.

May 7, St. Stanislaus, Bishop and Martyr

Gospel No. 10, page 257.

May 8, The Apparition of St. Michael, Archangel

Gospel of the Feast of St. Michael, September 29, page 436.

May 9,
St. Gregory Nazianzen, Bishop and Doctor

Gospel No. 14, page 264.

May 10, St. Antoninus, Bishop and Confessor

Gospel No. 12, page 261.

May 11, Sts. Philip and James, Apostles

Summary:

At the Last Supper, Philip asks Jesus to show them the Father and is told that to see Him is to see the Father.

WAY, TRUTH, LIFE

Lord, Jesus, Your merciful understanding of the human limitations of Your apostles is never more apparent than at the Last Supper where You reveal the deepest aspects of Your relation to the Father and the Holy Spirit, together with teaching on Your own nature, work, and future intentions. They are terribly sad at the Last Supper — sad at the news, now clear to them as never before, that You are about to leave them in some mysterious and frightening manner. You feel for them.

So You say to them: "Let not your heart be troubled. You believe in God, believe also in Me. In My Father's house there are many mansions. Were it not so, I should have told you, because I go to prepare a place for you. And if I go and prepare a place for you, I am coming again, and I will take you to Myself; that where I am, there you also may be. And where I go you know, and the way you know."

All this is not too clear to Thomas: "Lord, we do not know where Thou art going, and how can we know the way." Your answer to him is unforgettable: "I am the way, and the truth, and the life. No one comes to the Father but through Me. If you had known Me, you would have known My Father . . . ."

Now it is Philip's turn to draw from You one of the deepest of theological truths: "Lord, show us the Father and it is enough for us." There is a hint of disappointment in Your voice now, as though You wondered about the effectiveness of all Your special teaching to them: "Philip, he who sees Me sees also the Father. How canst thou say, 'Show us the Father?' Dost thou not believe that I am in the Father and the Father in Me? The words that I speak to you I speak not on My own authority. But the Father dwelling in Me, it is He who does the works . . . Amen, amen, I say to you, he who believes in Me, the works that I do he shall do, and greater than these he shall do, because I am going to the Father. And whatever You ask in My Name, that I will do, in order that the Father may be glorified in the Son. If you ask Me anything in My Name, I will do it."

WHATEVER YOU ASK

So You speak to the apostles at the Last Supper, Lord Jesus, of being one with the Father, of being our intercessor with Him, of being the carrier of our prayers to the Father. At this same Last Supper, You institute the Holy Sacrifice of the Mass with the result that now everything You have said and done and promised at the Last Supper is said and done and fulfilled in our midst.

At every Mass, knowing our worry, pain, fear and uncertainty, You say to us: Let not your heart be troubled. You believe in God, believe also in Me . . . I am the way, the truth, and the life. (You really are that in the Mass!) . . . He who sees Me, sees also the Father . . . The words that I speak I speak not on My own authority . . . Whatever you ask in My name, that I will do.

Lord Jesus, if that's the way You speak, I have only one answer: increase my faith, make it a living faith, so that all these truths may become the food for my spirit that You intend them to be. You cannot go back on Your promise: "Whatever you ask in My name, that I will do, in order that the Father may be glorified in the Son."

Lord Jesus, using this Mass which is offered in Your Name as my strong and violent prayer, I ask for faith in *You.*

Prayer for the day:
PHILIP, HE WHO SEES ME SEES ALSO THE FATHER.

* May 12,
Sts. Nereus, Achilleus, Domitilla and Pancras, Martyrs

Gospel of Twentieth Sunday after Pentecost, page 222.

May 13,
St. Robert Bellarmine, Bishop and Doctor

Gospel No. 14, page 264.

* May 14, St. Boniface, Martyr

Gospel No. 10, page 257.

May 15,
St. John Baptist De La Salle, Confessor

Gospel of January 31, page 329.

* May 16, St. Ubaldus, Bishop and Confessor

Gospel No. 12, page 261.

May 17, St. Paschal Baylon, Confessor

Gospel No. 15, page 266.

May 18, St. Venantius, Martyr

During Easter Season, Gospel No. 10, page 257.

After Easter Season, Gospel No. 5, page 248.

May 19, St. Peter Celestine, Pope and Confessor

Gospel No. 2, page 242.

* May 20, St. Bernardine of Siena, Confessor

Gospel No. 15, page 266.

* May 21-24, Mass of Preceding Sunday

May 25, St. Gregory VII, Pope and Confessor

Gospel No. 2, page 242.

May 26, St. Philip Neri, Confessor

Gospel No. 15, page 266.

May 27,
St. Bede the Venerable, Confessor and Doctor

Gospel No. 14, page 264.

May 28,
St. Augustine of Canterbury, Bishop and Confessor

Gospel of February 6, page 335.

* May 29, St. Mary Magdalen of Pazzi, Virgin

Gospel No. 18, page 272.

* May 30, St. Felix, Pope and Martyr

Gospel No. 2, page 242.

May 31,
Queenship of the Blessed Virgin Mary

Summary:

The angel Gabriel is sent to announce to Mary that she will bring forth a son who shall be called the Son of the Most High, and of His kingdom there shall be no end.

FULL OF GRACE

Lord Jesus, the Father sends Gabriel to a town of Galilee called Nazareth where Mary lives. The angel greets her very mysteriously: "Hail, full of grace, the Lord is with thee. Blessed art thou among women." She is puzzled and Gabriel sees it in her face. "Do not be afraid, Mary, for thou hast found grace with God. Behold, thou shalt conceive in thy womb and shalt bring forth a son; and thou shalt call His name Jesus. He shall be great, and shall be called the Son of the Most High; and the Lord God will give Him the throne of David his father, and He shall be king over the house of Jacob forever; and of His kingdom there shall be no end."

Lord Jesus, we know what follows — Mary's consent which brings You into her womb, the journey that You and she take to visit Elizabeth and John, John's birth and Your own. I never tire of recalling those blessed events.

But today we are celebrating the feast of the Queenship of Your Blessed Mother. Queen Mary is her title. She is Queen of Angels, of Patriarchs, Prophets, Apostles, Martyrs, Confessors, Virgins, Queen of all Saints, Queen conceived without original sin, Queen assumed into heaven, Queen of the Most Holy Rosary, Queen of Peace.

QUEEN MOTHER

Mary belongs to David's royal line, but she doesn't live in any palace. And the man she is engaged to — also of David's lineage — is a very humble carpenter. So she does have royal blood. But it isn't royal blood that gives her a right to be called Queen. It is because she conceives in her womb and gives birth to a King, to You, Son of God, Lord of the universe, King of Kings. "The Lord God will give Him the throne of David his father, and He shall be king over the house of Jacob forever; and of His kingdom there shall be no end."

If You are to be King over the house of Jacob forever, it is simple logic that Mary Your Mother will be queen, and if Your kingdom shall have no end, neither shall hers.

Lord Jesus, we know Mary most of all as our Mother, and that's all right with her, I'm sure. But being our Mother, she has to care for us, protect and guide us (just as she had to do with You.) Giving her her rightful title as Queen is simply turning the tables on her and giving her her due. Loving homage is due to queens. And that's what we want to give her in this feast, together with our fellow subjects in this world and the next.

And what is the best way of showing this homage? Here there can be only one answer. We give her what is most precious to her — You, her Son, in this sacrifice of the Mass. And we give ourselves with You. Lord Jesus, purify and perfect our love for Mary, Your Mother and ours. Hail, holy Queen, Mother of mercy, our life, our sweetness, and our hope!

> **Prayer for the day:**
> **DO NOT BE AFRAID, MARY, FOR THOU HAST FOUND GRACE WITH GOD.**

FEASTS OF JUNE

* June 1, Mass of the Preceding Sunday

* June 2,
Sts. Marcellinus and Peter, Martyrs; St. Erasmus, Martyr

Gospel No. 7, page 251.

* June 3, Mass of the Preceding Sunday

June 4, St. Francis Caracciolo, Confessor

Gospel No. 15, page 266.

June 5, St. Boniface, Bishop and Martyr

Gospel of All Saints Day, page 451.

June 6, St. Norbert, Bishop and Confessor

Gospel No. 12, page 261.

* June 7-8, Mass of the Preceding Sunday

* June 9, Sts. Primus and Felician, Martyrs

Gospel of Feast of St. Matthias, February 24, page 340.

* June 10,
St. Margaret, Queen of Scotland, Widow,

Gospel No. 19a, page 274.

June 11, Feast of St. Barnabas

Summary:

Jesus prepares His disciples for the apostolate by promising that they will be persecuted, delivered up and killed for His Name's sake.

SENDING YOU FORTH

Lord Jesus, when You send the disciples out to continue Your work, You predict the worst kind of life for them: scourging, scorn, hatred, disgrace, death. "Behold, I am sending you forth like sheep in the midst of wolves," You tell them. A sheep in the midst of wolves hasn't a chance in the world to survive. You know — and they suspect—that Your prophecy will be fulfilled. Nevertheless, You invite them into the apostolate, and they accept. It is madness.

Lord Jesus, as I try to figure out the why of it all, all the old clichés come to mind: that it is Your work they are to do; and as they persecuted You, so must they inevitably persecute Your workers; that the world immersed in materialistic philosophy feels offended and annoyed by spiritual ideals; that Your presence in the world implies the need for conversion on the part of those who adore the false god of self-will (and who wants to be converted?). All this is true; but there is still something very mysterious about it all.

Think as I will about what makes apostles so spend themselves, I always come back to the mysterious bases of all religion: the supremacy of Your Father, the absolute necessity for all men to worship Him, and the need of men to know how to fulfill their destiny in the light of the supremacy of God. "As the Father has sent Me, I also send you," You have said. Nothing can or must stand in the way of that sending — not the unwillingness of men to accept, nor the weakness of men to carry the message. It is so well stated in the epistle: "The Holy Spirit said: 'Set apart for Me Saul and Barnabas unto the work to which I have called them.'"

MY NAME'S SAKE

The infinite lovableness of the Father imposes itself on men, inviting from them the response and the desire for union with Him that alone can save and give joy. This and this alone matters. If lives are lost or torture inflicted, it simply means that torture and death are the necessary means that release love from its hiding place in the apostles' hearts. And it is only love that brings salvation . . . both for the "victims" and for those who inflict the persecution.

Lord Jesus, Your prophecy is still being fulfilled today in many parts of the world. Modern Barnabases, Peters, Pauls, Andrews and Thomases are being treated like sheep in the midst of wolves. But so spreads the Faith, so grows love for Your heavenly Father, and last but not least, so expands happiness and joy among men.

But what about us? In Baptism You have called each of us to be members of Your apostolic, missionary Church. Baptism and Confirmation commission us to be Your apostles now. Are we too to expect persecution and death? That is in Your hands. Bloody martyrdom is not the inevitable and only climax to being an apostle. But the will to do what You will for us, the desire to spend ourselves in prayer and active work (when possible according to our state of life) in order to make the Father more loved by all men — this is necessary and it is possible for all of us.

Lord Jesus, grant that the zeal and example of Your blessed apostle, Barnabas, may inspire us to live for You as he has done. By the intercession of Blessed Barnabas, Thy apostle, cleanse us from the stains of our sins—and from our unwillingness to work for You (secret).

Prayer for the day:
HE WHO HAS PERSEVERED TO THE END WILL BE SAVED.

June 12, St. John of St. Facundo, Confessor

Gospel No. 15, page 266.

June 13, St. Anthony of Padua, Confessor

Gospel No. 14, page 264.

June 14, St. Basil the Great, Bishop and Doctor

Summary:

Jesus demands whole-hearted service from those who would be His disciples.

EVEN HIS OWN LIFE

Lord Jesus, Your words are surely very startling: If any one comes after You and does not hate his father and mother, and wife and children, and brothers and sisters, yes, even his own life, he cannot be Your disciple. And he who does not carry his cross and follow You, cannot be Your disciple.

I do not believe You actually mean that we must hate anyone who stands in the way to being Your disciple, for that would go against all Your strong teaching about loving one another as You have loved us. The ordinary meaning of the word "hate" implies ill-will towards a person. Surely You do not want us to will evil to anyone — relative, friend, or enemy.

The note in my New Testament says that the word "hate" here means to "love less," and that makes sense. We must keep our values straight: no human attachment to people or things or self can stand in the way of following You and doing your apostolic work, once You have chosen us for that work.

This means total dedication to You even as You have been totally dedicated to the Father and to what He wants done in the world. Once more, it is the supremacy of God that is at issue. Once I see that one vital fact, all human objections fade to their proper stature of the important-but-not-the-essential.

In other words, this life that You have given me is not mine exclusively. It implies an obligation and a responsibility to You, to Your Church, to the saving of souls, to the glory of the Father. It is only in *selfless* living for You and Your cause that I will be saved and the world made holier. And any kind of interference with this selflessness from family, friends, possessions, and above all, from my own comfort and convenience must be put in its proper place. This is not easy doctrine, but Your cross has no mattress on it.

SALT IS GOOD

You go on to tell about the necessary preparations that have to be made for building a tower or for engaging in battle. There is no point in starting anything unless one has the wherewithal to carry it through. Then You conclude: "So, therefore, every one of you who does not renounce all that he possesses, cannot be My disciple. Salt is good; but if even the salt loses its strength, what shall it be seasoned with? It is fit neither for the land nor for the manure heap, but must be thrown out. He who has ears to hear, let him hear."

The lesson is unmistakable: to carry through in Your apostolic work, we have to be free from any attachments that might diminish full attention to You and Your saving will. The fullness of the apostolate demands fullness of renouncement and complete gift of one's life to You. This alone makes us worthy instruments for Your powerful work. For an apostle to be satisfied with anything less is to expose himself to the danger of being neither an apostle nor even an ordinary Christian; for he has lost his strength and is fit for nothing but to be cast out.

O God, the Rewarder of faithful souls, grant that, by the prayers of Blessed Basil, Your Confessor and Bishop, whose venerable feast we celebrate, we may obtain pardon of our sins (postcommunion). And may his example and intercession inspire us all to take up our cross and follow You according to the vocation to which You call each of us.

Prayer for the day:

HE WHO DOES NOT CARRY HIS CROSS AND
FOLLOW ME, CANNOT BE MY DISCIPLE.

* June 15,
Sts. Vitus, Modestus, and Crescentia, Martyrs

Summary:

Jesus sends His disciples into the towns to prepare the way for Him; he who hears them,
hears Him; and he who rejects them, rejects
Him.

HEARING AND REJECTING

Lord Jesus, in the preceding verses of this chapter You tell about Your sending the seventy-two disciples out in pairs into the towns of the countryside to cure the sick and to announce that the kingdom of God is at hand for them.

If they are not well received, they should go out into the streets of the town and say, "Even the dust from your town that cleaves to us we shake off against you; yet know this that the kingdom of God is at hand." If they reject You as their Savior, they cannot escape meeting You as their judge. "I say to you, that it will be more tolerable for Sodom in that day than for that town."

Now You seal the commission of the disciples in these terms: "He who hears you, hears Me; and he who rejects you, rejects Me; and he who rejects Me, rejects Him who sent Me."

So it is in Your day, and so it continues to be in ours. There is a chain of delegation from the Father to You, from You to the apostles, from the apostles to bishops, and from bishops to priests and the laity. You make the conveying of truth depend both on the zeal and conviction of the disciple and on the receptivity of the hearers, most of all the latter.

But You will never force Yourself on anyone, either disciple or hearer. The disciple should rejoice — not in results like having devils subject to them, or other sensational effects of their apostolate — but in the fact that they are doing Your work and that therefore their names are written in heaven. (I wonder if You mean by this that sincere dedication to Your apostolate is a sure sign of predestination?)

RIVER OF INTERCESSION

For the hearer now, just as in Your day, his rejecting of Your disciple bearing Your way of life and Your truth is his privilege as a free man. But if he decides against the disciple, he decides against You; and deciding against You, he decides against Your Father. So powerful is the freedom of man, either for his personal destruction or his salvation. That is the way You have made him. So be it.

Today's Feast is a feast of martyrs, two men and a woman who were rejected by those to whom You sent them. They preached the truth and it was refused. So they preached louder and more effectively by shedding their blood. "God is wonderful in His saints, the God of Israel is He who will give power and strength to His people: blessed be God" (offertory verse).

Their blood becomes part of a river of intercession that washes humanity even unto our time and unto the end of time, bringing forth greater and greater receptivity to Your Person and Your truth among men. "The Saints shall bless Thee, O Lord: they shall speak of the glory of Thy kingdom" (alleluia verse).

Lord Jesus, plunge me into that river of intercession by plunging me into this Mass that I may become more and more receptive to You and Your truth and may thus become more and more myself a carrier of Your truth and love into our world.

> *Prayer for the day:*
> REJOICE RATHER IN THIS, THAT YOUR NAMES
> ARE WRITTEN IN HEAVEN.

* June 16-17, Mass of Preceding Sunday

June 18,
St. Ephrem the Syrian, Confessor and Doctor

Gospel No. 14, page 264.

June 19, St. Juliana Falconieri, Virgin

Gospel No. 18, page 272.

(Same day, Sts. Gervase and Protase, Martyrs

Gospel No. 9, page 255).

* June 20, St. Silverius, Pope and Martyr

Gospel No. 2, page 242.

June 21, St. Aloysius Gonzaga, Confessor

Summary:

Jesus teaches that the whole Law is summed up in total love of God and love of one's neighbor as oneself.

GOD OF THE LIVING

Lord Jesus, You are saying to the Sadducees who do not believe in the resurrection, "You err because you know neither the Scriptures nor the power of God. For at the resurrection they will neither marry nor be given in marriage, but will be as angels of God in heaven. But as to the resurrection of the dead, have you not read what was spoken to you by God, saying 'I am the God of Abraham, and the God of Isaac, and the God of Jacob'? He is not the God of the dead, but of the living."

Lord, it might very well be that at the resurrection men will be like angels; but I don't believe You wish to teach that we are angels now, forgetting that we also have bodies. You have made us as we are — with bodies as well as spiritual souls. And we are to go to You as we are: as body-spirit beings.

That is the way Your Saint, Aloysius, did it. He was a man, every inch of him, despite the way he is sometimes pictured, as though he were in fact an angel who never knew he had a body, never knew what it was to be tempted. I cannot believe that this is so. His body was probably just as rebellious against his spirit as our bodies are.

But early in life he learned a secret that made all self-discipline seem — not easy, it never is for anyone — but logical and natural. The last part of today's gospel contains the secret. In answer to the Pharisee's question about the great commandment in the Law, You say: "Thou shalt love the Lord thy God with thy whole heart, and with thy whole soul, and with thy whole mind. This is the greatest and the first commandment. And the second is like it, Thou shalt love thy neighbor as thyself. On these two commandments depend the whole Law and the Prophets."

PURIFYING LOVE

Loving You as he did — with all the power of his heart — how could he help being pure? I wonder if that all-out love for You isn't still the best remedy for overcoming temptations to impurity.

Lord Jesus, there are materialists abroad today who do not believe in the resurrection of the body either. They want to consider man as an end in himself, made only for the pleasure of the moment. Your teaching, made flesh in the person of St. Aloysius, condemns such persons good and proper. If they let their bodily instincts control them, they will burn in hell as men, body and soul.

There are others in our midst who would like to forget that they are bodies and would enjoy hearing religion defined exclusively as spiritual relationship with You. But You say that in addition to loving God with our whole heart, we must also love our neighbor. And love of neighbor is more than a purely spiritual sensation or feeling. It must be made flesh in positive works of mercy like feeding the hungry, clothing the naked, visiting the sick and imprisoned.

There can be, You have told us, no true love of God if it is not shown outwardly in love of man. As You inspired St. John to write: "He who has the goods of this world and sees his brother in need and closes his heart to him, how does the love of God abide in him? My dear children, let us not love in word, neither with the tongue, but in deed and in truth" (I John 3:17-18). So neither can there be purity without love. But I must continue to think that St. Aloysius loved his body and did not despise it. He was a man, and he knew how You made man.

Love, being the basis of his purity, makes him Your glory. You have crowned him with glory and honor. In this Mass we praise You, Lord Jesus, we who are men, we who have bodies as well as souls. We join our voices to those of the angels in praising You for accomplishing Your will in Aloysius, who was not an angel, but a man who learned the lesson that love for You can do all things.

Prayer for the day:

> THOU SHALT LOVE THE LORD THY GOD WITH THY WHOLE HEART.

June 22, St. Paulinus, Bishop and Confessor

Gospel No. 16, page 268.

June 23, Vigil of the Nativity of St. John the Baptist

Summary:

> The Archangel Gabriel appears to Zachary to tell him that he will beget a son and call him John.

JUST BEFORE GOD

Lord Jesus, both Zachary and his wife Elizabeth are just and faithful, walking blamelessly in all Your commandments and ordinances. But they have no son, Elizabeth being barren these many years. And now both are quite old. Zachary has been taking his turn officiating in the order of his course as a priest before God when he is chosen one day by lot to enter into the temple to burn incense.

Outside the people are praying at the hour of incense. Within Zachary is going about his duty of offering the sweet-smelling smoke. Suddenly he senses that he is not alone. He looks to the right of the altar of incense and sees an angel standing there. He is troubled and filled with fear.

The angel speaks to him: "Do not be afraid, Zachary, for thy petition has been heard, and thy wife, Elizabeth, shall bear a son and thou shalt call his name John." So, Lord Jesus, Zachary has been praying for a son these many years; he is still praying in spite of the barrenness of Elizabeth and the advanced age of both of them. He has in fact been praying for a miracle. Well, the age of miracles is about to begin. Because of his perseverance and faith, he is to be heard. But the son he will beget will be no ordinary child.

The angel continues: "Thou shalt have joy and gladness, and many will rejoice at his birth. For he shall be great before the Lord; he shall drink no wine or strong drink, and shall be filled with the Holy Spirit even from his mother's womb. And he shall bring back to the Lord many of the children of Israel, and he shall himself go before Him in the spirit and power of Elias, to turn the hearts of fathers to their children and the incredulous to the wisdom of the just; to prepare for the Lord a perfect people."

FIDELITY'S REWARD

So do You announce the birth of Your Precursor to the Precursor's father. The following verses of St. Luke's gospel relate how Zachary is struck dumb because of his doubting Your angel's word, how the people realize that he has seen a vision in the temple, how he goes back to his house and the angel's word is fulfilled. Elizabeth conceives and secludes herself for five months, saying, "Thus has the Lord dealt with me in the days when He deigned to take away my reproach among men" (Luke 1:18-26).

Lord Jesus, it is a high moment in history, and it is fitting that the temple in Jerusalem should be the scene of this pressing and momentous announcement of long-awaited redemption. Many years of fidelity to the Law, of longing hope and preparation are summed up in this good man and his wife. Fidelity and simplicity of life with the privilege of bearing the son who will go before You to prepare Your way.

It is fitting too that the announcement should come at a serious moment in Old Testament worship, for it answers all the prayers that have been said these many years and it announces the fulfillment first in John and then in You of the perfection of all worship.

Lord Jesus, in holy Mass we share in the worship that sums up and fulfills all the longing of the Old Testament people and their praying—that sums up also all of the work of John and all of the redeeming work of the One whose way John has prepared, You, Jesus Christ our Lord.

"Sanctify, O Lord, the gifts we offer, and by the intercession of Blessed John the Baptist, cleanse us through them from the stains of our sins" (secret).

> *Prayer for the day:*
> **DO NOT BE AFRAID, ZACHARY, FOR THY PETITION HAS BEEN HEARD.**

June 24,
Nativity of St. John the Baptist

> *Summary:*
> **Elizabeth brings forth a son, and on the eighth day he is circumcised and given the name John.**

JOHN IS HIS NAME

Lord Jesus, I wonder if You were there for this big celebration. St. Luke tells us how Your Mother Mary goes off to help Elizabeth as soon as she receives You into her womb; how You thrill Elizabeth and John when they first behold Mary; and how Mary stays nearly three months with Elizabeth and then returns to her own house. The evangelist doesn't say so, but it seems to me about the most natural thing in the world for Mary to have presided over John's birth and then to have waited just eight days more for the joyous day of his circumcision. Well, if You and Mary aren't there in person, You know what is going on, and You know that You are the real center of the day.

It is, of course, altogether extraordinary and wonderful that this should happen to Elizabeth, a fact that is well recognized by Elizabeth's neighbors and kinsfolk who have heard that the Lord has magnified His mercy towards her. Now the rite of circumcision is being performed. The enthusiastic relatives want to call the child by his father's name, Zachary. But his mother will have none of that. The child has already been named by heaven itself. And she insists on the name John against all the protests of the relatives.

They can do nothing with the mother so they make signs to the father. He asks for a writing-tablet and writes, "John is his name." And they all marvel the more. But this is just the beginning. Zachary, who has been struck dumb because of his hesitancy to believe the archangel Gabriel, now opens his mouth and begins to speak, blessing God.

BLESSED BE THE LORD

Wonderment then turns to fear as the people begin to catch on that they are associating here with the workings of their mysterious, awe-inspiring, Lord and Master, their God. "What then will this child be?" they ask themselves, for obviously the hand of the Lord is with them. And now Zachary, being filled with Your Holy Spirit, prophesies saying, "Blessed be the Lord, the God of Israel, because He has visited and wrought redemption for His people."

What then will this child be? We know what he will be. "Thou, child," his father predicts, "shalt be called the prophet of the Most High, thou shalt go before the Lord to prepare His ways" (alleluia verse). He will fulfill that prophecy to the letter. No one has ever had a stronger sense of vocation than he; no one has ever been more humble (though next to Your Mother he is the greatest of the saints).

He knows that he is great, that he is born without original sin, that his work is a divine work. But he also knows that You are greater. The day will come when his followers will leave him and adhere to You. Then will come his beautiful tribute to You: "He who has the bride is the bridegroom; but the friend of the bridegroom, who stands and hears him, rejoices exceedingly at the voice of the bridegroom. This my joy, therefore, is made full. He must increase, but I must decrease" (John 3:29-30).

A man of such stature—loving You so much and being so loved in return—can never die. You live, and John lives. He still prepares us for You. Like a chosen arrow, he aims himself straight at our self-will, weakness, and pride—all obstacles to Your total ruling within us.

But he prepares us also by his example of interior intimacy with You. You are the Bridegroom, he is Your friend who rejoices exceedingly at Your voice speaking to him. Lord Jesus, through the intercession of John still living with You, grant me the grace to be like him, the friend of the Bridegroom, rejoicing constantly at hearing Your voice, and determined more and more to go before You preparing the way for You into the hearts of all those whom Your Father sends my way. "It is good to give praise to the Lord, and to sing to Thy Name, O Most High" (introit).

Prayer for the day:
BLESSED BE THE LORD, THE GOD OF ISRAEL, BECAUSE HE HAS VISITED AND WROUGHT REDEMPTION FOR HIS PEOPLE.

June 25, St. William, Abbot

Gospel No. 17, page 270.

June 26, Sts. John and Paul, Martyrs

Gospel No. 9, page 255.

* June 27, Mass of Preceding Sunday

June 28, St. Irenaeus, Bishop and Martyr

Gospel No. 6, page 250.

or

June 28, Vigil of Saints Peter and Paul

Summary:

Jesus demands a threefold confession of love from Peter.

LORD, THOU KNOWEST

Lord Jesus, it is after You have died and risen that this gospel takes place. The memory of his three-fold denial of You is still fresh in Peter's memory. Now You stand before him and say: "Simon, son of John, dost thou love me more than these do?"

Peter remembers all that You have done for him, Your having chosen him to be head of Your Church, Your having washed his feet, Your friendship. He answers: "Yes, Lord, Thou knowest that I love Thee." And You do know, Lord Jesus. "Feed My lambs," You command him, knowing that the lambs—the souls that You, Good Shepherd that You are, have laid down Your life for—will be in good hands.

The dialogue goes on. Three times denying that he knows You require a threefold declaration that he loves You (the formula is Your very own: love can wipe out the greatest sin). I don't suppose there is a more sincere and heartfelt declaration of love in all the Scriptures than Peter's final profession: "Lord, Thou knowest all things, Thou knowest that I love Thee." He is right: You know, but You want him to say it. He will remember it better that way. "Feed My sheep," You command him. And he will.

Then You look into the future, and You see the way in which he will prove his love: "Amen, amen I say to thee, when thou wast young, thou didst gird thyself and walk where thou wouldst. But when thou art old thou wilt stretch forth thy hands, and another will gird thee, and lead thee where thou wouldst not." St. John tells us that You say this to signify by what manner of death Peter would die.

THAT I LOVE THEE

Because of Peter's love, but above all, because of Your answer to that love when You say, "Feed My lambs . . . Feed My sheep,"

Peter is continued in our Holy Father. In his teaching and in the sacraments, the Pope continues to feed Your lambs and Your sheep with Your holy truth and Your divine Life. The Pope is the visible manifestation of Your love for us. He is our good shepherd.

But back to Peter for a moment and to a consideration of how much he really is our leader even after these many years. We do not need a leader in order to sin: we do that well enough ourselves. But to return to You, to know the way back from sin to Your forgiving Heart, is another matter.

Peter is so much one of us because of his sin. He is so much our head because of his repentance. He is so much our shepherd because of his love. We have all denied You not once, but many times. No matter how often we sin, You stand before us. You do not mention the sin, there is no need for that. Both You and we know it. You simply say, "My child, dost thou love me?" You say it in confession, You say it in this and all Masses.

Please, Lord, grant us the grace always to say with the sincerity of Peter, our head, "Lord, Thou knowest all things, Thou knowest that I love Thee." It is love like that that alone can fit us to be apostles today.

> *Prayer for the day:*
> **THOU KNOWEST THAT I LOVE THEE.**

June 29, Saints Peter and Paul

> *Summary:*
> Peter confesses that Jesus is the Christ, the Son of the living God.

BLESSED SIMON

Lord Jesus, I wonder if sometimes You do not get tired of the way we sophisticated modern Christians smile at the naïveté and "humanness" of Your first successor. You will admit, I think, that Peter is rather impulsive, braver in word than in action, and overly aware of those qualities he thinks should go with a leader. But Peter is solid. He comes through in the end (with Your help, of course): he justifies the faith You have in him. And that is all that matters. You have indeed proved him and known him (introit).

What I have always admired is the way You handle Peter and bring him along. There is something of the man-to-man approach in Your attitude to Him: You respect him as a man. To be a man is to be capable of mistakes. You do not take that capability away from Peter, for You see that it isn't freedom from errors that makes a good superior, but rather general good judgment, love, humility.

You train Peter, and his companions, in these qualities (especially in love and humility) Yourself. He learns by observing You. He learns very much from his own mistakes and falls. He is the kind of man You want as Your first Pope. And You get what You want.

What I especially like about Peter is His way of looking at and talking to You. In yesterday's gospel You ask him three times: "Simon . . . dost thou love Me?" You don't rub it in. Your respect for him is still there. You ask him three times because You know he wants it that way, so that he can put all his heart into his final: "Lord, Thou knowest that I love Thee."

UPON THIS ROCK

But it is time to get to today's gospel. You ask, "Who do men say the Son of Man is?" It is a rather impersonal question, and You get an impersonal answer: "Some say John the Baptist; and others, Elias; and others, Jeremias, or one of the prophets." It isn't the answer You want.

Then You say: "But who do you say that I am?" Peter answers for them all: "Thou art the Christ, the Son of the living God!" Peter makes You happy with his profession of faith, and You admit it: "*Blessed art thou*, Simon Bar-Jona, for flesh and blood have not revealed this to thee, but My Father in heaven. And I say to thee, thou art Peter, and upon this rock I will build My Church, and the gates of hell shall not prevail against it." Peter's faith and love win that promise and tribute from You. He is the only one ever to be so addressed by You.

"Who do men say that I am . . . Who do *you* say that I am?"

You continue to ask us those same questions today. There is a variety of answers, but there is only one that You want to hear from us; and we wouldn't have it were it not for blessed, good, honest Peter: "Thou art the Christ, the Son of the living God!" Wonderful! For Peter to make such a statement is to justify Your choice of him to continue Your work of love in the world.

Lord Jesus, if I make my own Peter's tributes to You, will You also support me in all my efforts to continue Your and his work in the world today?

> Prayer for the day:
> THOU KNOWEST THAT I LOVE THEE . . .
> THOU ART THE CHRIST, THE SON OF THE
> LIVING GOD!

June 30, Commemoration of St. Paul

Summary:
Jesus prepares His disciples for the apostolate by promising that they will be persecuted, delivered up and killed for His name's sake.

THE GENTILES' APOSTLE

Lord Jesus, it is no secret to You that St. Paul is one of the most excellent creations of Your divine grace. Few humans have ever cooperated with Your grace as he has, few have ever allowed themselves to be so dominated by You and still remained themselves. Paul states it so well: "He who worked in Peter for the apostleship, worked also in me among the Gentiles; and they recognized the grace of God, that was given to me. The grace of God in me has not been fruitless; but His grace always remains in me" (gradual).

Paul is not there the day You tell the other apostles that You will send them forth like sheep in the midst of wolves, that they will be scourged, persecuted and delivered up to death for Your Name's sake. He is not there, because he is still Your enemy, he still has to be knocked off his horse by Your strong grace.

You take care of his formation later on, after his conversion, when for three years in the Arabian desert You teach him even as You instructed the other apostles. So that Paul can truthfully say: "I give you to understand, that the gospel which was preached by me is not of man. For I did not receive it from man, nor was I taught it; but I received it by a revelation from Jesus Christ" (epistle).

No, Paul does not hear Your prediction about the perils of being an apostle. He finds out with first-hand knowledge about those perils: persecution, disillusionment and betrayal from his own converts, shipwreck, scourging, imprisonment, and finally death. Never once does he weaken or waver in his vocation of bringing You to the Gentiles. "I know whom I have believed," he said (introit), "and I am certain that He is able to guard the trust committed to Him, against that day, being a just judge."

FRUITFUL GRACE

"I know whom I have believed . . ." Lord Jesus, he is speaking about You; he knows You. You are personal and real to him at all times. There is an interchange of friendship and love between You and him—an interchange that is maintained by his thinking about You and speaking to You and that is manifested by his writing about You and his self-immolation for You.

Paul cannot keep You to himself. You are too good, true, beautiful, wonderful and glorious. And that is why he is the apostle he is. For me to live is Christ, to die is gain, he says. Love compels him to want to share You with others so that You will be loved more and more.

Lord Jesus, You did it for Paul. I am almost afraid to ask You to do it for me. I don't think I could take it as Paul could. But what would Paul say to that? I can hear him now: "By the *grace of God*, I am what I am." A final word then to him and to You: "Holy Apostle Paul, preacher of truth, and doctor of the Gentiles, intercede for us" (alleluia verse). And, Lord Jesus, *whatever* You want is all right with me.

Prayer for the day:

I LIVE, NOW NOT I, BUT CHRIST LIVES IN ME.

FEASTS OF JULY

July 1,
Feast of the Most Precious Blood

Summary:

Jesus dies on the cross, a soldier opens His side; and immediately there comes forth blood and water.

ALREADY DEAD

Lord Jesus, a few days ago in the Feast of Your Sacred Heart, we beheld Your open heart, burning with love for Your Father and for us. Now we look upon the blood that flows from that heart, and on the effects of that blood in our world today.

Your blood flows from Your body, and this separation of blood from body brings about Your death. Your blood, then, is the price You pay to win our freedom from hell's eternal slavery. "God has favored us in His beloved Son: in whom we have redemption through His blood" (tract).

You are He who came in water and in blood; not in the water only, but in the water and in the blood (gradual). "Thou hast redeemed us, O Lord, with Thy blood, out of every tribe and tongue and people and nation, and hast made us for our God a kingdom" (introit). We are the Kingdom, we are Your Mystical Body, Your Church. And we are founded on Your blood, that is to say, on Your love.

For Your blood is at once the price You pay for our freedom, it is the symbol of Your love for us, and it is the sign of growth in the kingdom. It is Your blood that flows again, as it were, each time You become active in one of Your sacraments; it is in that blood that we are "dipped" unto cleansing and rejuvenation in the sacrament of Penance; it is that blood that You offer up, now in an unbloody manner, in Your Eucharist unto our growth as a Kingdom.

"Take and drink ye all of this," You command, "FOR THIS IS THE CHALICE OF MY BLOOD OF THE NEW AND

ETERNAL COVENANT: THE MYSTERY OF FAITH,
WHICH SHALL BE SHED FOR YOU AND FOR MANY
UNTO THE FORGIVENESS OF SINS."

REDEEMED IN HIS BLOOD

So Your sacred blood is not a thing of the past, of Calvary, only;
it belongs to us, because You have given it to us and commanded
that we drink it. It is now our life blood as individual persons and
as a Church. Without it we die. We, who have been permitted to
approach Thy holy Table, O Lord, have drawn waters with joy
from the fountains of the Savior: may His blood, we beseech Thee,
be for us a fountain of water springing up into everlasting life (postcommunion).

But on Calvary Your blood flows on the ground, Lord Jesus.
Are we to understand by this that You want material creation, too,
to share in the freedom from slavery that You purchase at such a
price? There are some who might feel distressed at the thought of
Your blood flowing on the ground. But why? If all creation, groan-
ing, fell under the sway of Satan at the fall of our first parents, then
it too would need to be freed from that slavery.

Your blood is the price of freedom for the whole world of matter
as well as of men. There is no better cleansing power than Your
precious blood. Now, of course, Your blood no longer falls on the
ground. Now You smile on the things that are and are made, bringing them within the realm of Your redemption by means of Your
blessings, the sacramentals of Your Church. But there would be no
blessings, and no sacraments or sacramentals if first of all Your
blood had not fallen to the ground from out of Your heart as You
hung on that first glorious altar, Your holy cross on Calvary.

You have redeemed us, O Lord, in Your blood. How can I ever
thank You as You deserve? "The mercies of the Lord I will sing
forever: I will show forth Thy truth with my mouth to generation
and generation" (introit).

Prayer for the day:

ONE OF THE SOLDIERS OPENED HIS SIDE
. . . AND IMMEDIATELY THERE CAME FORTH
BLOOD AND WATER.

July 2,
Feast of the Visitation of our Blessed Lady

Summary:

Mary goes to visit her cousin Elizabeth and is joyfully greeted both by Elizabeth and by the child she carries in her womb.

WHEN ELIZABETH HEARS

Lord Jesus, the events just preceding this section of the gospel tell us how Mary is told that she is to become Your Mother, how she gives her consent and You take flesh in her womb. No other woman ever has or ever will have anything as wonderful as this happen to her; but what is the first thing she thinks of? Of Elizabeth, her old cousin, who has also miraculously conceived a child. She feels that Elizabeth needs her, so she arises and goes with haste into the hill country, to a town of Juda.

As she enters Elizabeth's house, an extraordinary communication takes place between Mary and Elizabeth and between You and Your cousin John, both of You still in Your mothers' wombs. You reveal Yourself to John; John rejoices vigorously in his mother's womb, and she in turn cries out to Mary: "Blessed art thou among women and blessed is the fruit of thy womb!" Surely Elizabeth is here the representative of all of us. She voices the love and the joyous gratitude of all humanity that each of us knows in his heart he should be constantly expressing. Blessed is Mary . . . Blessed is the fruit of her womb! We all owe Elizabeth a great debt of gratitude for teaching us what to do about divine visitations and for the words with which to clothe our feelings.

But Elizabeth is not finished. "And how have I deserved that the mother of my Lord should come to me? For behold, the moment that the sound of thy greeting came to my ears, the babe in my womb leapt for joy." She could just as well have asked, "How have I deserved that my Lord Himself has come to me?"

MAGNIFYING THE LORD

But that's the way You so often make Your approaches to us, Lord Jesus. You come in the person of others; You make use of human beings. So it was then and so it is today. Dwelling in us, You desire to visit all the Elizabeths and Johns of our world. And, of course, You often come in the person of Mary, Your Mother. The essential thing is that You come to us always.

You are the hero and the center of the original Visitation and You remain the center of this present Feast. It is You that Mary is thinking of when she cries out: "My soul magnifies the Lord, and my spirit rejoices in God my Savior; because He has regarded the lowliness of His handmaid . . . Because He who is mighty has done great things for me, and holy is His name."

It is Mary's prayer, the Magnificat. But she gives away and shares everything. She first shares You with Elizabeth and John; then she gives You to the apostles, the poor, the blind, the lame; she gives You to the Father, to Calvary, to the world, to all of us. And in doing this, she gives us the lesson we need most of all to learn in life: that in sharing You with others, we can best possess and keep You for ourselves.

Yes, Lord Jesus, it is a remarkable Mother You have picked out for Yourself . . . and for us. She is surely happy and most worthy of all high praise, for out of her has risen the Sun of Justice, You, Christ our God.

Prayer for the day:
BLESSED ART THOU AMONG WOMEN AND BLESSED IS THE FRUIT OF THY WOMB!

* July 3, Leo II, Pope and Confessor

Gospel No. 2, page 242.

* July 4, Mass of Preceding Sunday

July 5, St. Anthony Mary Zaccaria, Confessor

Gospel of February 27, St. Gabriel of Our Lady of Sorrows, page 342.

* July 6, Mass of Preceding Sunday

July 7,
Sts. Cyril and Methodius, Bishops and Confessors

Gospel of February 6, page 335.

* July 8,
St. Elizabeth, Queen of Portugal, Widow

Gospel No. 19a, page 274.

* July 9, Mass of Preceding Sunday

* July 10,
The Seven Holy Brothers, Martyrs, and Sts. Rufina and Secunda, Virgins and Martyrs

Summary:

Jesus claims that whoever does the will of His Father in heaven, he is His brother and sister and mother.

MOTHER AND BRETHREN

Lord Jesus, You are speaking to the crowds, fulfilling Your work as the voice of truth to people in need of truth. It is for this that You have come, and the rest of this gospel will reveal how essential You consider this work to be.

All of a sudden someone interrupts You, "Behold, Thy mother and Thy brethren are standing outside, seeking Thee." St. Matthew doesn't say why they seek You. It might be that they just want to pay their respects to You, or that they want to talk to You about some serious business, or that they seek You as men are supposed to seek their God.

Whatever their motive, they and all mankind must know that Your Father's will and work do in fact come before all purely human considerations. You have been teaching the crowds. Now You turn to Your relatives and to all of us, asking, "Who is My mother and who are My brethren?" And pointing to Your disciples, You say, "Behold My mother and My brethren! For whoever does the will of My Father in heaven, he is My brother and sister and mother."

I am sure You do not mean this as a rebuke to Your brethren and above all not to Mary. For if anyone meets Your condition— doing the will of the Father, it is she. She proves her dedication to the divine will by giving You up again and again. She even gives up one of a mother's choicest joys—the care of her Son—leaving that duty to the chance whims of Your official followers and friends. So it has always been with her from the beginning.

Your words then are far from a rebuke to her; they simply set the record straight. But what a lift Your teaching is to Your disciples then and to other mothers and disciples all through time! Doing the Father's will to the best of one's ability and desire, You say, is more precious than blood relationship to You. "Blessed be the name of the Lord, from henceforth now and forever" (introit).

WILL OF THE FATHER

"Behold My mother and My brethren," You say, and You point years ahead at today's martyrs, too. They meet Your requirements. And so is it possible with Your grace for us here and now to do Your Father's will and to become Your disciples.

But, Lord Jesus, how difficult is the condition! To do the will of the Father according to the example and the measure of Mary and even these saints. Once more I am brought face to face with the life-long conflict between Your ideal on the one hand and my fearful lack of courage on the other. Is *desire* to do Your will enough, as the spiritual writers say? It seems so unconvincing.

Once more I know (and maybe it is the one thing I need to know) that if I ever do make the grade, it won't be my achievement but Your powerful grace working its way into my life day by day through the instrumentality of the Food that makes saints, the

Food that identifies me with and feeds me more and more on Your will. Lamb of God, who takest away the sins and the weakness of the world, have mercy on me!

We beseech Thee, Almighty God, that by the intercession of Thy saints, we may experience the *effect of that salvation* of which we have received the pledge in these mysteries (postcommunion). Lord Jesus, I believe that the effect of Your salvation guaranteed by this Mass is the grace to do Your Father's will.

Prayer for the day:
BEHOLD MY MOTHER AND MY BRETHREN.

July 11, St. Pius, Pope and Martyr

Gospel No. 2, page 242.

July 12, St. John Gualbert

Summary:
Jesus teaches the love and forgiveness not only of friends but enemies.

LOVE ENEMIES

Lord Jesus, Your teaching in the Sermon on the Mount both corrects much of the wrong interpretation the doctors of the Law have given to the Law in the past, and it brings out new facets that can call forth a new way of life and a truly Christian culture in the future.

It goes without saying that Your teaching bridges the centuries and seeks a foothold in our minds and hearts. In regard to relationships between the injuring and the injured, the former teaching had it thus: Thou shalt love thy neighbor and hate thy enemy. But You tell us that we must love our enemies, do good to those who hate us, and pray for those who calumniate and persecute us.

And You go on to say that forgiveness of enemy and prayer for him are conditions for being children of Your Father in heaven, who makes His sun to shine on the good and the evil, and sends rain on the just and the unjust. For if we love those that love us, what reward shall we have? This is a bare minimum that anyone can achieve. And if we greet our brethren only, what do we do that is in any way heroic? Do not even the Gentiles do that? As Your followers we are not to be satisfied with a pagan minimum. We can have only one ideal: "You therefore are to be perfect, even as Your heavenly Father is perfect."

Lord Jesus, I have always thought of this command of Yours as practically impossible of fulfillment, even as I knew in my heart that You would not give us an order that would be beyond our powers. I suspect that I put too much stress on the words "perfect as the Father is perfect." I have been thinking too concretely along the lines of the theological perfections of Your Father, He being the sum total of all perfections so that there is no limit to His wisdom, goodness, power, love, and majesty.

HEAVENLY FATHER

We cannot be infinitely wise as He is, nor infinitely powerful or good; but if we can learn to forgive our enemies and others who injure us, we do something very God-like, something that He is always doing to us. When we sin, we become much more of an enemy to Him than any of those who offend us.

But He forgives. It is His very nature to forgive, and we can share in this nature when we make ourselves the carriers of His forgiveness to those who offend us.

Fortunately, You give not only the command to forgive, but You give us Your own example of effective forgiveness when on the Cross You pray for Your enemies: "Father, forgive them, for they do not know what they are doing" (Luke 23:34). And You inspire men down through the ages to use forgiveness of enemies as the springboard for holiness. Today's Saint, for example, was intent on avenging his brother's murder; changed by Your grace he embraces the assassin with forgiveness and goes off to become a saint. And the day of his conversion is Good Friday.

Best of all, You give us the Mass in which You share with us not only Your command to forgive (You do in fact make forgiveness a necessary condition for offering the sacrifice worthily), but also Your forgiving will, together with the strength to carry it through. Lord Jesus, make me ever more and more faithful to the spirit of the Mass, to the spirit of forgiveness.

Prayer for the day:
YOU THEREFORE BE PERFECT, EVEN AS YOUR HEAVENLY FATHER IS PERFECT.

* July 13, St. Anacletus, Pope and Martyr

Gospel No. 2, page 242.

July 14, St. Bonaventure, Bishop and Confessor

Gospel No. 14, page 264.

* July 15, St. Henry, Emperor and Confessor

Gospel No. 15, page 266.

July 16, Our Lady of Mount Carmel

Gospel No. 1, page 241.

* July 17, St. Alexius, Confessor

Gospel No. 17, page 270.

July 18, St. Camillus of Lellis, Confessor

Summary:

Jesus has chosen His apostles, not they Him: He calls them His friends.

NO LONGER SERVANTS

Lord Jesus, You are speaking here of Your apostles at the Last Supper; but everything You say here You also mean for us to observe. You tell them and us that we must love one another as You have loved us. This is not a matter of choice: it is Your commandment; and it is an essential aspect of being Your follower. We must love as You love, and You love to the extent of laying down Your life for us.

Lord, is it possible for us to love one another as You have loved us? I know Your answer: You say You would not command the impossible. In Baptism and above all in the Eucharist You give us the power to love as You love. But if we do not use this power, if we ignore it and do not trust in it, it leaves our lives untouched. We must *want* to love simply because it is Your desire for us.

But I must go on. We are Your friends, You say, if we do the things You command us to do (and after reading Your gospels, I can have no real doubt about what You command). We are not Your servants, because the servant does not really know what his master does. But You call us Your friends, because all things that You have heard from the Father You have made known to us.

Lord Jesus, You have surely fulfilled more than Your share in our friendship. On Your side there has been absolute openness, so that all along we have known Your divine intentions for us and for our world. Just ordinary friendship in this life is one of Your greatest and best gifts. Friendship with You is a foretaste of heaven. But in true friendship there has to be communication and sharing and mutual self-giving.

It is in our part of our friendship that we have failed. You have given us Your truth, You have thereby revealed to us the mind of God; You have given us Your life of grace whereby You and the Father and the Holy Spirit make Yourselves at home in us as individuals and as a community; You have given us Your Sacraments whereby You constantly act in and upon us. Lord, there is nothing You have not done for us. I am shocked and ashamed at my lack of realization and appreciation.

BUT FRIENDS

We have not chosen You, You say, but You have chosen us, and have appointed us that we should go and bear fruit, and that our fruit should remain; that whatever we ask the Father in Your name, He may give it to us.

Lord Jesus, You want our mutual friendship to be more than a sentimental attachment. You want it to be a permanent union between You and us, based on mutual communication, mutual sharing, mutual sacrifice. This is so important to You because You know that love and friendship in the lives of men are the best possible invitation to those who do not know You. So, love for You is not only the inspiration for all apostolic action; love for You binding men together is in itself the apostolate. This is the fruit that we must bear in our lives in this world.

I am afraid that up to now our friendship has been too one-sided, Lord Jesus. But what is this You say: Whatever I ask the Father in Your Name, He will give it to me? Well then, in Your Name here in this Mass wherein You make present for us the Last Supper, I beg the Father to make me want to do my share in our friendship, to make me want to give myself to You and to Your apostolate with all the enthusiasm and love of the saint whose feast we celebrate today. Praise be to Thee, O Christ!

Prayer for the day:
YOU ARE MY FRIENDS IF YOU DO THE THINGS I COMMAND YOU.

July 19, St. Vincent De Paul, Confessor

Gospel No. 16, page 268.

July 20, St. Jerome Emilian, Confessor

Summary:

Jesus blesses little children and invites a young man to give up all his possessions and to come and follow Him.

OF SUCH IS THE KINGDOM

Lord Jesus, You are not at all pleased with the disciples for rebuking the children and those who bring them to You that You might lay Your hands on them. "Let the little children be, and do not hinder them from coming to Me," You say to the disciples (and to everyone, everywhere). "For of such is the kingdom of heaven." And You lay Your hands on them so that they will know ever afterwards that they have been loved with a very great love.

Lord Jesus, You cannot help giving signs of affection to these little ones. You are drawn to them and they to You in an instinctive friendship that You insist must not be interrupted. I suspect that You so love them because of their holiness, their innocence unspoiled by worldliness. You love childlikeness because that is what Christianity is; and no one is a better witness to Your basic truths than a child.

And the disciples had better take the preaching of these children to heart. In St. Mark's account of this same incident, You say that whoever does not accept the kingdom of God as a little child will not enter in. In other words, whoever does not want to be in their presence and who does not trust in Your Father as a little child trusts in his Father, will have a hard time getting into the kingdom. And if he should get in, he might not know how to act there; because heaven is a place for little ones.

This is important doctrine; and now comes more of the same. A certain man comes to You and says, "Good Master, what good work shall I do to have eternal life?" You answer: "Why dost thou ask Me about what is good? One there is who is good, and He is God. But if thou wilt enter into life, keep the commandments." "Which?" he asks You. "Thou shalt not kill. Thou shalt not commit adultery. Thou shalt not steal. Thou shalt not bear false witness. Honor thy father and mother. And thou shalt love thy neighbor as thyself."

ONE THING LACKING

The young man says to You, "All these I have kept, what is yet wanting to me?" That is good. You love him for his fidelity to Your law and will. But You hope he will go on from there and choose heroism. "If thou wilt be perfect, go, sell what thou hast, and give to the poor, and thou shalt have treasure in heaven; and come, follow Me." And St. Matthew goes on to tell us that the man's face falls, and he goes away sad, for he has great possessions.

Lord Jesus, You invite both the children and the man to come to You: You really want both them and him. The children accept Your invitation, and their joy in Your presence now is a foretaste of heaven. But when a child grows up, more is expected of him. He has to remain a child, trustful and loving, and then he has to act maturely in keeping human values in their correct scale of importance. Your young man with the great possessions seems afraid of that decision.

You invite him to go all the way with You. He doesn't really have to. This is a counsel of perfection that You do not even expect all to accept. He thinks of his great possessions, he makes his judgment, and goes away sad. His wealth stands between him and You. He leaves You and Your invitation, and You alone know the final outcome of his decision.

Lord Jesus, today's Saint makes up for the failure of the man with the great possessions. He becomes a child and grows in childlikeness until he reaches the ultimate degree of childlikeness, leaving all things to follow You. Now he never has to leave You.

In every Mass You invite us to come to You. In the Mass You put Your arms around us and laying hands on us, You bless us. More than that, You feed us with the bread of childlikeness and true detachment in Communion. Help us always to see the Mass as the one force that can make and keep us little, that can help us to make the judgment that will always keep You in the first place in our lives.

Prayer for the day:

IF THOU WILT BE PERFECT, GO, SELL WHAT THOU HAST, AND GIVE TO THE POOR . . . AND COME, FOLLOW ME.

* July 21, St. Praxedes, Virgin

Gospel No. 18, page 272.

July 22, St. Mary Magdalen, Penitent

Gospel of Ember Friday in September, page 214. Or Gospel of
Thursday in Passion Week, page 113.

July 23, St. Apollinaris, Bishop-Martyr

Summary:

To correct the personal ambitions of the apostles, Jesus tells them that the only path to greatness is the way of humble service to others.

AS ONE WHO SERVES

Lord Jesus, this scene takes place at the Last Supper. Even at
this solemn moment, they are discussing and arguing about precedence and seniority. Their rising voices call forth from You a
last sad rebuke—and a great lesson—for them and for us. The kings
of the Gentiles lord it over them, You say, and they who exercise
authority over them are called benefactors. But this must not be the
way with Your followers.

On the contrary, let him who is greatest among them become as
the youngest, and him who is the chief as the servant. For which is
the greater, he who is guest at the table or he who serves? Is it not
he who is the guest? That is what they might think; but it is a
superficial view; and it is contradicted both by what they have seen
here tonight and by Your own words.

You feed them with Your body and blood; You wash their feet;
all Your public life You have served them with Your truth, Your
guidance, Your love. Now You climax it all with one of the loveliest
and truest descriptions You have ever given of Yourself: "I am in
your midst as he who serves." And the conclusion doesn't have to
be put into words: if they are really concerned with being great, let

them imitate You in being in the midst of their people as servants of the people, carriers of Your truth, Your life, Your love to them.

When and what kind of reward will they get? You tell them: "You are they who have continued with Me in My trials. And I appoint to you a kingdom, even as My Father has appointed to Me, that you may eat and drink at My table in My kingdom; and you shall sit upon thrones, judging the twelve tribes of Israel."

TRUE GREATNESS

Lord Jesus, it may take them many years to learn what true greatness means; but some day, with Your help, each of them will pass the test.

There will always be Christians whose desire for recognition and preferment will make them glory in being served, in dominating and lording it over others. Almost all of us act that way at times. It is always because we momentarily lose sight of You here at the Last Supper and forget Your words to *us*: "I am in your midst as he who serves."

Let popes, bishops, priests, superiors, generals, teachers, fathers and mothers—Christians one and all—remember that ruling others is primarily taking *Your* place in the midst of others, serving their needs for truth, love, life: serving by giving oneself to them.

This is the ideal You hold out to us. It is not impossible because all that You are and do at the Last Supper, You give to us at our Mass. Here You continue to be in our midst as He who serves all our needs. Not the least of those needs is that of learning true greatness, of learning that abandon to You can achieve—slowly, yes, but truly—that identification with You that permits us to say: I serve, no, not I, but You, Lord Jesus, You serve in me.

Prayer for the day:
I AM IN YOUR MIDST AS HE WHO SERVES.

* July 24, Mass of Preceding Sunday or St. Christina, Virgin-Martyr

Gospel 19a, page 274.

July 25, St. James, Apostle

Gospel of May 6, page 366.

July 26, St. Anne, Mother of Our Blessed Lady

Summary:

The kingdom of heaven is like a treasure hidden in a field, like a pearl of great price, like a net cast into the sea that gathers in fish of every kind.

THE KINGDOM

Lord Jesus, You say that the kingdom of heaven is like a treasure hidden in a field; he who finds it hides it, and in his joy goes and sells all that he has in order to buy that field. He strikes a good bargain. And so does the merchant who finds a single pearl of great price. He sells all that he has to buy it.

Of course, You are speaking about Your Church, the Mystical Body, which is truly a treasure hidden in the field of this world. It is worth everything, more than the field itself, more than all possessions, in spite of the fact that it contains all kinds of fish, big and small, good and bad (according to Your third image in this same gospel).

This treasure, Your Church, is worth so very much because it is You, it is Your presence in this world. You are the treasure; and to sell all that one has in order to possess You and to be caught up into the life-stream of Your worship of the Father and Your love for men is wisdom of the highest order; it is the best kind of keenness in the "business" that pays off in eternal dividends.

We might wonder why this gospel is used for the feast of St. Anne. She lived in the Old Testament, before You established Your Church. But living before You came is no barrier to giving up everything to purchase membership with You in Your Church. To long for You is to be ready in advance to sell all that one has in order to buy the treasure.

A GOOD GRANDMOTHER

Anne surely is full of this desire for You. And she is in direct relationship with You. You have seen to it that Your Mother, Anne's child, Mary, was conceived immaculately in Anne's womb so that never for an instant did Satan have any power over her. Anne carries in her womb and brings forth her who is to become Your own Mother. That makes her Your grandmother.

I am sure she is no different than any grandmother. She probably helps take care of You when Mary is busy; she surely enjoys You; and in You she undoubtedly feels that she lives on. But if she lives on in You, does she not also live on in us whom You have gathered into Your Church? That would make her our grandmother, too. That gives her a special place and work to accomplish in Your Church. Her life, of course, is centered in You. But you have died for us. She isn't going to let us get careless and thus expose ourselves to eternally broken hearts. In her quiet way she goes about binding up our cuts and bruises, winning grace here and protection there by her constant intercession for us.

Too often we take grandmothers for granted. We come to see them occasionally on a namesday or a birthday and give them a celebration, with some gifts as signs of our affection. Then we forget them again.

I suspect that many of us treat St. Anne the same way! So that should make us throw our whole hearts into the recommendation that Your Church has for us today: "Let us all rejoice in the Lord, while we keep this day in honor of blessed Anne, on whose solemnity the angels rejoice, and give praise to the Son of God" (introit).

Rejoicing is all right with her, and she does appreciate it; but there is only one thing she really wants: "Nourished by these heavenly sacraments, we beseech Thee, O Lord our God, that, through the intercession of Blessed Anne, whom Thou didst will to be the mother of her who brought forth Thy Son, *we may be found worthy to attain eternal salvation*" (postcommunion).

Prayer for the day:

THE KINGDOM OF HEAVEN IS LIKE A TREAS-URE HIDDEN IN A FIELD.

* July 27, St. Pantaleon, Martyr

Gospel No. 6, page 250.

* July 28,
Sts. Nazarius, Celsus, Martyrs; Victor and Innocent, Popes

Gospel No. 7, page 251.

July 29, St. Martha, Virgin

Summary:

Jesus tells the busy Martha that she should not be so anxious and troubled about so many things when only one thing is necessary.

A WOMAN NAMED MARTHA

Lord Jesus, when St. Luke says that Martha welcomes You into her house, he passes over the joy and satisfaction that Martha must feel at the unspeakable privilege. Martha is undoubtedly proud of her home: she has always enjoyed making it attractive to others, especially to Lazarus, her brother, and Mary, her sister.

And she is a good cook. She knows it, and others do, too, including You. Your recognition of her skill in that art is surely one of the reasons for her greater effort today. Usually she manages very well by herself; but the added guests, her extra care, and the closeness to dinner time press upon and excite her. "There's Mary," she says to herself, "you'd think she would see what a mess I'm in."

Maybe she even motions to Mary behind Your back. But how can Mary see Martha's signs? She is looking at You, drinking in Your divine wisdom. She's in a different world completely. Finally Martha can stand it no longer. If she doesn't get help, she'll fail You. If Mary won't pay any attention to her, You will. Standing before You, wiping her hands on her apron, she complains: "Lord, is it no concern of Thine that my sister has left me to serve alone? Tell her therefore to help me."

I suspect she feels ashamed of herself as soon as she says it; for there is implied blame and criticism of You Yourself in her voice. You are feeding Mary instead of her feeding You—a situation that just doesn't seem right to Martha. Now You speak to her—with understanding of human (and possibly feminine) frailty—but with a hint also of reproof: "Martha, Martha, thou art anxious and troubled about many things; and yet only one thing is needful. Mary has chosen the best part, and it will not be taken away from her."

THE BEST PART

So ends the episode, at least as much as St. Luke wants us to see. I suppose that Mary continues to sit there until Martha, calm and herself again, announces that dinner is ready. As You eat, both women watch You; and every once in a while You look up from Your appreciation of Martha's love-inspired creation, this dinner that she has made for You, to smile at her so that she will know that You have nothing against her.

I doubt that in the future Martha will give up her cooking for sitting at Your feet. But she'll see her cooking in a new light—as loving performance of the duty of her vocation rather than as an occasion for over-much pride in her accomplishments.

Lord Jesus, I like Martha very much: for her way of showing her love for You, for her fidelity to her vocation, but most of all for this slight fault of hers that calls forth Your words to her. For You are thinking and speaking not only to her but to all of us who, in the bustle of daily life become overly concerned with satisfaction-producing results rather than simple faithfulness to vocation and to love.

Martha learns, Lord Jesus. In this and all Masses teach us to sit at Your feet absorbing Your mind in the epistles and gospels; and then at the Meal of Your body and blood which You serve for us, fill us with full understanding—of You, of our vocation, of our whole life as dedicated service centered on You. Thus we will learn slowly but surely that only one thing is indeed needful—You, Lord Jesus!

Prayer for the day:

MARTHA, MARTHA, THOU ART ANXIOUS AND
TROUBLED ABOUT MANY THINGS: AND YET
ONLY ONE THING IS NEEDFUL.

* July 30, Sts. Abdon and Sennen, Martyrs

Gospel of All Saints Day, page 451.

July 31, St. Ignatius Loyola, Confessor

Gospel of Feast of St. Titus, February 6, page 335.

FEASTS OF AUGUST

August 1, Feast of St. Peter's Chains

Gospel of June 29, page 389.

August 2,
St. Alphonsus Mary de Liguori, Bishop and Confessor

Gospel of Feast of St. Titus, February 6, page 335.

* August 3,
The Finding of the Body of St. Stephen

Gospel of Mass of December 26, page 18.

August 4, St. Dominic, Confessor

Gospel No. 15, page 266.

August 5,
Dedication of the Church of Our Lady of the Snows

Gospel No. 1, page 241.

August 6,
The Transfiguration of Our Lord Jesus Christ

Summary:

Peter, James and John see Jesus transfigured on the mountain and hear the Father say: "This is My beloved Son, in whom I am well pleased."

AND WAS TRANSFIGURED

Lord Jesus, it is best for me to try to understand Your transfiguration by trying to grasp what it meant for the three apostles. For nearly three years now they have been with You. They have heard You speak, and their minds delighted in Your divine truth. You have spoken to each of them man to man, heart to heart; and they have received Your friendship with gladness and joy.

They have also seen Your mercy towards the poor and sick. They have been constantly proud of You, for You have been so true, so good.

But in all these experiences with You, You have appeared to them only as a man. Now for the first time, they see with their eyes that You are more than man. Your face shines as the sun, and Your garments become white as snow. They love it, especially Peter. He wants to settle down with You right there: "Lord, it is good for us to be here."

But their experience of Your divinity and glorification is just beginning. You have spoken to them before of Your Father. Now for the first time they hear the Father's voice: "This is My beloved Son, in whom I am well pleased; hear Him."

It is the Great God speaking, the God of Abraham, of Moses, the God of the Ten Commandments! God whose face no man can see with human eyes and remain alive. And He calls You "Beloved Son." Struck with awe, they fall on their faces.

You do not leave them long in their fear. They have seen and heard enough. Peter feels Your hand on his shoulder, and Your familiar voice sounds: "Arise, and do not be afraid." Obeying You, they raise their heads, stand and look around. The vision—and the heavenly voice—are gone. But You remain. You and they have work to do.

BELOVED SON

But now things will no longer be quite the same between You and them. Ever after, when looking at You and listening to You, they will remember how You looked with Your face shining like the sun. They will hear Your Father's voice, and they will remember how very good it was to have been there.

Lord Jesus, today You do not take Peter, James and John to the mountain: You take us. Because You died and rose again and instituted Your Church in which You yearly renew Your earthly life, we can now live that life with You.

Today You are transfigured before *us*. Your transfiguration is a living experience for us. We see You, we are with You. Your Father says to us: This is My beloved Son, in whom I am well pleased; hear Him. Contemplate Him, love Him.

I think I am going to enjoy obeying this command of Your Father, Lord Jesus. I want to look at You, I want to hear You all my life and all of eternity. "How lovely are Thy tabernacles, O Lord of hosts! My soul longs and faints for the courts of the Lord" (introit).

But I can only prepare myself for contemplating You in eternity by hearing and contemplating You as You speak to me now from the pages of the gospels.

Lord Jesus, You ask the apostles to tell the vision to no one till the Son of Man has risen from the dead. But now You have risen from the dead; therefore Your request no longer holds. To tell everyone of the vision of Your divinity, of Your glory, Your goodness and lovableness is what I want to do always. You are beautiful above the sons of men: grace is poured abroad in Your lips. You are the brightness of eternal light, the unspotted mirror, and the image of His goodness (gradual and alleluia verses). Praise be to You, O Christ!

Prayer for the day:

THIS IS MY BELOVED SON, IN WHOM I AM WELL PLEASED. HEAR HIM.

August 7, St. Cajetan, Confessor

Gospel of the Fourteenth Sunday after Pentecost, page 204.

* August 8,
Sts. Cyriacus, Largus, Smaragdus, Martyrs

Gospel of Feast of St. Francis Xavier, December 3, page 315.

August 9, St. John Mary Vianney, Confessor

Gospel No. 15, page 266.

or

Vigil of St. Lawrence, Martyr

Gospel No. 4, page 246.

August 10, St. Lawrence, Martyr

Gospel of Feast of St. Ignatius, February 1, page 331.

* August 11, Sts. Tiburtius and Susanna, Martyrs

Gospel No. 9, page 255.

August 12, St. Clare, Virgin

Gospel No. 18, page 272.

* August 13, Sts. Hippolytus and Cassian, Martyrs

Gospel No. 9, page 255.

August 14, Vigil of the Assumption of the Blessed Virgin

Gospel No. 1, page 241.

August 15, The Assumption of the Blessed Virgin Mary

Summary:

Elizabeth greets Mary and calls forth from her
the words of the Magnificat and the prophecy
that all generations shall call her blessed.

SHE WHO HAS BELIEVED

Lord Jesus, Mary has just entered Elizabeth's house; and at her
greeting John leaps for joy in Elizabeth's womb. Now Elizabeth,
filled by the Holy Spirit, cries out in a loud voice to Mary, Your
Mother: "Blessed art thou among women . . ."

It is a magnificent greeting and tribute both to Mary and to You
from a good and holy woman speaking in the name of all of us:
Blessed is Mary among all women, and blessed is the fruit of her

womb—You! And blessed is she who has believed, because the things promised her by the Lord shall be accomplished.

What are these things promised her, Lord Jesus? The Holy Spirit shall come upon her and the power of the Most High will overshadow her: she will conceive in her womb and bring forth a Son and will call His name Jesus. This Son will be destined for the rise and fall of many, His name will be a sign of contradiction, He will be put to death. Suffering with her Son, Mary's soul will be pierced with a sword. But the third day He will rise again, finish His work, ascend into heaven. There His Mother will join Him.

At the moment of this gospel, Mary doesn't know these things. She simply believes; and on the strength of her faith, she cries out: "My soul magnifies the Lord, and my spirit rejoices in God my Savior; because He has regarded the lowliness of His handmaid; for, behold, henceforth all generations shall call me blessed. Because He who is mighty has done great things for me, and holy is His name; and His mercy is from generation to generation on those who fear Him."

GREAT THINGS FOR HER

He who is mighty has done great things for her: He has made her Your Mother. In accepting You, she accepts all that You imply—those things of Your and her life that we have already recalled. She accepts Your death and hers, Your glorification and hers. "Mary is taken up into heaven: the host of angels rejoice" (alleluia verse).

"A great sign appeared in heaven: a woman clothed with the sun, and the moon was under her feet, and upon her head a crown of twelve stars. *Sing to the Lord a new song: because He has done wonderful things*" (introit).

Lord Jesus, it is a joy to obey Your Church in this command. The song we can always sing is Your Mass, the new song of thanksgiving that You give to us, Your Church. In it we can give thanks to the Lord our God for the wonderful things He has done in giving You to her and her to You and both You and her to us.

"May the offering of our devotion ascend to Thee, O Lord, and through the intercession of the Most Blessed Virgin Mary, assumed into heaven, may our hearts, fired by the flame of charity, incessantly long for Thee" (secret).

One thing we can be sure of: the more we sing, the more one with You we will become; and then the more we become the children of Mary herself. And isn't that what You wanted to accomplish in the first place?

Blessed be you among women, Mary. Lord Jesus, fruit of Mary's womb, blessed be You!

Prayer for the day:

MY SOUL MAGNIFIES THE LORD, AND MY SPIRIT REJOICES IN GOD MY SAVIOR.

August 16,
St. Joachim, Father of the Blessed Virgin Mary

Gospel of the Nativity of the Blessed Virgin, September 8, page 428.

August 17, St. Hyacinth, Confessor

Gospel No. 15, page 266.

* August 18, Mass of Preceding Sunday

August 19, St. John Eudes, Confessor

Gospel No. 15, page 266.

August 20, St. Bernard, Abbot

Gospel No. 14, page 264.

August 21, St. Jane Frances de Chantal, Widow

Gospel No. 19a, page 274.

August 22, The Immaculate Heart of Mary

Gospel of Mass of Blessed Virgin during Paschal Time, page 285.

August 23, St. Philip Benizi, Confessor,

Gospel No. 16, page 268.

August 24, St. Bartholomew, Apostle

Summary:

After a night of prayer, Jesus picks His twelve apostles.

NIGHT OF PRAYER

Lord Jesus, You have been attracting followers for months—men who see in You the answer to their hopes, who seem ready to follow You wherever You might lead. But Your plans call for more than followers. Once You have finished Your saving work and have established Your Church as the chief depository of Your salvation and Your truth, You will leave the world. Then You will want men to make Your truth and grace present throughout the world.

They must be good men, men of influence, capable of commanding respect and of exercising responsibility. Now You are ready to announce Your choices. After spending a whole night in prayer, You come down from Your mountain sanctuary and call the disciples to You.

You look at them and they at You. They all feel that this is a momentous and decisive day in their lives, and in that opinion they are not wrong. Perhaps You say a few words to explain what You are going to do, why it must be that only twelve are to be chosen, and what the work of the apostles will be. You tell them that, even though not all can be apostles, You still need and want them to stay close to You and to grow in the vocation that You have in mind for each.

Then You call out twelve names, and twelve men emerge from the crowd and come and stand before You. They are Simon (whom You named Peter), and Andrew, Peter's brother; James and John; Philip and Bartholomew; Matthew and Thomas; James the son of Alpheus, and Simon called the Zealot; Jude the brother of James, and Judas Iscariot, the one who will betray You. You look at them and slowly start walking down the mountain, the apostles at Your heels, (and surely they are joyfully congratulating one another at having been chosen).

TRYING TO TOUCH JESUS

Now You come to a level place, and before You know it You are in the midst of a great throng—not only of Your disciples, but of people from all of Judea and Jerusalem, and the sea coast of Tyre and Sidon who have come to hear You and to be healed of their diseases. And all the people seek to touch You because power goes forth from You and heals all.

Lord Jesus, it is truly a beautiful picture: You standing there in the midst of that sea of hands, giving Yourself to them with such love.

It is no accident that You relate the choosing of the apostles with teaching truth and channeling divine healing power through Your body to hands held out to touch You. That is the way it will always be in Your Church.

You will some day leave the world physically; but You will always remain in the midst of Your Church teaching and granting the power of holiness. You will be doing this because of the apostles You choose this day . . . and the successors whom they choose in Your name.

So it is that this scene of teaching, healing, and of hands held out to touch You is reproduced today in parishes throughout the world —parishes that are the fruit of the seed planted by the apostles.

"Almighty and everlasting God, Who, because hallowed by its being the festival of Thy blessed Apostle, Bartholomew, hast made this to be for us a day of pleasantness and of spiritual joy; teach Thy Church, we beseech Thee, ever to love what he loved, and ever to set forth what he taught" (collect).

Lord Jesus, help us to be worthy to carry on Your work in our world as the apostles did in theirs. Here are my hands held out to touch You. I believe that You will grant the power.

Prayer for the day:
POWER WENT FORTH FROM HIM AND HEAL-
ED ALL.

* August 25, St. Louis, King and Confessor

Summary:

Jesus tells a parable about a nobleman who gives money to his servants expecting them to use the money for gaining more money.

TO OBTAIN A KINGDOM

Lord Jesus, You tell this parable: A certain nobleman goes into a far country to obtain for himself a kingdom. Before leaving he calls ten of his servants, gives them a gold piece each with the instructions to trade till he gets back.

On his return, having received the kingdom he sought, he again summons the servants to learn what success they had with the trading. The first says: "Lord, thy gold piece has earned ten gold pieces." The lord says: "Well done, good servant, because thou hast been faithful in a little, thou shalt have authority over ten towns."

Then the second servant comes and says: "Lord, thy gold piece has made five gold pieces." And the lord says to him: "Be thou over five towns."

And another comes, saying, "Lord, behold thy gold piece, which I have kept laid up in a napkin; for I feared thee, because thou art a stern man. Thou takest up what thou didst not lay down, and thou reapest what thou didst not sow." The lord says to him: "Out of thy own mouth I judge thee, thou wicked servant. Thou knewest that I am a stern man, taking up what I did not lay down and reaping what I did not sow. Why, then, didst thou not put my money in a bank, so that I on my return might have gotten it with interest?"

And he said to the bystanders: "Take away the gold piece from him and give it to him who has the ten gold pieces." But they say to him: "Lord, he has ten gold pieces." The parable ends with the mysterious words: "To everyone who has shall be given; but from him who does not have, even that which he has shall be taken away."

FAITHFUL SERVANT

Lord Jesus, the lesson You want to teach us is fidelity to the interests of Your Father. You want us to make use of the gifts the Father gives us in order to win a greater tribute of devotion and love for Him from those we live and deal with.

St. Louis, King of France, was one who took this teaching of Yours to heart. He traded with the coin You gave him and gained ten more: by his example of detachment from his royal privileges and wealth, by his readiness to go into far off lands to fight for Your kingdom, and above all by his justness in all things, he has won much love for You and a great reward for himself.

Peguy puts these words in Your Father's mouth: "When St. Louis says that he loves me, I know that he loves me . . . When St. Louis loves me, says God, I am sure I know what is meant. He is a free man. When St. Louis loves me, I am aware, I know what it is to be loved" (*Men and Saints*, page 215).

For St. Louis' kind of love, You translate him from his earthly throne to the glory of Your heavenly kingdom. Lord Jesus, grant that by our fidelity to our vocation and by the merits and intercession of St. Louis, we may have companionship with You, the King of Kings (collect).

Prayer for the day:

WELL DONE, GOOD SERVANT; BECAUSE THOU HAST BEEN FAITHFUL IN A VERY LITTLE, THOU SHALT HAVE AUTHORITY OVER TEN TOWNS.

* August 26, St. Zephyrinus, Pope and Martyr

Gospel No. 2, page 242.

August 27, St. Joseph Calasanctius, Confessor

Gospel of Feast of St. John Bosco, January 31, page 329.

August 28, St. Augustine, Bishop and Confessor

Gospel No. 14, page 264.

August 29,
The Beheading of St. John the Baptist

Summary:

Salome dances, wins Herod's favor, asks for and receives the head of John the Baptist on a dish.

JOHN APPREHENDED

Lord Jesus, Your precursor John is headed for trouble. Loving God and His law as he does, he feels compelled to protest the king's open scorn for that law which he shows by marrying his brother's wife Herodias. How perfectly did the Psalmist prophesy of him: "I spoke of Thy testimonies before kings, and I was not ashamed; I meditated also on Thy commandments, which I loved exceedingly" (introit).

Herod is king, but that fact does not prevent John from telling him in fearless words: "It is not lawful for thee to have thy brother's wife." That kind of language incurs the woman's hatred. The dramatic stream of events flowing from Herodias' hatred is known to all: the dinner on Herod's birthday, Salome's dance, the king's mad promise to the girl; Salome's request for John's head, the beheading, and the daughter's presentation of the head to her mother.

There is no point in trying to unravel the cross currents of abnormality and hatred in the drama. It is not Herod or Herodias or Salome who is in the spotlight here: it is John . . . and You on whom John has centered his life.

How do You feel about all this, Lord Jesus? You must be say-

ing to Yourself that John is faithful and true to himself to the bitter
end. All his life he has been going before You, preparing the way
for You by leading the penitential life that is the background for
all his preaching of penance to others. He has given his disciples to
You, saying to them that You must increase while he decreases. For
him You are the bridegroom, while he calls himself the "friend of
the bridegroom." He has given You Your most descriptive title:
"Behold the lamb of God." Now at the end of it all, his disciples
lay his headless body in a tomb. And in suffering violent death, he
is Your precursor to the end.

THE JUST SHALL FLOURISH

How You must admire and love this great cousin of Yours! It is
admiration and love that You have bequeathed to Your Church so
that we can share in it and make it our own: "It is good to give
praise to the Lord; and to sing to Thy name, O most High" (introit).

We can rejoice thus because we know that John's death is not a
tragedy . . . not for him, at any rate. It might be for Herod, Herodias, and Salome; but for John it is simply the final act of love for
You and Your law. And such love wins its reward: "In Thy strength,
O Lord, the just man shall exult, and in Thy salvation he shall rejoice exceedingly: *Thou hast given him his heart's desire"* (offertory verse).

He exchanges his head and his life for his heart's desire—for
You, Lord Jesus, and from You he will never again be separated.

But he still continues his work on earth among us. He still prepares the way for You by preaching penance, speaking of Your testimonies before kings, and teaching us to meditate on Your commandments and to love them exceedingly. Lord Jesus, with Your
grace coming to us from this Mass and from all Your sacraments,
speed the example and the work of John in our lives.

Prayer for the day:

**IT IS NOT LAWFUL FOR THEE TO HAVE THY
BROTHER'S WIFE.**

August 30, St. Rose of Lima, Virgin

Gospel No. 18, page 272.

August 31, St. Raymund Nonnatus, Confessor

Gospel No. 15, page 266.

FEASTS OF SEPTEMBER

* September 1, St. Giles, Abbot

Gospel No. 17, page 270.

* September 2, St. Stephen, King and Confessor

Gospel as on Feast of St. Louis, August 25, page 421.

September 3, St. Pius X, Pope and Confessor

Summary:

To compensate for his triple denial, Jesus asks
Peter for a threefold expression of his love.

LORD, THOU KNOWEST

Lord Jesus, this scene takes place after You have risen from the
dead. You have just appeared to the apostles at the lakeshore and
have made breakfast for them. You are as natural as before, perhaps
even more so, for You notice how hesitant and awe-struck they all
are. The memory of those terrifying days of Your passion and death,

together with their own failure to stick by You, still clouds their joy. Peter in particular remembers his triple denial of You.

It is inevitable, therefore, that You should turn to him now that breakfast is over and say to him: "Simon, son of John, dost thou love me more than these do?" You are looking him in the eye as he answers: "Yes, Lord, thou knowest that I love Thee." You believe him and reply: "Feed My lambs."

You say to him a second time: "Simon, son of John, dost thou love Me?" Again Peter answers: "Yes, Lord, Thou knowest that I love Thee." And You repeat: "Feed My lambs."

A third time You say to him: "Simon, son of John, dost thou love Me?" I can see him standing there, eyes cast down, crushed with the memory not only of his denial but above all of the trust You have placed in him, and yet knowing as he has never known before what it means to be loved by God. "Lord," he cries, "Thou knowest all things, Thou knowest that I love Thee." And You do know, Lord Jesus. That is why You give him the final command: "Feed My sheep."

Feed My lambs . . . feed My sheep: what are You talking about, Lord Jesus? Who are these lambs and these sheep? Surely You are not talking about animals. You are talking about people, about Your followers, the lambs and sheep—bishops, clergy and people—whom You, Good Shepherd that You are, have redeemed and gathered together by Your saving death.

THAT I LOVE THEE

Peter is to feed lambs and sheep with the same food that You have always provided—with Your word of truth and Your life of grace. He is the one You delegate to continue the shepherding You have begun. Without truth and grace they will die; and then all Your work will have been in vain.

This, therefore, is a truly decisive scene in the history of the world, Lord Jesus; and it is essential to the whole plan of salvation that You inaugurated at Your coming into the world and which You will continue till the end of time.

Today we celebrate the feast of one of the newest and greatest of Your Saints, St. Pius X, Pope. On the day of his election, he too stood before You, and the same conversation took place: "Pius, lovest thou Me?" "Lord, Thou knowest all things, Thou knowest that I love Thee." And Your words were planted in his heart: "Feed My lambs, feed My sheep."

And like the first Peter, Pius obeys: he gives the same food—truth and grace—and with the same infallible guarantee that it is Your truth and Your grace that he hands out to all, hierarchy and laity.

He teaches through his encyclicals, he brings Your body and blood to little children, he invites his whole flock to the green pastures of daily Holy Communion, he tells the world that active and intelligent participation in the public prayer of Your Church is the primary and indispensable source of Your spirit, Your holiness.

Christ—Peter—Pius: truth, grace, love. And it is all for *Your* sheep and Your lambs, for us.

Lord Jesus, standing before You engulfed in the memory of his denial, Peter knows what it means to be loved by You. I think that this meditation has helped me also to know that fact as I have never known it before.

Prayer for the day:
LORD, THOU KNOWEST ALL THINGS, THOU KNOWEST THAT I LOVE THEE.

* September 4, Mass of the Preceding Sunday

* September 5,
St. Lawrence Justinian, Bishop and Confessor

Gospel No. 12, page 261.

* September 6-7, Mass of Preceding Sunday

September 8,
The Nativity of the Blessed Virgin Mary

Summary:
> The list of ancestors of Jesus from Abraham to
> Joseph, Mary's husband.

HUMAN ORIGINS

Lord Jesus, I confess that whenever this gospel meets my eye in the missal, I feel a little let down. In all Your gospels I see You preaching or doing good or suffering or teaching. This list of names hardly warms the heart.

But perhaps there is more here than one thinks. Who are these men and women mentioned by St. Matthew? Each is a person marked for a particular role in life. They have their own lives to live, and some of them are far from exemplary. Rahab is a prostitute, David is a murderer and adulterer, and the wife of Urias seems happy enough to get rid of her husband in order to marry David.

All of these people are sinners, descendants of our sinful first parents. But whatever they do or think, they have a God-given commission to be links in the chain of humanity leading from Abraham, the Father of Your race, to Joseph, Mary's husband; a chain of humanity in which You are preparing Your own flesh and blood.

Humanly speaking, the blood that You carry in Your pure body and which You have received from Your blessed Mother has a long —and sometimes a violent and turbulent—history. But it is human blood, and You have chosen to become human. As a matter of fact, looking at those names and remembering their personal history, there can be no doubt that You have really become man.

OF HER WAS BORN JESUS

You have received this blood from all Your ancestors, Lord Jesus. And You are going to pour it out again for them. And not for them only, but for all the rest of mankind, including us. I have never before thought of expressing gratitude to these ancestors of Yours, Lord; but I'll try to remember to do it from now on whenever this gospel comes along.

Maybe it is no credit of theirs that their line has produced the fairest of human flowers, Mary Your Mother. And surely it is Your divine intervention alone that sees to it that she is miraculously conceived without original sin. But You do not readily set aside the human and ordinary series of causes and effects: I believe that Mary is the achievement also of her ancestors.

But since Mary is their accomplishment under God, and since she is Your Mother, and You are our Savior and Redeemer and Head of the Body of which we are members, then all of us who are baptized into You belong to those ancestors too.

Now I see how right Pope Pius XI was when he said that "spiritually we are all Semites." It is a glorious heritage—a fact that Your Church unmistakably recognizes when she begs the Father to deign to accept Your sacrifice with the same gracious and kindly attention with which He accepted the offerings of Abel and the sacrifice of "Abraham our patriarch and that which Thy chief priest Melchisedech offered unto Thee, a holy sacrifice and a spotless victim" (Prayer after the Consecration of the Mass).

Maybe from now on, reflecting on these things and this list of names will make me all the more eager to offer myself with and to receive in Communion You who are called Christ, the Son of Mary, of the race of David and Abraham.

Prayer for the day:
OF HER WAS BORN JESUS WHO IS CALLED CHRIST.

September 9, St. Peter Claver, Confessor

Gospel of Twelfth Sunday after Pentecost, page 201.

Same day, St. Gorgonius, Martyr

Gospel No. 16, page 268.

September 10,
St. Nicholas of Tolentine, Confessor

Gospel No. 16, page 268.

* September 11,
Sts. Protus and Hyacinth, Martyrs

Gospel No. 9, page 255.

September 12, The Most Holy Name of Mary

Gospel of the Mass of the Blessed Virgin during Advent, page 281.

* September 13, Mass of the Preceding Sunday

September 14, The Exaltation of the Holy Cross

Summary:

Jesus predicts that He will be lifted up and will draw all things to Himself.

IF I BE LIFTED UP

Lord Jesus, You are close to the Last Supper and to Your death as You say these things: "Now is the judgment of the world; now will the prince of the world be cast out. And I, if I be lifted up from the earth, will draw all things to Myself." And John tells us that You say this to signify by what death You are to die.

The crowd as usual is mystified by Your words: "We have heard from the Law that Christ abides forever. And how canst Thou say, 'The Son of Man must be lifted up'? Who is this Son of Man?"

They seem so close to recognizing who You are, but yet so far away. You do not answer them outright. You simply say: "Yet a little while the light is among you. Walk while you have the light, that darkness may not overtake you. He who walks in darkness does not know where he goes. While you have the light, believe in the light, that you may become sons of light."

It is indeed a little while that You, the Light, will be with them. Your prophecy will be fulfilled, and You will be lifted up on the throne of Your Cross from which You will rule over the world and will draw all men and things to Your heart. "By the sign of the Cross, deliver us from our enemies, O Thou our God" (communion verse).

SWEET THE WOOD

Lord Jesus, a lot has happened since You first made these predictions. All has been fulfilled: You have been lifted up onto a cross and have died; You have risen from the dead and established Your Church, endowing it with Your own worship, the sacred Liturgy; Your holy sacrament of Baptism has drawn us to Your cross so that now we share in all its fruits of light and life. And today Your Church celebrates this sacred feast of the Exaltation of Your Cross.

"But it behooves us to glory in the Cross of our Lord Jesus Christ: in whom is our salvation, life and resurrection, by whom we are saved and delivered" (introit).

This is a needed feast for all of us, for it reminds us of what You have done for us and of what we are as Your members. It asks us questions, too: If You draw us to Yourself, do we allow ourselves to be drawn? Do we share the obedience unto death that You have and that we cannot escape if we would be Your members? (There is such danger of growing cold in Your service.)

But perhaps worship—and the thrill of this feast—can bring us back to our senses. Make us sincere when we cry out to Your Cross: "Sweet the wood, sweet the nails, sweet the load that hangs on thee: thou only wast worthy to bear up the King and the Lord of heaven" (alleluia verse).

But let the feast do more than raise up mere emotions. May it bring us the grace to become obedient unto death, even the death of the cross if need be; for only such obedience—laced with love—can identify us with You and make us worthy to share Your glory. "Be present with us, O Lord our God, and as Thou dost make us rejoice in honor of Thy holy Cross, defend us by its perpetual aid" (post-communion).

Prayer for the day:
> AND I, IF I BE LIFTED UP FROM THE EARTH, WILL DRAW ALL THINGS TO MYSELF.

September 15,
The Seven Sorrows of the Blessed Virgin Mary

Gospel of the Mass of the Blessed Virgin during Paschal Season, page 285.

* September 16,
St. Cornelius, Pope, and St. Cyprian, Bishop, Martyrs

Gospel No. 7, page 251.

September 17,
The Impression of the Stigmata of St. Francis

Gospel No. 4, page 246.

September 18,
St. Joseph of Cupertino, Confessor

Gospel of Nineteenth Sunday after Pentecost, page 220.

September 19,
St. Januarius, Bishop and His Companions, Martyrs

Gospel of Feast of Sts. Marius and Companions, January 19, page 324.

September 20,
St. Eustace and His Companions, Martyrs

Gospel No. 8, page 253.

September 21,
St. Matthew, Apostle and Evangelist

Summary:

Matthew, called by Jesus to follow Him, gives a banquet for the Lord to which he invites many publicans and sinners.

PUBLICANS AND SINNERS

Lord Jesus, You must be gratified at Matthew's prompt and unquestioning consent to Your invitation to follow You. Matthew, formerly called Levi, leaves all things, including that despised (but well-paying) job of tax-collecting, to go after You into the unknown.

And to top it off, he gives a big banquet in order to celebrate his change of vocations. Matthew's friends are not drawn from the best ranks of society, are they? There are fellow tax-collectors (an unpopular breed in any age), publicans and sinners—outcasts nearly all. And You in the midst of them, feeling quite at home.

"Well, did you ever . . .!" the Pharisees are saying to themselves; and soon they are no longer able to restrain their sarcasm, scorn and anger. "Why does Your Master eat with publicans and sinners?" they ask Your disciples.

You overhear the Pharisees and You answer: "It is not the

healthy who need a physician, but they who are sick." The application is unmistakable: You are claiming to be a physician, and Matthew's crowd of sinners are the ill. Sin is sickness, and they all have it bad. You are there to cure them.

You don't give them any medicine, any miracle drugs. You just give Yourself. They see You, eat with You, they bask in Your presence, they love You. For the first time in their lives they know themselves for what they are: sinners, yes, but human persons whom You visit and respect.

You identify Yourself with them now: You will die for them later. How can they help loving You? But love destroys sin. That's the kind of physician You are.

MERCY NOT SACRIFICE

Your words continue to the Pharisees . . . and to us: "But go, and learn what this means: 'I desire mercy, and not sacrifice.' For I have come to call sinners, not the just." Here You are speaking of Your Father, and You mean that the kind of work You are doing—curing sinners, loving them, being merciful to them—is much more precious in the sight of God than all the empty, loveless, mechanical sacrifices of the pure but heartless Pharisees in their careful observance of the letter of the Law.

Lord Jesus, help us all to take to heart and put into practice this lesson and example that You give us today. We Christians are Your witnesses; we are supposed to take Your place everywhere. That means that we, like you, belong among sinners. Sharing Your truth, Your grace, and above all Your love, we can give ourselves to those who need You today; and the more we give ourselves, the more the sinners in turn will come back to You.

And as far as we are concerned, if we give ourselves to sinners, Lord Jesus, maybe our mercy can become part, at least, of our sacrifice—our sacrifice and Yours, the holy Sacrifice of the Mass. Praise be to Thee, O Christ.

Prayer for the day:

I HAVE COME TO CALL SINNERS, NOT THE JUST.

September 22,
St. Thomas of Villanova, Bishop and Confessor

Gospel No. 12, page 261.

Same day,
Sts. Maurice and Companions, Martyrs

Gospel No. 7, page 251.

* September 23, St. Linus, Pope and Martyr

Gospel No. 2, page 242.

September 24, Our Lady of Ransom

Gospel No. 1, page 241.

* September 25, Mass of the Preceding Sunday

September 26,
Sts. Isaac Jogues, John de Brebeuf and Companions, Martyrs

Gospel No. 8, page 253.

Same day, Sts. Cyprian and Justina, Martyrs

Gospel No. 9, page 255.

* September 27,
Sts. Cosmas and Damian, Martyrs

Gospel No. 8, page 253.

* September 28, St. Wenceslaus, Martyr

Gospel No. 5, page 248.

September 29,
Dedication of St. Michael the Archangel

Summary:

Jesus teaches that little children must be protected from scandal: their angels in heaven
always see the face of the Father.

LIKE LITTLE CHILDREN

Lord Jesus, the disciples ask You: "Who then is greatest in the kingdom of heaven?" You answer by showing them a child and saying: "Amen I say to you, unless you turn and become like little children, you will not enter into the kingdom of heaven. Whoever, therefore, humbles himself as this little child, he is the greatest in the kingdom of heaven."

Then You go on to say that to receive a child for Your sake is to receive You. I suppose that simply means loving children, making them feel that they are loved. "But whoever causes one of these little ones to sin, it were better for him to have a great millstone hung around his neck and to be drowned in the depths of the sea."

These are strange words, as well as those that follow about the danger and malice of scandals. But the words are strange only to those whose idea of the greatness of Your Father and the hideous-ness of sin does not measure up to reality. "If thy hand or thy foot is an occasion of sin to thee, cut it off and cast it from thee! It is better for thee to enter life maimed or lame, than, having two hands or two feet, to be cast into the everlasting fire."

So it is the soul that counts; but more than that, it is the glory of Your Father that counts. You die to save souls, Lord Jesus. But You die most of all to join souls to Yourself so that through and in You they can worship the Father.

The real evil of scandal of causing little ones (or anyone) to sin is that sin offends the infinite, majestic, loving and lovable God and that persons whose goal, glory, and joy is to worship God are forever separated from Him. All sin deprives God of love, and when sin separates souls forever from Him, its malice is infinite.

THEIR ANGELS

So You say to us: "See that you do not despise one of these little ones; for I tell you, their angels in heaven always behold the face of My Father in heaven." Thus we finally come to the point of this feast: angels. Their chief function is to worship and adore God, always and forever beholding with love His holy face.

Why do You give us angels, Lord Jesus? Isn't it that You want them to help us all to the final fulfillment of our being, divine worship? We will not be whole until we stand with them in heaven, loving, adoring, praising God, the while we join their worshipful "Holy, Holy, Holy, Lord God of Hosts. Heaven and earth are filled with Thy glory. Hosanna in the highest!" (And surely the angels, knowing as they do the greatness and lovableness of God, must be most eager to succeed in the vocation You give them of protecting us and leading us to worship.)

But, Lord Jesus, we don't have to wait for heaven in order to be whole. We have worship, the essence of heaven, daily on our altars. And there too we have the unseen but very real presence of the angels and archangels, the cherubim and seraphim . . . and all the rest.

Lord Jesus, strengthen our faith so that this truth may not only sanctify us more and more, but most of all that You and the Father and the Holy Spirit may more and more be loved and admired.

Prayer for the day:
WHOEVER RECEIVES ONE SUCH LITTLE CHILD FOR MY SAKE, RECEIVES ME.

September 30, St. Jerome, Confessor and Doctor

Gospel No. 14, page 264.

FEASTS OF OCTOBER

* October 1, St. Remy, Bishop and Confessor

Gospel No. 12, page 261.

October 2, The Holy Guardian Angels

Gospel of the Feast of St. Michael, September 29, page 436.

October 3, St. Teresa of the Child Jesus

Summary:

Jesus teaches that to enter the kingdom of heaven it is necessary to turn and become like little children.

GREATEST IN THE KINGDOM

Lord Jesus, the apostles may seem human and selfish at certain times, but we can thank their very weakness for some of the most valuable lessons You give us. Here they want to know who is greatest in the kingdom of heaven. To say the least, their idea of the kingdom of heaven is rather faulty.

They are hardly ready for the truth You give them. You see a little child playing near by and You call to the child. The little one leaves the world of make-believe, looks at You, sees Your face, and runs to You with arms open wide. You receive him with affection and set him down in the middle of the apostolic circle.

They look at You, and the child looks at You and at them. Then You speak: "Amen I say to you, unless you turn and become like little children, you will not enter the kingdom of heaven. Whoever, therefore, humbles himself as this little child, he is the greatest in the kingdom of heaven."

You have just given them the essential direction for becoming

438

great in the kingdom of heaven, for becoming a saint. It might take them a lifetime to grasp the full extent of Your teaching, but they'll do all right in the end. Meanwhile, we don't do so well ourselves in humbling ourselves as a child does—even with two thousand years of object lessons from Your saints behind us.

WHO HUMBLES HIMSELF

Lord Jesus, Your child, St. Teresa of Lisieux, is one of the most striking of Your creations; and few of Your chosen ones have been so brilliant and perfect in following Your formula of sanctity as she . . . few have been so necessary and providential for *us* as she.

In our times we don't come to You asking who is to be greater in the kingdom of heaven: most of us are trying to figure ways just to stay inside Your Church and still live according to our worldly will and desires. So You set St. Teresa in our midst as if to say: you have to turn away from self as she has done, you have to become a child, you have to run to Me and trust in Me exclusively and explicitly, putting all of your life in My hands. Unless you do this, you cannot even think of entering the kingdom of heaven, least of all becoming great in it.

Lord Jesus, You say to Teresa: "I have loved thee with an everlasting love: therefore have I drawn thee, taking pity on thee" (tract). And so do You say to all of us. Your love shines on us as the sun shines on the seeds in the ground. Your love seeks to release the inner power of love in us. The degree of our response of love determines whether we will be mere ordinary unheroic Christians or be saints. St. Teresa goes all the way.

"May the heavenly mystery, O Lord, inflame us with the fire of that love by which Blessed Teresa, Thy Virgin, offered herself to Thee as a victim of charity for men" (postcommunion).

The way of Teresa is open to us: it is the way of humility, the way of the Scriptures, the way of the Eucharist, the way of littleness; and it is reinforced by her own well-known ambition to spend her heaven on earth making You more loved.

Lord Jesus, teach me to do Your will; teach me, help me to be a child as Teresa was.

Prayer for the day:

UNLESS YOU TURN AND BECOME LIKE LITTLE
CHILDREN, YOU WILL NOT ENTER THE KING-
DOM OF HEAVEN.

October 4, St. Francis of Assisi, Confessor

Summary:

Jesus praises the Father for revealing great
truths to the little ones; He invites all to take up
His yoke and learn from Him.

TO LITTLE ONES

Lord Jesus, You are always magnificent when You speak directly
to Your Father: magnificent and loving and very revealing of what
our relations should be to Him. Here You praise Him who is Lord
of heaven and earth for hiding deep truths from the wise and prudent and revealing them to little ones. You present Your Father as
a Father to men, deeply interested in winning the correct response
of creaturely love and admiration from them.

Those who are little—there is hardly a better exemplar than St.
Francis—who realizes their need for divine truth and help and who
see themselves as totally dependent on Your Father for all that they
have and are, these will always receive what they seek. Your Father
will open to them the truth that will satisfy their hearts' desire.

But You are the way by which this truth comes to them. How
right You are to say: "All things have been delivered to me by My
Father; and no one knows the Son except the Father; nor does anyone know the Father except the Son, and him to whom the Son
chooses to reveal him." The way, then, to the Father and to full
possession of joyous union with Him must be through You.

And there is no doubt about Your willingness to reveal Your
Father to those who are little. "Come to Me," You say, "all you who
labor and are burdened, and I will give you rest. Take My yoke
upon you, and learn from Me, for I am meek and humble of heart;

and you will find rest for your souls. For My yoke is easy, and My burden light."

Lord Jesus, aren't You contradicting Yourself in these two phrases? You admit that some of us labor and are burdened, and You invite us to come to You. But in the same breath You tell us to take upon ourselves another yoke, Your very own yoke; and we are to learn of You who are meek and humble of heart; and then we will find rest for our souls.

MEEK AND HUMBLE

Lord, this is strange language to our modern way of thinking. But it is not strange to the Saint whose feast we celebrate today. He takes You at Your word. He gives himself utterly to You as he gives up all earthly goods; and few human beings have ever been quite as happy and rich as Francis. I mean *rich* in the sense that by being unattached to all creaturely things, he was really able to possess and enjoy them. Above all he was able to possess the praise of all creation and to give it a voice: "My God and my all!"

So this is Your yoke, Lord Jesus, that You want us to take upon ourselves—the yoke of praise for the Father. Francis no longer possesses house, money, land, securities—he has nothing that the world thinks so essential. But "Francis, the poor and lowly, enters a rich man into heaven" (alleluia verse).

Lord Jesus, all the Saints shame us, but few of them so sharply as Francis. I can never hope to equal his love and his complete despoiling of self. But he wasn't always thus. There is a beginning of his holiness. There is a moment when You overwhelm him with Your love so that ever after he is a free and willing captive of that love.

Lord, if it happened to Francis, it can happen again . . . if I want it to . . . if I have enough courage to want it to happen again. Help me to know You so that I may know the Father. Then perhaps this knowledge can really penetrate my reluctant will and show me that only one thing matters: "My Lord and my God!"

Prayer for the day:

HE WHO LOSES HIS LIFE FOR MY SAKE WILL FIND IT.

* October 5,
St. Placidus and His Companions, Martyrs

Gospel No. 9, page 255.

October 6, St. Bruno, Confessor

Gospel No. 15, page 266.

October 7,
The Most Holy Rosary of the Blessed Virgin Mary

Gospel of Ember Wednesday in Advent, page 8.

October 8, St. Bridget, Widow

Gospel No. 19a, page 274.

October 9, St. John Leonard, Confessor

Gospel of Feast of St. Titus, February 6, page 335.

* October 10, St. Francis Borgia, Confessor

Gospel No. 17, page 270.

October 11,
The Motherhood of the Blessed Virgin Mary

Summary:

Jesus is lost and after three days Mary and Joseph find Him in the Temple in the midst of the teachers.

BOY LOST

Lord Jesus, one can feel the pain and terror that grip the hearts of Mary and Joseph when they come together after the first day's journey back to Nazareth, only to find that You are not with either of them. I can hear Mary cry out: "I thought He was with you!" And Joseph: "And I thought He was with you!"

They rush back to Jerusalem, and it doesn't take them a whole day this time. For three days they seek You, each hour piling pain upon pain. They have lost You, the light of their home, You, the God of their hearts. "O, all ye that pass by the way, attend and see if there be any sorrow like to my sorrow," Mary thinks in her heart (Lamentations of Jeremias, 1:12).

The third day of seeking brings them to the temple. (Did they come to pray?) There You are, but in what strange company for a boy of twelve! A group of the great Jewish teachers and Scripture scholars surround You, their faces filled with amazement at the wisdom of Your questions, Your comments and understanding of the holy Word (after all, it is Your word, isn't it?)

Your Mother and Joseph are hardly less astonished at finding You in such illustrious company; but the first comment of Mary is the comment of a mother: "Son, why hast Thou done so to us? Behold, in sorrow Thy father and I have been seeking Thee."

How strangely do You answer Your Mother, Lord. "How is it that you sought Me? Did you not know that I must be about My Father's business?" This is language they find hard to understand. Your Father's business? Who is Your Father? What is the business? Why does that business seem to imply such grief to them? No wonder St. Luke says that they do not understand the word You speak to them. There will be much for Mary to ponder in her heart in days to come.

MOTHER OF JESUS

Lord Jesus, Your Church, desiring to celebrate a feast in honor of Mary's divine motherhood, chooses this section of the gospel for our contemplation. I think I can understand why. Motherhood is a combination of almost divine joy, responsibility and privilege, together with enduring pain and worry.

No mother has ever loved a son as Mary loves You. Now she has lost You. Those three days of separation are a foretaste for her of the three years of Your public life during which You will be gone from her and of those three days of Your sojourn in the tomb in which You will be gone from this world.

Yes, it is the feast of Mary's Motherhood . . . of her Motherhood of You as Savior. And this gospel is chosen because nowhere in all the New Testament does her close relation to Your saving work emerge more clearly. As has been said so often, it is not so much her physical motherhood that makes Mary great as it is her dedication to You, to Your saving work, to Your Father's will.

"Let us celebrate with joyfulness the Motherhood of blessed Mary ever Virgin" (magnificat antiphon). Yes, Lord Jesus, let us celebrate. But there is only one way for children to celebrate, and that is all together.

Therefore, Lord Jesus, add our joy and gratitude and love to Yours not only in this feast but every day. And grant us through the intercession of Your Mother and ours to be more and more *one* with You, with her, with one another. "O sing unto the Lord a new song, for He has done marvelous things" (introit).

Prayer for the day:
DID YOU NOT KNOW THAT I MUST BE ABOUT MY FATHER'S BUSINESS?

* October 12, Mass of the Preceding Sunday

* October 13, St. Edward, King and Confessor

Gospel No. 15, page 266.

October 14, St. Callistus, Pope and Martyr

Gospel No. 2, page 242.

October 15, St. Teresa of Avila, Virgin

Gospel No. 18, page 272.

* October 16, St. Hedwig, Widow

Gospel No. 19a, page 274.

October 17, St. Margaret Mary Alacoque, Virgin

Gospel of the Feast of St. Matthias, February 24, page 340.

October 18, St. Luke, Evangelist

Gospel of the Feast of St. Titus, February 6, page 335.

October 19, St. Peter of Alcantara, Confessor

Gospel No. 16, page 268.

October 20, St. John Cantius, Confessor

Gospel No. 15, page 266.

* October 21, St. Hilarion, Abbot

Gospel No. 17, page 270.

* October 22-23, Mass of the Preceding Sunday

October 24, St. Raphael, Archangel

Summary:

The first sick person to go into the pool called Bethsaida after it is touched by an angel is cured of whatever infirmity he has.

ANGEL OF THE LORD

Lord Jesus, this section of the gospel introduces a miracle that You are about to work for a man who has been sick for thirty-eight years. In this part Your Church wants us to concentrate on one thing: on the fact that at certain times an angel comes down into the pool, troubling the water. And the first sick person into the pool after it is stirred by the angel is cured of whatever infirmity he has.

This is the feast of the Archangel Raphael, "one of the seven who stand before the Lord" (epistle). Your Church—relying on the opinion of some of her Fathers—seems to think that it is Raphael, restorer of Tobias' sight, who comes into the pool, troubles it, and gives miraculous power to the water.

Well, whether it is Raphael or some other angel, this feast and Raphael's personal history shows how closely related the angels and archangels are to You, Lord Jesus. Raphael does for Tobias what You do for us. He says to Tobias: "When thou didst pray with tears, and didst bury the dead, and didst leave thy dinner, and hide the dead by day in thy house, and bury them by night, I offered thy prayer to the Lord . . . And now the Lord hath sent me to heal thee, and to deliver Sara thy son's wife from the devil" (epistle).

Now it is You, Lord Jesus, who offers our prayers and our good works to the Father; it is You whom the Father sends to heal us of our sins and to deliver us from the devil. Only, what Raphael does in a limited manner, You do in a divine manner.

He praises the Lord and helps men. You are *the* praise of the Father, You are praise in person: by Your life and by Your death, You stand before the Father, showing Him Your wounds which perpetually intercede for us.

BLESS THE LORD

And that brings us in: not only do You divinize the waters of baptism (I recall how the Easter Candle, which stands for You, is plunged into the baptismal water) and restore us to life in Your holy sacrament of Baptism, but You keep us alive and growing by feeding us with Yourself in the Eucharist.

So You are much more of a wonder-worker than Raphael, or any archangel, and he would be the first to admit it. But You do want him to have a stake in our salvation and above all in our worship (which is an essential element in our progressive salvation).

I must not think of Raphael (or any of the angels or archangels) as beings far removed from us and our time. They stand now before the Lord. They stand before and around our altar of sacrifice where You offer Yourself daily to the Father in an unbloody manner. And there am I. "I will sing praise to Thee, in the sight of the angels, I will worship towards Thy holy temple, and I will give glory to Thy name, O Lord" (alleluia verse).

But we are not only one in worship: we are one in You. You are the life of the angels' souls even as of ours. May this feast — and a greater devotion to the angels — transfer some of their enthusiasm, reverence and love to all of us. "Bless the Lord, O my soul: and let all that is within me bless His holy Name" (introit).

Prayer for the day:
> I AM THE ANGEL RAPHAEL, ONE OF THE SEVEN WHO STAND BEFORE THE LORD.

* October 25, Sts. Chrysanthus and Daria, Martyrs

Summary:
> Jesus threatens and reproves the Scribes and Pharisees for the manner in which they approve the evil deeds of their forefathers against the prophets.

WOE TO YOU

Lord Jesus, it is frightening to hear You when Your just anger against the Pharisees and Scribes boils over. "Woe to you!" You cry out, "for you build the tombs of the prophets, whereas your fathers killed them. So then you are witnesses and approve the deeds ot your fathers; for they indeed killed them, and you build their tombs."

Lord, in this rather obscure language, You are evidently referring to the evil and murderous reception Your spokesmen, the prophets, have been receiving these many years from these experts in the Law and from their forebears. Men of God, devoted to God's honor and glory and determined to promote that honor, always run the risk of violent opposition from men who have learned to twist the Law and make it fit selfish ends.

So You go on to condemn them with Your Father's own words: "I will send them prophets and apostles; and some of them they will put to death and persecute, that the blood of all the prophets that has been shed from the foundation of the world may be required of this generation, from the blood of Abel unto the blood of Zacharias, who was slain between the altar and the temple."

"Woe to you . . . !" These are harsh words from the mouth of the Savior of the world, Lord Jesus. But when You speak in this harsh manner to these hypocrites, it is not out of any feeling of hatred for them. You rather wish to shock them into a realization of the possible hellish end that their self-deification and pride will bring them if they do not reform. Your anger and threats are a last attempt to make them come to their senses. Anger is sometimes the overflow of pity.

MARTYRS' BLOOD

You are not too successful in changing the Scribes and Pharisees, Lord Jesus. On the contrary, You are simply stating — as it were prophetically — what they will do to You. As their fathers in the past have poured out the blood of the prophets, so will these present hypocrites add Your own blood to the ever-growing pool in which the sins of the world must be washed away.

Today's martyrs have contributed their blood to this redeeming pool. They are thus co-redeemers with You. And now they plead with You for us — that we too may be ready to follow them (and You) along the way of sincerity even to death, if that be Your will.

"May the prayers of Thy blessed Martyrs, Chrysanthus and Daria, be with us, we beseech Thee, O Lord, and may we who honor them by this service continually enjoy their loving help" (collect).

Prayer for the day:

I WILL SEND THEM PROPHETS AND APOSTLES: AND SOME OF THEM THEY WILL PUT TO DEATH.

* October 26, St. Evaristus, Pope and Martyr

Gospel No. 2, page 242.

* October 27, Mass of the Preceding Sunday

October 28, Sts. Simon and Jude, Apostles

Summary:

> Jesus tells the apostles to love one another and to expect to be hated because they are His disciples.

CHOSEN OUT OF THE WORLD

Lord Jesus, You are at the Last Supper and You are speaking not only to Your apostles, but to all of us. You tell us that we must love one another; that if the world hates us, it has hated You before us; that we are not of the world since You have chosen us out of the world; that no servant is greater than his master; and if they have persecuted You, they will persecute us also.

All these things they will do to us for Your Name's sake, because they do not know Him who has sent You. He who hates You, hates Your Father also. If You had not done for them works such as no one else has done, they would have no sin. But now they have seen, and have hated both You and Your Father; but that the word of their Law might be fulfilled: "They have hated Me without cause."

Lord, Jesus, everything You say here will be fulfilled: fulfilled in You during the next few days, in Your apostles as they will go about continuing Your work, in us as we too do our part in sharing Your apostolate.

With what love do You speak to these friends of Yours . . . and to us! And how great is Your sadness at the stubbornness of those whom You so want to save! You know by experience what it means to be hated; and You can see how vicious hatred is, how it can poison the human heart.

Men hate You, men whom You so love (and whom the Father loves so much that He sends You to save them). But this is the really horrible fact: "He who hates Me hates My Father also . . . But now they have seen, and have hated both Me and My Father."

ABIDING IN LOVE

Lord Jesus, I think I am beginning to see the depths of Your Passion as never before. It is not so much the physical pain they will inflict on You that tortures You; it is this hatred that causes the deepest wound. But isn't love the remedy for hatred? If hatred destroys, love builds. If hatred wounds, love heals.

Isn't that why You spend so much time at the Last Supper telling them and us about love? Tomorrow You are going to hang on the Cross, the victim of hatred. You will suffer terribly; but even as You suffer You will know in Your heart that these beloved disciples of Yours, fearful though they be as they watch You from across the valley, love You with the love of sinners who grieve at their very weakness.

You know that they will some day make up for their momentary weakness by themselves dying for love of You. And then, of course, beneath Your Cross, holding You up on a scaffold of love stand Mary, Mary Magdalen, and John.

And here at this Mass, still beneath Your Cross, do I stand. There is still a lot of hatred against You in our world, Lord Jesus. But Your formula still holds: love can wipe out many things; it can counter-balance the hatred. Lord Jesus, help me to continue what the apostles so gloriously begin as they look at You there on the Cross. Help me to abide forever in Your love.

Prayer for the day:
> THESE THINGS I COMMAND YOU, THAT YOU MAY LOVE ONE ANOTHER.

* October 29-31, Mass of the Preceding Sunday

Last Sunday in October, Feast of Christ the King,
page 224.

FEASTS OF NOVEMBER

November 1, Feast of All Saints

Summary:
> Blessed are the poor in spirit, the meek, the merciful, those who suffer persecution; for their reward will be great in heaven.

BLESSED

Lord Jesus, it is always a joyous sight to see You in the midst of the multitudes. These people have come to You hoping for answers to the problems and mysteries of life. There are varying degrees of sincerity among them and of hope and longing in their eyes as they look on You. They will not be disappointed in their quest. In them the words of the psalmist will be fulfilled: "They that seek the Lord shall not be deprived of any good" (Psalm 33:11, gradual of today's Mass).

They look to You, and You feed them with life-giving words: Blessed are the poor in spirit, the meek, they who mourn, those who hunger and thirst after justice, the peace-makers, those who suffer persecution for justice's sake, and in general, all who are reviled and hunted down for Your sake. "Rejoice and exult," You tell them, "because your reward is great in heaven."

A great reward in heaven is surely good reason for rejoicing, because that is the only place where rewards endure. But the reward is not the only reason why all these people are blessed. They are blessed most of all because they are so like to You, Lord Jesus, they so share Your being.

What You really do in these Beatitudes is to describe Yourself.

Looking at You, we see You as perfect poverty of spirit, perfect meekness, perfect mercy. Blessed will we be who so let You live and grow in us that we too will be poor in spirit, merciful, and pure of heart. It is You, Lord, who are marvelous in Your saints.

HOW GLORIOUS

And it is You who say to each of us: "Come to me, all you who labor and are burdened, and I will give you rest" (alleluia verse). You are not talking here about physical refreshment, but of holiness, of Your presence in us. You issue that invitation to us today from the midst of this festival Mass.

We hear Your word, we come, and when You have gathered us together, You and Your Church cry out: "Let us all rejoice in the Lord, celebrating a festival day in honor of all the Saints: at whose solemnity the angels rejoice and give praise to the Son of God" (introit).

None of us can become saints without You. But we can come to You, we can rejoice in and with You, we can celebrate this and all the feasts of Your Church Year. And as we celebrate with understanding and love, You gradually become our holiness; for there is nothing like worship to make us realize Your attractiveness and to make us open our lives to receive You. You are holiness, but You require rejoicing, celebrating, adoring hearts in which to take root and grow. We may not be saints yet, but the way is open to us; it is that of adoration and praise.

Now I think I can understand Mother Church's enthusiasm when she cries out: "Oh! how glorious is the kingdom wherein all the saints rejoice with Christ; they are clothed in white robes; they follow the Lamb whithersoever He goeth" (magnificat antiphon)! Oh! How glorious are You, Lord Jesus; our hope, our desire, our life!

> **Prayer for the day:**
> REJOICE AND EXULT: BECAUSE YOUR RE-
> WARD IS GREAT.

November 2,
Commemoration of all the Faithful Departed

Summary:

At the resurrection at the end of time, the good shall come forth unto the resurrection of life, and the evil unto the resurrection of judgment.

THE DEAD SHALL HEAR

Lord Jesus, You say that the dead shall hear Your voice, and those who hear shall live. For as the Father has life in Himself, even so He has given to You also to have life in Yourself; and He has granted You power to render judgment, because You are the Son of Man.

The hour is coming, You say, in which all who are in the tombs shall hear Your voice. And they who have done good shall come forth unto resurrection of life; and they who have done evil unto resurrection of judgment.

Lord Jesus, You speak with such familiarity and authority about this world beyond the tomb . . . and with good reason. It is Your world, and You know each of its citizens personally, as they also know You. They do indeed hear Your voice, and You hear theirs in intimate conversation.

Lord Jesus, today is the day on which Your Church commemorates all the holy souls who have "gone before us with the sign of faith, and rest in the sleep of peace" (canon of the Mass). Many of these holy souls still wait and suffer. But it is suffering that is tempered by assurance of final eternal union with You.

And yet, because they no longer have the demands of their bodies to distract them, they must know, as we cannot, how finally and utterly desirable You are. Hence their most poignant suffering. Without our help they can only wait and hope.

ETERNAL REST

Lord Jesus, this Commemoration must recall to us more vividly that in You we are all one intimate family: You, Our Lady, the angels and saints, all the holy souls who have gone before us, and we who remain.

We really need this day. Our loved ones die and leave our world and our physical companionship. After a period of sorrow we gradually become accustomed to their loss, and eventually we run the risk of losing awareness of them as people.

But the holy souls still live as members of Your Body. We share with them the very same divine life of grace that You have within You. Far from going off into a nebulous world of vague impersonalism, they remain personalities even as we are.

Your Church says this so beautifully in the Preface of the Mass of the Dead: "For unto Thy faithful, O Lord, life is changed, not taken away: and the abode of this earthly sojourn being dissolved, an eternal dwelling is prepared in heaven."

Lord Jesus, while these loved ones were with us, we spoke to them and they spoke to us. Why should we not continue to speak to them now as we also have learned to speak to You, to Your Mother and the saints? This speaking will crack wide the wall of separation that death and forgetfulness have built up between us and them.

And gradually as we speak to them and they to us, we will learn familiarity with Your world, which is to be our world, our home, for all eternity. This familiarity is the best preparation for the moment when You and all Your holy departed ones will greet us and make us want to cry out: "Death is swallowed up in victory! O death, where is thy victory? O death, where is thy sting" (epistle)?

Prayer for the day:
> THEY WHO HAVE DONE GOOD SHALL COME
> FORTH UNTO RESURRECTION OF LIFE.

* November 3, Mass of the Preceding Sunday

November 4.
St. Charles Borromeo, Bishop and Confessor

Gospel No. 12, page 261.

* November 5-8, Mass of the Preceding Sunday

November 9,
Dedication of the Basilica of Our Savior

Gospel No. 20, page 279.

November 10, St. Andrew Avellino, Confessor

Gospel No. 15, page 266.

November 11,
St. Martin of Tours, Bishop and Confessor

Summary:

Just as light held up dispels darkness, so does the light of faith show us our way through life.

LAMP ON LAMP-STAND

Lord, Jesus, You say that no one lights a lamp and puts it in a cellar or under a basket, but upon the lamp-stand, that they who enter the house may see the light. So far, so good.

You go on to say that our eye serves as a lamp for us, and if the eye is sound, our whole person has light; whereas if the eye is defective, our whole person is in darkness. You tell us to see to it that the light that is in us is not darkness. "If, then, thy whole body is full of light, having no part in darkness, it will all be illumined, as when a bright lamp illumines thee."

You have been clearer than this, Lord Jesus. I think we can begin with the certainty that You are speaking about Yourself and Your relation to us. "I am the light of the world . . . I have come a light into the world, that whoever believes in Me may not remain in darkness" (John 12:46).

And we always remember our Easter Vigil experience: "Light of

Christ . . . Thanks be to God!" That night we had our candles lit
from the Easter candle that stood for You. You are our light because You are our life. "To believe means to share not what Christ
believes, but what He is," says Msgr. Guardini.

In giving us the virtue of Faith (which You give in holy Baptism) You give us the power to see things, people and events — our
present world and the world to come — with *Your eyes*. We share
in Your vision. If this eye of Faith is sound, our whole body will
be full of light.

NO PART IN DARKNESS

But You say, "take care that the light that is in thee is not darkness." If I allow my faith in You, my sharing in Your life and
vision, to be dimmed by materialistic principles and practice, by
carelessness about prayer and holy reading, if I give up speaking to
You, then I shall soon walk in darkness.

But more tragic than that, others depending on me will also
walk in darkness. For no one receives the light from You for himself
alone. You make this plain when you tell us: "You are the light of
the world . . . Even so, let your light shine before men, in order that
they may see your good works and give glory to your Father in
heaven" (Matthew 5:14-16).

Your words and the example of today's Saint accuse me. "My
truth and My mercy shall be with him," You predict through the
Psalmist (offertory verse). But more than Your truth and mercy,
You are with him; and the light for all future times resulting from
the combination of Your grace, mercy and truth and his love never
will be extinguished.

Lord Jesus, to believe is to share not what You believe, but what
You are. I live, no, not I, but You live in me.

Lord, through the intercession of St. Martin grant that I may
see myself dwelled in by You. Help me to experience the living
reality which You are as You live in the saints, in the sacraments,
in this Mass, in my fellow members of Your Church. Grant all this,
not for any kind of self-gratification, but that through me You may
continue to be the light of the world. I believe in You.

Prayer for the day:

NO ONE LIGHTS A LAMP AND PUTS IT IN A
CELLAR . . . BUT ON A LAMP-STAND, THAT
THEY WHO ENTER IN MAY SEE THE LIGHT.

* November 12, St. Martin, Pope and Martyr

Gospel No. 2, page 242.

* November 13, St. Didacus, Confessor

Gospel No. 16, page 268.

November 14, St. Josaphat, Bishop and Martyr

Gospel of Feast of St. Thomas of Canterbury, December 29,
page 26.

November 15,
St. Albert the Great, Bishop and Confessor

Gospel No. 14, page 264.

November 16, St. Gertrude, Virgin

Gospel No. 18, page 272.

* November 17,
St. Gregory, the Wonder Worker, Bishop and Confessor

Summary:

Jesus demands that we have faith, for everything is possible for him who believes.

FAITH IN GOD

Lord Jesus, You say that a mountain will obey a man who does not waver in his heart, but believes that whatever he says will be done. You tell us: "All things whatever You ask for in prayer, believe that you shall receive, and they shall come to you."

Lord, I remember wondering about this when I was small. I knew You must have been serious when You said this, and that if You promised it, so it would happen. And I remember being tempted to try You out; but there weren't any mountains in our part of the country. Besides, I don't believe I would have had the courage to issue that rather terrifying command.

Ever since, whenever You talk about faith, I always get the feeling that I am stepping into an area that is very mysterious indeed. Your Church teaches us that faith is a free gift from You and that You grant it to whomever You will. And yet, in this gospel You seem to insist that its strength and effectiveness depend also on us. "Have faith in God," You say, "believe that you shall receive."

How can I have the faith You demand? Why have I been so fearful of obeying and going all the way with You?

If I have been afraid of speaking to mountains and requiring obedience from them in Your name, could it be that I have never really known Your actual presence in me? In the past You have existed too much as a figure who lived long ago rather than as One who lives here and now in me.

The laws of nature, the solidity of the world around us, the human relationships, the power of wind and storm . . . have always seemed more vitally real and demanding than You who are the author of nature, You who can command, direct, and suspend any of her laws.

ALL THINGS WHATEVER

So, Lord Jesus, I shall continue to talk to You about Yourself and Your gospels. Talking to You (and listening, too) is one thing I really believe in. This is a human work that is within my power. It makes awareness of You grow in me. And as You grow in me, so do Your promises fill me with the necessary confidence to take You fully at Your word.

I don't know if I'll ever get up enough courage to tell a mountain to take off and cast itself into the sea. There are many complications that such tampering with scenery could bring about. And there are many more, and greater, needs for our world.

Lord Jesus, show me Your face. "Thy face, O Lord, do I seek" (Psalm 26). Live and grow and make Yourself known to me more and more so that whatever I ask You in prayer, especially for those who are in need, it may come to me, and most of all, to them. Live and grow in me so that all my asking may be in conformity with your will.

To You do I lift my soul: in You, O my God, I put my trust (Psalm 24). I stretch out my hands to You; my soul thirsts for You like parched land . . . Show me the way in which I should walk, for to You I lift up my soul . . . Teach me to do Your will, *for You are my God* (Psalm 142)!

Prayer for the day:
HAVE FAITH IN GOD.

November 18,
Dedication of the Basilicas of Sts. Peter and Paul

Gospel No. 20, page 279.

November 19, St. Elizabeth, Widow

Gospel No. 19a, page 274.

November 20, St. Felix of Valois, Confessor

Gospel No. 16, page 268.

November 21,
The Presentation of the Blessed Virgin Mary

Gospel No. 1, page 241.

November 22, St. Cecelia, Virgin and Martyr

Gospel No. 18, page 272.

November 23, St. Clement, Pope and Martyr

Gospel No. 2, page 242.

November 24,
St. John of the Cross, Confessor and Doctor

Gospel No. 14, page 264.

November 25, St. Catherine, Virgin and Martyr

Gospel No. 18, page 272.

November 26, St. Sylvester, Abbot

Gospel No. 17, page 270.

* November 27-29, Mass of the Preceding Sunday

November 30, St. Andrew the Apostle,

page 313.